MW00991417

PRAISE FOR *FOOD FOR THE FUTURE: STORIES FROM THE ALTERNATIVE AGRO-FOOD MOVEMENT*

"In a moment when despair is not unreasonable, this book makes it clear that at least it's not mandatory—it's like a seed catalogue of hope, showing example after example of people who put their minds and bodies to doing the right thing."

—**Bill McKibben**, Schumann Distinguished Scholar in Environmental Studies, Middlebury College, author of *The End of Nature*, and other books

"Sociologist John Brueggemann examines the stories of people actively engaged in today's small-scale food and farming movement toward healthier and more sustainable food systems. Their commitment, passion, and pragmatism are so inspiring that we will all want to join or support this movement in every way we can."

—**Marion Nestle**, professor of nutrition, food studies, and public health, Emerita, New York University, author of *Unsavory Truth, How Food Companies Skew The Science of What We Eat*, and other books.

"Brueggemann has authored an insightful study of the 'little victories' of the 'beautiful' alternative agro-food movement. It is a refreshing alternative to the tendency of critical sociology to focus on the 'ugly' and 'illogical' aspects of the existing food system. Similarly refreshing is the fact the analysis resists airy generalizations and instead offers conclusions that are based on a series of very concrete analyses of some of the alternatives to that food system."

—**George Ritzer**, distinguished professor emeritus, University of Maryland, author of *The McDonaldization of Society*, and other books

"In this wonderfully rendered account of how ordinary people are working to change our food and agricultural systems—from production to consumption and everything in between—Brueggemann does the invaluable service of giving eaters the conceptual and practical tools they need to play their roles in building healthy lands and communities. *Food for the Future* is indispensable reading for precisely this moment in time."

—**Norman Wirzba**, research professor of theology and ecology, Duke University, author of *Food and Faith: A Theology of Eating*, and other books

"In grappling with the moral dimensions of agriculture, a social scientist relates inspiring stories from the front lines of the agro-food movement and shows how greed shaped the modern food system."

—**David R. Montgomery**, professor of geomorphology, University of Washington, coauthor of *What Your Food Ate: How to Heal Our Land and Reclaim Our Health*, and author of other books

Food for the Future

Food for the Future

Stories from the Alternative Agro-food Movement

John Brueggemann

LEXINGTON BOOKS
Lanham • Boulder • New York • London

Published by Lexington Books
An imprint of The Rowman & Littlefield Publishing Group, Inc.
4501 Forbes Boulevard, Suite 200, Lanham, Maryland 20706
www.rowman.com

86-90 Paul Street, London EC2A 4NE

British Library Cataloguing in Publication Information Available

Library of Congress Cataloging-in-Publication Data

Names: Brueggemann, John, 1965- author.
Title: Food for the future : stories from the alternative agro-food movement / John Brueggemann.
Description: Lanham : Lexington Books, [2023] | Includes bibliographical references and index.
Identifiers: LCCN 2023011267 (print) | LCCN 2023011268 (ebook) | ISBN 9781666930719 (cloth ; alk. paper) | ISBN 9781666930726 (epub)
Subjects: LCSH: Food supply—Environmental aspects. | Food supply—Health aspects. | Sustainable agriculture. | Food industry and trade.
Classification: LCC HD9000.5 .B748 2023 (print) | LCC HD9000.5 (ebook) | DDC 338.1/9—dc23/eng/20230309
LC record available at https://lccn.loc.gov/2023011267
LC ebook record available at https://lccn.loc.gov/2023011268

Contents

Preface   ix

Acknowledgments   xi

Introduction   1

Chapter One: Moral Foundations and Market Culture   13

Chapter Two: The Ugly Story of the American Food System   25

Chapter Three: Grounding   49

Chapter Four: Extraction   75

Chapter Five: Processing   93

Chapter Six: Distribution   113

Chapter Seven: Consumption   137

Chapter Eight: Stewardship   159

Chapter Nine: Communication   179

Chapter Ten: Patterns Among Engaged Sustainers   197

Chapter Eleven: Social Sources of Engagement   235

Chapter Twelve: So What?   259

Appendix A: Methods and Data   273

Appendix B: The Central Cast of Characters   277

Appendix C: Glossary   281

References 287

Index 301

About the Author 309

Preface

Over the years, I've heard numerous students ask why sociologists so often focus on gloomy issues. It's a fair question. I spent about twenty years studying class and race stratification, examining how different groups, including workers and people of color, were marginalized by the main institutions of American society. That research was all about exploitation, domination, oppression, inequality, and poverty. I later turned my attention to people who are "successful," and examined how the main institutions in American society have failed them. That work highlighted patterns of overscheduling, workaholism, hyper-consumerism, isolation, and mental health concerns. Both strands of my work, and that of many sociologists, do emphasize ugly aspects of society.

In recent years, several thoughts about this apparent gloominess of sociologists occurred to me. First, the reason why many of us spend so much energy documenting problems is that we think things can be better. The focus on grim stuff often reflects underlying optimism. Possibilities for improvement start with naming and understanding the issues. Second, while many sociologists think that much of what is going in the world is harmful and unnecessary, we are often not very astute at generating specific, concrete solutions. A lot of inquiries never move past analysis. Of those that do, the plans are often abstract, utopian, or quixotic. Third, to make matters worse, we sociologists often present our ideas in ways that are not comprehensible to the people central to our concerns.

Those insights got me thinking. How could the world be a better place? Who really has answers to that question? How can more people tap into such answers? That's how this project started.

The first time I spoke with a subject for this research was about ten years ago. A lot has happened since then, needless to say. It took me a while to realize what I was investigating, what the specific topic would be. I initially cast my net widely, trying to find people who do interesting, life-giving things that actually make the world a better place. I have no particular expertise related to agriculture or food. As I spoke to people, though, those topics kept popping up. Over time, what I was looking for came into focus, as you will see in the pages below.

Most of the research for this book was conducted between 2017 and 2020, though some of it began well before that, and some of it occurred after that. This is basically an investigation into the cultural shift toward a greater concern for healthy food and the social movement that has driven it. The evidentiary basis of this work is a series a semi-structured interviews, and participant observation, as well as consultation of secondary sources. What I try to show here is a snapshot of a part of the world. It is one image from a particular time period. I am not attempting to describe deep history, or make predictions about the future, though the past and future come up quite a few times.

There are two rather significant topics that I do not really address here, which may seem like a curious choice. This book is not about Donald Trump or COVID-19. To be candid, I am rather sick of both topics. I followed a hunch that more than a few readers might feel the same way and wouldn't mind reading a book in which the ex-president and disease are not central topics. They are mentioned here and there, but I do not spend any real time talking about them. For now, my impression is that the empirical snapshot I attempt to present is not fundamentally altered by those two factors.

I hope the result of the research, this book, will be of interest to social scientists interested in agriculture, food, social movements, morality, inequality, community, and civil society. The material here would be relevant for academic courses focused on those topics. My aspiration is that the stories from the alternative agro-food movement relayed here will also appeal to anyone who cares about the well-being of American society and the prospects for living a good life in relation to food. Amid all the madness loose in the world today, I believe we can do better, and the cast of characters introduced in these pages offer some concrete ideas as to how.

Acknowledgments

I am deeply indebted to all the people who agreed to be interviewed for this research. They shared time, information, insights, and in many cases, the precious gift of hopefulness. Several folks helped connect me with key research subjects who proved especially informative. They include Rose Cherneff, Hans Kersten, John Richardson, and Naomi Tannen.

A bunch of splendid research assistants helped bring this project to fruition. Sarah Rosenblatt, Willa Jones, Maggie Griesmer, Lizzie Benkart, Tegan O'Neil, Nat Cabrera, Rosa Desmond, Arden Pradier, Shannon Reilly, Brianna Cochran, Miles Chandler, Adelaide Scenti, Sarah Spruill, and Shiloh Hurley helped gather data and other materials, conducted and transcribed interviews, gave critical commentary and editorial feedback, and, most importantly, provided ongoing inspiration and encouragement. I feel fortunate to have worked with every single one of them.

I taught two courses that drew from and informed this research. One was Food for the Future: The Sustainable Food Movement in the United States and the other was Food for the Future: The Sustainable Food Movement in the United Kingdom. Those were edifying experiences for me, and I appreciate the thoughtful engagement of everyone involved.

A number of researchers were generous with their time, energy, and expertise, offering crucial feedback and guidance. Thanks to Carolyn Cherneff, Pat Fehling, Stephen Gasteyer, Karen Kellogg, Michael MacQuarrie, Juliet Schor, Sheldon Solomon, and Kenji Tierney.

I have benefitted from spending many years in a vibrant professional setting, the Department of Sociology at Skidmore College. Thanks to all my colleagues there for supporting me in countless ways. I am grateful to our administrative assistant, Linda Santagato, who makes our department functional and fun. Special thanks to Andrew Lindner and Rik Scarce who did everything they could to bring the best out of this work.

I am very appreciative of several folks who read the manuscript and gave me incisive feedback. Cliff Brown, Patrick James Miller, Christina

Brueggemann, Shiloh Hurley, Ivy Ken, Andrew Lindner, Joya Misra, Barbara Purcell, Shannon Reilly, Rik Scarce, Sarah Spruill, I couldn't have done it without you!

Kudos to my two talented buddies, Martha MacGregor and Katie McWheenie, who offered creative expertise in designing the cover of this book. As you can see, Martha, who is a graphic designer, and Katie, who is a multidisciplinary artist, do marvelous work. Martha also designed the figures.

Having thought seriously about food for a few years now, I have been recalling with fondness and appreciation the people who prepared lots of meals for me over the course of my life. I am thinking in particular of Hilda Hallman Brueggemann, Lila Bonner Miller, Mary Miller Brueggemann, Jim Brueggemann, Lisa Simcox Brueggemann, Lorraine McHugh and Christina Brueggemann. There is a special place in heaven for such talented cooks and generous hosts.

As always, I am grateful to the most important teachers in my life, my parents and brother, Mary, Walter, and Jim Brueggemann. Among countless other lessons, they taught me about one of life's great joys, breaking bread with people you love.

Finally, I want to say thank you to those folks with whom I have shared the most meals, Christina, Emilia, Anabelle, and Peter Brueggemann. From highchairs and bibs, and coaxing you to eat what I cook, to enjoying what you cook, and all the conversation and fun along the way, it is a sweet gift to share the journey with you.

Introduction

HORTON EATS A FORKFUL

This book is about different foods, the stories they embody, and most of all the people in the stories. It's about where food comes from, what's in it, why people choose to eat one food versus another, and why we should feel happy about what a lot of people are eating right now.

Does a forkful of food matter? How many times have you put one in your mouth and not thought about it for even a millisecond? How many unhealthy or bad tasting bites do people take without even a smidgen of consequence? Does it matter if a small child throws a forkful of food or an adult drops one? Maybe a single forkful of food doesn't matter very much—for most of us, most of the time.

But what would a starving person say about a single forkful? Or a person with intense food allergies? It's easy to think of other poignant circumstances: a frustrated parent who can't get her child to eat enough or to stop eating too much, a farmer who has barely made ends meet but managed to pay the bills and put food on his table, a proud, new restaurant owner serving her first customer, a seasoned chef whose restaurant just went out of business serving their last customer, and so on.

What do we make of any given 100 forkfuls? Or a million or a billion? Every single forkful is usually related to many other forkfuls. Thus, each forkful is part of a larger story related to a meal's quality, a person's health, a community's well-being, a nation's economy, global weather, and market patterns. Does a forkful of food matter? In some real sense, no. But in another sense, a sociological sense, big time.

The answers to those questions all relate to the rise of the alternative agro-food movement. In this book I attempt to document what this movement is and why it matters. Along the way, I explore the characteristics and relational patterns of people active in this movement, their ideological, moral and social commitments, and what motivates them to do what they do.

I interviewed sixty people across nine states, and observed dozens more in farmers' markets, stores, restaurants, churches, conferences, and other social

1

settings. What I found is that among all these diverse people there are robust patterns: ordinary people are quite capable of doing extraordinary, lifegiving things. I also learned that some particular social forces shape these people, nurture their habits, and in some sense bring the best out of them. Overall, I believe the lessons of the alternative agro-food movement offer inspiration both in terms of our food system in particular, but even in some ways with respect to our society as a whole.

Layers of Dirt

If one plant dies, we might wonder what happened to it. Was there a beetle, rabbit, or a lumberjack? But if lots of plants fail to thrive, we start to look for something broader, maybe a late frost or disease. And if numerous species become endangered, we look for an even deeper story. Does the soil have too little phosphorus or too much salt? That's when we look to edalphologists, who study the viability of soil for growing things. They are especially concerned when dirt gets ruined on a large scale. This is the condition we find ourselves in in American society. *The soil has been depleted of fertility and vast tracts of land are no longer suitable for life.* This statement is true both literally and figuratively.

The literal fact is that due to overuse of fertilizers, pesticides, and plowing over the last century, some half of the organic matter of U.S. soil has been lost. The organic matter is crucial for fertility.[1] Practices of agriculture and animal husbandry that started during the Industrial Revolution have damaged natural resources in a number of ways. Indeed, human collectives have a troubling track record on this score in general, as Yuval Noah Harari documents in *Sapiens: A Brief History of Humankind.* Some cultures are more ecologically careful than others, but generally speaking, where humans go, extinction of other species often follows.

The new monocrop system brought about by the Industrial Revolution came hand in hand with the certain perception that nature had to be conquered (see Bittman 2021). Indeed, one of the most important patterns during modernization was the increasing capacity of humans to harness natural resources for their own ends. Steam engines, ships, canals, trains, electricity, cars altered the leverage humans have in this endeavor and thereby transformed the subjective experience of time and space. The time it takes to get to town to buy or sell crops has been hugely reduced, which effectively means town is not as far away as it used to be, and there is more time for other things. Few people want to undo those human triumphs. But the gains have not come without costs.

This idea conquering nature proved devastating in terms of soil. "Since the dawn of agriculture," the geomorphologist David Montgomery laments, "society after society faded into memory after degrading their soil" (2017, 301, p. 9). An industrial farm might yield more crops in the short or even medium run. But along the way, there would be more plowing, more fertilizers, more chemicals. Those practices diminish the microbial biodiversity so crucial to healthy soil, which then decreases the fertility of the soil (Catton 1980). This then reduces the health of plants grown there, and by extension the nutritional value of food derived from their harvest, and the ecosystems surrounding them. Moreover, the greenhouse emissions from soil caused by industrial farming are also harmful to the atmosphere in general. One estimate suggests that since the Industrial Revolution began, some 135 billion metric tons of carbon has been released into the earth's atmosphere (Valasquez-Manoff 2018).

Just as increasingly unhealthy soil harms the world, though, increasingly healthy soil can repair it. Good soil has the ability to store and sequester CO_2 emissions. Plants draw carbon out of the air and then inject some of it into the ground via their roots, where it is fed upon by vital microorganisms. This process can literally heal the atmosphere by removing the carbon emissions generated by other sources.[2]

The material reality of soil is urgently important. A broader point here, though, extends from the causal argument linked to metaphorical soil. *The soil has been depleted of fertility and vast tracts of land are no longer suitable for life.* The figurative expression of this claim is about moral life. That is, the moral grounds of American society can be thought of as metaphorical soil. They have been poisoned and are becoming inhospitable for *social* life. The settings where we learn how to live with one another in durable ways are shrinking.

Confidence in American institutions has been deteriorating for a long time. This skepticism includes doubts about banks, organized religion, organized labor, corporations, medicine, newspapers, education, criminal justice, and of course government.[3] American citizens themselves have regarded such authorities with enormous distrust—even before Donald Trump and his allies actively started undermining them. The decades-old trend of political polarization in the United States continues to grow.[4]

Basic norms of decency, altruism, delayed gratification, reciprocity, and other ethical standards are weakening. Anxiety about our neighbors, much less strangers or foreigners, is mounting. Many have increasing tolerance for overt expressions of rudeness and hostility, especially if it is directed at "the other," whether that is a matter of race, sexuality, religion, or, increasingly, politics. This affinity for incivility includes bullying in public places, call-out/cancel culture on social media, and the harassment and mockery of public officials. The behavior we see and participate in during road rage has jumped the curb and spread across society. The road used to be one of the few places where shouting obscenities at a stranger was kind of expected. Sadly, vulgarity is the new normal in increasingly more social spaces.

In short, I am making two related claims about soil that I think are not particularly controversial, one literal and one figurative: (1) the ground in which we grow what we need to eat is deteriorating; and (2) the moral foundations that provide the basis of society are crumbling. In addition, not only are these literal and figurative claims related to soil each significant, but they are also intercausally related to one another.

That is, our depleted soil has made generating the resources necessary for life—plants, animals, technology, and medicine—more difficult. Without sufficient food, shelter, clothing, and security, it is harder to get along. And it is harder to live a good life. Those who starve have a difficult time thinking about feelings, meaning, cooperation, or learning. That is, actual soil affects the moral health of society.

Given that we seem to be facing what is basically a human-made problem, though, how the moral sickness of society affects real soil is also important. The health of figurative soil affects the health of literal soil. To be specific, the use of fossil fuels, artificial fertilizers, salinization, plowing, and other production processes, extending from our way of life, are contributing to a steady trend of land degradation. Our culture, our moral habits, are implicated in this causal chain. For instance, the expectation one can readily get every kind of fruit or vegetable twelve months a year, or the choice to eat meat ten times a week affects the use of fossil fuels, which can directly or indirectly impact soil health.

With the right balance, soil gives rise to life. Seeds take hold, grow, and transform into plants that become part of a viable ecosystem, and end up providing calories for animal life. What is left over, the detritus of living things that have died returns to the ground, contributing once again to its lifegiving balance. Instead of corrupting, the cycle can be regenerative. This sort of equilibrium has evolved in countless settings around the world under wildly different circumstances, many of them home to human beings. There are plenty of places where people managed to live in harmony with the ecosystem around them. In *Collapse: How Societies Choose to Fail or Succeed*, for example, Jared Diamond discusses a number of cultures that have managed natural resources effectively for some time, including Polynesian Tonga, New Guinea, Denmark, and the Pueblo peoples (Diamond 2021).

However, soil can also fail. As noted above, the record of *Homo sapiens* in participating productively in the cycle of life is, on the whole, not that favorable. The growing problems with today's soil are vast. Edalphologists estimate that we have collectively spoiled about a third of the world's agricultural land (Montgomery 2017, p. 17). That is in large measure due to industrial practices that degrade soil. Of course, there are ways that plants can be destroyed besides poor soil—poisoned air or water will do it too. Good soil is necessary, not sufficient.

The same is true of moral foundations. Just as different soils with varied compositions produce a wide range of flora and fauna, moral foundations can be arrayed in varied ways that foster vibrant culture. Large societies as diverse as China, Rome, or the Maya, and smaller, more isolated cultures like the Pueblo peoples, the Yanomamo, or the Bushmen of southern Africa have all maintained viable societies over a long period of time. There is no single formula or pathway. It is a matter of developing some workable constellation of moral foundations that sufficient members of a society find credible and compelling. Not that every human society is a promising role model, of course. I am glad I don't live in Assyria, Sparta, or North Korea. More to the point, no culture is perfect, obviously, but many develop a way of life that is morally sustainable for a long time.

Even in functional, lasting societies, though, moral foundations can crumble. Contradictory internal values, military overextension, or neglecting the well-being of sufficient numbers of members are just some of the problems that have proven catastrophic across history. No doubt, solid moral foundations do not guarantee integrity and longevity in a society. Natural disasters, war, famine, population fluctuations, for example, have all done their fair share of damage. By definition, though, moral disasters are human-made. Just as ideals and normative habits have to be invented and cultivated, the departure from or defilement of them is done by people. Again, the point is that moral order is a necessary but not sufficient premise for viable, sustained human culture.

In the pages below, I describe alarming circumstances related to our dominant food system, which I call the ugly story. It is one among many bad stories in our society. "What the hell just happened to our country?" is the subtitle of Steve Almond's book, *Bad Stories*. It's about how certain narratives, which may be untrue and/or cruel, lead other people to think and do bad things. Each chapter addresses a different story, like "What amuses us can't hurt us," "Trump was a change agent," "There is no such thing as fair and balanced," or "America is incapable of moral improvement." The upshot in each case is that we become inured to pessimism.

A Word after a Word after a Word

The idea in *Bad Stories* is that such narratives tap into subjective perspectives and thereby shape how we think about the world. This contradicts the widespread belief in the academy that facts speak for themselves. "Just give them the data, however complex or counterintuitive," according to this canard, "and they'll get it." Almond shows otherwise. Stories that are transmitted from influential mouthpieces, told in persuasive ways, and repeated over and over, gain traction. Those that speak to strong impulses already in motion become reality. As Margaret Atwood said, "a word after a word after a word is power."

If there is anything Donald Trump has taught us, it's that if you repeat a lie often enough some people will believe it. Death by a thousand lies. His dishonesty has left a large hole in our civic life, a chasm so wide and deep many credulous followers can't seem to find their way out of it, and many others can't stop worrying about everyone else falling into it. Trump's hollowing out of American culture has, of course, been abetted by certain media companies that both feed Trump some of his soundbites and receive some of their own from him. This mutual admiration society involving cynical power-hungry politicians and greedy, right-wing "news" outlets has facilitated a loud symbiotic voice that speaks through the bullhorn of social media. Can anyone picture Trump mattering in politics before Roger Ailes built Fox News or before the iPhone? It's a perfectly designed system for bad stories.

In the film, *The Natural,* a baseball team on a bad losing streak is subjected to a speech delivered by what appears to be an incompetent quack. The desperate manager will apparently try anything. "What is losing? Losing is a disease . . . as contagious as polio. Losing is a disease . . . as contagious as syphilis. Losing is a disease . . . as contagious as bubonic plague . . . attacking one . . . but infecting all." The winsome hero, Roy Hobbs (played by Robert Redford), walks out in disgust. The irony is that this assessment appears to be exactly right. The players seem to have a losing attitude, which has become a self-fulfilling prophecy.

Steve Almond's specific point is similar: cynicism is deeply infectious; cynical words are powerful. In reading the stories Almond tells, and thinking about his main claim, I started to see relevant evidence everywhere. *They got away with it; I might as well try it, too. If everyone is pointing a finger at those people, how can they not be guilty? If I can get it for free, why not try, even if I have to cut corners? Even if only part of the criticism is right, then the so-called facts don't matter. He became famous for his killings; maybe I will too. His behavior is so outlandish I'm tired of paying attention to any of it. Yeah, maybe we did something wrong but that doesn't matter because they did, too.*

How right Roosevelt was that we should indeed fear fear. In our world today, we have an epidemic of cascading fears. "Fear leads to anger," a great Jedi master once said. "Anger leads to hate. Hate leads to suffering." Think about how many different kinds of people feel victimized right now. Folks from different religions, races, sexes, genders, vocations, political parties. I do not mean to suggest that no one is ripped off, stigmatized, or mistreated in some authentic, lasting way. Countless images of law enforcement officers assaulting people of color is only the tip of the iceberg. What is striking, though, is how the air we breathe is rife with the stench of resentment and cynicism.

Even the most dominant, powerful people can feel like nothing is going their way. Not just those who have suffered historical harm, such as poor people, people of color, Jews, Muslims, atheists, immigrants, disabled people, LGBTQ folks, old people, but also Christians, men, "incels," straight people, white people, political centrists, cultural conservatives, those condescended to by elites.

No doubt there is at least a grain of truth in many cases. Is it possible to muster some compassion for the most privileged—white, male, cisgender, straight, affluent, educated, Christian—in recognition that the world is changing around them in ways that are not easy? I hope so because that is who I am. The world really is changing in mindboggling ways, and every one of us, every single one of us, needs compassion sooner or later. If we can offer that, can't we also feel compassion for those with heavier burdens? For those whose oppression runs deeper? If we can recognize how much fear and anger there is, then we might grasp the vast risks of escalating hatred and suffering.

So, what's the good news? Remarkably, many people in this world rank with fear resist despair. Moreover, actively resisting despair—applied hope— is also highly contagious. Bad stories lead to bad things. Good stories lead to good things.[5] "Darkness cannot drive out darkness," Martin Luther King Jr. said, "only light can do that. Hate cannot drive out hate; only love can do that." This is a book of good stories filled with light and love.

"Losing is a disease," says the shrink in *The Natural*, "attacking one but infecting all. Ah, but curable!" Even though he didn't cotton to the uninspiring psychologist's words, Roy Hobbs lends support to the claim with his actions. Discipline, hustle, integrity, faith, and even talent can be contagious too. When he hit his most important ball and literally knocked out the lights, Hobbs was still a rookie.

In the pages that follow, you will meet a number of winners who demonstrate the same qualities. Like Roy Hobbs, they are ordinary people who do extraordinary things. As I grappled with my own frustrations about the state of the world, flirting with despair, I sought out such people. I did this after consulting a wide range of scholarly research literature. I looked for answers in books for quite a while and came up short. After much reflection, I decided to speak with people who do interesting things that are positive and consequential.

These are people who take action against the odds and get things done. I initially cast my net widely, speaking with activists, artists, and teachers, for example, folks engaged with a range of issues like gun safety, the exploitation of musicians, overly scheduled children, military disarmament, mentoring young victims of trauma, using art to heal damaged communities, the discipline of genuine craft as a form of resistance, corporate responsibility, and addiction to social media.

Along the way, I was edified and inspired. As I tried to gain some insight into applied hope, I kept running into people linked to a particular issue: stuff related to food. More specifically, I found people responding intelligently and creatively to the mess that our food system has become. So that became my focus—I initially came to this particular focus on food inductively. I asked where good things are happening and was led to this topic. As I dug into it, I learned so many things.

One is how food is at once simple and complex. Eating is one of the very first things a baby does after birth. After we fully develop teeth, we spend about 35 minutes each day chewing.[6] If a person is hungry, it's hard to think about anything else. Food is so elemental. However, it is also vastly cultural. Eating food is one of the few organic functions around which humans build visible, public culture. That is, we share and ritualize eating much more than we do sleeping, sex, or excretion, for example. A number of other material resources share characteristics with food, things like housing, clothing, transportation, and medicine. They are all valuable assets that we need to survive, which are entangled in complex social dynamics. But food alone has this distinctive quality of being so elemental and so culturally embedded at the same time.

Another lesson was that food touches most every aspect of society in some way. If you study food, you will eventually also learn about family, gender, race, nationality, politics, economics, religion, education, and various other social phenomena. The converse is true, too. One has to study all those other things to really understand food. As a sociologist, that is part of how I came to the topic as well. It was through my interests in power, inequality, and morality, and the social currents that shape those issues that I backed into the topic of food.

In terms of agriculture and food, I was an ignorant outsider when I started this project. I know a bit more now, but I'm still a person describing something from a distance. To find people to interview, I used what social scientists call snowball sampling. I kept asking, "who should I talk to?" The response was very much of a rolling snowball. Even when I was just chatting with people and didn't ask for names, many folks would say, "oh, you need to interview my neighbor . . . cousin . . . friend." As a result, I met lots of interesting people doing inspiring things. Over time, I came to think of each project being carried out by different individuals as part of something larger.

A few years ago, *The New York Times Magazine* ran a story entitled "Can Dirt Save the Earth?" (Valasquez-Manoff 2018). It details new agricultural techniques for getting carbon out of the air and into the soil, which slows global warming and enriches soil—a win-win, as it were.[7] The problems with degraded soil, unhealthy consumption, wasted food, climate change, and a range of other challenges are connected. There is no silver bullet that will address all of them. In fact, dirt can't save the earth, not dirt alone, at least. As noted above, though, revitalizing soil is a step toward reducing the harm. That is the core point of each one of the good stories here: reducing harm.

This way of thinking is historically associated with the practice of social work. Harm reduction, as it is known among professional social workers, is a practical approach for addressing substance abuse, which accepts, for better or for worse, that substance abuse is a part of the world. It holds that users have a role to play in addressing abuse, that individual and community well-being are both important goals. The harm reduction model seeks to fully acknowledge the harm caused by substance abuse while also affirming drug users themselves. It steers away from absolute solutions, condemnation or turning a blind eye.

No doubt the long-term prospects of this approach will be unsatisfying to anyone who takes seriously the health of our world, in ecological and moral terms. It's not enough to do one small thing. In my view, though, the social workers rightly regard "all or nothing" thinking as a dead end in practical terms.

As a sociologist who aspires to see connections, structures, and systems, I have come to think of it—all or nothing thinking, that is as an overly rigid and limited way of understanding the world. When you work to develop a data-driven comprehensive plan for change, and you're honest, you never finish. Most grand theories pertaining to social life have either fallen well short of their claims or led to disaster.

In any case, the main characters in the stories I've heard reject the all-or-nothing view. These people, whom I've interviewed and observed, typically evince a distinctive combination of idealism (strong enough to keep pushing) and pragmatism (focused enough to chalk up actual victories). They don't attempt everything, they achieve something.

Outline of this Book and Which Parts Matter Most

Every word of this book is important, and each should be read in the order it appears. As much as I hope for such commitment on the part of readers, I understand certain sections of this text may be of more interest to some than others. In the next chapter, I elaborate on how the moral foundations of our society function and why I think they are crumbling. My argument there is that expansive market culture has led to social arrangements that have weakened our moral foundations. If you want to dig into the main theoretical argument underpinning this book, read chapter 1 carefully. If not, I trust you'll feel free to skip it.

Chapter 2 is about how expansive market culture has brought about the ugly story of our dominant food system and all the moral erosion that entails. If you are well aware of how problematic our mainstream food system is or can't bear any more bad news, gliding past chapter 2 is fine too.

However, the chapters after that, which focus on the beautiful story, are essential reading. The people with whom I spoke mostly behave in ways that are foreign to me. They live lives that are agrarian, physical, and entrepreneurial. They pay attention to material things, dirt, weather, bodies, and specific places. I have no expertise related to those things. I have spent my adult life working as a teacher, researcher, and administrator in a small town in upstate New York. To this work I bring sympathy for my research subjects, an eagerness for a hopeful future, and some tools of a social scientist. I regard their stories (relayed in chapters 3 through 9) as the most important part of this text.

As I gathered them, I came to believe that they are not simply the last few smoldering embers of a dying fire, but the catching cinders that may well blaze up and illuminate the world. Each narrative is different but part of what is appealing about them is that they are part of the same warm brightness. They are only stories. I have not investigated individual claims with eyewitnesses or anything like that. However, I did read widely among primary and secondary sources to see how such claims align with other points of view.

In chapters 3–9, I share specific stories of several individuals. (Brief descriptions of those subjects can be found in Appendix B.) In chapter 10, I offer a summary of how all those folks are similar and different in comparison to one another. I then review the networks of organizations that connect, socialize, and energize those individuals in chapter 11, which is the most sociological part of this text.

In the final chapter, chapter 12, I answer the main research question: what is the alternative agro-food movement and why does it matter? I summarize the key empirical findings of this research and then highlight how this movement contrasts the themes of market culture. Finally, I explain how it can help restore moral foundations in our society.

The body of this book is followed by three appendices. The first one, Appendix A: Methods and Data, summarizes how I gathered the empirical evidence for this project. The second one, Appendix B: The Central Cast of Characters, provides a list of the main research subjects featured in chapters 3–9 and a brief summary of their respective activities. It might be useful to consult that appendix as readers come across different names in various chapters. The final one, Appendix C: Glossary, offers definitions of several terms I introduce. They are all defined in the text of the book, but the glossary provides a convenient inventory of them in one place.

NOTES

1. Thanks to David Montgomery for explaining the details of how this works to me (Montgomery 2022).

2. Lots of varied sources document this pattern. See, for example, Montgomery (2017), National Public Radio (2017), Forelle and Wolfe (2018).

3. See Jones (2022).

4. See Pew Research Center (2022).

5. See *Braiding Sweetgrass: Indigenous Wisdom, Scientific Knowledge, and the Teachings of Plants* by Robin Wall Kimmerer (2015), for a great example.

6. The way we masticate food is just one of many adaptive traits related to eating from which our species benefits (see Golembiewski 2022).

7. See Montgomery (2017); Jackson, Lajtha, Crow, Hugelius, Kramer, and Pineiro (2017).

Chapter One

Moral Foundations and Market Culture

ON MORALITY

In this research, I spoke to many people who consciously try to minimize the damage they cause in the world, maximize the ethical benefits of their actions for the long run, and even try to repair damage that others have done. At the center of such endeavors were concerns about the planet, nature, land, food, human well-being, and that of other species. This general sensibility—minimize damage, maximize benefits, make repairs if possible—was constantly evident to me in the words and actions of people I encountered. Some of them had common language for describing such efforts, like environmentalism, regenerative agriculture, or food justice. However, the conceptualization of such individual and collective efforts, and the words used to describe them were, overall, varied, layered, and often fuzzy.

I started using my own language to capture all of this good work without really being aware of it. I later realized the ontological journey I had made. A lot of people rightly think about how many miles a package or vehicle travels to get somewhere because it reflects how much fossil fuel has been used in transit. A more expansive concern involves how much greenhouse gas is emitted by human actions, those of an individual, household, company, or country, for example, predominantly known as a carbon footprint. Carbon footprint is obviously a better term than carbon miles because one can emit lots of greenhouse gases without traveling very far.

As anyone trying to be responsible in their consumption patterns knows, food is closely related to carbon footprint, but there is so much more to consider in addition to greenhouse gases.[1] A household could monitor its carbon footprint and do very well—that is, keep their use of fossil fuels to a minimum and use technology that emits very few greenhouse gases—and still be involved in destructive behavior. It might be a matter of poor nutrition, harsh treatment of labor, cruelty toward animals, or handling waste in ways that directly harm people.

The term I was using in my mind to think about such matters more broadly is *moral footprint*. And I realized I was using it in a particular way, differently than how I had heard it previously used. I offer all of that as context for what follows in this chapter, which is a fairly abstract summary of how I am thinking about the notion of moral footprint.

The bases of moral behavior can be conceptualized in different ways. There are *places* or institutions, like communities, homes, schools, or churches, for instance. Using "sticks and carrots," they socialize people into a sense of accountability: how we treat one another matters. We might think in terms of certain *habits*, like manners, decorum, or ethics. Some norms are well-known but unspoken. Like how neighbors treat one another, or how young people relate to old people. Not all such practices are equal. Sexual mores matter. The width of neckties not so much. Some habits are better, more durable, and beneficial to human well-being than others.

Or we advance formal *principles*, such as the Golden Rule. They are familiar, celebrated theories, schemas, or systems of thought. It is worth thinking carefully about the guidelines that inform our choices. We should aspire to be coherent and consistent in how we understand our choices. For instance, parents have to practice what they preach if they expect their kids to really accept their guidance.

We can also talk about revered *authorities*, like generals, surgeons, or grandmothers—what certain people think is worth paying special attention to. All these elements together comprise the moral fabric of society.

Another, particularly useful way to think about this fabric is in terms of basic *moral foundations* (see Brueggemann 2014a). The conceptual categories I have in mind were developed by Jonthan Haidt.[2] Building on extensive empirical research, Haidt and his colleagues contend that every viable society must maintain six essential moral foundations: care, fairness, liberty, loyalty, authority, and sanctity. Each category is comprised of a combination of social commitments to a particular ethic and a critical mass of trust on the part of society's members toward that arrangement. People need to know they are standing on morally solid ground.

MORAL FOUNDATIONS

The foundation of *care*, for instance, consists of material resources arranged so that most people receive sufficient sustenance to survive, and perceive that their needs are met. They have to not starve and have some awareness of that fact. If they do in fact starve, they may believe the system is configured for *harm*. Because the goal of providing care for most members of society is not always fulfilled, we can think of this as *the problem of care*, which must be resolved by any society that will last.

The foundation of *fairness* involves a widespread recognition that the logic on which the distribution of resources operates is sound. Fundamental standards of fairness must be consistently used in terms of how group members are treated. Depending on the culture, the standard may be based on some combination of different ideals such as "blood," piety, strength, beauty, or skill, for example. There is enormous variety across societies in how things may be distributed. What matters is a shared belief that the logical basis itself is sound and that it is reliably integrated into the system. In a feudal system, a subset of families owns most of the property. In a capitalistic system, claims of noble blood have little to do with owning property.[3] In any system, making sure that most people do not acquire resources in a way that contradicts the basic rules—that is, by *cheating*—is the *problem of fairness.*

The foundation of *liberty* varies across cultures in other ways. This is about balancing what individuals receive from and give to the group. If one individual forcefully dominates others, or if group dynamics overly repress enough individuals, the resulting sense of *oppression* may become volatile. A radically progressive taxation system designed to provide a foundation of care or a greedy, hoarding autocrat both might foster a sense of tyranny. Finding the right balance between what the group needs and what individuals need is the *problem of liberty.*

Any group that holds together must also have a secure foundation of *loyalty.* The reality of liberty, especially in modern society, often entails a certain amount of mobility whether in terms of geography, education, vocation, religion, or family. People move and change in terms of such issues. Cultivating a critical mass of buy-in, solving the *problem of loyalty*, is no easy feat in modern society. Without sufficient commitment, though, whether it is a matter of secretly marrying multiple spouses at the same time, working against one's employer, or polluting one's own neighborhood, the perception of *betrayal* becomes problematic.

A closely related issue is the foundation of *authority.* "Our group" must respect certain standards and the human carriers of them, whether it is elected officials, clergy, parents, teachers, soldiers, or healers. People need to know that someone is in charge, at some level, and they deserve to be in charge. Deserving could be based on strength, popular support, wisdom, age, or other assessments. Exerting one's individuality, independence, or a commitment to a different culture can only go so far before it is regarded as *subversion.*

Multicultural, pluralistic society faces a steep, uphill battle in addressing the *problem of authority.*

Again, there are close connections to the next and final foundation of *sanctity.* Society must maintain certain ideals above all others that are set aside and revered. Such hallowed ideals are usually embodied in certain myths, rituals, and symbols, whether it is a religious text, high holy day, or national flag. A certain level of continuity in what is sanctified makes for meaning, stability, and psychological health. Some statues should be torn down because the perception of what they stand for has changed. Even in those moments, though, there is sometimes an unexpected cost to pay, like a loss of respect for authority or public life in general. Not every moment or thing can be sacred. If everything has the same value, none of it is particularly special. On the other hand, if enough of culture is defiled, the resulting sense of *degradation* will have rippling implications. The tendency toward disenchantment in modern society made the *problem of sanctity* acute well before Donald Trump began his daily assault on decorum.

Our Moral Footprint

These six foundational principles can, at least conceptually, be considered the components of a moral footprint. To be clear, the categories formulated by Haidt and his colleagues were not intended for the kind of repurposing of them that I am doing here. Nevertheless, I believe an individual or group can be evaluated in terms of their moral footprint according to how well their behavior serves care, fairness, authority, liberty, loyalty, authority, and sanctity in the setting in which they live.

A moral footprint is like a carbon footprint, at least conceptually, in that the less harm or the smaller, the better. I prefer the idea of a moral footprint to the more commonly used notion of moral order for several reasons.

First, moral footprint is reminiscent of carbon footprint and suggests that how we tread morally matters. It denotes movement, choices, agency, rather than some fixed state of affairs.

Second, moral order implies that there are moral keepers of order. That may be true in some sense; moral authorities matter. People like our grandparents, clergy, or Holocaust survivors, for instance. But I want to emphasize a broader sense of responsibility for morality implicating institutional leaders like the Vatican or the Supreme Court yes, but also regular people, ultimately every single one of us.

Third, I think the idea of moral footprint allows for a certain kind of clarity about how we think of morality as being stronger or weaker. A moral footprint, I'm suggesting, can be smaller (better) or larger (worse). Maybe we should call it immoral footprint, but moral footprint sounds better. Each of us leaves a mark on this earth while traipsing through life, like a kid tracking mud through the kitchen after playing outside. But those who persistently make morally wise choices, who tread lightly as it were, leave a smaller mark. Of course, there are other ways to conceptualize such a metric, but this approach seems to balance brevity and clarity.

Fourth, I also think the notion of a moral footprint can be thought of in both collective and individual terms. We can talk about various levels of fossil fuel emissions, food waste, or degraded soil in a nation or a community. And we can talk about how any given individual contributes to such problems. "Each man's life touches so many other lives," Clarence observes in *It's a Wonderful Life*.

So how are we doing? How are moral foundations in our society holding up? What does the moral footprint of 21st-century America look like? As my father, Walter Brueggemann, and I argued in *Rebuilding the Foundations: Social Relationships in Ancient Scripture and Contemporary Culture* (2017), these moral issues are both ancient and currently aligned in particularly ruinous configurations. Even if it remains a subject of vigorous debate, the basis for this pessimism is well documented. That American culture pushes some people to the side and leaves some behind is well known. Unlike many other industrialized societies, who have in recent decades shown how high the floor can be and how much mobility up the social ladder is feasible, we continue to unnecessarily fail many of our most vulnerable citizens. The "American dream"—that is, the realistic aspiration for genuine social mobility—is in some real way more alive in many other nations than it is here. The World Economic Forum's Global Social Mobility Index 2020 ranks the United States as twenty-seventh behind nations as diverse as Denmark, Slovenia, Japan, Australia, and Ireland.

As I argued in *Rich, Free and Miserable, the Failure of Success in America* (2012a), dominant social arrangements afflict the affluent and empowered as well the impoverished and excluded. Evidence of this can be seen in patterns of workaholism, hyper-consumption, environmental degradation, mental and physical ailments due to persistent behaviors known to be unhealthy, marital disruption, social isolation and loneliness, neglect of loved ones, waste, greed, rudeness, and frustration. In my view, the obvious, devastating problems that harm the marginalized, such as hunger, housing insecurity, unreliable healthcare, lack of political representation, inadequate education, and the less obvious problems that affect the affluent, as noted above, are all related—not identical across groups, but connected. They stem from deteriorating moral foundations.

What does that mean? Just as robust moral foundations come in many different configurations across societies, the disintegration of foundations may vary greatly in terms of causes and character. There is obviously more than one source of trouble in our society. I believe, however, that much of the damage can be traced back to a particular cluster of problems. The main source of deteriorating moral foundations is expanding market culture. The idea that everything is for sale has pushed beyond the boundaries of the economic sphere into other parts of society. Exhibit A: the American political system put into its most important office a salesman—I mean no disrespect to smart, hardworking salespeople—whose main product was a brand name and who, arguably, was otherwise wholly unsuited for the presidency.

The expansion of market culture has occurred, as other important institutions that have historically provided countervailing balance have grown weak. This includes core elements of civil society such as organized religion, organized labor, the media, and education, as well as government in particular. As a result, the market has more sway over our values and norms than it did in the past (see Brueggemann 2012a). Without romanticizing history, we can acknowledge that in this way there was more balance in American society in previous eras. In a society partly built on conquest, abduction, and enslavement, some people—indigenous peoples, people of African descent, and other people of color—have been brutally abused. What I am arguing is that, in addition to those moral failures, even people who have historically benefitted from how American society has been arranged are now suffering weakening moral foundations. Plus, peoples of color face the legacy of historical discrimination, ongoing systems of marginalization, as well as the impact of weakening moral foundations that others face.[4]

The Power of Institutions

Such countervailing institutions (organized labor, organized religion, the media, education and government) have at times advanced the wellbeing of many people in our society. I am not suggesting that any of these countervailing institutions was ever perfect. By definition, all institutions leave someone out, and these institutions are no exception. Such problems were better or worse at different times, but even now some people can't vote or don't have their interests represented fully in the polity, some can't join a union, some are declared sinners by virtue of some immutable identity and cast out, some have access to low-quality education or no education, and some don't have their story told truthfully. Indeed, these institutions have directly enabled the domination of different people, most notably Native Americans and people of African descent, and other people of color, but also women, immigrants, LGBTQ+ people, Jews, Muslims, and other non-Christians.

Nevertheless, such institutions, which have at times provided this important counterbalancing weight against market logic, fulfilled basic functions that are inherently noble. Religion engages the sacred and offers spiritual comfort. Education helps young people find their way in the world and at times levels the playing field. Unions provide bargaining leverage for the exploited. Media and journalism hold the powerful accountable and offer the first draft of history. Government provides security, manages collective resources, and oversees important decisions.

To dismiss such institutions because they are flawed, because they have at times been harnessed for oppressive purposes, is wrong on at least two counts. First, it represents an overly simplistic understanding of history. All institutions are imperfect because they are comprised of human beings who are inherently limited and because no single institution can be everything to everybody. However blemished they are, these institutions have each made invaluable contributions to the well-being of society. To use any shortcoming of an institution as justification for abandonment is to fold before the game begins.

Second, to scoff at the failings of all organized, sustained, normatively guided collective enterprises—that is, institutions—is to yield without a struggle to the corrupt, the greedy, and wasteful. The ruthless often have armies, treasure, and/or formidable friends. The most pitiless and destructive antagonists in history, the Nazis are, arguably, a striking example. Resisting such a force requires social power, the collective energy and skills of a group. And no group, such as the Allies of World War II, can hold together without compromise and commitment. The same is true for a community group wanting to improve local schools, secure clean water, or resist mishandling of environmental waste.

Some fights are worth having, as anyone who works in a large organization understands. Some intraorganizational battles are worth waging to the end, even if they rip institutions apart, as abolitionists rightly claimed. For modern society to have any chance, though, we must buy into some level of institutionalism. We have to accept that no individual can singlehandedly confront pandemics, war, sex trafficking, economic depression, homophobic or misogynistic family norms, or other large-scale problems. And that acts of conscience, symbolic gestures, "likes," "shares," "reposts," and such may matter but will only take us so far. If that is so, then these particular institutions are among our most important social resources. At least they have been in the past, and perhaps may be again.

These countervailing institutions (organized labor, organized religion, the media, education and government), on their best days, provided a kind of *moral hardware* (see Brueggemann 2012a). As such, they were structural settings with stable traditions and norms that engendered a conservative kind of rootedness that facilitated memory *and* a progressive sense of hopeful possibility that seeks society's improvement. In such contexts, individuals could cultivate *moral software*—the capacity for wise decisions, self-awareness, reasoned reciprocity, delayed gratification, or altruism. For instance, we might learn how to share in school, show reverence in church, work as a group in the union, find out what's going on in the newspaper, or protect our and others' rights in the Constitution.

Or put it this way. Show me a principled, disciplined, formidable individual who speaks truth to power, who acts one step at a time with integrity and strength, who persists, and I'll show you someone embedded in some community of discourse and moral intent.[5] It's probably someone who is networked with compatriots who share ideas, resources, and buttress one another's resolve, or at least someone drawing from previous experiences and socialization in such a network (see Etzioni 1996; Stout 2010). Sometimes that special person may look like they are distinctively courageous in taking a singular, bold stance. But more often than not, behind her are mentors, allies, supporters, or silent partners, who provide a moral reservoir from which to draw guidance and energy (see Press 2012). In short, acquiring and making use of the moral software is contingent on encounters with and lessons from the moral hardware.

Market Culture

For varied reasons—some related, some independent—each of the countervailing functions of these institutions has grown comparatively ineffectual, which by extension has undermined the moral capacities of our society. This enfeeblement has unfolded simultaneously alongside the growing impact of the market. In the most affluent era of the most prosperous society in human history, think of the attention, energy, and anxiety Americans manifest in relation to shopping, investing, planning, gambling, producing, or consuming. In a setting with more disposable income than ever before, think of how little time is left over for noneconomic activity. And don't forget the level of poverty that we consider normal in this context. The market, writ large, is seductive, capacious and jealous. It will take as much as we will give (see Brueggemann 2012a).

I should acknowledge that people mean lots of different things when they use the word "market," including *the* stock market, a given supermarket, various other settings where buyers and sellers exchange money, goods, and services, or a particular type of societal-level economic system. Unless otherwise stated, I generally use the term in the latter sense, to refer to the large, complex systemic infrastructure of the market economy.

As I critique aspects of our society related to how our economy operates, I want to be very clear about one thing. I do not think the market is inherently bad. It is a crucial component in the great history of Western society, and indeed in the moral foundations of our culture. A market is an economic system with many buyers and sellers. It presumes that some property is privately owned by individuals and those individuals compete to sell and/or buy goods. With some important exceptions (e.g., cryptocurrency), a market is a material reality. The purpose of any given economic system is at least partly accessing some part of nature, refining it, and then converting such forces into stuff that people want. In the case of commodities, buyers acquire physical objects comprised of animals, plants, or minerals, for example. In the case of market-based services, buyers make use of others' labor—the energy of humans, which of course is a force derived from nature, too—and their skills.

"The market" is also a legal fiction or social construct (see Harari 2015, p. 28). It is a set of practices that lots of people agree is important. A market only works if enough people agree to play by the rules, not just the laws, but also the norms. No one wants to do commerce in a place where highway robbery (the literal kind) is common. Bandits are bad for business. So are xenophobic tribalism, rigid traditionalism, and undependable infrastructure. In effect, the market both requires and advances a certain level of stability. A foundation of trust, reliable transportation and communication, a certain level of openness, and other stabilizing features are necessary.[6]

In that respect, the market can be part and parcel of social order. A social system must generally serve the greater good to some minimal extent to provide a context in which a market economy is viable. It must allow the activities necessary for buying and selling (e.g., free labor, ownership of property, freedom to move around, an infrastructure that makes transportation possible, minimal random violence, sufficient sustenance and shelter). Needless to say, not everyone has to be free (e.g., slaves, women, infidels) for a market to "work," but some critical mass must be. Indeed, most market economies have significant populations that are not fully folded into such freedom and security. Markets can function quite effectively for a segment of the population in combination with sustained brutality. For any sizeable element to benefit from market logic, though, these arrangements must be in place.

Let me pause here and say that the lack of fairness and equality in such settings reflects a failure of those involved. I do not condone it or passively accept that it is necessary. My point is that market systems have operated functionally in many settings, even if they had such significant shortcomings.

The real genius of the market, according to Adam Smith, Alexis De Tocqueville, Emile Durkheim, and others, is how it captures and negotiates the self-interest of many individuals (again, not necessarily all individuals, but many). In some ways, that coordination is the core social good of the market, the crucial value of this institutional logic to society. At its best, the market negotiates the basic paradox of human nature. Each of us is an individual with singular consciousness and at the same time we are all part of a social species that always lives in collective organization.

In other words, the market is like the internet. It is built by the varying contributions—most small, a few significant—of individuals, the totality of which becomes a sizeable resource and opportunity for any particular person with basic freedoms. Just as any individual can find lots of varied kinds of information on the internet that was put there by countless other people, any given buyer in a market has a plethora of options to choose from for a single type of commodity, which were produced by many different sellers. Likewise, someone who posts something on the internet may reach countless readers, just as someone selling a product in a market may transact with many customers. Remember, the most basic definition of a market is an economic system with many buyers and sellers. (A secondary point of this analogy is that the internet is in many ways itself a market, both for financial transactions but also the exchange of attention.)

This particular institution, this set of practices and norms, this economic logic—the market—has captured vast powers of nature and humanity. It "has created more massive and more colossal productive forces than have all preceding generations together," Marx and Engels wrote in their famous pamphlet. Irrigation, fertilization, transportation, medicine, plumbing, electricity, digital communication . . . think of the wonders. The market has had a hand in a lot of that. Even the most fundamental innovations that weren't invented within market societies—use of fire, written language, advanced math, and agriculture, for example—have been magnified in effect through the application of market principles over time. The market has thus facilitated increasing literacy, widespread mobility, more calories, better housing, nuclear power, and lifesaving vaccines.

As with all social constructs, the patterns of behavior we call a market have to be reproduced. Anything that is constructed can be deconstructed or reconstructed. Force, corruption, distrust, scarcity, war, revolution, disease, natural disasters, and numerous other phenomena—natural or human-made—have the capacity to destroy markets. And they have done so in many cases (see Diamond 2011). So, at the end of the day, the market is both breakable and changeable.

The dominant pattern, however, is that the market economy has proven to be a remarkably durable institution. While it is an earthly creation, history has shown that the market is in fact not fragile. Indeed, it is hard to think of a kind of organizational logic that has held up better under varying conditions across time. It is like a plant that is fertile, attractive, and keeps growing. In many cases, it spreads beyond what the planter intended. What's the right metaphor? Hostas, pachysandra, Sweet Annie? And in some cases, it takes over.

Expansive and consuming. Bamboo? When out of control, it can overwhelm and kill other flora. Kudzu, knotweed?

For some such plants, one key to maintaining healthy proportions is clear, firm boundaries. What is the setting? What contains the plants in question? Rocks, streams, other robust plants? The same is true of the market. It can play a vital part of social life when it is embedded in the right cultural and institutional environment. Countless critics and advocates of the market have made the rudimentary error of thinking the market is present or absent, on or off, and therefore good or bad (or vice versa). This simplistic reasoning contradicts how most every system works.

Let's assume that the market is here to stay. In most systems—both natural and human-made—too much of any one thing is often a bad thing. Lack of biodiversity is harmful to ecological balance. Likewise, human history shows us that any society that is dominated by a single kind of narrowly oriented institution (e.g., government, military, religion, family, caste) is in for trouble. Modern complex human society is not really possible under such conditions.

For us, here and now, the issue is not simply the logic and functioning of the market itself. It is not that market forces are loose in the world. It's that they are inordinately influential and untempered relative to other social forces. This is evident in the way several key market principles permeate our culture: efficiency, profit, consumption, individualism, competition, and short-term thinking. Each of these elements has value, and under the right circumstances contributes to the wellbeing and advancement of humanity. However, we do not have the right circumstances. These values are not embedded in institutional contexts alongside broader ethical considerations and normative habits.

Narrowly defined *efficiency* that goes too far can be dehumanizing, as production, service, and retail workers in various industries well know. Not to mention the white-collar jobs so familiar to us from *Dilbert* and *The Office,* and other popular representations. Numerous industries, such as tobacco, firearms, and fossil fuels pursue *profit* without serious consideration for other ethics, such as health or safety. We all have to consume to survive, but the unnecessarily high rates of obesity, heart disease, and addiction in the United States clearly demonstrate that something is amiss in our *consumption* patterns. Who wants to live in a society in which you can't express and exert your own will? But the widespread loss of community, the epidemic of incivility, and the growing sense of isolation in American society suggests that excessive *individualism* can be self-defeating. *Competition* was deeply woven into the American ethos well before the phenomenal rise of reality TV. The election of an ethically challenged, repeatedly bankrupted, womanizing reality TV star to the most important office in the world might be a sign that our aspirations tied to ugly competition are out of control. Any *short-term* gain, material or otherwise, that seems like a win but destroys valuable resources in the long run is not worth it, as we are learning from climate scientists.

CONCLUSION

In sum, our collective moral footprint is broadly toxic because the foundations of morality are out of whack. Various institutional patterns are arranged in such a way as to undermine the basic moral foundations of care, fairness, liberty, loyalty, authority, and sanctity. There appear to be a number of factors behind this cluster of problems, including intense and increasing political polarization. That said, I think that the most enduring and important factor is expansive market culture. The logic of the market has expanded beyond the economic sphere into other parts of our lives. The vast institutional infrastructure of the market has grown stronger while other countervailing institutions have grown weaker. The resulting culture facilitates overemphasis on efficiency, profit, consumption, individualism, competition, and short-term thinking. The loss of balance related to expansive market culture is the main cause, I believe, of crumbling moral foundations. How does that relate to food? What can be done about it? The former question is addressed in the next chapter, the latter question in those that follow.

NOTES

1. See Schor (2011), Tobler, Visschers, and Siegrist (2011).
2. See Haidt (2006; 2007; 2012), Haidt and Graham (2009), Haidt and Joseph (2004).
3. There are, of course, often large numbers of people who are excluded, marginalized, or brutalized. Many societies have endured intact for some time with such arrangements. A viable society need not be just. Indeed, stratification is built into every society in one form or another. I do not mean in any way to condone such injustice. Inequality varies a great deal across societies. The extreme forms are abhorrent. The point here is that, according to Haidt's moral foundation theory, a critical mass of individuals have to accept that the arrangements are reasonable—even if that means some are systemically mistreated.
4. See Brueggemann (2012a), Hochschild (2016).
5. This point has been demonstrated in various settings. See, for example, Hunter (2010) and McKnight and Block (2010).
6. This is a key point often underappreciated by critics of neoliberalism. See Fukuyama (1996), Hall and Soskice (2001) and Hetherington (2005).

Chapter Two

The Ugly Story of the American Food System

THE FAILURES OF EXCESSIVE MARKET CULTURE

A few years ago, my dad and I took a road trip across rural Missouri and Kansas, where my grandfather had been a pastor of several rural churches and where Dad had grown up. We saw the reality of the long-term trend among American farms; they were growing larger in size and smaller in number. In each case, the town had nearly vanished. Endless fields of monocrop rows are everywhere, but not many people. Houses laid out in a grid sit empty in serenely quiet, melancholy towns. No sounds of cars driving by or kids playing. "That's where the store used to be," Dad would say, or "that was the Post Office . . . bank . . . school." But almost nobody is visible in any of those places today.

Later, I thought of a little vignette from Khaled Hosseini's novel, *The Kite Runner.* "It was a dark little tale about a man who found a magic cup and learned that if he wept into the cup, his tears turned into pearls. But even though he had always been poor, he was a happy man and rarely shed a tear. So he found ways to make himself sad so that his tears could make him rich. As the pearls piled up, so did his greed grow. The story ended with the man sitting on a mountain of pearls, knife in hand, weeping helplessly into the cup with his beloved wife's slain body in his arms" (Hosseini 2003, p. 23).

For most of the 20th century, the quantity of American farms was shrinking while the average size of them was growing.[1] The small number left, with huge tracts of land often owned by a single family, are like the poor man who has accrued a wealth of pearls. The pile of pearls are the profits, no doubt large profits in some cases, reaped by the few owners. The murdered wife and other tragedies that were exchanged for the pearls are the costs: bankrupt farmers and hollowed-out towns (see Graham 2005). Some families surely benefit, but even those who do then live in dilapidated communities.

The market, as discussed in the last chapter, has been a remarkably durable institution that has advanced the well-being of humanity for much of recorded history. In terms of food, it must be credited in part for the immensely increased volume and diversity of food products generated since the Industrial Revolution, especially during the 20th century. What we are seeing now, though, is that market logic alone makes for a problematic food system. Left to itself, the market does not ultimately care about the feeding of people. Or we could say that when people are only thinking in terms of what they can buy or sell, they may well overlook the basic importance of healthy calories for large segments of the human population (see Guthman 2011).

In the United States, many of us have in fact done just that. We neglect the importance of healthy food for ourselves and our neighbors. Sometimes, quite frequently actually, food sits unused on a store shelf while people nearby go hungry. Of course, the same thing is often true in terms of other resources. The market has helped generate large amounts of housing, clothing, cars, and medicine, for instance, while many are homeless, poorly clad, lacking transportation, or unable to access the drugs they need.

As I suggested in the last chapter, several themes that characterize excessive market culture are now evident in most institutions and in the conduct of many individual Americans. This includes inordinate concern for efficiency, profit, consumption, individualism, competition, and short-term thinking. Conventional social science organizes the economy into three phases: production, distribution, and consumption. These six aspects of market culture are in play in all three phases. In each case, though, one of these themes tends to be more prominent. This chapter provides a brief overview of how each of these themes plays a role in the failures of the Industrial Food Complex and our dominant food culture.

Efficiency

The emphasis on efficiency in food production can be traced back to the development of monocropping, which began in different places around the world thousands of years ago (see Berry 2009; Harari 2015). The idea was to focus on one crop, produce as much as possible, as inexpensively as possible, and then take it to market to sell. Instead of growing something for one's own family or tribe, a farmer generated commodities to sell. Over time this logic would become central to modern, scientific farming. The monocrop system was enabled by and helped expand mechanization. Increasing use of plows, fertilizers, and herbicides, as well as standardized practices for packing, shipping, and marketing were all part of this shift (Scott 1998).

It was hugely productive. This new paradigm was so effective that it overwhelmed many traditional, local practices of farming throughout the world (see Patel 2008; Bittman 2021; Jackson and Jensen 2022). Central to the objective of efficiency was uniformity. Trade required predictability. This entailed standardizing practices as much as possible, regardless of distinctive geographical or cultural features of different agrarian settings. It also meant reducing human error, creativity, or folk wisdom. The uniformity, which was fundamental to the increases in yields, also reduced biodiversity. While many more people could be fed in such a productive system, there were new risks such as greater vulnerability to pests and diseases. This partly explains the Irish potato famine, for example.

The "Green Revolution" was a global movement that unfolded in the 1950s and 1960s, which involved increasing use of new technologies that generated huge amounts of crops, especially high-yielding varieties of cereals (see Patel 2007; Bittman 2021; Jackson and Jensen 2022). The crucial technological inputs were chemical fertilizers that ultimately led to both large increases in the volume of food produced and the decline in biodiversity in U.S. agriculture. This process was enabled in the United States by hundreds of millions of dollars of government subsidies. At the time, though, the enormous benefits in terms of feeding people, especially in less developed countries, were considered by many to be well worth the costs (Roberts 2008). The impact of this movement globally remains a subject of debate (Patel 2007; Bittman 2021; Jackson and Jensen 2022). What is beyond dispute is that this change in agriculture entailed a decisive shift toward greater reliance on synthetic fertilizers. This would be a key factor in the growing dependence of American farmers on technological innovation.

In *The End of Food*, Paul Roberts describes a kind of "tragedy of the commons" playing out over and over. The key for a wheat farmer in the Midwest, for example, is to grow more wheat while keeping costs down, which is to say becoming more efficient. To do that, conventional reasoning has held, he has to purchase more technology, perhaps a larger tractor combine harvester, and spread the costs of that investment out over time. He will produce more wheat and make more money in the short run. However, other farmers will then do the same thing and there will be an oversupply of wheat, driving prices down. And the cycle begins again for the original farmer, without any lasting gains combined with the debt from the capital investment.

Other problems abound in meat production. Large scale industrial meat production practices gained momentum in the 1930s. Today the industry is dominated by Concentrated Animal Feeding Operations (CAFOs), which, by definition, hold at least 1,000 animals for more than 45 days a year (see Natural Resource Conservation Service 2020). By the 1980s, most chickens, cows, and pigs were raised in CAFOs, and the concentration has intensified since then.[2] For instance, in 1987, the median number of hogs coming from American farms was 1,200. In 2002, that number was 23,400 (MacDonald and McBride 2009 p. 6). Such large production centers are in some sense much more efficient compared to more traditional methods of pastoral feeding (Garcés 2019; Fountain 2020). In industrial farms, it takes less time to raise a fully grown animal ready for the market.

Yet, there are hidden costs. They are "externalized" costs generated by producers, not directly passed on or visible to consumers, but rather borne by society as a whole, including taxpayers, and often the most vulnerable communities.[3]

While most American farms remain in the hands of families, they are not exactly family farms in the historical sense. In many cases, the animals on the farms are owned by or under contract with big agri-food companies.[4] Thus, family farms are often constrained in terms of how they can operate and what they can do with their products.

Today, many CAFO's hold 10,000 animals. Some hold 40,000 and the biggest hold up to 150,000! As *Jurassic Park*'s Dr. Ian Malcolm (played by Jeff Goldblum) said, "That is one big pile of shit!" The manure contains feces, urine, and often blood, birthing fluids, production area waste, antibiotics, and various other chemicals. It generates enormous amounts of methane and other gases. This contributes to the United States being the second leading country in the world in terms of greenhouse gas emission, behind China.[5] We have the second largest, most shitty moral footprint in the world.

In this instance, the readily available meat that provides huge amounts of calories might be thought of as the pile of pearls, though the nutritional value of such calories is in many cases dubious. Or perhaps the pearls are the wealth accrued by the giant ranches and meatpacking companies. Here, the horrors that generated all those tears include environmental damage, cruel treatment of animals, and rippling risks for humans.

Paul Roberts argues that overproduction is built into the industrial food system, which is hard on farmers but keeps prices down for consumers (see also Guthman 2011). American consumers spend less on food as a percentage of household income than those of most other countries (see Battistoni 2012). The true costs for consumers, though, as explained later in this chapter, are much higher than we realize.

Part of the problem, Roberts contends, is that the strategic goals of large food providers have put pressure on producers in terms of what they should generate and on consumers in terms of what they should buy. He says that mega-grocers like Walmart, Safeway, Kroger, and Albertsons, as well as fast food chains like McDonalds, Burger King, and Wendy's have had the scale and thus the leverage to shape both ends of the food system. The "hyper-efficient" system led by these big players has made for more volume, more diversity, more convenience, more calories, and lower costs. But also, less quality and less nutrition.[6]

All of this makes it very tough to stay in the black for the average family farm. Related problems in the dairy industry have been identified as contributing to high suicide rates among dairy farmers. According to the *New York Times*, one dairy co-op, "Agri-Mark, even began enclosing lists of suicide prevention resources with the checks it sends to farmers twice a month" (Yaffe-Bellany 2019).

The goal of efficiency is also evident in production practices that are unhealthy for workers. Companies as diverse as Kentucky Fried Chicken, Walmart, and Applebee's have all been implicated in this problem.[7] Speed-ups, demanding quotas, and inadequate training all contributed to high rates of injury in meatpacking and made it one of the most dangerous industries in the country in the late 20th century.[8] Other industries have been expanded through a range of strategies associated with McDonaldization and Disneyization, always with efficiency as a primary goal, and often with dehumanizing effects. See *The McDonaldization of Society* by George Ritzer (2020) and *The Disneyization of Society* by Alan Bryman (2004).

Now we can add another strategy to the list, *Amazonification*, which has a new twist on an old trick. The old trick is the privatizing of profits and the socializing of costs. Hence, Jeff Bezos is one of the richest people in the world and his employees need food stamps (paid for by taxpayers). The new twist involves digital technology, the growing addiction to hurried "one-click-living," unparalleled scale, the integration of independent suppliers, and reliance on vast global transportation. See *Fulfillment* by Alec MacGillis and *Amazon Unbound* by Brad Stone (2021) for details.

As central as the goal of efficiency is to the production and distribution of food, it is also very much connected to consumption, not just what we eat but how. The culinary historian, Annie Gray, said that fast food goes back to "at least the Roman period" (History Extra Podcast 2021). People would proffer trays with lamb chops on the street in Rome, for instance. "If you've got humans," she continued, "they're going to want to eat fast." Efficient consumption is very old, probably an adaptive trait from long before the classical period. Eating quickly before predators or bad weather came along might have helped certain members of our species to survive long enough to pass down their genes.

But *Homo sapiens* does not always eat quickly. Meals linked to formal rituals, diplomatic functions, life course milestones, and ordinary family gatherings have often taken a ton of time. In that way, they are often decidedly inefficient. These aspects of human culture have presumably been adaptively beneficial too in the form of political alliances formed while breaking bread (e.g., peace treaties or weddings), psychological coping over food (e.g., mourning rituals, sacred meals), or just social bonding while eating (e.g., birthday parties, family picnics, dinner with friends).

Thus, how fast we eat is actually quite variable. Then, the question is what are the circumstances that make us eat quickly or slowly? One decisive factor is the availability of food on the quick. Modern fast food like hamburgers came along in the early 20th century. McDonalds and Burger King really got going in the middle of the 20th century. New forms of refrigeration were crucial to that shift. Food courts in malls, schools, and other places popped up in the late 20th century. The strip malls with lots of places to grab a quick bite showed up around the same time. Now this infrastructure for efficient food is widespread and integral to American culture. This includes fast food and food courts, as well as frozen food, processed food, preprepared meals, drive-through, and food delivery. A rapidly growing sector of this regime is delivery attached to the gig economy like Uber Eats, Doordash, and Grubhub. Another is the fresh meal delivery services like Blue Apron, Home Chef, and Factor.

For many low-income families, efficiency is an urgently necessary aspect of their lives. Those who work multiple jobs to make ends meet have scarce time for home-cooked meals with fresh ingredients (see Bowen, Brenton, and Elliot 2019). In such cases, the need for efficiency is based on other problems, namely poverty and inequality.

Among affluent households, the story is different. As numerous labor-saving, time-saving devices as many enjoy, they still find it difficult to find the time to shop for fresh ingredients, make a meal from scratch, or sit down and eat it together (see Fielding-Singh 2021). Do you know any people who eagerly embrace the employment of gadgets, servants, outsourcing of household tasks, or other time-saving steps without any thought? Many have traded health for time. In her book, *How the Other Half Eats: The Untold Story of Food and Inequality in America* (2021), Priya Fielding-Singh documents the enormous amount of stress folks in affluent households feel around their food consumption habits. Getting it right feels like an immense burden to many.

The comedian Jim Gaffigan has a couple bits where he makes fun of people who hike or camp. He jokes that he is decidedly "indoorsy." It occurs to me that the goal of efficiency makes many of us indoorsy. Of course, many households have no time to waste. However, my focus here is on the addiction to hyper-efficiency. Sure, many Americans understandably appreciate their comforts, air conditioning, heat, and other wonders of modern technology. But this sensibility, something related to an attraction to ease, cuts us off from the mysteries and messiness of nature. As Max Weber explained a century ago, efficiency is usually rational in the short run, but often comes with a less visible, noxious cost in the long run.[9]

Profit

Denying people access to healthy calories is an old tradition in America. The conquest of the Americas on the part of Europeans is an ugly foundation for everything that followed and continues to shape the contours of our world. The kidnapping and human trafficking of African bodies into forced labor camps is another fundamental part of the story that continues to have rippling implications. The ongoing wrongs of broken treaties, appropriation of natural resources, legal segregation, debt peonage, enslavement of prison labor, various protections of immorally acquired wealth are not just by-products of our history. They are integral to it. Just like structured inequalities built into the educational, health, and criminal justice systems remain crucially important now.

Not all profit is bad, of course. Nevertheless, this grotesque history is in fact all linked to the pursuit of profit.[10] And all of it is related to food, how it is produced, and who has access to it. On this score, William Faulkner had it right: "The past is never dead. It's not even past." That part of our past helps account for the more than 30 million Americans who are food insecure today, including disproportionate numbers of people of color.

Moreover, the profit motive is implicated in ongoing systems of injustice related to food. White people own 98 percent of rural land. But people of color comprise some 62 percent of agricultural laborers.[11] It's worth recalling that farm workers lack most of the protections found in other industries (see Brueggemann 2002). People of color are also overrepresented in the animal slaughtering and processing industry, work settings with some of the unsafest conditions in society (see Brueggemann and Brown 2003). Minority and low-income communities also endure disproportionate amounts of environmental waste with immensely damaging consequences (Washington 2019; Addison 2022).

More generally, the practices of Big Food and Big Ag generate profit in ways that are broadly harmful (see Roberts 2009; Leon and Ken 2017; 2019). "It's a throw-away world we live in," my plumber recently declared to me as we investigated a major leak in our house. He was explaining why parts we've used for our plumbing system fall apart now more frequently than they did in decades past. For a lot of companies, what matters most is selling stuff, not the quality of what they make. Between planned obsolescence and cutting corners to keep production costs down, there is a lot of crap out there.

Can you imagine an automobile manufacturer whose executives would never choose to buy one of its vehicles, a university whose faculty would not send their kids to school there, or a hospital whose physicians wouldn't take their sick loved one there? There is a widespread belief that employees who work for Big Food corporations do not consume their own products.[12]

One of the people to whom I spoke, Mark Maraia, owner of Carbon Neutral Investments LLC, said "You go to any farmer or rancher and go, 'okay, do you eat your own products?' That's the test." Many fail it.

In *Salt, Sugar, Fat*, Michael Moss tells the story of an historic meeting in 1999. Eleven men, the heads of America's largest food companies, met in Minneapolis. With some 700,000 employees among them, these competitors spent a great deal of their time thinking about how to ruthlessly outmaneuver one another. But in this extraordinary gathering, they sat together to confer about their industry. A vice-president of Kraft named Michael Mudd made a presentation in which he advised a bold shift. Obesity is a national epidemic, he explained, and anyone who seriously considers the problem recognizes that the products generated by the companies represented in that room contribute to it in significant ways. His recommendation was a paradigm shift in which these companies reduce the ingredients in their products most responsible for the cravings linked to obesity and related health issues. Mudd found some sympathetic ears among his audience. But not enough. In the end, the profit motive and the competition among those CEOs led the group to circle wagons around the status quo.

What Mudd seems to have known, Michael Moss documents, is that the Big Food companies have chosen, repeatedly, to produce and sell products that they know are harmful to consumers. They have put ingredients understood to be unhealthy at high levels—including salt, sugar, and fat—into "food" products. What concerned them was not nutrition, but purchase, not how the food affected people's health, but whether they would buy it. The key to that, Moss shows, was taste. For sugary sodas, this was about finding the "bliss point," the perfect amount of sugar to foster ongoing craving—a well-known concept associated with the market researcher Howard Moskowitz.

One of the amazing feats of Big Food has been their ability to convince so many of us that their products are delicious and fun.[13] I have thought about that when talking to European friends whose lives revolve around traditional cuisine and fresh foods. Somehow, it's hard to explain Diet Coke, Cheetos, and Twinkies to someone who relishes what's in season or their grandparents' recipes.

What Mudd was really concerned about, according to Moss, was not an obesity epidemic, not the well-being of Americans, but that consumers would at some point get wise about Big Food's role in it and turn on them. He was wrong, at least in the short run. Most consumers have stayed in the dark for many years.

Does it need to be said again that there is nothing wrong with profit? Certainly not as a reasonable goal situated alongside other values. Indeed, our species is hard-wired for trying to secure and accumulate resources. Surplus is what allows us to survive winter, establish security, make art, and dream about the future. Return on investments is what shareholders expect executives to worry about.

That said, there are problems with how profit has been realized in the American food system. In 2017, the top 25 global companies in the food and beverage industry collectively hauled in $741.2 billion in revenue and $86 billion in profit (McGrath 2017). Nestle, Coke, and Pepsi topped the list. As a group, those 25 corporations secured revenues greater than the Gross Domestic Product of every country in the world except for the most productive 18. So what is wrong with this picture?

First, profit has been narrowly defined as a singular objective at the expense of other values. The real word for that is greed, which seems to have induced a fundamental lack of honesty. Big Food is notoriously cagey about its production. This includes lack of transparency, nondisclosure clauses in employee contracts, misleading labels, huge investments in marketing, legal action against critics demanding transparency, and funding self-serving "science."[14]

Some food is not what it seems, like Parmesan cheese made out of wood pulp, honey cut with corn syrup or fructose syrup, expensive Japanese wagyu beef produced in North Dakota, lobster that is actually squat lobster (a creature more closely related to a hermit crab), red snapper that is often not red snapper, or overpriced American port wine that does not involve the geographical location, grapes, or production method of real port (Olmstead 2016).

The dairy and meat industries have been especially effective at facilitating government classification of their products as basically healthy despite ample scientific evidence bringing such claims into question.[15] No matter what the competitive pressures are, only greed could motivate you to produce toxic chemicals dressed up as food and try to convince parents to feed it to their children.[16]

Caveat emptor big time. Why invest in buyers being unaware? No doubt it would be unsettling for many people to see the realities of food production, especially oblivious suburbanites like me who live a relatively sanitized life. Peering through the doors of the factory to see how the sausage is actually made might be shocking, in any case.

Still, that doesn't change the fundamental right people have to know what they are eating and where it comes from. Especially in the age of trans-fatty acid, high fructose corn syrup, sodium benzoate, butylated hydroxyanisole, butylated hydroxytoluene, salmonella, E. coli, other harmful pathogens, and various additional legitimate concerns. What they are hiding above all appears to be a corrupt system that is dependent on unhealthy ingredients, mistreatment of employees, inhumane handling of animals, and degradation of natural resources.[17]

Just as food producers and distributors will go where the profits are, even if that requires cutting corners, they are less likely to go where there are no profits. The big players won't invest in settings with low marginal returns. Where people can't pay the normal price, you won't see big grocery stores. Where jobs are scarce and poverty is rampant, in other words, we can expect to see few stores, which is to say food deserts and food insecurity. As long as investors only pay attention to the bottom line, distributors narrowly define profit, and government doesn't take responsibility for creating alternative possibilities, we can expect many Americans to go hungry.

Consumption

In 1900, Marion Nestle shows in *Food Politics* (2013), the top ten most lethal illnesses in the United States were largely beyond our control. They included illnesses poorly understood by medical experts and citizens alike. Fast forward 100 years. To a much greater extent, the ailments on the list are collectively well understood. In many cases, such as coronary heart disease, certain forms of cancer, diabetes, stroke, and liver cirrhosis, for instance, we know that the illnesses could be ameliorated or even prevented by way of healthy diets (see also Brownell and Horgen 2004). So why doesn't that happen?

Huge interests are dependent on keeping consumers addicted and ignorant. Food producers traffic in numerous unhealthy commodities. Behind this pattern is a cluster of problems. While there are often large yields and more calories generated in agriculture, the products sometimes have little integrity. Many foods have combinations of ingredients that include toxic levels of salt, sugar, fat, and various preservatives. Marketing and rigged science intended to obscure such problems are common. Labeling and lobbying in ways calculated to hide all of the above is common. As a result, many consumers know less and less about where and how their food was produced.

No doubt there are large numbers of Americans who do not have access to or knowledge about healthy food. If you grow up in a household situated in a food desert, securing healthy ingredients is really tough. If your high school-educated parents work three jobs to make ends meet, how do they prepare real food, and how do you learn to do it? If your parents are highly credentialed overworked professionals, and your family never sits down for a home-cooked meal, how do you develop the habits? It's easy to imagine that the Food Network's show *Worst Cooks in America* never has a hard time finding comically inept folks from a broad range of demographics to serve as contestants (see Patel 2008, p. 289).

And many of us are susceptible to the unfiltered, uninterrogated claims of advertisers presented to us on billboards and in magazines, as well as in our living rooms through television, and increasingly into every other space through digital technology. Big Food spends a fortune on marketing with good reason: it works.[18] "Beef. It's what's for dinner." Anyone remember that ad campaign from the 1990s? Along with the sound of Aaron Copland's Hoe-down from Rodeo, we heard the voices of American icons like James Garner, Robert Mitchum, and Sam Elliot reminding us that eating beef is linked to patriotism, family, masculinity, security, and comfort.

Is inexpensive beef from grain-fed cows loaded with antibiotics raised in a filthy Concentrated Animal Feeding Operation to maturity in a year just as good as more expensive beef from grass-fed cows raised on a small farm for at least twice that long? Does Fruit Roll-up really have fruit in it? Care for some "all-natural non-dairy creamer" made from corn syrup?

In truth, there is no real shame in being susceptible to such offerings of food, however farfetched. Deep in our genetic roots is a survival instinct that evolved in the context of scarcity. As Annie Gray suggested, our hunter-gatherer ancestors who survived to procreate mostly said yes to any food they could get their hands on with as little trouble as possible, and then passed on the predisposition to eat what they could scrounge on to their offspring, which is to say all of us. As deep as that instinct to efficiently secure sustenance is in us, though, it's not the only factor (see Ulijaszek and Lofink 2006). In *Food Fight: The Inside Story of the Food Industry, America's Obesity Crisis and What We Can Do about It,* Kelly D. Brownell and Katherine Battle Horgen (2004) estimate that at least 60 percent of population body weight can be attributed to environmental circumstances, like availability of certain foods, education, marketing (vs. biology).

One expert on body weight, George Bray said, "genes load the gun, the environment pulls the trigger" (quoted in Brownell and Horgen 2004, p. 24). The psychologists, artists, lawyers, and compromised "scientists" working in the marketing regime are sophisticated.[19] As genetically evolved suckers for available calories, many of us are an easy mark—it's like shooting fish in a barrel (Brownell and Horgen 2004; Herz 2018).

In the case of beef, this is especially damaging (see Roberts 2008, p. 209). The environmental impact is very bad. Most estimates say about 1800 gallons of water are required to generate one pound of factory farm beef—a serious drain on a vital resource. The manure, about 120 pounds per day per animal, indirectly pollutes water sources. Deforestation, greenhouse gas emission, and loss of biodiversity are other deleterious effects of the mainstream beef industry. Plus, there is the question of health. Too much beef is bad for us. The United States consumes more beef and buffalo than any other country in the world (except Argentina) averaging some 82 pounds a year per person (Christen 2021)—almost a quarter pound every day.

There are, of course, plenty of Americans committed to eating wholesome food. This includes many affluent households invested in nutritious, organic, sustainable, local sources. They can and are willing to pay more at Whole Foods, Trader Joes, farmers' markets, and CSAs and take the time necessary for cooking healthy meals, or they outsource those tasks to hired labor. And there are low-income households, especially in the country but increasingly in the city, devoted to both old practices of preparing and eating food, as well as new, innovative, nutritious ways of cooking. More about these folks later.

Yet, there are many Americans across the socioeconomic spectrum with access to relatively healthy food—whether it is produce from Walmart, other retail stores, farmers' markets, or gardens—who are not committed to eating well. Ironically, this includes people who are avid consumers, people who think very carefully about the quality of what they purchase and securing a genuine bargain. The Bureau of Labor Statistics reported in 2017 that families with the median household income (around $75K) spent nearly $20K on consumer goods. Even though a large chunk of that is for food, we spend less on food now than we did in the past.

For most Americans, there is another twist. While over time we have spent less on food, there has been a huge increase in the amount we spend eating out. That means that the overall decline is mainly driven by less being spent on food we prepare at home, often the most well-rounded calories we could consume. By well-rounded I'm talking about the *moral footprint*—again, think of where the food comes from, depletion of natural resources, management of human labor, how animals are treated in production, nutrition, and the like.

Lots of families, especially in low-income neighborhoods, make the understandable decision to buy inexpensive fast food over more costly organic ingredients for home-cooked meals (Roberts 2008, p. 291). That may be what is available in a food desert or what feels doable in the context of long hours at work. While fast food may be less expensive for consumers to purchase or producers to generate, though, that does not necessarily mean its production is in fact cheaper. A key point here is that enormous government subsidies pay for a small number of agricultural products that anchor the fast-food industry, especially corn, wheat, soy, dairy, and meat.[20] Who pays for the subsidies? Taxpayers. Plus, there are the costs passed on to future generations, as discussed below. This includes the use of fossil fuels, which currently contributes to degraded soil, depleted water supply, and climate change (see Graham 2005). If the price of oil goes up a lot, which many analysts expect, that will be extremely disruptive to the production of food. In any case, the oil will eventually run out. All of these costs are part of a misguided calculation, akin to the pearls and murdered wife in *The Kite Runner.*

Individualism

One of the historically distinctive features of American culture has been the sovereignty of the individual. Jefferson articulated this value most clearly in his famous words in The Declaration of Independence. The notion that each person has inherent worth and undeniable rights, regardless of where they come from, is justly revered. There has always been another side to it, though. Obviously, part of the problem is that some people were defined as being less than a man—including women, of course, as well as indigenous peoples, people of African descent, and other people of color. Jefferson himself was a slave owner and serial rapist. From the beginning, the ideal of individualism left some out, even including some carrying the privileges of whiteness and masculinity, such as men who didn't have property or credentials, members of other faiths, and foreigners.

The phrase "rugged individualism" was ironically coined by Herbert Hoover. Has there ever been a time when the idea of each person figuring things out for himself was less workable than during the Great Depression? While the phrase didn't emerge until the 1930s, the ethos is an older artifact of American history (see Bell, Ashwood, Leslie, and Schlacter 2020).

The problem with this mixed bag of cultural heritage in terms of food is that while the overall system has for some time been very lucrative, the returns only flow to a fraction of our citizens. That is how the pattern of increasingly large and increasingly productive agricultural operations ends up in the hands of fewer and fewer farmers. That is how the same country with the most billionaires ends up with the greatest levels of hunger in the industrialized world.

The term "food desert" refers to a residential area that does not have available distribution of healthy food in geographical proximity. No good markets, no fresh produce, little affordable food, especially healthy food (see Ver Ploeg, Mancino, Todd, Clay, and Scharadin 2015). Food deserts are settings generally associated with food insecurity, the lack of reliable access to healthy food. Obese consumers who live in such places are confusing to some. How could one be underfed and overweight? The desert refers to a scarcity of healthy calories. For instance, corner markets in poor, urban areas often have an abundance of relatively affordable food that is highly processed and loaded with sugar (Moss 2014). If that is all you have to eat, weight gain follows, and then in many cases the medical ailments associated with being overweight, such as diabetes. Needless to say, one can also be food insecure while living near an abundance of food due to other obstacles. Poor people sometimes live near rich people but can't afford to eat what they do.

In a food desert, even those with some resources and motivation have a hard time securing healthy food. It's just not there. Some critics suggest that this phrase is misleading because a desert is a naturally evolved geographical phenomenon with a viable ecosystem that supports life. Perhaps a better way to express this problem, they suggest, is the term "food apartheid."[21] That is an arrangement made by human beings that systematically separates a category of people from valuable resources and opportunities related to food. Apartheid literally means "apart-hood." Through residential segregation, unequal access to quality education, economic development, gentrification, environmental discrimination, and other divisive structures, this kind of system inhibits "food sovereignty," that innate authority humans have to generate what they need to survive.

There are clearly various factors that contribute to this problem, including a tradition of racial discrimination built into American culture before the Revolution. The individualistic ethos embedded in our political economy has old roots as well (Bell et al. 2020). That certain categories of people have been and still are methodically excluded from full access to the American dream is well known. In the food system, that is manifest in high rates of food insecurity. Inadequate nutrition for young people has rippling implications in terms of educational achievement, employment, and crime. Individuals who face material scarcity, ample research shows, are more likely to manifest cognitive deficits and dysfunctional behavior, which then contributes to additional cycles of scarcity and inequality (Mullainathan and Shafir 2013).

What is sometimes less recognized is that this same ethos plays out in other destructive ways that harm not only low-income households, but also the affluent. Various contingent factors have exacerbated the individualism undermining our food culture. This includes the privatization of American life after World War II, as well as the valorization of individualism among men, and among women, in different ways, during the 1960s and 1970s (see Brueggemann 2012a). No doubt, we can also look to the endemic workaholism of upwardly mobile professionals during the second half of the 20th century, the overscheduling of children, and most certainly the spread of digital technology and social media.[22]

These patterns related to individualism influence consumption, not just what we eat but also how. Each of them is implicated in the rise of easily accessed food (frozen, processed, preprepared, fast, drive-through), as noted above, the related decline of home-cooking and family meals. Such developments have contributed to less nutritional habits and by extension higher incidence of health problems. The loss of shared family meals may well weaken socialization processes that were previously important for teaching young people important values and cultivating family cohesion (Ochs and Shohet 2006; Purnell 2019). In *Going Solo,* Eric Klinenberg (2013) documents the astonishing rapid increase in the number of Americans living alone. This trend no doubt contributes to the increase of people eating alone as well.

These cascading problems, which involve individualism, as well as the goals of efficiency and profit, affect many affluent households, families that have both the means and the knowledge to eat differently. Some of these problems most certainly hurt lower-income families as well. If a household head works two or three jobs and access to fresh food and time for preparing it is limited, the result will predictably be individuals eating processed food on the fly when they can.

Competition

Many companies offer lovely messages in their advertising: *Resourceful by nature* (Archer Daniels Midland); *The miracles of science* (Dupont); *Performance with purpose* (PepsiCo); *Growth for a better world* (Monsanto); *Make today delicious* (Kraft); *Good mood food* (Arby's); *Eat fresh* (Subway); *Your way, right away* (Burger King); *Good food, good life* (Nestle); *It's what your family deserves* (Tyson); *I'm lovin' it* (McDonalds). Can you imagine how fabulous life would be if these companies delivered on such promises? So many beautiful, heartwarming sentiments. The reality in much of the agricultural, food, and beverage industries, though, is that the most successful companies are the most ruthless. "To be competitive, we've got to add fat," a Kraft executive once acknowledged (quoted in Moss 2014, p. xxii). What if they were all thoroughly truthful? *Don't ask what's in it; We hope no one finds out; Getting rich at others' expense; No, I would never eat what we sell; Loyal to nothing but profit; The community is not our problem; Crushing our competitors; Blame anyone but us.*

As we've seen, the health of consumers who can afford to pay is often a low priority. Of course, the well-being of consumers who cannot afford to pay generally doesn't even register (Patel 2008; Moss 2014). Certainly, efficiencies and scale can be adjusted and prices can be lowered to draw more low-income buyers in, as Walmart has demonstrated most lucratively. But the prevalence of food apartheid and food insecurity reveals a different kind of pattern for those who can't afford to pay.

The hard-nosed, take-no-prisoners approach among the many dominant companies, moreover, is evident in other ways. Even though top executives throughout these industries would extol the benefits of free-market competition, the reality seems to be that they don't really want to be in competitive markets. This likely accounts for the numerous oligopolies that characterize the economy of American food (Patel 2008; Leonard 2014). Of course, various economic variables are in play here. Nevertheless, the dominant ethos of vicious competition is a central factor. A number of corporations have intentionally helped to run other companies out of business (Wu 2018).

Two soft drink brands control 70 percent of the market. Fast food has about a dozen companies dominating nearly three-quarters of that market. Campbell's Soup produces about two-thirds of American soup. Candy is all about Mars, Hershey, and Nestle. For breakfast cereal, it's General Mills, Kellogg, PepsiCo, and Post Foods. More generally, a small number of large food companies with dozens of brands each command huge leverage in different food sectors. This includes in order of overall size Pepsico Inc., Tyson Foods Inc., Nestle, Kraft Heinz Co., and Coca-Cola Co. In 2016, despite growing concerns about obesity and its medical implications, Coke did nearly $20 billion in sales. Pepsico did roughly twice that. The others on this list are in between. These companies are, together, what we mean when we are talking about Big Food.[23]

The problem with oligopoly is that many of the beneficial aspects of market logic are inhibited. Competitive pressures are reduced, motivation for innovation is curtailed, transparency declines, and information for consumers is more limited. The scale of a few large players can make it harder for smaller firms to get started. In the case of a monopoly, the logic of supply and demand collapses. If consumers don't like the product, too bad. If the quality sucks, too bad. If the price seems unreasonable, too bad. If wages go down, too bad. You can't go elsewhere. All those same problems plague oligopolistic industries to a lesser degree.

Agribusiness is similarly characterized by oligopolies.[24] Five companies account for almost half of the food sold in American supermarkets. Four companies control more than three-quarters of the meat products industry. About six companies dominate the world's seeds and fertilizer industries. Two of the biggest, Monsanto and Bayer, recently merged in a $66 billion deal.

One of the problems of this particular oligopoly is that it forces small farmers to buy its products. Say a farmer takes up the ancient tradition of saving and using his own seeds. But he finds that seeds patented by one of the big companies, which are being used on farms around his, blow into his field and grow on their own. He can then face legal penalties for infringing on the patent. Monsanto itself holds some 1700 patents. If he does buy seeds from Monsanto, they may be inordinately expensive. Plus, they are designed to be used in combination with other Monsanto products such as pesticides and herbicides (see Maya-Ambia 2015).

All of these pressures incentivize a certain compliance on the part of family farms: get on board with Monsanto (see Kucinich 2014). You may own your own farm. It may be a "family farm" in some real way. Yet you often have to dance to someone else's tune. Farmers lose control. Their work becomes less about how they want to farm, what makes for healthy food, or what is good for the environment and more about not being run out of business. Some critics, including people I interviewed, think that this entire system is designed to run small farms out of business so the big guys can get control of more land (see also Stull and Broadway 2013).

Monsanto's "first GMO product, the patented Glyphosate-resistant, 'Round-Up Ready' soybean," as Lessley Anderson (2014) explains, "was approved by the USDA in 1994." This product, and others like it, is sold in conjunction with Round-Up, its key ingredient being glyphosate, which kills unwanted weeds but has also been associated with various health risks. In 2017, CNN reported that some 800 plaintiffs were suing Monsanto for health problems related to its products. One of them was a grounds keeper name Dewayne Johnson who had been diagnosed with terminal cancer.

During that suit, the jury learned that Monsanto executives attempted to mislead the public about scientific facts established by experts, bully scientists whose research implicated their products, and even generate bogus scientific research supporting their cause. The focal point of this research is glyphosate, which is registered for use in 130 countries on more than 100 different crops. One of the leading agribusiness companies (after the merger it is now the largest) actively lies about the toxic nature of the most widely used weed killer in the world. In 2018, a California jury awarded Johnson $289 million for the role Round-Up played in his illness.

Growth for a Better World. That is the slogan most associated with Monsanto. Without much consideration for farmers or the health of the people who use their products, Monsanto wants to win and win big (see Patel 2008). It apparently does not matter how. *Growth for a Better World?* Growth for a richer company? The outcome matters, the process doesn't. Is Monsanto exceptional in this way? Perhaps. It may be the most relentlessly cunning, pitiless player in the game. Monsanto has been on the top 20 most hated companies in the United States for some time, next to such organizations as Facebook, The Weinstein Company, University of Phoenix, and the Trump Organization.

Or Monsanto may just be one that got caught and incited public outcry (see also Addison 2022). Other corporations have been shameless in co-opting marketing labels such as "organic," "free range," or even "natural." Coca-Cola has repeatedly arranged for bogus science that pushes responsibility for the obesity epidemic away from its sugary products (Nestle 2017; 2018), a sadly common sort of practice, however outrageous (see also Patel 2008). As Marion Nestle reports in *Unsavory Truth: How Food Companies Skew the Science of What We Eat,* numerous food producers fund science that definitively demonstrates the healthy benefits of their products (see also Leon and Ken 2017; 2019). We are talking about carefully planned, well-funded, "expert"-approved lies, which is to say systemic corruption.

In any event, what is obvious for anyone who really cares to know is that Big Food is dominated by a small number of players whose loyalty to consumers, truth, or integrity is sometimes outweighed by their ruthless desire to compete and win.

Short-term Thinking

Anyone who raises children knows that teaching them to clean their rooms and figuring out how to motivate them to do it regularly takes time and energy. In the short run, it is a lot easier just to clean their rooms for them. In the long run, though, the relative benefits of learning to do it on their own are bounteous.

The same thing applies to developing the habits of preparing and eating meals in a decorous, civilized way. In addition to the time it takes to learn skills, stock and organize a pantry, plan meals, buy real food, prepare it, sit down together, and clean up, it takes energy to socialize an entire household to such routines. In the short run, it may well be easier to assemble frozen food, drive through, or eat out. It may also appear cost-effective in the short-run to multitask, run errands, watch screens (TV, phone, computer, video game), or do work (jobs, housework, or homework), all while eating.

The advantage in terms of long-term benefits, however, goes overwhelmingly to home-cooked meals shared together as a household (see Curran 2021). Commensality—eating together at the same table—is the gift that keeps on giving: more nutrition, more practice and insight about planning, budgeting, cooking, cleaning and work ethic in general, more social time nurturing relationships, more cultivation of life skills across generations, more "buy-in" to the household's well-being. Moreover, for young people better communications skills, self-esteem, and social resilience, more awareness of where food comes from, and more consciousness of how slow, quiet social interactions carry deep, subtle meaning that is usually sacrificed by way of easily accessed food quickly consumed.

This is not to say that any family who cuts corners once in a while by way of take-out or frozen food is doomed to miss out on all those good things. Obviously one can eat healthy fresh food in a rush, or really enjoy a slow meal with good conversation while consuming fast food—and receive some of these benefits. The point is that in the long run, in some general sense, the more real food we collect, prepare, and consume thoughtfully, the better off we will be.

As problematic as short-term thinking built into our daily lives is, the most significant risks are tied to large systems that lack vision. Corporate executives in Big Food and Big Ag understandably focus on certain short-term goals: productivity, quarterly reports, shareholders' returns, job security, salary, promotion, new job opportunities, and the like. Farmers obviously pay attention to short-term issues like the price of milk, this year's yield, or this week's weather. Such concerns are in some sense rational, but like a driver looking only at the road right in front of her car, one might miss the hazards down the way before it is too late. Perhaps it seems rational to try to exert some control over what's right in front of you. Nevertheless, it is decidedly nonrational when you don't pay attention to long-term implications.

As previously noted, *Homo sapiens* has a bad track record in managing natural assets in general. There are important, consequential variations across times and places in terms of how different cultures protect nature. A lot of different societies, though, have exhausted crucial resources (Diamond 2011; Harari 2015; Jackson and Jensen 2022). As geomorphologist David Montgomery explains in *Growing a Revolution* (2017), a common pathway for human self-destruction is through ruining soil. He goes so far as to say that the plow is one of the most destructive inventions in modern society precisely because it is so damaging to soil. The problem is that plowed soil is so vulnerable to wind, rain, and erosion (see also Catton 1980).

The plow represents a particular agrarian orientation that is problematic: thinking of the land as needing to be mastered. As long as the plow has been at work, Montgomery contends, soil has been declining in health and quality. This trend has more recently been exacerbated by the increasing reliance on pesticides, herbicides, fertilizers. The widespread use of nitrogen-based synthetic fertilizer is especially harmful to water, soil, and air (Roberts 2008, p. 217).

Plows and fertilizers both represent a modern sensibility oriented toward conquering nature. This perspective emerged during the Enlightenment, gained enormous traction through the industrialization of the 19th century, and then was applied to agriculture to great effect after World War II. The new agricultural system generated huge amounts of food for consumers and thereby profits for producers. Again, though, there are hidden costs, "externalities" in the parlance of economics. For example, Paul Roberts (2008) explains, it takes 20 tons of grain to produce a ton of industrial beef and it takes 20 tons of water to generate a ton of grain. At 400 tons of water per ton of beef, the roughly 12,500,000 tons of beef the United States produces a year requires about 5 billion tons of water.

More generally, this enterprise is harnessed to a "technology treadmill" (Roberts 2008, p. 218) because nature adapts to various synthetic fertilizers and herbicides. The system is built on an ongoing need for escalating volume and intensity of the inputs. At some point, that is, this year's weeds will not respond to last year's herbicide. So we need more, stronger herbicide. It is simply not sustainable because the necessary water is finite. So are the fossil fuels required for all the synthetic products of agribusiness (see Graham 2005; Maya-Ambia 2015). One environmentalist I talked to, Mark Maraia, said to me that "the only thing that the big producers care about is one thing:

the single bottom line. Again, they don't care about the effect on our immune system, or the soil. They don't care about the ecosystem."

Much of the food produced through such processes is short on nutritional value.[25] Soil saturated with nitrogen and glyphosate and other chemicals produces crops that are less healthy, which are in many cases fed to animals who are then less healthy, much of which ends up as a forkful of food that is less nutritious. In the meantime, our air, water, and soil are degraded, further exacerbating the requirement of technological innovation to maintain previous levels of productivity. To make matters worse, other countries are starting to emulate U.S. patterns by adding increasing amounts of meat to their diets (Roberts 2008). This sort of unsustainable production is the main problem with such short-term thinking.

In effect, industrial farming requires gambling the resources of tomorrow in service of abundance today. What happens to soil, water and air as a result of CAFOS with 10, 40 or 150 thousand animals is a case in point. We now know, though, that the odds are stacked. It's a bad bet. The best science we have has spoken loudly and clearly—with as much certitude as a group of professional skeptics can muster on most any topic—that climate change is a problem that puts our planet's flora and fauna at risk, and that human beings continue to play an ongoing role in exacerbating this problem.[26]

In *Our Final Warning: Six Degrees of Climate Emergency*, Mark Lynas (2020) traces the effects of how our use of fossil fuels raises global temperature. The cumulative effect of some 35 billion tons of CO2 emitted into the atmosphere by way of human reliance on fossil fuels so far has been more than one degree Celsius, which has helped trigger a broad range of problems like massive melt rates in permafrost regions, collapse of numerous species, devastating fires in places like Australia and California, stunningly high temperatures in urban areas, and destructive, extreme weather events in countless settings. The trajectory of another degree of increase over the next several decades, Lynas (2020) argues, will be catastrophic. This includes the effects on water, soil, and air in connection with the viability of food production.

CONCLUSION

This brief overview indicates various ways that our food system is failing to provide our society's sustenance (see Brueggemann 2012b). Each element of market culture is implicated in this failure. Again, none of these values is inherently immoral. *Efficiency, profit, consumption, individualism, competition,* and *short-term thinking* have all been important, benign ideals at one time or another. The point is that as values they are out of balance relative to other important social commitments. Collectively, these patterns make for a horrendous moral footprint and comprise a bad story. It is a story in which our most important resources—human and natural—are debased. The patterns are so robust and entrenched, the story is so familiar, that it is tempting to accept all this as given, normal, and inevitable. Despair is so tempting.

The "problem of economy" is basically the question of how society generates what it needs to survive. It is fundamentally a material issue. How will we feed, clothe, and shelter ourselves? The solution to the problem is a viable economic system. It could be based on hunting and gathering, agriculture, conquest, industrial production, digital technology, and so on. Different technologies, norms, and practices are built into production, distribution, and consumption. Notice the linear way of thinking in this process. Human beings approach untouched nature, extract resources, usually transport them to another location, alter or refine them in some way, put them in the hands of those who will use them, possibly those who acquired them in the first place or perhaps not, and then those resources are utilized. Waste is often placed in a setting where poor people live, typically people who did not benefit from the production and consumption of the resources in the first place.[27]

Picture a road leading into a virgin forest. The further you go, the rougher and more untouched it gets. Producers go down the road to pull out something useful, maybe rubber, bananas, or timber. They take the stuff from its place of origin in the forest via the road to a place where it is processed, conceivably a village or factory. After that, maybe it is taken to a setting where it is sold for currency, bartered for different goods, or just used. In this conventional understanding of economic processes, the activity of human beings is emphasized throughout the entire process, focusing on the acquisition of some material, and its relocation from a natural environment to a built one. This way of understanding an economy is useful, to a point. The problem of economy is a basic challenge in every society that must be resolved by human beings. This sense of things obscures a deeper truth, though.

Our mainstream food system today, what I am calling the ugly story of American food, is aligned with this understanding of economy: harness nature for human use. This is the "mechanistic view of nature," Robin Wall Kimmerer says, "in which land is a machine and humans are the drivers" (2013, p. 331). More generally, this understanding of the economy is consistent with Juliet Schor's (2011, p. 4) idea of business as usual (BAU), which refers to "current economic rules, practices, growth trajectory, and ecological consequences of production and consumption."

What we now know is that this whole thing, BAU, is a mess. To keep extracting natural resources in this manner, producers are forced to drill deeper, scrape off more materials, farm larger fields, fish out greater proportions, add additional pesticides, breed for shorter maturation, make use of transgenic technologies, and so on. If you think of the earth as simply a natural store from which to draw, the options are limited. There is only so much to take.

Perhaps this is an oversimplification. New technologies, most notably those brought about by the Green Revolution, can change the size of the pie. And that is often a good thing, at least in the short run. However, there are two things with which we need to reckon.

First, and most important, the modern industrial food system, which started in some sense during the Enlightenment and is clearly responsible for many marvelous advances, is now burdened by increasingly weighty failures we cannot ignore. At the core of this mess is a simple logical flaw: we are working against nature. Domination has proven to be an inadequate and ultimately self-destructive way to think about the relationship between humanity and nature (see Bell et al. 2020). That is a large part of what makes the ugly story so ugly.

The other thing we need to realize, happily, is that we have other choices. There have always been some who thought about it differently, cultures where people conceptualized their relationship to nature in terms that were not hierarchical, acquisitive, and exhaustive. Some of those sensibilities live on, as you will see in the pages to come.

NOTES

1. This robust pattern has been brought about by a number of factors. See Dimtri, Effland, and Conklin (2004), Graham (2005), Food and Water Watch (2015), Hossfield, Kelly, Smith, and Waity (2015), United States Department of Agriculture (2020).

2. Leah Garcés (Klein 2022) estimates that 99 percent of animals produced for eating in the United States are raised in industrial animal farms.

3. See Garcés (2019), Klein (2022), Addison (2022).

4. See Edwards and Driscoll (2009), Stull and Broadway (2013), Leonard (2014).

5. See Foer (2009), Schor (2011), Food and Water Watch (2015), Fountain (2020).

6. See Roberts (2008, p. 59) and also Guthman (2011), and Estabrook (2018).

7. See Ritzer (2020), Ehrenreich (2001), McMillan (2012).

8. See Brueggemann and Brown (2003), Leonard (2014), Leon and Ken (2022).

9. See Weber's *The Protestant Ethic and the Spirit of Capitalism* (2010) for the original formulation, but also Scott (1999), Ritzer (2020) Honore (2004), and Taylor (2014) for more recent commentaries.

10. I am thinking of profits here in broad terms, as in income, dividends, revenues, compensation. A lot of people might be get rich without a company turning a large "profit," per se.

11. See Philpott (2020a; 2020b), Bittman (2021), and Horst and Marion (2019).

12. See, for example, Bilger (2006), Moss (2014), and Genoways (2016).

13. For documentation associated with these patterns, see Nestle (2017; 2018), and Leon and Ken (2017; 2019).

14. See Schor (2004), Lesser et al. (2007), Chernin (2008); Oreskes and Conway (2011); Genoways (2016), Nestle (2018).

15. This is demonstrated by Nestle (2013; 2018) Kearns, Schmidt and Glantz (2016), and Garcés (2019).

16. For a range of evidence, see Schor (2004), Andreyeva, Kelly, and Harris (2011), Chernin (2008), Brownell and Horgen (2004).

17. See, especially Foer (2009), as well as Oreskes and Conway (2011), Moss (2014), McMillan (2012), Montgomery (2017), Nestle (2018), and Garcés (2019).

18. This is another well-documented pattern. See Schor (2004), Brownell and Horgen (2004), Chernin (2008).

19. This is one of those things known by many people but somehow still accepted as normal. See Brownell and Horgen (2004) Chernin (2008), Moss (2014), Schor (2004), Andreyeva et al. (2011), Oreskes and Conway (2011); Nestle (2018). Recent research on several countries indicates that when advertising to children is restricted, the consumption of fast-food decreases (see Herz 2018, p. 272).

20. See Guthman (2011), Nestle (2013) Foley (2013), and Klein (2022).

21. See, for example, Sevilla (2021).

22. See Schor (1992), Brooks (2001), Wallis (2006).

23. See Patel (2008), Food and Water Watch (2013; 2015), Leonard (2014), Wu (2018).

24. See Stull and Broadway (2013), Leonard (2014), Addison (2019), and Garcés (2019).

25. As Brownell and Horgen (2004) and Bittman (2009; 2021) show, this is a well-documented criticism.

26. There is a ton of research on this. See, for example, McKibben (1989) and Intergovernmental Panel on Climate Change (2014).

27. See Clark, Millet, and Marshall (2014), Maya-Ambia (2015), Zimring (2016), Bell et al. (2020).

Chapter Three

Grounding

THE CYCLE OF ENGAGEMENT

There is also a beautiful story. It is old and new, singular and multifaceted, linear and circular. It's post-modern! And modern. And pre-modern. As I mentioned at the outset, I started this project with the intention of learning from people who do interesting things, who respond to all the madness loose in the world with wisdom, creativity, generosity, and optimism. As I spoke to different people doing a wide range of things, I soon learned that food is a focal point in society that is full of this kind of vitality. I became captivated by the stuff that nourishes us and inspired by the people who handle it. This led me to the alternative agro-food movement.

In this research, I am focused on a particular set of activities, which some refer to as the alternative agro-food movement. These activities are part of a cultural shift with distinctive interactional dynamics not easily controlled. They are also embedded in an organized social movement directed by intentional people (see Starr 2010; Guthman 2011).

As a social movement, it actually intersects with a cluster of collective endeavors that go by various names. They include environmentalism, the small farm movement, the regenerative agriculture movement, the organic movement, the good food movement, the new food movement, Slow Food, localism, vegetarianism, veganism, simple living, the back to the land movement, the fair trade movement, the alternative energy movement, the anti-GMO movement, the labor movement, some other forms of social justice advocacy, some other philosophical traditions, and some other subgroups. Some of these efforts are distinctively different things (e.g., the labor movement versus environmentalism), and some are overlapping groups with varied names (e.g., the small farm movement, the regenerative agriculture movement). In short, it's complicated (see Sumner 2015).

I prefer the name alternative agro-food movement, even though it is a little clunky, because it implies a contrast compared to our mainstream food system, and references both agriculture and food. When I say "the movement," I have a particular set of activities in mind that lie at the heart of the alternative agro-food movement, which I will delineate in detail. As I try to describe all this social terrain, when the tendrils of other movements reach into this movement, I will say so.

As I talked to people who handle food, I encountered folks who *do* things, whose lives are characterized by hearty verbs. "The best things in life," Edgar Allen Poe observed, "make you sweaty." When speaking about this project with family, friends, colleagues, or those I interviewed, almost everyone quickly thought of someone else I should talk to, some interesting person involved in farming, gardening, cooking, healing, sharing, preserving, conserving, advocating, stewarding, teaching, storytelling. (Poe no doubt had a few other things in mind, as well.)

In almost every case, the folks I spoke and listened to have two qualities. First, they actively handle physical materials, like soil, water, seeds, crops, trees, grain, meat, food, meals, waste, land, or in some cases, human bodies. This includes farmers, especially, as well as chefs, nutritionists, clergy, and physicians, for example. Second, they aspire to make the world a better place, by either advancing some positive goal or reducing a certain kind of harm, or both. They have some sense of purpose, vocation, or activism. The most resourceful efforts are those that link positive goals to harm reduction, like using waste for fertilizer, for instance.

As I started talking to people, I wanted to know what is important to them. I was intentionally trying not to look too far. I thought attempting to view the whole story too quickly might lead me to a false sense of coherence or a phony kind of optimism that is not grounded in reality. I was trying to be inductive.

After I encountered about 60 people, though, I realized that each of them has a story, most interesting, and many of them feel like they are part of a larger story. This chapter and the six that follow are organized in terms of some individual stories and how I came to understand that larger story. I now think of the focused activities of many individuals as unfolding at different, related stages in a broader *cycle of engagement*. (Each term I am introducing like this is defined again in the glossary in Appendix C). This is necessarily speculative, to be sure, but is much informed by what people on the ground told me.

Based on what I've learned, I picture this cycle as having six stages that primarily involve material activity (the handling of stuff), plus one that is largely symbolic and conceptual. The first stage is *grounding,* which is about how human beings relate to plants, animals, sun, water, earth, and air, and specifically how we impact or channel those resources. The second stage is *extraction*. This includes farming, especially harvesting, which is central to the movement, as well as gardening, fishing, slaughtering, milking, and other ways human beings procure natural resources.

The third stage is *processing*. This involves the work of transforming natural resources into useful food, so it includes cooking, refining, preserving, and other forms of conversion.

The fourth stage is *distribution*, which is just what it sounds like. The private sector is of course the main context for distributing food, including supermarkets and health food stores. But distribution also occurs at hospitals, religious settings, farmers' markets, community supported agriculture, and other food hubs.[1]

Whereas those places sometimes focus primarily on getting food to people, there are other settings more focused on getting food in people, which is to say *consumption,* the fifth stage. Such work occurs in homes, restaurants, schools, soup kitchens, and, again, religious settings.

As resources are used up through consumption, some people worry about restoring them through *stewardship*, the sixth stage. In my thinking, this is actually a multifaceted cluster of activities that involves the protection of natural and human resources, which is to say plants and animals as well as people. Unlike grounding, stewardship is more about the big picture, attending to large swaths of resources over time. Here I have in mind conservation, preservation, "buy-local" organizations, "organic" and other credentialing organizations, food sovereignty advocacy, labor unions, public health professionals, and animal rights groups.

Many of the folks I spoke to think of these activities as being connected. One thing leads to another. None of the subjects described the whole thing the way I am explaining it, but my portrayal of the big picture reflects my interpretation of their aggregated stories. Thus, grounding leads to extraction, which then requires processing and distribution (sometimes in a different order). That journey then allows for consumption, which motivates stewardship. Concern for the big picture by way of stewardship then allows for specific inputs through grounding.

This image of the cycle of engagement is what Max Weber termed an "ideal type." It is a theoretical version of how things work that is conceptually clear but perhaps tidier than how things actually work in real life.

As noted, every stage mentioned so far involves the handling of material things—soil, water, plants, animals, food, and human bodies. There is one other cluster of activities important to this movement, *communication*. Some people spend a lot of time articulating how aspects of the cycle of engagement work, how different stages are related to one another. Those folks are active in advocacy, lobbying, research, education, marketing, religion, and

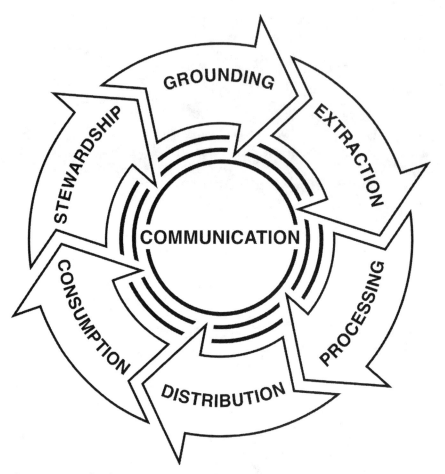

Figure 3.1.   Cycle of Engagement. Created by Martha MacGregor

storytelling. They deal primarily in symbols, such as words, images, and sounds (e.g., journalism, documentaries, lectures), as they try to make the connections intelligible, accessible, and resonant.

For now, I realize the cycle of engagement (see figure 3.1) sounds rather abstract. But I plan to remedy that in this chapter and the following six chapters. Each of them focuses on one stage in the cycle of engagement and features several subjects that I interviewed who are active at a given stage. Most of those mentioned by name are actually involved in multiple stages, but I put several individuals forward in each of these chapters to try to illustrate what I have seen in the movement writ large.

GROUNDING

Michael Pollan famously said, "you are what you eat eats." That means you are the "Round Up Ready corn" or bluegrass, eaten by the cow that becomes your hamburger, depending partly on whether it is grain-fed or grass-fed. The people who care about *grounding*, would add a third "eat." You are what you eat eats eats. That is, you are also the thing eaten by the thing eaten by the thing you eat. Grounding is about the most basic foundations of food. It is the seed that is planted, the soil in which it is placed, the water that hydrates the soil and seed, the fertilizers, and so on.[2]

There are people who spend a lot of time thinking about soil. This includes the likes of the distinguished geomorphologist David Montgomery, who has

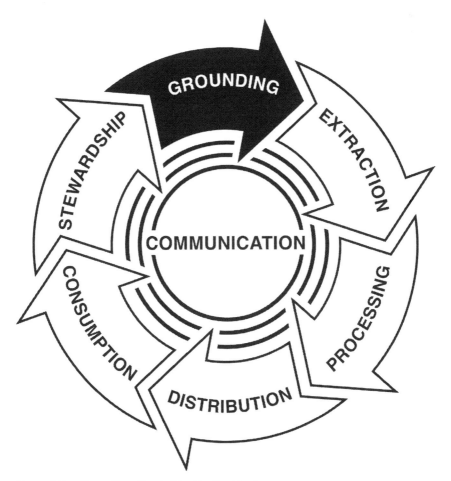

Figure 3.2. Grounding. Created by Martha MacGregor

written a series of illuminating books about soil. And it includes Elizabeth Forelle and Kailyn Wolfe, recent graduates of Skidmore College, where I teach, who wrote their senior thesis in Environmental Studies about the effects of tilling on soil health. Needless to say, the studies such researchers do are important. More about them later.

But the folks I first sought out are the ones who get their hands dirty. Most grounders don't only pay attention to grounding. Lots of farmers care about soil, but that is hardly the main point of their work. What really distinguishes grounders from others removing resources from nature is the recognition that in the long run the front end matters as much as the back end; what we put into the soil matters as much as what we take out.

As I studied farming, a certain topic kept popping up that I did not expect: earthworms. If you are fortunate, you eat a lot of their poop. That is, you eat food that comes from soil that has a lot of earthworms in it because they thrive amidst diverse microbes found in healthy soil. Earthworms help enrich soil by consuming dead vegetation that is not directly useful for plants, digesting it, decomposing it, and releasing waste that contains nutrients now useful to plants. Earthworm poop, what is actually called castings, then grows into kale, beans, carrots, or grass eaten by cattle. Plants from soil with lots of earthworms are much more nutritious and tastier than those grown in soil without them. "Compost," Leah Penniman wrote, "is proof of life after death" (Penniman 2018, p. 94).

This icky imagery of earthworms is one of the first lessons of real food, at least for "indoorsy" (I'm borrowing Jim Gaffigan's term) people like me who grow up knowing very little about where their food comes from. When you first hear about the realities of the origins of food, it sounds repulsive. Food comes from dirt, as well as worms, rotten plants, bugs, shit, and murdered animals.

"One thing I've discovered is that a lot of people are squeamish," one farmer told me. "And I'm quite intolerant of squeamish people, including my grandchildren. Like, you know: 'ah! There's bees, there's bugs.' They don't like to get bitten, don't like to get their hands dirty. . . . So, you know, in terms of why more people don't do it," she said about farming and gardening, "it's down to the earth. It's grubby, dirty. You get a bit dirty. A lot of people don't like insects. I'm amazed at the number of people who don't like insects."

Because they use no artificial pesticides, I asked folks at one urban community farm how they handle pests. The most senior farmer there—who has been at it for some three decades—explained that they try to create a natural habitat in which the predators of the pests will thrive. The farmers are trying to assist in the murder of pests. Even so, he added, things don't always work out, you win some and you lose some, the pests occasionally wreak havoc. He doesn't have a naïve sense of harmony according to which plants and animals are all buddies, but rather a respect for a system in which everyone has a part to play, life and death are part of the deal, and the long term is viable.

As I came to understand, the more one learns about all this, the organic realities of our food, the more it is demystified. Indeed, when you learn about what is under the ground on a regenerative farm (which those invested in regenerative agriculture are eager to talk about) and compare it to what is behind the closed doors of a Big Ag corporate operation (which those invested in industrial production are not), the earthworm poop starts to look pretty darn good. Indeed, the mystified products of Big Ag and Big Food, which is to say the stuff deceptively presented to us as sanitized, clean, innocent are made up of lies: *don't think about the dirt, poop, chemicals, murdered animals, exploited workers, or ecologically irresponsible packaging connected to what was produced.*

For many engaged sustainers, this is a very important point. It's partly about reducing unnecessary things that are destructive like toxic chemicals and wasteful packaging. And it's about looking clearly at the icky stuff that is essential, and honestly facing difficult things like suffering and death. The cycle of life inescapably involves pain.

Different folks commented on the strain of the labor, for sure, but also the trauma inflicted on animals and even the harm to plants. Some feel strongly about being upfront and compassionate about the uncomfortable stuff. I spoke to a Methodist pastor named Dee Lowman who situates food in the center of her ministry. She endeavors to relay to her parishioners that "there's a connection in our spiritual life with the animals who give their lives for our food. I'm a vegetarian," she told me, "but others aren't."

Leah Penniman writes about all the young people she encounters in educational programs who eat chicken but want nothing to do with their slaughter. "I shared that I voluntarily raise and kill hundreds of chickens every year even though I am a vegetarian because I know our community eats meat and I want that meat to be humanely and sustainably raised" (2018, p. 169). In her book, *Farming While Black*, she goes on to describe in detail the techniques carefully used at Soul Fire Farm to end the lives of chickens. It's not all easy or happy. But there is something appealing about the honesty and gentleness.

MORT MATHER: LIVING THE GOOD LIFE

Many of the people I spoke to evince a kind of youthful urgency. The dynamism of the collective project, the "movement" of this social endeavor, feels to many of them like something fresh, something that is happening here and now. Like most social movements, however, the alternative agro-food movement did not spring up out of thin air. It is like a waterway that has been fed by numerous little springs, brooks, and creeks. As one gazes on the wide stream, it is easy to forget that lots of things had to happen across vast terrain for this water here to flow.

I met several energetic folks who have been around a while, who are active in the movement now, but who were busy in "this work" back when it was more solitary and countercultural. This includes a couple different fellows from Maine who identify with the "back to the land movement." Richard D'Abate and Mort Mather were each influenced by Helen and Scott Nearing's iconic book *Living the Good Life*. They were each born in New York City. For various reasons, including the desire to be less dependent on oil and closer to the land, they independently moved to Wells, Maine, in the 1970s where they met and became close friends. Richard is now in his late seventies and Mort in his early eighties, and both still live in Wells.

I met Richard through a good friend of mine, Matt, who is his son. Richard has been a poet, teacher, academic administrator, and the executive director of the Maine Historical Society. He and his family have endeavored for many years to tread lightly on the land. To heat their house, he "spent most of 1973 to about 1980 cutting wood," Richard told me. As a matter of resisting mainstream consumer culture, for years they had no television (until the Boston Red Sox won the pennant in 1986). They gardened, baked their own bread, and cultivated a community of countercultural artists and intellectuals. Matt loved his childhood, by the way, but still complains about the wood-chopping and the absence of a TV.

Richard introduced me to his buddy Mort. (A short summary of the activities of every primary subject like Mort who is featured in a subheading is listed in Appendix B.) Even though he was born in NYC, Mort grew up on a farm in rural New Jersey. After graduating from high school there, he went to college at the University of Wisconsin where he earned a degree in theater. Mort has been a freelance marketer, a member of the Coast Guard, a stage manager of big theater productions in Chicago, Milwaukee, and New York, and nightclub manager in San Juan. After many rich experiences, he turned to a simpler life in Maine, settling there permanently in 1972

"Our first garden was fairly small," he wrote in one of his books, *How to Improve Your Life and Save the World.*

Small though it was, we still got potatoes, tomatoes, beans, peas, spinach, lettuce, beets, radishes, onions, cucumbers and zucchini. I had made the break with New York and was living in Maine with Barbara just dubbing around less than two years after realizing I was unhappy. I loved being in the garden. It was so quiet; seldom even a car passing or a plane. I was more likely to be taken from my thoughts by honking geese overhead or the distinctive sound of the Baltimore oriole. Barbara said that one of her favorite things was to look out at the garden and see me leaning on the hoe gazing out over the field contemplating the universe (Mather 2019).

Over time, Mort became an accomplished organic farmer and sustainable agriculture guru. He has published numerous books, essays, and columns, and worked with various groups and organizations all linked to organic farming.

Today, he runs a 1.25-acre operation called Easter Orchard Farm that provides fresh produce for his son's restaurant, Joshua's Restaurant and Bar in Wells, Maine. Mort's wife and Joshua's mother Barbara is a hostess there. On the farm, Mort has one fulltime employee. "I have got a farm manager. I call him my sous farmer." The two of them grow some 9,000 tons of Certified Organic vegetables a year, almost all of which go to the restaurant. A couple extra people are hired during the busy times of harvest, Mort told me.

Mort moves the crops around on a three- to five-year rotation, changing what is growing where, adding compost and horse manure, so as to maximize the richness of the soil. He's been at it long enough to have a good handle on things. For example, "if plant leaves are yellow then you're probably deficient in nitrogen," he explained. Still, he still runs into challenges that require the input of trained experts. He has soil tests done on a regular basis, as most organic farmers do, in this case through the University of Maine's Cooperative Extension.

During one recent year, Mort brought in a specialist from the Maine Organic Farmers and Gardeners Association to examine a corner of the garden where the plants were inexplicably smaller. Through careful investigation they speculated that some combination of which way the rows of vegetables were planted (east-west is preferable) and the proximity of a particular type of trees whose root systems grew underneath the garden may well have contributed to this issue.

As Mort spoke to me about Easter Orchard Farm, he exuded confidence derived from ample experience. It was tempered, though, by humility based on the inherent challenges of the work. Weather, market pressures, technological problems, and puzzles like the one mentioned above pose regular dilemmas. I was reminded of Wendell Berry's words: "No expert knows everything about every place, not even everything about any place" (Berry 2010, p. 5).

Mort is thoughtful and articulate about no-till farming vs. conventional tilling. He does some of both. He thinks a great deal about soil health, as all grounders do. Working quietly in the garden in the 1970s, reading far afield to learn about best gardening practices, building a small community of like-minded folks committed to an "alternative" lifestyle, Mort added more than his fair share to the upstream antecedents of the current movement. In the 1970s, there were surely hopes among Mort, Richard, and their fellow travelers about what their subculture might amount to in the long run. But the real focus was "living the good life" rather than changing the world. "We didn't know we were part of a movement," recalled Mort. "We were just living our lives" (quoted in Haskell 2016).

The upscale bistro run by Mort's son Joshua and stocked by Mort's farm is more like the coursing waterway we see now. It is visible, cosmopolitan, exciting, and mainstream, even in a small Maine town. Joshua's website mentions Mort's farm, includes blog entries about the sourcing, and describes the fresh ingredients in each dish. You can get a honey-lemon-ginger chicken skewer with a bulgur-mint-tomato salad, pork osso bucco with shrimp brushed with pesto, or a bourbon apple Manhattan. Like many such farms and restaurants today, Joshua's is explicit about being attached to elements of this movement.

I haven't learned about anyone else with this same story—a farming parent growing produce to stock a child's restaurant. That said, there is an aspect of this relationship that is actually pretty typical. Lots of people interested in food, including chefs and other cooks, develop that passion through the influence of older family members. The same is true of gardening and farming. Most every farmer I interviewed talked about some aspect of the work as being self-taught (usually the business side of things), but they always had mentors and role models, too, folks who were older and more experienced. This of course is how culture and socialization work in general. We learn to see the world a certain way and value particular activities as we grow by watching those around us. We often acquire things and skills from older generations in our families.

I asked Mort how he measures success personally and collectively. It's something about which he's thought a lot. "The only way I measure success is 'am I happy?'" Then he laughed and said, "I'm happy! So that's my success." "As far as measuring success in organic farming in the world," he paused, "the only thing I can do is what I can do. And that is to live my life in a way that has integrity. And the integrity is not based on anybody else's set of values. It's not based on the Bible. It's not based on laws. Those things are probably figured in. But it's based on what I feel is right. . . . I can't say 'this is how you do it.' Each person has to find their own way. I can only say 'this is how I do it.' Will the world ever become all organic? Are we moving in the right direction? Maine is moving in the right direction. Other places, I don't know."

This combination of convictions—a strong sense of personal responsibility and deep engagement with others in pursuit of a larger purpose—was not unique to Mort. My impression is that the younger farmers feel more identified with this social movement per se. Even if Mort resists being didactic in his call to siblings in arms, though, his actions suggest deep commitment to the larger enterprise, too.

Mort twice served as President of the Maine Organic Farmers and Gardeners Association. In the early 1970s, he helped form a group called Friends of Intelligent Land Use, an activist group that successfully resisted the development of an oil refinery in the nearby town of Sanford. Mort was pivotal in an effort during the mid-1970s to protect an historic 250-acre property, Laudholm Farm, from commercial development. In collaboration with others, Mort helped transition the property to an estuarine sanctuary for research and education, the Laudholm Trust (Haskell 2016). He may not feel comfortable telling people what to do, but he has a lot to say, and his actions are broadly instructive. Such organizations that Mort and others in his generation helped develop established an important legacy for younger engaged sustainers.

MATTHEW LEON AND CORINNE HANSCH: LOVIN' MAMA FARM

That includes Matthew Leon and Corinne Hansch, who operate Lovin' Mama Farm in upstate New York. Driving my minivan to meet them, I was enchanted by the verdant, hilly farm country, just a few miles from downtown Schenectady. I drove up their very steep driveway, smiling as I read the lyrics of Strawberry Fields Forever, which are intermittently posted on half a dozen signs located every 15 feet. Strawberry Fields Nature Preserve is adjacent to Lovin' Mama Farm.

Matt and Corinne work an acre, producing 30 types of microgreens, 150 different vegetables, and 100 varieties of flowers, selling mostly through direct marketing to customers at farmers' markets, as well as a little wholesale to restaurants and supermarkets.

We met in their kitchen to talk. Their three young home-schooled kids were nearby. Their niece, who was my student at the time and introduced us, entertained the youngest one and listened to our conversation. Their home is functional, lived in, warm, and comfortable. Matt has dreadlocks and was wearing a t-shirt and a gentle smile. Corinne has the intelligent eyes of a leader. She served homemade coffee cake and tea in mismatched mugs. Fortyish, white, earthy, they looked like hippies to me. As a parent of three, I was immediately struck by how calm their household is.

I asked them how they got into regenerative farming. Corinne grew up in Santa Cruz and the Sierra foothills of California. "I read *Anne of Green Gables* so many times as a kid. I read incessantly, and I read a lot of older literature. I wonder if that might have influenced me. Learning about compassion, I think that does help, with some sort of morals."

Her parents nurtured such moral engagement. "When I was fourteen I said I didn't want to go to church anymore," Corinne recounted, "and my mom said I had to start volunteering. I did a hospice training course and just being around people at that stage of life, I think influenced me a lot to understand compassion and care for people." Her parents helped found a farmers' market in their town, Corinne recalled. She grew up gardening, and then working at a flower stand in high school.

While attending Lewis and Clark College, she told me, Corinne studied abroad in east Africa. The academic social science she had read about in books took on new meaning as she was exposed to real life consequences of global inequalities. Along the way, she got drawn into permaculture, which is agriculture intended to be sustainable and self-sufficient for the long run.

Matt grew up in Manhattan, surrounded by vast complexities of a diverse urban population. Over time, he came to appreciate the varied perspectives and different kinds of vulnerabilities people have. Unlike many peers in the city, Matt "had a lot of nature experiences" in the Northeast hiking, camping, and skiing. During those trips he learned to see and hear the different kinds of complexity and diversity of nature.

He recalled a solo on an island in the Canadian wilderness during high school. Having not eaten any real food for several days, in the wild alone, Matt remembers it as a profound experience. Nature plus solitude plus low blood sugar equals mind-altering. "I'd see my animal friends nearby. Little pike fish would swim by." He had never gained any traction in organized religion or formal philosophy, but that particular adventure sparked something. "Mother Earth," as he calls "her," had a hold of him.

Matt's parents placed a lot of emphasis on education. He attended a Montessori school for pre-K and after that went to a prestigious private school in Manhattan. He then attended a truly exceptional Quaker school in Indiana, Earlham College (which happens to be my alma mater). While there, he went on a program called Southwest Field Studies, which involves an extended stay in the high desert of southwestern states, learning about natural history and sustainable living.

I had several friends in college who went on the same program. They each came back deeply affected by the experience (and completely ungroomed). Several months of camping, hiking, studying, and living communally in the desert leaves a mark. For Matt, it was a turning point. After that, being in school didn't feel quite right (a familiar sensibility among those I knew who went on that trip). He "went to Colorado to ski" and then ended up in Portland, Oregon, where he met Corinne.

Of course, private schools, selective colleges, and skiing in Colorado reflect a kind of privilege that few have. Farming, especially in innovative, morally ambitious ways, entails significant risk, which is no doubt easier to take on with some sort of buffer, perhaps a strong educational background or some capital. The opportunity to adopt this vocation is not available to everyone in the same way.

Later, Matt and Corinne rented land and farmed it together in Mendocino County, California, for some eight years. Water shortages and weeds made it a tough setting in some ways, they told me, but demand for local food was high and the farm thrived. That part of the world has a strong culture of gardening, localism, and treading lightly on the earth. At that time their production was certified Mendocino Renegade, which they believe meets or exceeds Certified Organic standards.

For all of that time they were plowing their fields, they explained, but thinking about how they could move toward no-till farming. After a falling-out with the landlord, they "lost the farm," a painful episode that made them rethink their plans. Matt's dad encouraged them to try farming in Amsterdam, NY, where he lives. The land where they live and farm now is owned by him, they told me, so the rent they pay is below market pricing. Along with one part-time employee, Corinne and Matt basically do all of the farm work. Their kids and some family members help out on occasion. Corinne handles most of the office work, accounting, taxes, marketing, and so on. Throughout our time together, I heard about different people who exposed them to nature, gardening, and business, but as farmers they seem largely self-taught.

In Amsterdam, they decided to go no-till, a momentous decision that was a long time coming, they noted, and has proved very fortuitous. In New York, water and weeds are less of a problem, but the season is shorter, regulations and politics are more burdensome, and the market is more competitive. They also decided to become organic (partly due to the competition) and believe they are the only no-till/Certified Organic farm in the area.[3] They have two fields, totaling an acre and a half, plus two greenhouses, and 60 chickens. They use lots of compost and some fertilizer.

Each fall they extract soil samples from about six inches down from several places around the field, place about a gallon in a Ziploc bag, and send it to nearby Saratoga 4-H, which is associated with Cornell Cooperative Extension Saratoga County. The samples are shipped to Cornell University, where scientists generate a report about the chemical makeup of the soil. Matt and Corinne then do some math and decide what kinds of fertilizer to add.

They work hard, especially from May to October, and even in the winter there is always something that needs to be done. But Matt said "saving the planet, getting people healthy food, and educating people about the healthy food" energize them. And the work is paying off. The organic matter left from decayed plants helps enrich the soil. In just two years, the health of the soil has improved greatly, they reflected. Not plowing keeps carbon sequestered in the earth where it helps plants grow, rather than releasing it into the atmosphere where it is harmful. The system responds well to droughts or storms, more effectively than conventional farms.

Plus, their yields are tremendous, they exclaimed. In California, where the season is longer, when they were still plowing, they would get about four rounds of lettuce in a season. In New York, they get ten. That means they are getting more production out of the land, generating more food with more nutrients, while enhancing the soil, and making the air cleaner. They keep using the same land but carefully rotate what they grow on it. Rather than damaging the soil with each round of plowing, seeding, fertilizers, and herbicides, this organic, no-till method leaves the soil richer each round. Their first season in Amsterdam, they indicated, the farm grossed $90,000. In September of their second season, they had already reached $100,000. On an acre and a half.

It's worth emphasizing that current research suggests this example of productivity and profit through no-till methods is not exceptional. It appears that over time no-till farming pays for itself through abundant crop yields, plus it adds to the cumulative health of the soil and reduces the amount of carbon released into the atmosphere.[4]

Matt and Corinne are explicit about being located in and invested in the social movement advocating regenerative farming. They mention Paul Kaiser of Singing Frog Farms in Sonoma County, CA, and Connor Crickmore of Neversink Farm in the Catskills of New York, gurus of this movement on each coast who have influenced how Lovin' Mama Farm does things. They are active in the Northeast Organic Farmers Association, New York, which is similar to the Maine Organic Farmers and Gardeners Association that Mort has helped lead.

A central contention of this movement shared by Matt, Corinne, and Mort is that small, ecologically sound farms can be profitable. It is their conviction that scaling them up, getting more land and more technology, is not the solution. Getting more out of the land, by putting more into it, or rather working with it, is the key. They are exuberant about this point.

Corinne and Matt exude ambition about their craft. They care about what they do, what they produce, how they produce it, and the life they are able to live. They want to be good at all of it. "I have lots of dreams for projects we could grow off the farm, like cooperatives," Corinne suggested. "I'm excited about creating jobs and community . . . drawing from people's talent. As an entrepreneur, that's what keeps me excited."[5] They both draw a parallel between the systemic harmony that is required for vital soil, microbes, earthworms, and plants in the ground, as well as vibrant individuals, relationships, community, and culture above it. Both agricultural ecology and human ecology involve idiosyncratic, local contexts and resources, synergy, and cooperation.

Corinne and Matt aspire to be "tuned in" on both counts, being alert to the worms in their field and the people in their community alike. Not that people are insignificant like worms, but that worms are significant like people. Life matters, the system linking different forms of life matters.

"Like in Schenectady they're starting a food coop," Corinne said. They plan to join. "By getting tuned into the community you're benefiting yourself," Matt observed. "Rather than introducing new ideas you're seeing what's already going on and building, not reinventing the wheel. It's just like doing a soil test. Like what does the soil need? I'm going to apply that but not these other things, because if you get too much phosphorus, then you mess with the soil and have a problem."

I was a little surprised to not hear a more strident, rigid sense of the one right way to do things from them, or from others I spoke to who are a part of this movement. "People can be pretty self-righteous about it," Corinne observed, "but we use lots of methods." Nearly all of the regenerative and organic farmers I encountered are careful not to vilify conventional farmers. That sensitivity or omission is definitely part of the script that over time became familiar to me.

Given how much success Corinne and Matt are having with no-till farming, though, I asked about why more farmers aren't adopting such practices. The first answer they gave is that a lot of farmers are in fact moving toward no-till. This practice is spreading. It's not easy. There's a learning curve. Weeds are always a challenge. Learning how to manage them without adding a lot more herbicides is apparently pretty tricky.

Matt offered a related comment about why so many farmers resist this approach. "We see this in people all the time. I've heard that when men are downtrodden in society, they go home and beat their wives, because they want to control something." Plowing offers a sense of control, he believes. It allows a farmer to manage the weeds, to wake up and see a neat, field with tidy, clean rows. Amidst variable weather patterns (which are becoming more extreme due to climate change), government regulation, dependence on government subsidies, Big Food, Big Ag, competitive pressure, and all the other uncertainties, this purported desire for control made sense to me. "I may be a cog, but I've got my tractor and, man, I love this," Matt parroted a hypothetical farmer. Yet the control is an illusion, he pointed out. If too much rain comes right after plowing, "they'd lose their soil."

"At the root of it there's a cultural perspective that it's 'man versus nature.' We don't agree with that. We believe it's a circle of life. By looking at nature and saying we have something to learn from her, that's where you get back to these ancient indigenous agricultural methods." This sense of synergy between humanity and nature is a message I heard from engaged sustainers repeatedly, in different forms. For many, it is a core value that informs and energizes a bunch of other stuff.

I asked about the most important challenges confronting farmers. Matt basically said it is about the domination of corporations in the food system. Big companies provide farmers with seeds and then later buy their crops, setting prices on both ends, and reducing the control farmers have along the way.

In answer to that same question, Corinne didn't hesitate in identifying glyphosate, the compound in Monsanto's Roundup. What concerns her is how ubiquitous this herbicide is in farming and how so many illnesses have been linked to it.

These two answers together represent another pattern. When asked about ugly things facing farmers, Matt described the big picture, the proverbial "forest" as it were, whereas Corinne described a particular chemical, the "trees." Engaged sustainers do this a lot. They think about big things like philosophy, ideology, climate, land, community. And they think about little things like chemicals, earthworms, seeds, yields, profit margins.

In the end, Corinne and Matt both attributed these problems to the greed woven into our economic system and culture. Matt said, "the human race is consuming itself." It's not like that everywhere, though, they hastened to add. Corinne mentioned her travels to other countries where she witnessed people with much less stuff and way more joy. The ancient, simple wisdom of that joy, as evident on Matt and Corinne's farm, struck me as entirely viable. This is what grounders do. They attend to fundamentals and make connections.

Since I interviewed them, I learned that many of their ambitions were coming to fruition. They sell their produce through the Troy Waterfront Farmers' Market, the Schenectady Greenmarket, Saratoga Springs Farmers' Market, Honest Weight Food Co-op, and their own CSA. And they offer tours of their farm.

Matthew and Corinne seemed special, in many ways. But they are not the only ones who think or work this way. One measure of this shift is consumer demand for products that are generated responsibly. This includes direct purchases from farmers like them, but also distributors and restaurants who want their products. An illustrative example of this is the stunning rise of the fast-casual salad/grain bowl company Sweetgreen. Their fresh salads and commitment to sustainability, local sourcing, animal welfare, treatment of employees, recycling, composting, and transparency has proved a winning combination. From 2007, when the company was founded, to 2020, they grew from 1 to 100 locations (Berscovici 2020). I will say more about Sweetgreen in the pages to come, but wanted to note here that the demand for the kind of stuff being produced by the likes of Lovin' Mama Farm seems to be growing.

Another sign that Lovin' Mama Farm is part of a trend relates to the use of soil. The National Resources Conservation Services (NRCS) reports that between 2003 and 2006 some 86 percent of U.S. cropland used some form of "conservation tillage" for at least one crop. For many farmers themselves, the gains are concrete and immediate. The NRCS (2016) reports that, as a result, "Fuel use has been reduced by 812.4 million gallons of diesel equivalents, roughly the amount of energy required annually by 3.2 million average households. Emissions have been reduced by 9.1 million tons of CO_2 equivalents, enough to offset the annual CO_2 emissions of nearly 1.9 million passenger cars. Continuous no-till has been adopted on 21 percent of acres and accounts for 35 percent of the reductions in fuel use and emissions. Corn Belt and Northern Plains production regions account for 58 percent (~29 percent each) of the fuel and emission reductions" (See also Starapoli 2016). Together, Matt, Corinne, and the others committed to the "soil health movement" in particular and "regenerative agriculture in general" are making a difference (see Greenaway 2018).

Matt and Corinne were alert to small things happening in their household—how else to explain young well-behaved children, and home-made treats?—and in their fields—no-till farming is all about building biodiversity in soil. But they also showed interest in broad patterns like CO_2 emissions and the well-being of their community, as well as the big picture, like the momentum of the national movement advancing regenerative agriculture, and their relationship with Mother Earth. Their orientation, which draws from different spiritual traditions, brought to mind the Buddhist monk, Thích Nhất Hạnh, who said: "You carry Mother Earth within you. She is not outside of you. Mother Earth is not just your environment. In that insight of inter-being, it is possible to have real communication with the Earth, which is the highest form of prayer. In that kind of relationship, you have enough love, strength and awakening in order to change your life" (Confino 2012).

JAMIE AGER: GRAZING THE WAY
NATURE WANTS TO BE GRAZED

Sustainable agriculture is largely focused on produce. And rightly so. Our health and our earth will both benefit from greater reliance on plants in the Western diet. But an important objective of this movement is also figuring out how to generate protein, including meat, with more integrity. How do farmers raise animals in ways that are responsible?

There have always been farmers and ranchers who raise cattle, poultry, hogs, and other animals with care.[6] Industrialized meat processing began in the early 19th century. By the middle of the 20th century, meat production was dominated by large-scale factory farms commonly known as Concentrated Animal Feeding Operations (CAFOs). A CAFO, by definition, holds at least 1,000 animal units (i.e., basically 1,000 pounds of live animal weight), which could mean 1,000 beef cattle, 700 dairy cows, 2,500 pigs, 125,000 broiler chickens, or 82,000 egg-laying hens (USDA 2020). Quantitative thresholds are usually at least a little problematic. For instance, a farm with 999 animal units is presumably not a CAFO. But a farm with one more unit is. As previously noted, it's not uncommon for a CAFO to hold 10,000 or even 50,000 head of cattle. The largest ones may hold up to 150,000 head. The most carefully managed CAFOs produce meat on a large scale at a fast rate with relatively low cost. It takes about six weeks now to grow a chicken to "slaughter weight" (Garcés 2019) and as little as ten months for a steer (Roberts 2008).

However, they generate numerous problems, too (Foer 2009). Cattle raised on CAFOs are generally fed corn. Much of what they are fed is not edible by humans. Because of their numbers, the large amount of concentrated manure is problematic for the environment on numerous levels. The resulting ammonia, hydrogen sulfide, methane, and particulate matter contribute to contamination of air and water. Plus, farming corn uses a lot of water in general. CAFOs usually require government subsidies to function, either directly or in support of grain farmers. From the perspective of animal welfare, many critics believe, all CAFOs involve systematic atrocities (Foer 2009; Garcés 2019). The grain-fed cattle produce meat that is less nutritious and sometimes carries pathogens unsafe for human consumption (Sierra Club (no date); Hribar 2010; Fountain 2020).

The concentration of manure is so unhealthy for animals that it is believed that they cannot survive without antibiotics. One estimate indicates that 70 percent of medically important antibiotics is used for animals—and it's precisely because they cannot survive in such filthy conditions without them (Klein 2022). As bad as this situation is for animals, it's very dangerous for humans because the risks of antibiotic-resistant diseases passed from animals to humans are very real and lethal (Food and Water Watch 2015).

In short, CAFOs generate enormous quantity with low expenses for owners but lots of costs for others. "The only people that are for those are the ones that own them," one farmer said of CAFOs. "People *hate* those farmers. What must it feel like to have a job where people hate you?" another asked (quoted in Foer 2009, p. 173).

In contrast to this system through which the vast majority of American meat is produced, however, there is a movement afoot to combine tried and true traditions with modern technology. I visited such an operation involved in this movement near Asheville, North Carolina, called Hickory Nut Gap Farm and met Jamie Ager, co-owner of the business. "Eighty percent of beef sold in the United States is done by four companies," I heard Jamie point out at one point. "So, where do we fit in?"

Jamie's storied family has owned and run the farm for five generations. The day I was there, there were four other people on the tour, all fellows associated with Mother Earth Food distribution company. Graham DuVall, co-owner of Mother Earth Food, and his colleagues were there to see if Jamie would be an appropriate vendor for his business. More on him later.

Jamie's great grandparents were named James Gore King McClure Jr. and Elizabeth Skinner Cramer. The two affluent Chicagoans married in the spring of 1916. He was a graduate of Yale and an ordained minister, and she was a painter who had studied in Paris. They spent part of their honeymoon camping in North Carolina and became smitten with Hickory Nut Gap Farm. They bought it that summer and moved in the following spring. Four years later, McClure started the Farmers Foundation, a co-op of farmers, which he ran until his death in 1956 (Ager 1991).

Over the generations, the family has included soldiers, ministers, musicians, educators, businesspeople, politicians, and especially farmers. The most famous family member was the grandson of James and Elizabeth McClure, James "Jamie" McClure Clarke, who graduated from Princeton, served in the Pacific theater during World War II, ran the Farmers Foundation, worked as an editor at the Asheville Citizen-Times, served in both the North Carolina House and Senate, and then the U.S. House of Representatives.

In learning about this interesting family, I could see quickly that they have always valued education. That included schooling at Yale, Princeton, Williams, Vassar, Duke, Davidson, and the University of Illinois, for example. Jamie Ager and his wife both attended Warren Wilson College—where Jamie Clarke had once been special assistant to the President.

A strong sense of history permeates the way the family presents the farm to the world. Its website today mentions Cherokee and other Native American peoples who occupied the area before white settlers; Sherrills Inn, which was in operation on the same site in the mid-19th century; and diary entries from James McClure, the first family member to purchase the land. I perceived genuine pride in this history on the part of the farm's current management, but also a savvy, forward-looking sense of marketing. Somebody has done a great deal of thinking about how to present all this information.

Jamie Ager has studied up on "triple bottom line" bookkeeping, which emphasizes people and planet, along with profit, or communal, environmental, and economic concerns. He has visited Joel Salatin's Polyface Farm in Virginia—which has been something like the Vatican or Harvard for ambitious young farmers eager to pay homage to and learn about regenerative agriculture. Jamie has also visited Will Harris's farm, White Oak Pastures, several times. This is a well-known operation that has received widespread media coverage for "radically traditional farming" and meat production. Jamie regularly attends the Grassfed Exchange Conference ("The conference for regenerative producers and sustainable food supporters," its website advertises). He is, in short, dialed into the industry and the movement.

From my visit to the farm, talking to Jamie, and reading about the farm, I learned that this is a large, thriving enterprise—and a very different kind of operation from Lovin' Mama Farm in Schenectady. Jamie and his crew work four hundred acres, 200 around the original farm and 200 they rent nearby. Any given year, they have about 120 head of cattle, 150–200 pigs, 3500 broiler chicks, 600 laying hens and 350 turkeys. They also grow apples, blueberries, and blackberries.

Like many farms today, Hickory Nut Gap Farm has a slick website that extols the family's values, in this case: stewardship, authenticity, relationships, and leadership—all terms one hears associated with this movement a lot. Being around Jamie for a couple hours, I sensed a man who is motivated and proud. He wants to do great things with the farm so as to enhance the family legacy further. I heard the words authenticity, transparency, and ambition several times.

Hickory Nut Gap Farm actually includes several businesses. They raise cattle, pigs, and chickens, which is the primary farm enterprise (or ranch, depending on how you define that word). The website says the animals are all pasture-raised with no antibiotics or added hormones. The cattle are grass-fed, the "chickens thrive on pasture where they can forage for their own food and move around with freedom" and the pigs are "heritage breed" (which is a kind of pure-bred classification system).

Even my ignorant suburban nose could sense something special on this farm—the smell of healthy animals. In my youth, I had volunteered on a large ranch, cleaning out pigsties, and visited a family friend's industrial chicken farm. This was rather different. At Hickory Nut Gap Farm, I was astonished by the pleasant fragrance of the hogs (that is a sentence I never thought I'd write!)—earthy and pungent, but seemingly clean, hale, and happy. The pasture includes fescue, red clover, white clover, yellow dock, cockleburs, and chicories. "All the different grasses throughout the year create a really good summer grazing medley that really does work with the cattle," Jamie said.

There is a wholesale business, a community-supported agriculture, and a retail shop where you can buy fresh or frozen meat. That is connected to a deli where you can get a sandwich and drink (including an adult beverage), or a t-shirt. The farm also has a catering company and a venue available for rental. There are classes on butchery, making your own sausage, or yoga. And there are events involving apple-picking, live music, star-gazing, and other activities. The property has a summer camp where they teach horseback riding. "What I've learned over the last couple years is that now, not only are we going to have an interesting farm but sort of a whole organization. It's a much more ambitious play but I feel like the world is ready for it as well."

Plenty of evidence suggests Jamie is right. Consumers increasingly want to know what they are eating and whether it was produced responsibly.[7] Part of that includes the question of how animals are treated. Nicholas Kristof (2021) reported in the *New York Times* that more than 200 companies, even big brands like Burger King, Popeyes, Chipotle, and Denny's, have signed on to Better Chicken Commitment, which is a pledge to make sure chickens are treated humanely. Needless to say, these companies aren't making this shift because of some newfound tenderness for the animals that end up in their products. This change is driven by a recognition that consumers care about grounding.

Hickory Nut Gap Farm's website lists more than two dozen employees in addition to the owners, general manager, and farm manager, including a head butcher, a head baker, a head chef, as well as a graphic designer and digital marketing specialist, an events manager, a community outreach and education coordinator, a systems manager, and a director of marketing and internal relations, among others. "I think you can get too complicated," Jamie explained to our group as we toured the farm, "and it gets crazy at some point." There are certainly a lot of moving parts, already.

Not every place is as ambitious as this operation, but through my research I noticed a lot of farms that have added various activities and programs which transcend the traditional purpose of agriculture. Education and marketing are often intertwined. Products not made on the farm, such as prepared foods, adult beverages, pottery, t-shirts, and other merch are often part of the experience. Activities intended to enhance the setting as a destination, such as fresh picking, live music, playgrounds, and classes, too.

In my view, however, what is most special about Hickory Nut Gap Farm, what presumably drew Graham DuVall of Mother Earth Food here to investigate a possible partnership, is how the meat is produced. The moderate weather and abundant water help grass grow, Jamie explained to us, which makes western North Carolina a fine place to raise cattle. More grass means more cattle. "If you have the pasture-based model," Jamie said, "your costs are going to be more." Conventional grain-fed cattle take somewhere around 10 to 18 months to raise from birth to full-grown size of a ton or more when they are ready for slaughter. Jamie said it takes him 20 months to raise a steer on grass and they are smaller at the end of the process (see also Roberts 2008). But there are benefits.

> The cool thing, I think, about grass-fed beef in particular is that you're talking about sustainability. At the end of the day sustainability is about biodiversity, right? How do we build biodiversity? How do we enhance life? Like, how do

we change the conversation away from humans, mitigating our relationship with nature and sort of mitigating our environmental impact, using less? . . . How do we build environmental systems with biodiversity? When you take grass and you're turning that grass into food. And in the process from a systems standpoint, you're managing an ecosystem. You're managing the grass. Nature wants a mixture of grass in the fields or woods. So that edge effect is where the hotspots are. So, if we can use the animal's natural instinct for grazing, or in the case with hogs we'll stick them in the woods, and let them root out an area that's full of rose bushes or whatever, and then we'll come back through planting that into something good. You're taking grass, which humans can't eat, and you're turning that grass into high quality food. In the process, you're building soils through the process because you practice rotational grazing. You let it grow up big, thick and deep.

Instead of quickly raising animals as fast as possible, which is the main approach at CAFOs, thereby producing meat that is less nutritious, and creating a mess of the soil, water, and air in the area, the pasture approach is better in almost every way. The animals are happier as they grow, the meat is healthier, and many would say tastier, and the water is less polluted (Nation 2005).[8] The soil and air are actually better, cleaner in some real sense, after the fact. Of course, Jamie wants his farm to be profitable, but there is much more to his thinking.

He recalled to us a mid-summer drought several years back when it hadn't rained for over a month. He was out walking around checking on things.

I could reach down in the morning and even that dew would settle onto the soil. And because it had a thatch like this, even at noon, if you walk through the grass your feet got wet. Whereas in the continuous grazing situation, when you graze like that, the dew burns off by 8:30 or 9:00 in the morning. So, you know, it's all about sort of building that grass base, grazing the way nature wants to be grazed, which is rotation. Then that thatch goes down, builds organic matter. You're taking carbon out of the atmosphere, sinking it down into your soils and turning your soil into higher organic matter.

Because the soil is rich and generates healthy grass, Jamie can grow pasture on a larger proportion of the land, some of which wouldn't be flat enough for continuous grazing. His approach reflects what he called a "systems-level management" that takes advantage of a broader range of resources (e.g., sloped fields) in a sustainable way (e.g., rotating grazing).

A big issue for businesses like Hickory Nut Gap Farm is having a customer base that cares about things besides cost. "You've got to have an urban market with dollars to buy it." Asheville is a foodie place. I would say it is a hub for this movement in general. Needless to say, different elements of the movement are not perfectly aligned in Asheville or anywhere. Some folks care more about sustainability, justice, health, profit, treatment of workers, or animal welfare.

And sometimes the different priorities are in tension. For example, Jamie said, "I get the whole sort of plant-based movements that we're all sort of paying attention to right now. I just don't see how that interacts with the land. To me, the Impossible Burger, I went and ate one and it was fine. But that's like the most lab industrial grown food ever created, right. It's ironic to me that there's sort of this Vegan all-natural love affair with those types of products that are not even food really. It's a lab product."

He also has a realistic streak both in terms of the industry and the movement. "I know all the flaws in the industry." He speaks fondly of mentors, partners, and customers, evincing genuine pride and nostalgia for what his family and he are doing. However, he understands marketing and symbolism, too. "There is nothing more that *New York Times* journalists love to see than a bunch of ranchers talk about regenerative agriculture. I mean, that is just right for like the emotionally happy urban person."

I got the feeling lots of the pieces seem to be falling into place. When he talks about scaling up, this sector of agriculture—pasture-fed animals—is emphasized as part of the context. Jamie sounds like he feels the need to be a leader in the industry to make his particular business really work. "To me, what's cool is this whole sort of natural production method. That is, the systems are getting there. We're figuring out how the model works and that's what we want to really be, is a facilitation point for all those conversations, and have annual meetings."[9]

CONCLUSION

Grounding is about trying to shape the human impact on natural resources, including plants, animals, earth, sun, water, and air. I encountered other grounders besides the people featured in this chapter. Most of them were farmers or gardeners, but not all. Some notion of a moral footprint is very much in the front of their minds.

I met a master electrician named Brian Valle in the summer of 2021. At that time, he was working for ReVision Energy, a company focused on alternative energy, primarily solar. It's a for-profit, employee-owned company that carries B Corporation certification, which reflects a commitment to "high social and environmental performance" (bcorporation.net) and recognizes the intersectional "relationship between environmentalism and social justice" (revisioneergy.com). Brian installs solar panels for residential and commercial properties.

At my request, my research assistant, Miles Chandler, interviewed his father, David Chandler, professor of Civil and Environmental Engineering at Syracuse University. David studies green infrastructure, among other things, focusing on the management of usable water. Beyond the basic science involved in this work, the application of his research is manifest in the development of viable infrastructure and sustainable development.

All the folks I talked to who think about carbon emissions in relation to their consumption habits are in some sense grounders as well. Chapter 7 focuses on them. Along with Brian, David, and those consumers, I encountered lots of other engaged sustainers paying attention to how humans can be linked to the sun, water, and air in viable ways. In this chapter, though, the focus was on plants, animals, and soil, which are in fact the elements that garner the most attention in this movement.

The grounders featured in this chapter explicitly draw from ancient practices. They evince respect for "the past" and foundational knowledge related to the land and the community. But, as in the cases of Mort, Matt, Corinne, and Jamie, they are not captive to old traditions. Tried and true practices are neither clutched onto as a matter of unthinking habit, nor abandoned just because they are old. New ways of doing things, like drawing on scientific experts, innovative technology, or sophisticated marketing, are certainly viable options when demonstrated to yield returns.

I discerned a certain kind of idealism in the productive process. *Let's do this thing with integrity.* One hears a kind of zeal about healthy soil, happy animals, and the synergy of working *with* nature. This kind of grounding is at its core noble. *Let's leave the place better than we found it.*

Yet, such convictions are alloyed with realism too—realism about the need to think about what sells. The customer may not always be right, but they have a large say over how things are going to go. The presence Joshua's Restaurant and Grill has on social media, and the narrative attaching it to Easter Orchard Farm exemplifies explicit engagement with the public (which would have been unimaginable when Mort first started gardening). Lovin' Mama Farm is moving into Certified Organic partly to compete more effectively in local markets. Jamie and his family have converted Hickory Nut Gap Farm into a multifaceted destination for both educational and marketing purposes. Such work is about revealing the nobility of grounding to the world, helping the public understand what goes into responsible agriculture, but it's also about selling not just a product, but a brand linked to experience and identity. Noble and cunning.

NOTES

1. A community-supported agriculture (CSA) is a system in which a farm is supported by shareholders who make periodic payments to receive shares of fresh produce as it is harvested (see Woods and Ernst 2017; Schnell 2007; Graham 2005).

2. In *The Hidden Half of Nature*, David Montgomery and Ann Biklé (2016) show how intimately the health of human beings is dependent on the health of soil. What's in the soil becomes what's in the gut.

3. This kind of strategic pragmatism appears to be fairly common in this movement (see Qazi and Selfa 2005).

4. See Plumer (2013), Starapoli (2016), Greenaway (2018), Cusser, Bahlai, Swinton, Robertson, and Haddad (2020).

5. This is also part of a larger pattern. "Building community around the plight of regional farmers," Qazi and Selfa (2005, p. 66) document, "has recently gained momentum."

6. By the way, I've heard various definitions of the difference between a farm and a ranch. Most say ranches have livestock intended to generate meat whereas farms have mostly produce and maybe livestock used for dairy. Others say ranches are bigger than farms. And still others say ranches and farms are the same thing, but the former are known as such out west and the latter in the east.

7. See, for example, Hunt (2007), Gumirakiza, Curtis, and Bosworth (2014), and Leonard (2014).

8. Grass-fed meat has lower fat content, more protein, fewer calories, and more omega-3s (see Nation 2015).

9. See Qazi and Selfa (2005) for evidence of this orientation spreading among farmers linked to the alternative agro-food movement.

Chapter Four

Extraction

Where will we get our food from? Will we have enough? These primordial concerns preceded the emergence of *Homo sapiens* from our primate precursors. Most consumers in industrial society no longer think about such issues, not really. Stores and restaurants provide what they need. A lot of farmers do think about it, though. All farmers worry about the volume, frequency, and quality of their harvests. This is also true of others involved in extraction processes such as foaling, milking, fishing, slaughtering, and reaping. Generating resources that can be used *directly* to feed one's family and other people is surely a concern for many extractors. So, lots of operations produce kale, green beans, broccoli, and other vegetables. The primary goal for most extractors in contemporary society, though, is to generate resources that can be sold for money to pay the bills—to *indirectly* feed their family—and, if they're fortunate, turn a profit. For example, corn is the number one crop in the United States, three-quarters of which is used for biofuel or livestock feed. Of that which is used for food, a large portion becomes high fructose corn syrup (Foley 2013).

What you get out of the soil depends on what you put into it. Extraction in general is based on grounding. As one leads to the other, many who are concerned with either are concerned with both. But for a lot of farmers and others involved in agriculture, extraction is the main business. Our primal concern with food has made the volume, frequency, and quality of extractions immensely important throughout the human experience. What seems to have gotten lost at some point, perhaps in part due to the Green Revolution, is the concern for quality. Remember, the Green Revolution was comprised of a vast dispersion of agriculture technologies related to irrigation, pesticides, fertilizer, and so on, during the middle of the 20th century that helped increase yields in a big way across the globe. The goal of "more," Bill McKibben (2004) has explained, eclipsed the goal of "better." That is certainly part of the story behind the massive amounts of corn produced in the United States, a pattern that unfolded in the later part of the 20th century.[1]

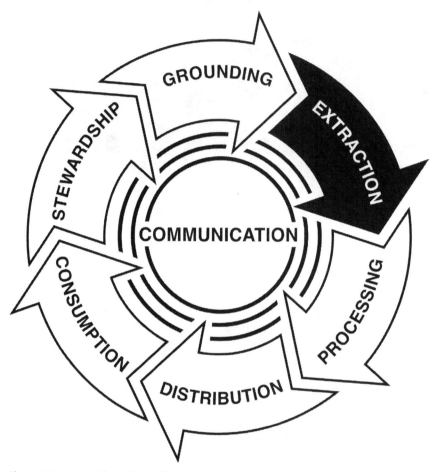

Figure 4.1.   Extraction. Created by Martha MacGregor

For the extractors I encountered, quality has been reclaimed as a primary goal. The health and vitality of what they grow and the nutrition and taste it holds when it is converted into food matters. None of them are growing corn for livestock feed or high fructose corn syrup. It may take surrendering control of a field by giving up the plow, or it may take longer to raise a steer, but quality is in the equation, at least competing with volume and frequency as important objectives. It is still a relatively tiny percentage of overall farmland, but the number of acres of Certified Organic cropland has been increasing by nearly 150,000 acres per year for a while, a trend that is expected by some experts to hold steady.[2] As noted above, no-till farming is literally gaining ground, too. The USDA expects this pattern to continue for many crops (Plumer 2013).

MICHAEL KILPATRICK: YOU LEAVE IT
BETTER THAN YOU FOUND IT

I live in a small town in upstate New York that has a vibrant tradition of farmers' markets. As I learned from talking to different people, the idea of a "farmers' market" is increasingly popular and contested. Does it include conventional or non-local farmers? How do you define local? How can the fish monger be local in a landlocked setting? How about pottery, soap, prepared foods, or knife-sharpening? What do you do about competing farmers' markets? What should the relationship be between a municipality that loves its farmers' market and the farmers who live outside of it? How do the stakeholders navigate fault lines between disproportionately urban, Democratic consumers and disproportionately rural, Republican producers? (Voters in our city, who comprise a large portion of the customers, voted for Clinton in 2016 whereas voters in the surrounding areas, who comprise a large portion of venders, voted for Trump [*New York Times* 2018]).[3] More generally, how do the farmers' market vendors make collective decisions about all this? I find these thorny issues to be fascinating. As I learned from two successive coordinators of one of our farmers' markets, a lot of local farmers find them quite vexing.

In our town there is one main farmers' market, which is held in particular times and places each week, depending on the season. (There are other markets opened at other times and places, which sell produce, prepared foods, and other products.) When you walk through the main one, several vendors make an especially strong impression. The quantity, variety, and quality of what they sell stands out. Plus, depending on seniority, they have a better location in the market. For these reasons, I was well aware of the Kilpatrick stall before I met Michael. As I sought out several people so I could learn more about how things work, I was encouraged to speak with Michael Kilpatrick.

Sometimes you meet people and think, *this guy must be a great brother, uncle, or neighbor . . . his parents must be so proud of him . . . gosh, the world would be a better place if there were more people like him.* That is how I felt when I met Michael. I also had the feeling within a few moments that Michael accomplishes more before breakfast than most people do in a week.

When I first met him in 2013, he was 26 (he easily could have passed for 20) and already running a farm that was one of the most profitable businesses associated with our local farmers' market. I found myself envious of Michael for the preternatural wisdom he expressed alongside his youthful energy and fearless candor. So much of what he told me seemed like the kind of obvious after-the-fact knowledge that usually comes from a lifetime of experience.

As I interviewed him at that time in the small city park where the farmers' market is held, he was bursting with ideas. "You can have a micro farm. In the city limits, you can actually feed yourselves. Why doesn't this park have a little garden?" (Within a couple years of that conversation, Michael proved that this wasn't idle talk.) "Why is this park not being grazed by cows? Why is this town mowing? Do you know how much America spends on feeding their lawns every year? Billions of dollars," he said.

Michael has quick eyes and seems to understand the gist of a question before it is done being asked. He never seemed rude but was eager to have an efficiently productive conversation so he could get on to the many other things on his list of things to do for that afternoon.

He told me his family—two parents and seven kids, white, and identified as Christian—relocated from suburban Massachusetts to rural New York in 1999. At first, they had ducks, chickens, and a small garden. A couple years later, Michael and his brother, both still teenagers, made a plan for turning this enterprise into a real farm. Their parents were around but not really involved in the farm. By 2005, Kilpatrick Family Farm was selling to multiple weekly farmers' markets, including most importantly, Saratoga Springs Farmers' Market, which is more than 50 miles from their land. Within seven years, multiple people had told me it was one of the most profitable farms associated with the market.

By the way, self-provisioning is an important part of this movement as a whole. One of the few analytical studies done on home gardening, by Justin Schupp and Jeff Sharp (2012), used data from Ohio to identify factors most strongly associated with this practice. They found that people who live on a farm or in a standalone house are likely to have a garden. Interestingly, being in an urban, suburban, or rural setting did not make a difference. Nor did income level or geographic region. However, they did find that households who had faced economic hardship (which is about recent struggles versus baseline income level), manifest pro-environment behaviors, become engaged with the local food system, and are more likely to have a garden. I didn't find out about all these factors in relation to Michael, but it is clear that he is engaged with environmentalism and local food systems. In his case, it appears that home gardening was some sort of gateway to farming.

As of 2018, the Kilpatrick farm's website reported that it had a staff of 12 people that manage some 500 acres, including 15 acres of vegetables rotated on 50 tillable acres, and 100 acres of pasture for broiler chickens and turkeys. Kilpatrick Family Farm was selling at multiple farmers' markets, to multiple wholesale buyers, and providing a CSA for some 250 families (Kilpatrick Family Farm website). Michael also keeps a busy schedule of speaking engagements, conferences, organizing, and blogging. Plans were in the works for making their farm a destination where kids can go to celebrate birthdays, mingle with livestock, and learn about farming and food.

When I asked how he measures success, he didn't blink: "If you're making money." He referenced a couple—older, more experienced farmers—who are influential mentors. "They really knew the business side and so they shared that with us," he explained. They ran a "very profitable" farm. It was clear to me, though, that he is a self-starter, too. He's read books and taken some business courses. He referenced Jim Collins, Eliot Coleman, Wendell Berry, and the Rodale Institute. He also did an internship at Polyface Farms, a kind of Mecca among regenerative farmers led by a well-known farmer and writer named Joel Salatin.

As I learned more about Michael during that conversation, in several lectures I've heard him give, and from his website, I realized that money was just the beginning of his answer about success. "Basically, our mission, what we believe," he said to me, "is to change people through food."

This purpose also extends from religious conviction. "We're Christian and we believe that we're stewarding the earth. That's the other big 'why?' behind it." The "it" here is his commitment to a specific way of thinking, working, and living.

> As long as they choose the Bible, it doesn't matter. It talks about in Genesis the creation mandate, the dominion over the earth. And dominion over the Earth doesn't mean you rape and pillage and abuse the earth. It means you care for the earth, and you leave it better than you found it, how God created stuff and trying to model that. And that just gives you that little "umph" to get up every day because farming is hard and tough. So when you believe you can tie your faith into it, there's so much more connection to it.

Michael's moral convictions also relate to a thorny issue that many in this movement contemplate: organic certification (see Guthman 2004). Organic cropland in the United States has been growing steadily for about two decades, usually by about 8 percent per year. Demand often exceeds supply. That is real change, obviously. But it may appear to be less significant than it really is. Most importantly, organic acreage still only accounts for one or two percent of all cultivated cropland in America. Just a tiny fraction. Nevertheless, the baseline proportion really reveals the full story. As an idea, "organic" has taken off. More on related processing and consumption patterns in subsequent chapters. Suffice it to say here that the rising number of consumers paying attention to how nutritious and natural their food has moved the needle.

That is why the phrase "all natural" can be seen everywhere throughout the grocery store. All natural—all as in every part, really? As dubious as such claims often are, advertisers now recognize that they have to at least make a gesture toward the shifting demand. It's also why farmers like Michael ponder such matters.

"We're not Certified Organic because it's a government program and there are so many things we think are wrong with that. One of the big reasons that Certified Organic is always wrong is because we've left the principles and gone to just a list of rules." Such a list is too rigid and narrow. He said, "we're Certified Naturally Grown, which is the same standards as organic, but a different certifying agency." He also said his farm has embraced the "New York Farmers' Pledge, which actually goes beyond Organic. It talks about fair labor practices. It talks about, you know, your run-off and your marketing and stuff like that. We take it pretty seriously is what I'm trying to say."

A number of farmers I spoke with echoed similar ambivalence (see also Savage 2016). The idea of Certified Organic is not inherently wrong, I heard, but involves too much bureaucratic prescription. A lot of farmers bristle at the idea of government imposing politicized regulations on them (see Qazi and Selfa 2005). Jamie Ager, the cattle farmer mentioned in the last chapter, said to me, "I wouldn't say 'Organic' because agriculture is way too complicated to be described in one word. But at the same time, I'm a dad who goes to Food Lion on Sunday and has to buy food for the kids for school tomorrow. . . . So, as a consumer I appreciate the label. As a farmer, the label makes some sense but not a lot of sense."

Polyface Farms in Virginia—where Michael and his brother and Jamie all visited—organizes around several principles consistent with the spirit of Organic but other ideals, too: transparency, grass fed, individuality, community, nature's template, earthworms. Its website offers guidance about "scaling up without selling your soul" (polyfacefarms.com/principles). The idea that the salvation of one's soul is related to how one extracts resources from nature, for many of these people, is not a tongue-in-cheek matter. Regardless of whether the standard a farmer follows is Certified Organic or some other parameters, this is serious stuff.

Shifting from conventional to organic farming is an expensive, time-consuming, multiyear undertaking. It involves different equipment and crop rotation. Farms have to be free of chemicals for three years before they can be called Certified Organic. The farmers who maintain those standards mostly spoke of meeting consumer demand and/or distinguishing themselves from competitors. Corinne Hansch and Matt Leon (also mentioned in the previous chapter) and Jamie Ager, despite his ambivalence noted above, generate products designated as Organic at least partly for this reason.

All of the farmers I interviewed expressed commitment to agricultural practices that have basic integrity, regardless of what government or consumers think. Sometimes that may be easier than Certified Organic. But sometimes it is harder. No-till farming creates particular challenges when paired with Certified Organic standards. As previously noted, both are doable together, but not easy. No-till farming can make weeds a problem, which is especially difficult if a farmer is not using synthetic herbicides in order to meet the Certified Organic standard. Specific techniques have been shown to be successful, but they are a bit complicated. As a result, some opt for no-till but not Certified Organic. In any case, what came up in numerous conversations, including the one I had with Michael Kilpatrick, is a commitment to viable, long-term agriculture that generates healthy, nutrient-dense crops or livestock. What did not come up was condemnation of other farmers using varied techniques, which surprised me a bit.

Michael spoke of lucrative possibilities extending from an acre or two of farming but said "you've got to be focusing on growing the business, researching new stuff, doing the stuff only you can do." In addition to growing food, Michael wants to "grow more farmers," which motivates his commitment to education. His website includes numerous blog posts and PowerPoint presentations with lots of concrete guidance about growing various crops, diverse technologies, marketing, accounting, regulations, networking, and so on. He strongly encourages farmers to crunch the numbers. See what works, get feedback, and make adjustments. "Soak up information like a sponge," he advises, "visit other farms, invest in mentoring, read, or listen to podcasts. Don't give up!" (Stone Barn Center for Food and Agriculture 2016).

I asked him what it's like to grow food people will eat. "It makes you feel happy," he declared. Happiness is also a common theme among engaged sustainers. "You're changing their lives. So many people are disconnected, and to get them to actually connect to something on an earthly level because people now are into TV, video games and that kind of stuff, stuff that's just meaningless in so many ways. So to get them back to how we were created to be." You can see on their website a persistent emphasis on "relationships," "interactions," "connections," "building trust," "exceeding customers' expectations."

"We came from the earth!" Michael exclaimed to me.

To connect people back to the earth, I think, is very important. So feeding people and knowing you're making them healthy too. . . . Knowing people that have cancer and knowing what causes that and then knowing you're feeding people good food that's not going to give them that, that can make them actually healthier and heal them. We've had CSA members that had cancer when they came to us and they've beaten it since then, eating healthy vegetables, and that's just huge!

His exhilaration was infectious as he spoke about "the power of nature and healing, the power of regenerative farming, the power of looking at nature and how it was created to function and then trying to duplicate that." This "healing" is an expansive notion for Michael. To be a "regenerative" farmer is to think about the whole system, including healthy soil.

"We just picked up 13 new acres . . . prime river bottom. It was corn land. . . . We know 36 months from now we're going to bring the cows across it, the chickens across it, you know, do the whole circle of life thing to it, get the bacteria counts up, the worms back in there." Growing corn every year degrades soil. Bringing cows and chickens across the land refers to intermittent grazing. The Kilpatrick Family Farm makes use of cover crops, like annual ryegrass, crimson clover, oats, oil-seed radishes, or cereal rye. They are planted in between the usual crops such as corn, soybeans, or wheat. Careful rotation of cover crops and livestock greatly enhances the nutritional constitution of the soil, which makes the ecosystem more vibrant in general.

As much passion and clarity as Michael expressed about his values, he still grapples with tricky ethical questions in practice. In our conversations, his website, and other venues, he extols the value of doing right by hired labor. "We realize people are worth money and you have to treat them well to get good people, and you want everyone to feel like they mean something." But he opposed the proposal to raise the minimum wage in New York State because it would keep from hiring young people in part-time jobs. Hiring kids is important, he explains, yes, from a business point of view, but also so they can develop a work ethic, see how farms work, and learn where their food comes from.

This ambivalence seems characteristic of a broader pattern. I interviewed several farmers whose operations are so small that hiring other people is not really an issue. But I also encountered owners of larger operations who do hire 5, 10, 20 or more people. In general, they all spoke about the importance of treating workers well. But agriculture, even the sustainable agricultural movement, is known for not always treating laborers that well.

Margaret Gray (2014) documents some of the movement's failures in this regard in her book, *Labor and the Locavore: The Making of a Comprehensive Food Ethic*. In particular, she shows that the vibrant local food movement in the Hudson Valley of upstate New York is fueled in part by terribly underpaid migrant labor.

I didn't speak to enough people to get a complete picture of this issue. But one farmer told me a "dirty secret about organic farms" is "that they're relying on interns, which they don't pay hardly anything." The idea that Gray's characterization of the Hudson Valley is far from unique is very credible to me. It's not easy to make money off a little bit of land. And who is going to tell an interviewer, "Oh yeah, we exploit the hell out of our employees"? The ideal of doing right by one's community, neighbors, and employees is rhetorically very prominent in this movement. I suspect, however, as Oscar Wilde noted, "the truth is rarely pure and never simple."

Michael told me he wants his employees to learn, and he is eager to learn himself. He seeks out new information, evidence, ideas, feedback. He is what liberal arts college devotees like me call "a lifelong learner." But he is cynical about formal credentialing processes. He was shocked—horrified, I think—when I told him how much tuition costs at the college where I work.

In some basic way, Michael is a businessman. He aspires to be a highly successful one, I think. But not one who is captive to an unalloyed profit motive. "What they have, is they've taken the soul out of business," he said of big food companies. (I was reminded of John C. Bogle's important book, *The Battle for the Soul of Capitalism: How the Financial System Undermined Social Ideals, Damaged Trust in the Markets, Robbed Investors of Trillions— and What to Do about It*). "Did you know," he asked me, "Monsanto will not allow GMOs in their cafeteria?"

He is also an activist and a leader. "It's a national movement," he said about the new wave of innovative farmers. Michael speaks with respect and gratitude about older farmers like his mentors, and his paternal grandfather, but his heart seems to be with young farmers. He is a member of the Young Farmers Coalition.

Farmers and ranchers are on average much older than most other professions and as a group, aging. Michael explained:

> Those are the people who are holding those old farms. So their kids and grand-kids are wanting to come into this [the alternative mode of farming]. And the grandparents won't let them do it on the home farm because "we need every acre to feed the cows." But what they don't realize is that eroded slope that they get one bale of hay out of, if they were to put in the Christmas trees or to put in the grapes, could produce ten times that amount of money. Older people hate change so to make a 75-year-old farmer feel that he's been wrong for 50 years, that psychologically is very tough. It's easier to change the farmer than to change the ideas.

Big business and big government, he thinks, are more part of the problem than the solution. "You have Republicans who don't want to spend money on that [support for low-income families], they want to spend money on the farm. And you got Democrats who want to spend money on this [support for low-income families], but don't want to spend money on the farm. So, it's a nightmare!" He's skeptical about government subsidies in general and identifies as a Libertarian. But he's frustrated by the lack of common sense and compromise and thinks government should protect the best farmland from development for future generations. I found his admission that "I don't know quite how to rectify this" as a sign of wisdom and maturity, rather than incoherence. Michael has different views on a range of issues that do not all fit together into some tidy theory about how the world works.

A couple years after I interviewed him, he was instrumental in developing the Pitney Meadows Community Farm in Saratoga Springs, NY. This is a 166-acre farm right inside the boundaries of an incorporated city. There is a community farm, a high-tunnel greenhouse, a recreational event space, a children's educational area including a garden and greenhouse, a pick-your-own CSA, a large self-service vegetable stand, a mile-long path around the property for walking, and aspirations for maximizing intelligent use of the 120 tillable acres. With support from the city government, the private sector, hundreds of volunteers and donors, including a remarkable community leader named Barbara Glaser (more on her later), there is great excitement in our community about this project.

What I find especially encouraging, in addition to watching this amazing venture take shape in my own community, is that I have come across a number of similar endeavors in other places, such as Abundance Farm in Northampton, MA., Community Involved in Sustaining Agriculture in South Deerfield, MA, Glynwood Farm in Cold Spring, NY, the Hudson Valley Farm Hub near Kingston, NY, Soul Fire Farm in Petersburg, NY, Polyface Farms in Swoope, VA, and Sankofa Community Farm at Bartram's Garden in Philadelphia, PA. Each one is very different, but they all involve extraction and also a profound commitment to stewardship of the land, of the community, and education.

In a 2016 interview conducted by folks from the Stone Barns Center for Food and Agriculture, Michael was asked what plans he had for the future. "I see us having started a new farm in five years, focusing this time on how much money we can make on an acre. I think it could easily be over $200K if we focus on the right crops in the right area of the country. I would also like to continue innovating techniques and tools for the small farm."

A while later, last I heard, Michael had bought and moved to a farm near Dayton, OH. Most importantly for him, no doubt, his wife had a baby. Upon reflection, I sensed there was something familiar about Michael. Young, white, male, a little iconoclastic, and proudly agrarian in his sensibilities, he has a whiff of a hero in a Hollywood movie set in farm country. As someone who respects the past and the land, though, he is not confined by traditions or a particular "place." He is energetic, hungry for information and success, and ready to try new things. I wouldn't want to bet any money on what he'll be doing in ten years because I just don't think it is predictable. For now, though, he is the face, or at least a representative face, of the leaders in this social movement, of young farmers committed to regenerative agriculture. He is active in several stages of the cycle of engagement, including extraction.

ROSE CHERNEFF: PAYING ATTENTION
AND RELATING AND NOTICING

I recently contemplated the wonder of a ruby-throated hummingbird as I watched it in my backyard. Its wings were beating so fast, more than 50 times per second, while it hovered, and drank. It seemed joyfully frenzied and incongruously calm at the same time. I perceived something similar about Rose Cherneff when I first met her on a summer afternoon at Abundance Farm in Northampton, MA. Another farmer and mutual friend, Naomi, introduced us there, where Rose is farm manager. During the couple hours we spent together, Rose shared lunch with Naomi, my research assistant, Miles, and me, greeted a dozen or more people who came by to pick vegetables, called out to a couple different colleagues, and completed several chores here and there—flitting among these activities with ease. She also listened to my questions patiently and answered them carefully. She is, to borrow a phrase she uses, "very blendy."

Rose grew up in Belmont, MA, a suburb of Boston. "I definitely don't have an academic brain," she told me, "so school was really hard for me." I found that a little difficult to swallow since Rose graduated in 2013 from Carlton College, an institution that accepts 20 percent of its applications and is ranked in the top ten of national liberal arts colleges. And also, because it takes only a few seconds of listening to Rose to recognize that she is thoughtful and expressive. But I understood Rose's underlying point, which is that she thrives in getting her hands dirty. "I don't like work that's not grounded." Or, more to the point, she loves work that is.

In high school, she had joined a program in Boston called The Food Project. "Their idea is that they do youth development work and leadership training for teenagers, bringing a very intentionally racially, socioeconomically, geographically diverse group of teenagers together and grow food on what were once vacant lots in Boston," she explained to me. The Food Project focuses on community organizing, leadership development and workshops on social identity, power, and privilege.

This particular combination would prove pivotal for Rose, who finds deep resonance with plants but is also engaged with her own Jewish heritage, and broader questions of how different cultural traditions are related to the earth. The Food Project runs a CSA and participates in a local farmers' market, too.

She learned through The Food Project that "the world is crazy and unfair." Along with such sobering lessons as she was coming of age, though, she said that the experience helped her develop valuable tools, both in terms of practical skills for growing food, and intellectual insights about power relations. "It was a powerful combination," she exclaimed.

Another farmer named Leah Penniman, author of *Farming While Black: Soul Fire Farm's Practical Guide to Liberation on the Land* and farm manager of Soul Fire Farm, was also deeply affected by that combination at The Food Project. As a 16-year-old, she applied there for a summer job and was "hooked on farming" from the get-go (Penniman 2018, p. 1). For Penniman as for Rose, the emphasis on "integrating a land ethic and a social justice mission" was crucial. Penniman wrote that it is a relatively rare combination but then describes dozens of agricultural training programs across the country that are led by people of color and/or maintain a commitment to social justice.

Two other alums from The Food Project helped found Rooted in Community, which has for more than two decades hosted national conferences around the country on food, community, and justice and run numerous youth education programs. One of the achievements they extol most on their website (rootedincommunity.org) is the generation of a Youth Food Bill of Rights. More on that later. This sort of catalytic impact seems common among such organizations. Over time, I encountered subjects who knew other subjects I had met, and various links from one organization to another.

Anyway, back to Rose. During college, she was active in Food Truth, a student club at Carlton: "Food Truth revolves around celebrating all things food," its mission statement reads. "It is a place for those who are passionate about sustainable agriculture and improving our broken food system as well as those who love cooking and savoring delicious wholesome meals."[4] In that work she helped draw the campus's attention to local sourcing, organic farming, and the potential impact of the college community's consumption patterns.

During that time, she also got to know local farmers in Minnesota and did various farm-related work activities. Her senior research project in Environmental Studies was about how regenerative farming practices spread depending on the social networks among farmers. She also did an internship back in Massachusetts with CitySprouts, an organization that supports the development of gardens in the public schools of Cambridge.

More farming followed after college. She worked on a "horse-powered" CSA that runs year-round and provides "whole diet" foods to its customers. In winter during those years, she worked in California landscaping and pruning fruit trees.

After nearly a decade of experience Rose became the farm manager at Abundance Farm in 2017. The mission there emphasizes food security and justice, community, and education. It is associated with Congregation B'nai Israel (a Conservative Jewish synagogue) as well as a Jewish day school, and the Northampton Survival Center. "The Northampton Survival

Center strives to improve the quality of life for low-income individuals and families in Hampshire County by providing food and other resources with dignity and respect. The Center runs two pantries—one in Northampton and one in Goshen, distributing approximately 650,000 pounds of food each year."[5]

The day I met Rose, she, Naomi, Miles, and I sat at a picnic table and ate lunch next to an acre or so of vegetables and fruit, as people came by to pick. "I'm glad we're sitting out here," she said, "because this is almost typical." As we talked, folks kept wandering by and having a quick word with Rose. "I think I calculated it one day . . . every fifteen minutes I get interrupted" by somebody coming by to volunteer, pick their own produce, or discuss some upcoming event.

But she loves the emphasis on human relationships. Rose lights up each time a person walks by. Some ask her where to find strawberries. Some show her what they've picked. She offers a kind word and a smile to each one.

"This is a unique job . . . it's very blendy," she said. It entails extensive interaction with plants and people. "It works well for my brain. I like switching tasks," fluttering from one thing to another. She runs a summer education program with about 15 teenagers, including some associated with the temple, some other Jews in the community, and some gentiles who live nearby. "They take on a leadership role in the farm, so they run the pick-your-own program and then we have workshops also around social identity.",

As for Michael Kilpatrick, religious faith is integral to her work on the farm. In her case, though, Rose is actively exploring her Jewish heritage. She spoke of "ancestral pain" that she carries in her body and the importance of "healing work through getting to know your ancestors." Much of the ancient wisdom, she explained to us, is written in terms of laws and practices related to agriculture because that was such an important part of life.

She mentioned several Hebrew words and their significance for farming. "There's something that we're moving toward in Judaism. The word *tzedakah* can be translated either as charity or justice," she explained. Abundance Farm is "part of this ecosystem of food justice organizations and we're not doing lobbying and we're not doing systemic change, but we thrive at what we call relational justice. So we're making these one-on-one relationships across lines," including ethnic, racial, class, religious, and cultural boundaries.

For instance, "we're really trying to move away from this idea of 'some people are giving, and some are receiving.' . . . I have needs that I need to get from my community and have things that I can give and . . . every person who walks into the farm is giving and receiving . . . it's important that 'pick your own' is the entire community and not just people who are food insecure at this moment."

According to the ideal of *orlah*, one is "not allowed to harvest fruit from a tree for its first three years of life. A lot of these rules, when I read them as a farmer, I understand them on a biological level, the wisdom of it . . . so helping the tree put its focus into root development and foliage the first couple years would have been important." Spirituality is often functional.

Pe'ah is "leaving the corners of the field unharvested so that others"—those in need—"can come harvest that." The needs of the land and the neighbor are both anticipated.

"And then *shmitah* is a really beautiful one, which is once every seven years you're not supposed to cultivate crops. You're allowed to cultivate perennials, but it's like a rest year. And it's also like debt is forgiven, right?" A Jubilee for fields?

What I found especially interesting about Rose's journey into her Jewish roots is how that exploration has motivated her learning about other cultures as well. Rather than crouching defensively, she has become more open to other traditions. "We are trying to grow one of the varieties of okra actually called Star of David" because its cross-section looks like a hexagram. "Okra is really popular, and a bunch of people who were born in the South have stories around that."

"That's amaranth," she said, pointing to a plant nearby. "There are very popular relatives of it all across America and South America. Amaranth and quinoa are staple grains across South America. A woman came last year who was a recent refugee from Rwanda." A lot of pigweed, a relative of amaranth "grows in our garden, which is like a staple green over there" in Rwanda. "She was excited because she couldn't find it in the grocery store. And we were weeding it" until she explained its value.

"We're doing Syrian greens," Rose said. "We grow tons of cilantro and people make Puerto Rican sofrito . . . it's a really beautiful cultural sharing pathway." "There's a tomato variety that we're growing called Plate de Haiti that was featured in art about the Haitian revolution."

Sometimes it's hard for two people from different cultures to relate to one another, Rose comments. "Everyone has stories about these plants, however. Having a third thing" beside two different cultural identities "that you can connect around is really helpful." She talked about meeting a woman from Haiti the year before.

She knows plants in a way," Rose said, "like even the way she touches plants is a type of fluency that I don't have." They discussed different foods her new friend missed from home. This happens a lot, Rose said—people miss food from home that they can't find.

Rose explained how her friend came with a squash she bought at a grocery store, which is usually hard to find. She had "sprouted it and cared for it and tended it." Then she brought it to Abundance Farm hoping to plant it. "And

I was like 'Amazing! Where should we plant it?'" They walked around the farm together. Rose suggested a chain link fence. But her friend said, no, Rose explained to me,

> it should be a tree "because that'll keep it warmer at night," which is just like a level of understanding of the whole ecosystem that I just don't have. So, we found the perfect spot for it and we planted it, and trellised it, and she came back a couple days later to check on it, and that was a relationship. We both love plants and there was cultural sharing.

Abundance Farm provides a kind of hub for this sharing, Rose explained. People harvest something one year and then the following year they bring new plants to add to the garden and share the produce with others. The land gives and takes. The people give and take. "It's a true community garden," Rose declared. "It's really heartwarming."

I was struck by the idea of fluency with plants and asked her about it (see Kimmerer 2015). "I remember as a child I transplanted some chard in my little, tiny side garden and it wasn't doing well," she said. She would come back each hour to check on it. "In some ways I was more in touch back then than I am now that I'm busy and have a 'to-do list.' And that, to me, is fluency. All that is, is paying attention and relating and noticing. And then I think, probably just genuine in the way that some people come alive with music or something . . . my enthusiasm is genuine."

For example, she recalled some eggplants about which she was concerned. They had been eaten by flea beetles the previous year.

> But when you plant plants, I've noticed that there's this period when they're just needy, like a young baby. And you're trying to basically wean them off of needing you. And basically there's this moment when you're being very tender, you're putting Reemay[6] there and you're making sure they get the exact right amount of sunlight and handpicking bugs off them and then there's this moment when you literally, I can't explain it what it looks like but you're like "oh, you're gonna be fine." And I think, I'm not a parent, but I think there's a moment when your child is a teenager and you're like "oh, you don't need me in the same way anymore and you have deep enough roots, and you're photosynthesizing on your own, you don't need to add nutrients."

The eggplants need to grow up. "Quick, quick!" She felt better when she left for vacation, she relayed because they had just gone into "I can handle it mode . . . thank God."

As Rose spoke in reference to plants in parental terms, I also perceived a studious eagerness to learn from them. I'm sure she agrees with the environmental biologist, Robin Wall Kimmerer, who said, "To replenish the possibility of mutual flourishing, for birds and berries, and people, we need an economy that shares the gifts of the Earth, following the lead of our oldest teachers, the plants" (Kimmerer 2021).

The goal of fluency in the context of the sacred became a pattern I noticed in speaking to engaged sustainers. Corinne and Matthew, mentioned in the last chapter, expressed similar concerns. In their reasoning, a loving kind of relationship is at the center of their work with the earth, which is understood by them as feminine and divine. Others were more vague but also spoke of deep meaning, attentive generosity, and alert gratitude in their work.

As I witnessed Rose's exuberance in talking about the different aspects of her work—like a hummingbird's wings beating 50 times a second—I started to wonder how such a social person could spend so much quiet time with plants. "I go slow, too," she reflected. "I think Judaism offers an amazing reminder to slow down, value moments of gratitude and noticing. And it's been a real joy, because I was working on a production farm and it was 'go, go, go bunch kale as fast as you can,' and it's been really amazing to value, and have my coworkers value pausing and noticing."

I realized later that valuing slowness is a common quality of engaged sustainers. Slow Food was one of the first organizations to gain traction in the effort to promote local sourcing and preserve culinary traditions (see Honore 2004; Patel 2008; Schor 2011). Slow Food International now emphasizes three points in its stated philosophy: (1) Good: quality, flavorsome, and healthy food; (2) Clean: production that does not harm the environment; and (3) Fair: accessible prices for consumers and fair conditions and pay for producers. All three points are central to the alternative agro-food movement.

It's worth noting, though, that this way of thinking about food is linked to slowness in general. It entails deliberation about how what we are doing "here and now" is related to what we and others will do "elsewhere and later." Thus, various thoughtful people speak of slow design, slow money, slow medicine, or slow parenting. There are analogues related to art, fashion, travel, leisure, and so on. Such intentional perspectives have been expressed in many ways, from ancient spiritual traditions like Buddhism and Yoga to newfangled self-help books, like *Deep Work: Rules for Focused Success in a Distracted World*.

Michael and Rose are in many ways quite fast. Like plenty of others I spoke with, they move quickly and cover a lot of ground. But there is also something deeply slow about these two and other engaged sustainers I encountered.

CONCLUSION

A constant pattern I ran across in my research was running into ordinary people doing extraordinary things. With very few exceptions, I believe none of the people I interviewed came from money. They do not command large organizations. Not a single one of them exhibited the qualities we would associate with matchless genius. And yet. People like Michael and Rose take little steps every day that add up to something. Malcolm Gladwell made famous the notion that through 10,000 hours of practice a person could become an outlier in terms of achievement. Each hour is a little step in the cumulative journey toward brilliance. How many people do you know who talk about putting their 10,000 steps in toward daily health? That's how I think of Michael and Rose. Constant, incremental steps toward fitness and achievement.

They are clearly special but far from unique. In addition to energetic striving, Michael and Rose manifested behaviors I witnessed in many others. They—Michael and Rose—aspire to greater fluency (to borrow Rose's term) in their vocations. Engaged sustainers often derive deep meaning from their craft. Like grounders previously mentioned, they explicitly reference ancient practice and contemporary innovation. Interestingly, Michael and Rose each speak of land in general with reverence, but do not seem overly attached to a particular place. That is true of a number of other farmers I met. Having relocated from Massachusetts to New York state, Michael poured huge amounts of energy into Kilpatrick Family Farm for a number of years and then apparently after a good bit of planning moved to a new one several hundred miles away in Ohio. Rose has already garnered a great deal of farming experience in her young life across three regions of the United States.

It's worth emphasizing that their work as extractors is extremely relational. Even as they take something from the earth, they think about sharing it. Michael wants his own farm to be successful but is overtly attached to the national movement of regenerative farming and constantly trying to teach others about his successes. Rose is active in her spiritual interior, but also externally connected to Jewish traditions, the community she lives in, and various friends and relations not linked to her religious traditions or community.

It occurs to me that for people whose waking hours are largely consumed by material things, they are quite attentive to nonmaterial abstractions as well: meaning, relationships, cultural memory, and the divine. This sort of awareness of the linkage between immediate practical challenges and larger, more abstract concerns appears central to a benign moral footprint.

NOTES

1. This emphasis on "more" is also related to disordered eating, obesity, and other eating issues, as I explain in chapter 7, which addresses consumption patterns, marketing, and availability of healthy calories.

2. See ongoing reports put out by Mercaris (e.g., "The Organic and Non-GMO Acreage Report"), and the United States Department of Agriculture (e.g., "Organic Survey").

3. Laura Sayre (2011) has argued that organic farms tend to be concentrated in Democrat-leaning states. In short, it's complicated.

4. See apps.carleton.edu/ccce/issue/environmentenergy/food-truth/.

5. See abundancefarm.org/partnering-organizations/.

6. Reemay is a type of fabric used in gardening and farming that lets sunlight in and keeps bugs out, among other things.

Chapter Five

Processing

Whenever I wash some fresh produce that recently came out of the ground, I often think about how hard farmers must work to clean their fruits and vegetables for sale at farmers' markets. After all the toil to grow and harvest the crops, they then have to wash them. I occasionally wonder about the process of certain crops ending up in food that looks so different in the end, like wheat becoming bread. Often, when I taste a subtly delicious dish that is complicated to prepare, I marvel at the talent of the cook.

The journey from a raw natural resource to a food item ready for digestion varies in distance and complexity, depending on what it is. An apple can be picked and immediately eaten. A chicken that ends up in coq au vin will travel farther. Whatever the pathway, all the different kinds of human energy spent converting the natural resources gathered through extraction into food ready for consumption comprise the category of processing. This includes, for example, de-hulling, milling, dressing, butchering, cleaning, washing, fermenting, pickling, pasteurizing, refining, jarring, canning, preserving, packaging, or, most importantly, cooking.

As little as most consumers know about farming and other kinds of extraction, the vast majority of processing is not only hidden and therefore out of sight, but largely out of mind. Have you ever seen a cow slaughtered or butchered? Or the process of black beans going from a field to a can? Many of us have scant firsthand information about such matters, and I suspect we think little about them either.

However, a meaningful shift is unfolding that became evident to me through the processors I spoke with. Many of them are committed to some kind of localism. The proximity of the origin of their food has become a priority along with other criteria, like cost, taste, health, and choice. For local sourcing, by definition, that means the conversion from natural resource to food is comparably quick. The processing of food for one's neighbor is on the whole more transparent than for those sending their products across the world

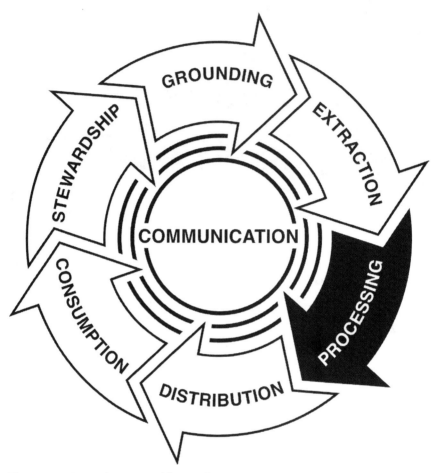

Figure 5.1.   Processing. Created by Martha MacGregor

(see Hunt 2007). For starters, it is easier to see what is close. Also, though, neighbors don't want to sell garbage to neighbors, so they have a stake in processing with integrity, which enables more transparency. They have nothing to hide. Likewise, the sunshine of transparency helps integrity grow. Plus, food that is not moved as far needs fewer preservatives, less refrigeration, or other kinds of intervention that would keep it from perishing.

Of course, the handling of some agricultural products is much more opaque than others regardless of where they are from. Most of us probably have more familiarity with what happens to an apple picked in New Zealand than we do with beef cattle raised in our own county. Some critics have argued that the metric of carbon miles is problematic for just this reason. Something could be produced with more uprightness and transported a fair distance compared to something produced with lots of fertilizers and preservatives in our own region. Ecological footprint is probably a better way to think about it (see Roberts 2008, p. 286). It's not just about where food comes from but how it's handled.

"Eat food," Michael Pollan said, "Not too much. Mostly plants." Several messages are implicit in this iconic advice. Think about what you eat. Eat stuff that is raw or cooked with integrity. Avoid "bechemicaled" food in general (that's Wendell Berry's lovely word). Eat less meat than most Americans have been eating. Pay attention to portion size.

Food production is not just about extracting natural resources, of course, but also how it is subsequently processed. It's not all healthy or sustainable, but we now have The Food Network and the Cooking Channel, not to mention various shows on other channels, fully devoted to food preparation. There is more attention devoted to the processing of food now than there ever has been since modern, industrial society started generating more than enough calories than society collectively needs. Processors are engaged sustainers involved in the conversion of natural resources into food. A good example is Marti Wolfson.

MARTI WOLFSON: COOKING ALLOWS US TO TAP INTO THAT CREATIVE SIDE OF OUR BRAINS

"Uhmmm, oh my gosh, I'm sorry. . . . I'm pregnant and things are just . . ." Marti stopped midsentence because she couldn't remember what she was about to say, as I interviewed her. As I thought about her since then, having learned how important movement, bodies, feelings, and senses are to her, I realized that that moment was somehow loaded with symbolic meaning about who she is. Needless to say, being pregnant is a defining experience for most women in that situation. Knowing Marti a bit, I figured it was deeply resonant, poignant, and lifechanging. I should add that during our conversation she had been speaking with clarity, insight, and passion for some time and remembered more details about various topics than most folks can ever pull off. The good-humored self-effacement is part of her affable personality.

I first met Marti Wolfson in 2001, when she was a student at Skidmore, a double major in Dance and Exercise Science. Two of my best friends were her faculty mentors in her respective majors. Encountering her during brief conversations and as she performed her senior dance recital, I could see at least part of what they saw: a light, a zeal for life. My friends told me she was passionate about movement, the body, health, and creativity, which I was able to learn more about when I interviewed her.

Like many I talked to, Marti started spending time in the kitchen early on. "Always my mother's little sous chef." A dancer since she was six years old, she told me, "it always comes back to the body, or what we call the somatic experience of being a person first." As with many young people, Marti initially started cooking for real when she lived in an apartment for the first time. No parents and no dining hall because she was a college student living off campus; she had to fend for herself. At the same time, she was completing assignments in Exercise Science courses that required her to systematically use and compare different diets. Her growing awareness of how varied combinations of foods affected her own body was shaped both by hands-on learning and academic training. She loved the creativity and lessons involved in such experimentation. "I started playing with healthier ingredients." Soon she would need all the skills and insight of such practice.

After graduation in 2002, Marti went to New York City and became a certified Pilates instructor. She then taught Pilates at Canyon Ranch Wellness Resort in the Berkshires. During that time, she became ill with an undiagnosed and apparently chronic digestive condition. As she was helping others build strength in their bodies, her own was letting her down. The medical professionals she consulted were ineffective. "Nobody was helping me. They were just throwing pills, antibiotics. No one was talking food."

She began experimenting with a new sense of purpose. But her efforts were uninformed, as I learned from her TEDx–CapeMay Talk. "Trying one extreme diet after another. I was so afraid of the physical pain and emotional unease after a meal. I micromanaged my diet to the point that eating was not pleasurable anymore and cooking, well, the kitchen felt like a spider web I was trapped in."

At Canyon Ranch, Marti got to know doctors and nutritionists who taught her about integrative health. From them she learned about "mind-body medicine" or what is formally known as functional medicine. This is a "biology systems" approach to medicine that seeks to identify the root causes underlying illness through scientific evidence and naturalistic treatments. Practitioners attend to the mind, spirit, and body of their patients. They might order lab tests and recommend yoga or meditation, or some other combination of conventional medicine and naturopathy.

For about four years, Marti worked hard to manage her health, study this approach to healing, and learn more about nutritional cooking. Over time, she determined that her illness was caused by a parasite and through careful trial and error figured out how to treat it with "food as medicine." By methodically eliminating inflammatory foods, she told me, she slowly healed her gut.

One of the hubs for functional medicine is The Natural Gourmet Institute for Health and Culinary Arts in New York City. Its motto is: "Kale, Quinoa & Community since 1977." A young woman by the name of Annemarie Colbin founded the Natural Gourmet Cookery School in the kitchen of her Upper West Side apartment. Well before many others, she grasped, studied, wrote about the important connection between food and health. She argued that a healthy diet is not just good for us, but that "food as medicine" can actually cure illness. The school she founded would go on to train more than 2,500 chefs from over 45 countries. Colbin wrote numerous books and was a celebrity chef frequently seen on television before The Food Network existed. In a 2006 letter to the *New York Times* editorial page, she wrote: "Intellectual knowledge is considered superior to intuitive knowledge. Sometimes it may be; often it's not." Marti is now working in this tradition.

Of that school, Marti told me,

> picture the yogic version of the Culinary Institute of America. You learn much more than classic French and Asian techniques, but also where your food comes from, the supply chain, health and nutrition. It is really a holistic approach to sustainability through the culinary arts. You learn how to properly prepare beans and sea vegetables, tempeh and coconut and spelt. I had never eaten so cleanly in all my life. But different than years prior when I thought I was eating healthy, I didn't feel compelled to micromanage my diet so much because all of the flavors were so satisfying and, most of all, my body felt good.

Marti trained at the Natural Gourmet Institute, finishing in 2008, and became a chef. In what she calls her "CALM approach"—for culinary and lifestyle medicine—nutrition is central, but the work is holistic and broad. "The majority of my work is food based, but I do a lot with mindfulness, exercise, and other lifestyle factors. I really like the whole range."

Marti's thinking is evident in various strands of the alternative agro-food movement. For example, my wife recently returned from a weekend retreat at a yoga center. She told me about a workshop she attended about "mindful eating" in which she learned to ponder the source of her food, where it comes from, who helps produce it, how it tastes, how it feels to digest it. Teachers there suggested that the circumstances of food production—how animals are treated, how plants are cultivated and harvested—all have a material impact on what food does to our bodies. A dairy farmer I spoke to at a local farmers' market told me the same thing. The comfort of the cows very much affects the quantity and quality of the milk they produce, he said. Jamie Ager said the same thing about the beef cows he raises.

The movement Marti is helping to lead is part of a broader pattern in medicine. Mainstream medical practitioners are starting to see food as medicine. Some physicians are prescribing fresh fruits and vegetables to their patients (see Hans Kersten, who is featured in the next chapter). "Culinary medicine" is an emerging field in medical school training (see Brown 2018; Kalaichandran 2018).

Such mindfulness in Marti's work is akin to the idea of "slowness" mentioned in the last chapter, as in Slow Food, the organization founded in Italy in 1986 by Carlo Petrini (Honore 2004). The idea gave rise to a global movement that emphasizes slowing down in general, as well as local ingredients, heirloom varieties, culinary traditions, minimizing waste, and resisting industrial and fast food. Just as real cooking requires patience, so does any genuine craft.

Again, this connotation of the adjective *slow* has become synonymous with sustainable, and responsible and has been subsequently applied to various activities like spending, design, film, fashion, parenting, leisure, education, consumption and thinking in general (see Honore 2004; Tayor 2014). In each case, the aspiration is to resist dominant modes of *fast* activities that emphasize efficiency, profit, and short-term thinking. The goal is to unsettle industrialized "timescapes" (see Snyder 2016, p. 13) that have commodified time, undermined craft, and devalued human relationships.[1]

Even though she is not really a steward of particular culinary traditions, Marti is, in more general terms, decidedly slow. Deliberate awareness and attentiveness are central to the CALM approach. Balance is key. This perspective on well-being and how so much revolves around it is expressed in frequent, diverse ways by sustainers. They talk about the soil where earthworms and microbes dwell, the plants that grow in it, the animals that eat the plants, and the bodies and the minds of humans. Health, broadly construed, is dependent on mindfulness of such connections.

Marti is working to expand such mindfulness. Having been to culinary school, she started her own business as a chef, educator, and consultant. "I was already an educator. I was teaching movement. I switched into cooking very easily," she told me. Marti is proud of her training and skills. When she says the word "chef" it sounds like an honorific title that should be capitalized, like Colonel or Monsignor. She was invited to give a talk for TEDx–Cape May in 2014 and has made numerous other appearances. In those moments she talks about struggling with her own illness and finding a way to well-being through food.

Marti is explicit about the countercultural thread in her work. Those of us ensconced in mainstream American culture have a hard time being mindful. "We're in a state of culinary confusion today." She laments the "Food Court," not the one at the mall (though that one is implicitly rebuked by her work) but the culture of fear and judgment we have built into our food system (see Herz

2018, p. 31). We worry about what people will think of what we eat because food says a lot about who we are. And of course, we worry about what to eat, whether anyone is watching or not. Is it fat, sugar, carbs (or rather bad carbs) I'm supposed to avoid?! Think of the cravings, the guilt, the shame, the disordered eating.

Sometimes it's not a taboo on where or what you *shouldn't* eat; it's strong pressure related to where or what you *should* eat. Marti told me about a client who was dealing with multiple health issues. Marti was trying to help her figure out dietary solutions. But the client faced an additional obstacle at work. The dining hall of her corporate employer serves three meals a day and employees are expected to eat there. If you don't eat with everyone else, Marti relayed to me, "you're going to be looked down upon." The food served in the dining hall was not helping and the woman didn't want to be a "pariah." "She was totally depressed about this workplace." I was thinking of my own experiences in family settings where there are pressures to consume what has been prepared. Or friends teasing me about being high maintenance when I ask about gluten-free options. That's what happens in a court—judgment.

Marti tried to convince her client to bring her lunch with healthy food in it. The key to figuring this out, Marti thinks, is to recognize the layers of connective issues. We know that any understanding of how a food system works must encompass consideration of economics, politics, culture, religion, medicine, law, and other institutions. So of course, it follows that the habits of any given individual related to food involve other aspects of her life. Diet matters, obviously, but Marti said it also ties into exercise, stress management, mind-body techniques and social relationships, too. We could add social context, demographics and other social factors that affect individuals (Brownell and Horgen 2004; Bittman 2021).

If one tries to pay attention to so many things at once, how does she make a meal? Or more to the point, how does she maintain viable habits of cooking and eating over time? "The kitchen is a daunting room in the house for many people," Marti observes.

Current patterns in the American kitchen are alarming. A growing number of us don't know how to cook. Only about a third of adults in the United States do, Marti said, despite unprecedented numbers of celebrity chefs. "Cooking at home is becoming a lost art," Bruce Peterson told *Beef* magazine in 2003 (Roberts 2008, p. 73). At that time, he was the head of perishables at Walmart, who has worked hard to accommodate the demand for ready-made meals. Mass-produced, heavy on the meat, intended for quick preparation and of questionable nutritional value, such meals are exactly the sort of thing Marti is working against.

As one research study reported:

> US adults have decreased consumption of foods from the home supply and reduced time spent cooking since 1965, but this trend appears to have leveled off, with no substantial decrease occurring after the mid-1990s. Across socio-economic groups, people consume the majority of daily energy from the home food supply, yet only slightly more than half spend any time cooking on a given day. Efforts to boost the healthfulness of the U.S. diet should focus on promoting the preparation of healthy foods at home while incorporating limits on time available for cooking (Smith, Ng, and Popkin 2013).

The biggest declines in home preparation appear to be among low-income households. It is worth noting that working people endured persistently shrinking real income from the 1970s through the 1990s. Since then, purchasing power on the low end of the socioeconomic status has gone up very little. That could mean more work for the same take-home pay and therefore less time for food preparation and/or just less income for expensive, fresh ingredients (Bowen et al. 2019). In any case, compared to fifty years ago, Americans across income categories are preparing and eating food at home much less.[2]

But there is something else going on among middle- and upper-class households. Many of them feel quite stressed about the need to consume food wisely (Fielding-Singh 2021). Relatively speaking, needless to say, they have the resources they need to cook meals with fresh foods. But many of them somehow do not cultivate such habits.

I thought of this trend when a friend told me a funny story. He was at a little party at another friend's home, in their large, fancy house with a state-of-the-art kitchen. At one point everyone smelled some weird noxious odor. It turned out to be plastic burning in the oven. One of the guests had put some dish in to warm it up without consulting the host. The plastic was the lining the new oven had on it when they had bought it two years earlier. No one had used the oven or even looked inside to notice the plastic in it all that time.

As easy as it must be for the Food Network to find guests from all walks of life for the popular TV show *Worst Cooks in America*, many like Marti are more devoted to the culinary arts than ever. From some teachers, such as her mother and Annemarie Colbin, Marti learned to value traditional ways of food preparation. Countless generations have accumulated deep knowledge about what works over the fire and on the stove. Such conventions provide a viable starting place. But Marti learned different lessons from other sources, including Exercise Science professors and functional medicine practitioners, as well as her own illness. Evidence matters. Experimentation allows us to learn new things to complement established customs.

If tradition and evidence are both guiding principles in her cooking, there is a third, surprising theme in Marti's approach that she got from Colbin: intuition. That made me think of young Marti, the six-year-old dancer who helped her mom in the kitchen and loved the human body's movement.

In some elemental sense cooking is integral to the human experience. Early humans uncovered the secrets of fire and fire is the basis for cooking. All of us have ancestors who succeeded in securing nourishing food with what they had. Anyone who had babies that survived into adulthood figured it out.

But the intuition Marti has in mind for the kitchen is not the extemporaneous inclination of a child. One has to know some basic things, like at least the rudiments of cooking. A better image might be an accomplished jazz musician who, after learning how to play the instrument, practicing, and listening to other musicians, improvises freely and creatively. Competence and experience combined with playfulness. How does a musician know if her choices work? The music sounds good. For Marti, the same is true of intuitive cooking. How does a chef know if his choices work? The food tastes good. If you want to do it the same way next time, fine. If you want to mix it up, that's alright too.

In a culture of fear where we are losing the knowledge, skills, and habits of cooking, Marti suggests, intuition can be empowering. Just as it transcends logic and reason in general, intuition in cooking can free a person to be inventive and spontaneous. The key, Marti said, is making it taste good. In other words, if you start with fresh, local, seasonal, whole ingredients, and then seek to make the dish taste good, how you get there doesn't matter.

"Just as we use art, music, dance, and writing to express ourselves," Marti said in her TEDx Talk, "cooking allows us to tap into that creative side of our brain too. When we use intuition, we tap into the limbic or emotional side of our brain, that brain which helps us feel nurtured. It makes sense, right? How we feed ourselves can be extremely nurturing." More broadly, Marti's aim in her own cooking and that of her students is to advance the health of those who eat the food. If it tastes good and makes someone feel better (physically and emotionally), that is success.

She describes her friends and colleagues in culinary nutrition as "artists" and "do-gooders." What they are not—by way of inclination or systematic training—is businesspeople. But Marti understands how important such acumen is for her and the "movement" of which she is a part. She has effectively used Wix.com, which is a cloud-based web development platform. That has allowed her to establish an online presence for her business and market her services. And she has benefitted a lot, she told me, from one training course at a local university for new small business owners. In 2016 Marti also completed a master's degree in human nutrition and functional medicine to add formal credentials to the many years of hands-on experience she now has under her belt.

Marti lives in a wealthy community. Many of her clients are corporate and affluent. Her hired services are not cheap. You have to pay attention, she explained to me, to "your numbers as a business owner." But the returns are not simply monetary. For example, Marti regularly cooks at a farmers' market. She arrives early with some of her own interns, asks farmers what they want to push, and then she and her team improvise with those ingredients for several hours. This provides guidance and encouragement to shoppers who then purchase the produce the farmers want to sell. "You don't have to think too much about what's in the food. It's fresh. Still, people need inspiration about what to do with the ingredients. So, that's what our table serves. It's another piece of education."

Overall, the setting provides a kind of "therapy" from the "very stressed-out world of eating." In a farmers' market people connect with one another, Marti pointed out. They learn about the source of their food and get to know farmers. "It's just a great place to come and socialize. It's a very healing place. I look forward to it every single week. It's such a high. There is nothing like the beauty of fresh food and I think that alone inspires your intuition."

One of her ambitions for the future is to build a community center that pulls together trained chefs, other professionals, volunteers, and sourcing from local organic farms, to serve free food to members of the community in need, especially those with health concerns, like cancer patients. "It's like Meals on Wheels but the uber-healthy version of it." As with many of the people I spoke to in this research, Marti is persuasive. I couldn't help but believe that her aspirations are realistic.

On top of all the stress and illness related to conventional cooking habits, and the fact that we are collectively losing the capacity to cook in the first place, Marti lamented familiar problems involving Big Agriculture and Big Food. Farmers who grow corn and soy are subsidized while those who grow fresh produce have a harder time. Processed vegetable oils that contribute to chronic diseases are marketed and sold widely. Companies like Kraft and Pepsi are still "manipulating people's palates." Companies such as Monsanto continue to squeeze out small farms. Things are bad and, in many ways, getting worse.

But there are also hopeful signs. Part of that is the normative appeal of "good food," which is growing. The "food court" Marti mentioned was about public norms reducing the possibilities for healthy food. But shame runs in different directions, as the comedian Jim Gaffigan has observed in a funny bit. Two friends accidentally run into one another at McDonalds. "I'm just here for the 99 cent ATM, what are you doing here, Jim?" "Oh, I . . . I'm just meeting a hooker. I'm certainly not eating here. That's for sure."

Beyond such observations about changing norms, Marti rattled off a bunch of concrete examples of progress to me. Schools are taking more seriously the need for healthy food and finding partners among farmers and gardeners. She drew my attention to the work of Stephen Ritz, a well-known author and teacher in NYC who has demonstrated "in one of the nation's poorest communities, his students thrive in school and in life by growing, cooking, eating, and sharing the bounty of their green classroom" (Ritz 2019). She talked about The Wellness in the Schools Program that helps tens of thousands of students in public schools in NYC eat healthy meals every day. She said the Lenox Hill Hospital in NYC is not alone in starting a rooftop garden. Various universities, like Johnson and Wales, and Tulane, are integrating the importance of healthy food into their medical education curricula. Wholesome Wave is a nonprofit organization linked to a network of nearly 1400 farmers' markets in 49 states that tries to make fresh produce affordable and accessible. She cited Ceres, a nonprofit organization with more than a hundred employees, working on a range of issues related to sustainability, including food and agriculture. "These small fights" matter, Marti declared.

Such efforts are aligned with some basic facts, which ground Marti's work. "I know in my heart that there are just certain truths in nature, and they will never change. That doesn't mean that mankind isn't messing around with nature. It just means that we have to get smarter and smarter about how we do things for ourselves and our planet. But there's always going to be the same truths about how to nourish ourselves that will keep us healthy and the planet healthy. That keeps me jazzed. There's a consistency in this work and for me it's just staying creative in how I deliver that, and inspiring people that they have the power to be their own healer." What would it mean if we were all healers?

Actual cooking at home is correlated with healthy eating (Smith, Ng, and Popkin 2013). So, the decline of home cooking is obviously concerning. But that is not the only thing happening. In the next chapter I discuss the spread of farmers' markets and community-supported agriculture, both of which are associated with home-cooking. Here I want to point out how the public places we eat in are changing.

One sign of this shift is the rise of the "fast casual restaurant" sector (e.g., Chipotle, Panera Bread). This is hardly the epicenter of pure, fresh, healthy food. (That would be the farm.) But the rapid rise of this type of restaurant reveals something important about shifting consumer demand. It is still fast food but has more made-to-order tailoring, fresh ingredients, fruits and vegetables, and less frozen and preserved foods. Citing the market research firm Euromonitor, Tim Carman of the *Washington Post* reports that sales for fast-causals jumped from $15.7 billion in 2007 to $26 billion in 2016 (Carman 2017). By 2020, it was $60 billion (Dunn 2020). Moreover, this explosion has had rippling implications for conventional fast food, Carman explains, who now feel pressure to make their products healthier.

Vegetarianism reflects the long-term trend of increasing concern for health and is important to both this shift among restaurants and to the larger alternative food movement. But meat is important too: how animals are raised and treated, as demonstrated in Jamie Ager's story in the last chapter, and how meat is processed, as demonstrated by Casey McKissick's.

CASEY MCKISSICK: WE DON'T WASTE ANYTHING

Another important subcategory here is the farm-to-table or farm-to-fork movement. It first became visible in restaurants but increasingly involves schools, hospitals, religious settings, and of course homes. I interviewed several chefs who are betting their livelihood on this trend. They have developed relationships with suppliers, either food hubs or farms, from whom they secure fresh ingredients. Compared to centuries past, obviously, we grow less of our own food. Compared to recent decades, as noted above, Americans are cooking and eating at home less. However, what is also clear from numerous sources, is that the farm-to-fork movement is not a flash in the pan. Think about the menus from any restaurants you've visited in the last few years and how many of them document where their ingredients come from. That includes, for example, Joshua's Restaurant and Bar in Wells, Maine, as previously described. Now think back to menus from 30, 20, or even 10 years ago and ponder the same thing. Several folks I spoke with spend most of their time getting products from farms, converting them into digestible food, and putting them on tables. One of them is Casey McKissick.

I interviewed him at a table on the patio of his restaurant in Black Mountain, North Carolina, over a couple beers, where he told me about his background and business. Casey grew up gardening. He studied experiential education and sustainable development at Appalachian State University. After that, he worked as a rapid river guide, climbing guide, and backcountry guide, he told me. Spending a lot of time in wilderness sparked questions for Casey about the way people relate to nature. Over time, such questions evolved into a more focused concern about food production. "I said," Casey quoted himself, "'maybe let's all go back to the woods.'" After the wilderness programs, Casey worked as a high school teacher. In his 20s, he learned about agricultural production and got into farming. "It turns out gardening and commercial farming," Casey acknowledged, "were very, very different things."

He then became an educator at the university level with North Carolina State's agricultural extension program. This was another formative experience through which he gained valuable insight into agricultural production systems. He got interested in supply chains and business. He was teaching and running his own family's farm at the same time. At its peak, he said, their farm had five acres of diversified vegetables devoted to direct marketing to restaurants and farmers' markets. They started with produce and cut flowers but got into livestock with the hope of having a more manageable work schedule. Through this combination of experiences, he explained, Casey learned lessons from multiple vantage points about the process of meat production.

Over time, he has become a largely self-taught farmer, butcher, chef, and restaurateur. When I interviewed him in the fall of 2018, Casey was no longer farming. He owns several businesses associated with the brand Foothills, including a butchery, two restaurants, a food truck, a catering company, and a meat-based community supported agriculture. Meat is central to all of it.

Bloomberg News reported in 2017 that the supply of "small-scale meat" could not keep up with demand (Shanker 2017). The main problem is the shortage of slaughterhouses. Due to the necessary capital, they are difficult to start. The work is hard and gritty. But they tend to be profitable, Casey told me. "Honestly, the modern meat slaughter facility is highly efficient. It's highly regulated. It's not like it's dirty. There are high volumes. So they're high line speeds and at times, depending on who you ask, that can cause additional stress to animals and people." The speed that is so hard on the people who work in such settings is crucial to low production costs. "That is why a pork shoulder at Sam's Club costs $1.29 per pound," Casey noted (in 2018 when I interviewed him).

In 2017 there were 1,100 slaughterhouses certified by the USDA. This is way down from the 9,627 establishments on record in 1967. Of the 1,100 today, about a quarter of them have 500 or more employees and are therefore designated as "large slaughterhouses." The big establishments are focused on their own supply chains. They will slaughter tens of thousands of animals every day, something around 70–90 percent of all the meat produced in the United States (Shanker 2017). "Those guys aren't interested in food," Casey said of such slaughterhouses. Just because you put something in your mouth doesn't mean it is food. And just because you are involved in "food production" doesn't mean you care about food per se.

Farmers running relatively small-scale farms, where the welfare of animals and quality of meat is important, don't use the big slaughterhouses, for the most part, Casey explained. They spend months raising an animal and then a slaughterhouse spends a few hours processing it. He noted that a lot of farmers do not like how the animals are treated in many large establishments. So they travel further and pay more for a greater amount of care and skill. Working conditions are usually better in such places too (Shanker 2017).

Keeping skilled butchers is important to Casey's business. "Whole animal butchery is absolutely a lost art. There's not a lot of people that actually know how to start from the beginning and take it all the way. And we have a tough time keeping skilled butchers."

Casey told me in 2019 that he pays $2.65 a pound to buy a whole pig. He gets meat mainly from three farmers. That means he knows exactly where every single meat product he sells comes from and who is responsible for its soundness. He wants animals raised in pastures where they are treated humanely, without extra hormones or antibiotics. "At the end of the day I would rather buy non-organic-fed pork from a farmer that I know, that all that money benefits his family, than to buy Certified Organic pork products from a national distributor who gets it from a bunch of different places around the country." Echoing Michael Kilpatrick's thinking described in the last chapter, Casey thinks the internal spirit of responsibility in production is more important than external bureaucratic criteria. "You lose transparency in that type of chain," he told me, "even though third party verification and all that kind of stuff is certainly rigorous. But at the end of the day, it's just people's signatures."

Casey then has to mark up the price further for his own margin. His website says that Foothills "holds the animals, farmers and the environment in the highest regard." At the core of such regard is thrift. "Like the butcher shops of the olden days, we don't waste anything." Low numbers seem to be a pattern underneath certain practices more likely to have integrity—low numbers of sources, acres, ingredients, collaborators, carbon-miles, and wasted parts. Such low numbers help make for a benign moral footprint.

As simple as it sounds, though, there is some sophisticated thinking behind this orientation. Casey channels the mindsets of a businessperson, ethicist, farmer, and cook all at the same time. "You have to use the whole thing for the economics to work out. It's like waste nothing! That's an economic principle. But it's also a philosophical principle that means that if we're killing an animal, we're going to use the whole thing. It goes back to ancient civilization, and we don't waste things. Honestly, more as a farmer, the entire product line is built upon every single piece of animal being used for something delicious and profitable."

As I kept hearing about a keen awareness of supply chains on the part of engaged sustainers, an image formed in my mind. Lots of people involved in extracting natural resources and lots of people focused on converting them for human use pay attention to supply chains. How do we get food from the field to the market? But extractors and processors think more deeply. That is, they think very carefully about the segment of the chain around them, and they look further up the chain and often further down from where they are.

The image that formed was that of someone fly fishing in a stream who thoroughly investigates details of the part of stream where they are. In thinking about the trout or bass, astute anglers look all around and consider potential predators, water temperature, hiding places, changes in depth, current seams, bank obstructions, and tributaries. To fully comprehend all those factors, one must think about conditions upstream and downstream as well. Where do the waters and fish come from and where do they flow to? A lot of engaged sustainers are thus *supply chain anglers,* including both Marti and Casey.

The word *angler* refers to someone fishing with a rod, line, and hook. *Angle* is an old word for hook. Like a person fishing in a stream, a supply chain angler looks carefully around where they are, up the stream and down the stream to see how the water is flowing, and how they can likely get what they are looking for.

Their part of the stream is their main work, culinary and lifestyle medicine on her part and "whole animal philosophy" butchery on his. Exploration of upstream encompasses the conventional supply chain, where the food comes from in connection with sustainable agriculture, viable community, humane treatment of animals, and so on. Concern for downstream is about the nutritional payoff of the food, the handling of waste, and the impact on social relationships.

As a supply chain angler, Casey is creative and ambitious about how all this can fit together. Yet, he's also a little skeptical about how much scaling up is possible. One of the pitfalls, he told me, is that medium-sized companies that do well get bought up by Big Food corporations such as Tysons. After such acquisitions, he suggested, such companies do bend toward the quality and transparency of the small companies because little guys have demonstrated that consumers value that. But corners are cut too, Casey said. Sometimes big companies just alter "labeling in a way that tells customers what they want to hear."

Consumer habits are a big deal for anyone trying to provide an alternative to Big Food. Competing against expansive marketing, the efficiency of easy access, and the cultural inertia of American consumption patterns is no small feat. In this case, though, the demand for high-quality meat from pasture-raised animals is soaring, which is both why there is a market for an independent company like Foothills and why the Tysons of the world are gobbling up other companies.

Casey said he's not terribly worried about consumer demand. Partly, consumers are seeking the kind of quality he offers. "I think that we're in the right place at the right time for what we're doing," he told me. "I think we've got the concept down that people will accept and then buy into the bigger picture." He also said, "I know that people always want burgers and hot dogs and beer. That's what the business is built on. It just happens to be that those products are made the way I want them."

Nonetheless, he sees this venture as risky. Whether he can actually make the business work even with robust consumer demand is very much in question. He said a lot of "alternative food producers" are in the same boat. A common problem is volume. He cited the high volume of Walmart and Amazon—two companies famous for treating employees poorly—as examples of successful business.[3]

According to Casey, there are two problems confronting "the small farm movement" related to volume. The first is immediate for many businesses and that is whether they can sell enough stuff to make a living. If producing something with quality is expensive, then you either have to charge a high price, in which case many consumers won't pay—consumer demand may be there but there is a ceiling—or you have to sell a lot of volume. If demand is there, then it's a question of supply. And we are back to the lack of independent slaughterhouses willing to treat animals as humanely as possible and process the meat with care.

A related issue is the larger purpose of this movement. "I worry about small farmers and the small farm movement," Casey said. "I worry about them thinking they can feed the country or even the world with this because they cannot." Remember, the big slaughterhouses processing animals from CAFOs handle 70–90 percent of all the meat produced in the country.

As we talked, he reflected on teaching disadvantaged students. "I was teaching them sustainable agriculture. I just remember at one point someone said, 'teacher, I don't worry about this shit; I don't even know what I'm going to have for dinner.' That really hit me hard back then and I'm like 'you're right!'" Not everyone can afford the products Casey sells. And not everyone has the time or money to think about the quality of what they consume (McMillan 2012; Bowen et al. 2019). Social class is a hugely important factor that shapes how people relate to this movement.

"My background in agriculture production does not lead me to believe that this is the secret, the key to feeding the world," he said of the alternative agro-food movement. "I think that large production can come a long way toward being more sustainable. But scale is a bitch. You can't get around that."

Casey is skeptical of any portrayal of our food system that is overly simplistic, as in small, local, and organic equals good versus large, global, and conventional equals bad. So low numbers (of acres, suppliers, wasted parts) are associated with good things, as noted above. But somewhere along the way, large numbers are necessary too—large numbers of slaughterhouses, farms, acres, hours, and calories.

CONCLUSION

There are lots of different kinds of processors involved in this movement. Some work at one stage of a process versus another, like pasteurizing milk or making cheese. Some work with a specific type of material, like dairy, versus a range of materials, like fresh produce. Both Marti and Casey represent common profiles. While their vocations and actual work are very different, there are some aspects of their endeavors that are similar, which typify what lots of processors do.

Localism involves keeping supply chains as short and simple as possible. If you buy a McDonalds hamburger, the beef likely comes from one of 20 processing companies across the globe, which has procured the meat from one of 400,000 cattle farms. The chain is neither short nor simple. If something is wrong with the meat on your Big Mac, it's not just that the person who sold it to you doesn't know where it came from, in all likelihood where it came from is simply unknowable. That's the consumer's view looking upstream in the supply chain.

If we think in terms of the reverse, starting at the beginning of the supply chain and look downstream, what does it mean for a rancher to produce meat for people he won't ever know? He probably doesn't know their names, culture, or even country. As he ponders the most important factors in his enterprise, say overhead, market fluctuations, speed and volume in production, regulations, relations with his buyers, and so on, at what point will he think about the interests of the people who will end up eating a burger from the meat he produced? Intermittently, rarely, never?

In contrast, both Marti and Casey secure material resources for their processing from people they know as nearby as possible. Physical proximity reduces carbon miles, minimizes the need for preservatives, and allows for personal relationships with buyers and sellers. Relationships tend to foster accountability, trust, and integrity. What they can see upstream and downstream in the supply chain is close and clear. Slow Food that is generated in a way that is thoughtful, conscientious, and responsible requires and contributes to slow relationships.

That Casey gets meat from only three farmers for his multifaceted business reflects a simple supply chain. He has a personal relationship with the owner of the small slaughterhouse, too. If something goes wrong with Casey's products, the source of the problem will be known. He is explicit in emphasizing the interests of the people he buys from and sells to.

Likewise, Marti works at farmers' markets turning the produce into delicious food, thereby assisting the farmers trying to sell their products. The well-being of those she sells her services and products to is a top priority in Marti's business.[4]

In both instances, Marti and Casey have customers committed to a particular lifestyle. Sustainability, health, and more generally what I call the moral footprint of their work matters to their customers. These are people, at least many of them, who believe that conscientious consumption is part of who they are.

Perhaps that is a luxury of sorts. Beggars can't be choosers. Only the affluent can. Just to be clear, I don't support wealthy people gorging themselves on extravagant delicacies while the poor starve. But it seems clear that middle-class households have to embrace morally responsible consumption as an ideal for it to become a norm in our society for people of all economic means.

Another unifying feature of Marti's and Casey's work as processors is how they define their goals. Like most processors, they worry about money. They have to get paid to keep doing what they do. But like engaged sustainers in general, they worry about other things, too.

In some sense, Marti is not just selling carefully crafted dishes and Casey is not just selling high-end meat. She is explicit about the fact that her services and products really center around the healthy bodies of her customers. If you buy a hamburger from Casey (and I have—wow!), you are purchasing humane treatment of animals and the happiness and well-being among them that results from such work, and you are buying the relationships Casey has with three farmers who supply his meat.

Marti and Casey are, like all of us, complicated. As individuals, there is much more going on in their lives than I have described here. But the aspects of their work that they share in common are important for this movement and, at least to some extent, representative of the handful of other processors I observed.

In sum, processors involved in the alternative agro-food movement tend to participate in short and simple supply chains that involve personal relationships, and the trust and integrity that goes with them. They think in broad, holistic terms that blend idealism and pragmatism in what they are doing, which, again, is a hallmark of a benign moral footprint.

NOTES

1. See also Brueggemann (2020, chapter 4). Al-Anon has a saying that captures some of this logic: "Don't just do something—sit there!"

2. There are complex patterns, but this basic shift has been clearly established. See Barbas (2002), Smith et al. (2013), Warde, Cheng, Olsen, Southerton (2007), Bowen et al. (2019).

3. Various problems related to food in these two behemoths are respectively documented by Ken (2014) and Stone (2021).

4. A group of Italian researchers have demonstrated the value of short supply chains in particular in an article entitled "The Hidden Benefits of Short Food Supply Chains: Farmers' Markets Density and Body Mass Index in Italy" (Bimbo, Bonanno, Viscecchia, and Nardone 2015).

Chapter Six

Distribution

A strange thing happened to me in the supermarket a while back. I found myself in the organic section! I used to make fun of people who ate tofu, granola, "twigs," or "hamster food"—all disparaging words my friends and I used in reference to healthy, organic, natural, fresh foods, I'm ashamed to say. Around that time Rupert Holmes captured our thinking: "I am not into health food. I am into champagne." Actually, we thought of granola as a kind of person, as in "yeah, that granola only eats tofu and hamster food." Tofu didn't need a nickname, we thought, because it mocked itself. Then, one day, it wasn't funny anymore, and as I looked at the long lists of ingredients on different "food" products, I made my way over to the organic section, and spent more and more time in produce.

Then something funny happened on the way to the supermarket. I took a turn and headed toward the farmers' market. There, you don't have to read any lists of ingredients and you don't have to wonder what the true meaning is of "heart-healthy," "nothing artificial," "no artificial colors, flavors, or preservatives," "all-natural," or packaging with various shades of green. It's like the absence of advertisements on produce that comes straight from farmers is the ultimate marketing. Just as there are increasing numbers of extractors who want to yield vital, natural, nourishing resources, there are more and more processors thinking seriously about how to responsibly transform those resources into food, we are witnessing a significant shift in how food is distributed. Distribution of course happens at supermarkets and restaurants, but also schools, hospitals, religious settings, health food stores, farm stands, farmers' markets, CSAs, and other food hubs.

Several encouraging trends along these lines have unfolded at the same time. First, lots of people care about taste and health. They have become more informed about what goes into most products in the food system. The Healthy Eating Index 2010 total score, which is an aggregate measure nutrition scientists use to monitor our collective eating habits, has been steadily rising for more than two decades.

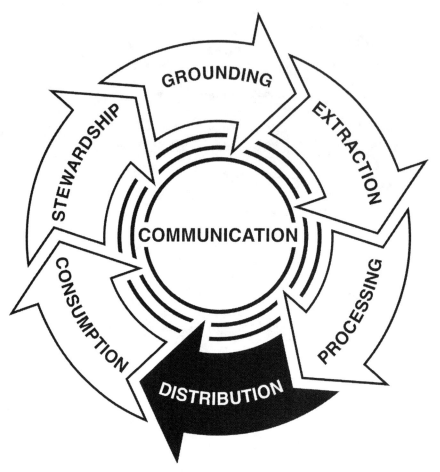

Figure 6.1.   Distribution. Created by Martha MacGregor

Everyone around me nodded approvingly as Neil Young repeatedly implored us to stop by the farmers' market during a concert in my hometown a couple years back. Farmers clustering in open markets to sell their produce is a very old tradition (see Schupp 2019). After significant farmers' markets fell out of favor during the post-WWII era, they began to emerge again in the 1970s (Schupp 2016). The U.S. Department of Labor started paying close attention to their numbers in the 1990s. The USDA's Agricultural Marketing Service counted 2,410 in 1996. As of 2017, the USDA listed 8669 farmers' markets in the United States (see Schupp 2019).[1] They are increasingly common in every geographical region (though less so in the Midwest), especially in areas that are disproportionately populous, white, affluent, and older (Schupp 2014).[2] Organic farms tend to be concentrated in states in the upper

Midwest and on the coasts, which is to say Democratic-leaning areas (see Sayre 2011).

The Farmers' Market Coalition (farmersmarketcoalition.org) extols a broad range of benefits of farmers' markets, including increased availability of healthy ingredients, including for low-income families by way of Supplemental Nutrition Assistance Program (SNAP or "food stamps") and Women, Infants and Children (WIC) vouchers. Farmers' markets reduce carbon miles by way of selling local produce. They often energize local economies for the same reason. People speak with each much more frequently and thereby build relationships and social capital in farmers' markets, compared to supermarkets (Gumirakiza et al. 2014; Purnell 2019).

The other important thing about farmers' markets is what is not happening there. Every time an item is purchased at a farmers' market, there is less chance that unsustainable agricultural techniques were used, animals were treated cruelly, or large numbers of carbon miles were involved in transportation. To visit a farmers' market is to turn one's back on the Industrial Food Complex.

This cultural shift has helped fuel an explosion of other food hubs, including conventional CSAs as well. The number of community supported agriculture outlets, it has been estimated, grew from basically zero in 1980 to more than 8,000 in 2018. CSAs are also clustered on the coasts and in the upper Midwest, and especially in the Northeast (Qazi and Selfa 2005; Schnell 2007; Galt 2011). The USDA has suggested that new business models used by CSAs are contributing to growing profits (Woods and Ernst 2017; see also Patel 2008). Innovative food hubs are setting up in tons of places. For instance, Headwater Food Hub serves a large region based around Rochester, New York, and offers a vast range of seasonal produce. Field Goods, which is headquartered in Athens, New York, on the Hudson River, also serves a large region, including eastern New York, western Connecticut, and northern New Jersey, and offers various fresh products generated through "sustainable practices," including produce but also baked goods, yogurt, and prepared foods.

At the same time as this shift toward healthy, fresh food, there is growing awareness that the richest country in human history has a hunger problem. For a lot of people across the political spectrum, it makes no sense that some 13 million American children do not have reliable access to healthy food. The USDA calculated that about 11 percent of U.S. households were food insecure in 2018. That number is closely related to the poverty rate. Again, one can be underfed and overweight, as lots of Americans who face food insecurity are, since not all calories are equal. In many cases, the only "food" available and/or affordable is highly processed.

What these trends seem to have in common is a connection to the failures of two large institutions. Government and corporations in the food and beverage industries have been ineffective in overseeing a food system that makes healthy food available to all Americans. A number of factors, which I will discuss later, helped foster this recognition on the part of many observers. The result, in part, has been an end-run, whether by choice or by necessity, around these institutions in the creation of alternatives.

GRAHAM DUVALL: TRUSTING PEOPLE
TO MAKE GOOD CHOICES

In 2012 Graham and Andrea DuVall founded a food distribution business in Asheville, North Carolina. When they started Mother Earth Produce, the two of them did almost everything. They worked with local farms to collect fresh produce, processed it, packaged it, and delivered it. And of course, they ran the business. I first ran into Graham at Hickory Nut Gap Farm in Fairview, NC. Graham came with three colleagues to meet the owner Jamie Ager (mentioned in chapter 3) and look over the farm, in the hopes of adding him as a vendor for Graham's food hub. Graham and I got to chatting that day as we walked around the farm and later, I called him to have a more extensive conversation.

He learned ornamental horticulture at the University of Georgia. "Just kind of being around local food, growing plants and sustainability educated me enough to direct my purpose." His wife Andrea had worked in the Georgia public school system and for a publishing company in Maine. When they met, Graham told me, they were both eager for a career shift. So they founded Mother Earth Produce.

As they set out to start a business based on food that does not directly involve farming, food processing, supermarkets, restaurants, farmers' markets, or cooking, they faced some big questions. How do you reach people? How do you make money? How do you make a difference? Graham is characteristically philosophical in thinking about those questions.

You have to listen to your gut and be willing to make mistakes, he believes. The passion that Andrea and he both feel for local food is like a calling. Like many engaged sustainers, Graham and Andrea are largely self-taught on the business end of things. They benefited from mentors and friends but had to figure lots of stuff out along the way, partly because they were rookies but also because this sort of food distribution system is a new species. When I spoke to him in 2018, Graham reckoned there were some 150–200 food hub companies in the United States like theirs, each of them at different stages of development in this evolving industry (see Woods and Ernst 2017). He talked about growing the business, treating employees well and helping the community to prosper.

Asheville is a quirky, kind place where one can imagine lots of people seeking out local, fresh food. Graham's enterprise is not big enough as a single entity, he thinks, to really register as a competitive threat to big grocery stores. (My guess is that the big players are actually quite concerned about the Graham's segment of the food distribution industry as a whole.) At any rate, as I learned about the business, it became clear to me that this is not an easy way to make a living. Their bread and butter is consumers who want fresh produce and other farm products but don't want to grow a garden or visit a farmers' market all the time. Mother Earth Produce is a new kind of middleman.

However challenging it is to compete in this growing market (see Woods and Ernst 2017), Graham's zeal and optimism are resounding. He believes in what he is doing, not just because it will help make the world a better place—he is passionate about that—but because he is confident that people want what he has to offer.

One key is information. The corporate industrial farming operations in Mexico and California try to brand their products with words like "community" and "love" in the messaging, Graham observed. "It's detrimental to the well-being of those of us that are really doing those things." Big Food sows confusion. Nevertheless, substantive information, Graham believes, or "authenticity," a word he frequently uses, sells. Indeed, for the movement writ large authenticity is the needle in the haystack of chaos (see Smith Maguire, Ocejo, and DeSoucey 2022).

Graham and Andrea have developed a kind of hybrid model, and it's working. They changed the name of the company to better reflect a broad range of offerings. "Mother Earth Food," their website declares, "harvests the healthiest organic and non-GMO food from local farms for weekly delivery to families in Asheville, Greenville, and Charlotte. It's like a Farmers Market delivered to your door!" They distribute boxes of fresh produce, as you would find in a conventional CSA, but provide a broad range of other commodities from local sources (e.g., meat, cheese, chocolate, baked goods, prepared foods) available through a slick online interface.

The day I met Graham at Hickory Nut Gap Farm, I also met another farmer, his colleague and chief information technology officer, Sandeep Goel. Sandeep told me about new technology being developed by The Bionutrient Food Association (BFA), in which he invested. It is based on large, expensive scanners that have been miniaturized into a handheld device. Within a couple years, he said, there will be an affordable, small system that can be used to identify ingredients and sources of foods. Eventually a phone app, what else? "How do I convince the mama with the Mercedes SUV, the soccer mom?"

Sandeep asked. "She doesn't know any different. So if she thinks that straw-berries there and those that we deliver are the same, I'm screwed." But with this device people will be able to point a phone camera at a random food product, say an apple, some beef, or even a plate of lasagna, and find out what it is and where it's from.

Sandeep said the technology will be able to distinguish between Advil brand ibuprofen and the generic equivalent. He indicated that different food products could then be "normalized," say on a scale of 1 to 10. So a shopper could pick among different boxes of strawberries for the best ones based on their scores. This would then motivate sellers to seek out the very best score by doing everything possible in the production process.

I confess it sounded like science fiction to me. But later Graham con-firmed that BFA is working on this device, the Bionutrient Meter, which will use blockchain technology to inform consumers what is in food. That is, it would have a decentralized inventory of information built and monitored by a peer-to-peer network, linked to sophisticated food testing labs. This could facilitate a radically new level of transparency. Graham extolled the distinc-tive vision of a fellow named Dan Kittredge, the founder and executive direc-tor of the Bionutrient Food Association. The BFA's website indicates that the first models of the Bionutrient Meter went on sale early in 2020.

What Graham, Sandeep, and Kittredge all believe is that with more information about what they are eating, consumers will seek out real food. Quality will win. Maybe it already has. Again, that is why claims of "natural," "healthy," "fresh," "unprocessed," or "no preservatives" can be seen every-where. Advertisers know that is what consumers want. So we get the nice labels, even if the reality of what is in food is often not quite so pure.

In any case, evolving ideals are a good sign. We have come a long way from being a culture that regards a TV dinner or a Big Mac as a special treat, at least for most people. Today, a true feast includes the freshest ingredients. An actually "balanced breakfast" is made of natural foods. The trick Graham believes, though, is to make real quality easily identifiable as such.[3]

On one hand, that doesn't seem that difficult. Get your food from farm-ers. Fresh produce sells itself without spin. But in this age of confusion, it is harder than it seems. For instance, "the USDA is making everything so challenging for people that are growing higher quality standards," Graham lamented, "because of their continual watering down of the USDA Organic certification." You may buy "organic" products such as milk, eggs, or pro-duce that come from massive, industrial operations, or other production prac-tices that lack the spirit of what is implied by the label.[4]

Sandeep thinks the new device will help people see through the misinfor-mation. "When you bring light to truth," he declared, "what happens is amaz-ing." He envisions this technology triggering "a race to the top." Corporations will embrace it, he thinks, and "they will claim it was their idea." Everyone will want to buy, and therefore producers will want to generate fresh, nourishing food. What is already clear, whether we see that device widely available for sale or not, is that a cultural shift is afoot. People want real food and customer preferences matter. Remember, demand for organic food is outpacing production of organic food. All of this is right in the middle of Graham's wheelhouse. I heard numerous other farmers say the same thing. Changing consumer demand is changing how food is produced.

Graham works in a narrow niche of food distribution. He is trying to provide an alternative way to access food that has integrity. Mark Maraia, owner of Carbon Neutral Investments LLC, and a board member of Graham's company, whom I also met at Hickory Nut Gap Farm, told me that Mother Earth Foods is "looking for the best quality farmers and the people who are most interested in eating high quality food." With food hubs like Graham's "you'll eliminate the middleman. The middlemen are absolutely devastating to all these small farms." The key, these guys believe, is for the small farmers to band together and cut out the *corporate* intermediaries. Mother Earth Foods is an intermediary, too, despite what Mark said, but more responsible and collaborative.

Like most engaged sustainers, Graham sees this project as embedded in a larger system, not just economically but also ecologically and socially. The economic bet, as noted, is that consumers will increasingly want *and* recognize quality, which is not sufficiently available through Big Food outlets.

Mother Earth Foods says they are "working directly with our local farmers to not just create an economic model of viability and sustainability, but working toward helping them regenerate their soil, so they can have a stronger, more nutrient dense product that is far more resistant to pest and disease and climate change."

For Graham, this is a matter of livelihood but also a moral stance. On a daily basis, he focuses on what's in a given crate, where it is going, and its marginal return. But he increasingly looks up, too. One of the things that motivates his work is the potential impact on climate change. Graham told me that he believes regenerative agriculture has the capacity to sequester all the excess CO_2 in our atmosphere—within a generation or two. He gets excited thinking about it. You might recall the *New York Times* article entitled "Can Dirt Save the Earth?" that I previously cited. A lot of smart people agree with Graham's audacious thinking.

A key to the business model is to keep viable local farms committed to quality. That means paying them a higher rate for their products, some 60 or 70 cents on any dollar worth of products, Graham said, compared to 20 cents they get from the supermarkets. What he offers his customers is an easier way to get high quality products. His material and labor costs are much lower than supermarkets, he explained, so he can pay farmers more than the corporations do and still turn a profit.

It is a combo of resisting the homogenization and dominance of Big Food while yielding to the emphasis on busyness in American culture. In some sense, Graham is offering a trade: giving up hyper-efficiency in production (e.g., CAFOs, assembly lines) and consumption (e.g., frozen, processed food easy to prepare) for gaining greater quality and retaining some level of efficiency in distribution (e.g., bringing good food to your door).

Another ideal at odds with mainstream market culture woven into their business plan relates to employee relations. Graham told me they have always paid at least a living wage to employees, which is so far doable because his overall costs are relatively low. The key contrast compared to Big Food is fewer intermediaries involved in processing, transportation, marketing, distribution, and so on. Again, the concern for farmers and employees, for agriculture and justice, for balancing the practical challenges of running a business and the goals of sustainability, in combination, are vital to the enterprise.

As with so many people I interviewed, Graham evinces a certain character: he is a kindred spirit to many others, and at the same time uniquely interesting. When you talk to him, he seems sincere, gentle, and thoughtful. I asked about the origins of his moral convictions, about his sense of generosity toward other people. "My parents are both evangelical Christians and I grew up in that thing. I would say that definitely had an influence." More generally, "I'm a bit of a kind of tender heart just by nature." To me, as someone who grew up in a family of clergy, he seemed familiar: a pastor who is nourished by the lives of his parishioners.

After our last conversation, I felt sort of protective of Graham. He's a nice fellow trying something hard and a little risky. In 2018, at least, the plan was working. They had changed their name to Mother Earth Foods to better reflect their expanded offerings. They were getting produce from about 40 farms, plus other commodities from various local sources. They had 12 employees, a customer base of 3,000 in Western North Carolina and upstate South Carolina. Graham had backed away from day-to-day operations to focus on a bigger vision. An important question for Graham and other food hub distributors like him is whether the project is scalable. Can fresh, healthy food be produced with integrity and distributed on a widespread basis? Can a company committed to such integrity, both in terms of regenerative agriculture and sustainability, but also in terms of the treatment of labor, the ethics of animal welfare, and the well-being of communities in which they operate, go big?

RICH FRANK: CLOSE TO IT

A lot of folks I talked to were skeptical about scaling up; they think it's probably not worth the trouble, or even viable. The oldest health food store in my town, Four Seasons Natural Foods, has been in operation for more than 30 years. The owner, Frank Rich, likes to be directly involved in every aspect of the business, and have personal interactions with customers. When I interviewed him, he explained that he carefully reviews what his store sells. We met in his cluttered office in "the new store," the second location associated with his business. I was surprised it didn't have a funny smell.

As a kid growing up in Philadelphia, Rich told me, he worked in a natural foods store. He spent lots of time during summers in the Adirondacks. Dealing with asthma first motivated him to think about how diet could affect his health, which led to a broader interest in healthy food and vegetarianism.

Rich bought the original store from a couple who owned it, "maybe not the best businesspeople," in 1991. At the beginning he had no competitors nearby. "When we opened, we were 100 percent of the pie, or close to it." For a long time, as Rich worked hard to build a successful business based on healthy food, he told me, the store and clientele were very countercultural. It was a funky place.

The first time I went in Four Seasons was in 1994. The original store always had an odd aroma—one not altogether unpleasant—and all kinds of products unfamiliar to me. Over the years, I have been in many times. During that period my attitudes toward the place evolved from amusement to curiosity, then adventurousness, and now a certain sense of loyalty.

As he built the business, questions related to meat, sugar, gluten, veganism, Certified Organic standards, sourcing, GMO, artificial coloring, and flavoring, and so many other dilemmas people who care about healthy food wrestle with have been a part of Rich's considerations. He confessed that he is flexible, and even cuts some corners once in a while, because certain products are popular, and he respects his customers. "I don't know 100 percent what's right for me all the time. So how do I know what's 100 percent right for you? And if you think it's good for you, I'm ok with it. As long as it's not full of just absolute garbage."

As we talked, he mentioned lycopene, monoculture, omega 3, and macrobiotics. I was thinking, *this guy knows a lot of stuff.* For 24 years, the business grew "a little bit, one percent, three percent" every year, he said. He then added the second location in 2014. The original site has an expanded café, and the new site has a larger store, with a small café. It was a huge shift that took time to pull off and adapt to.

Unlike most people I interviewed, Rich started his work with a solid background in business, he told me, partly because his father was a businessman, so he was exposed to lots of relevant lessons while growing up and benefitted from ongoing guidance from his father and grandfather. Because of Four Seasons' success, Rich recognized he could expand further if he had wanted. But he likes being "close to it," intimately involved in the whole business and relating to people. "That was more my bag than thinking about having ten stores." Just adding the one store has required him to be "a different kind of manager" who is more detached and who delegates more.

Four Seasons is still flourishing. But things are very different from when it first opened. Instead of "100 percent of the pie," Rich guesses he has "four percent of the pie" but the pie's gotten "huge." He recognizes a certain tension between his business's success and the momentum of the larger cultural shift. Four Seasons isn't countercultural anymore. (I feel personally entangled in that shift.) Consumer demand is immense but there are many other suppliers. As other stores emulate his approach, it gets harder to define and protect his niche. More health food stores compete, and the supermarkets make inroads in terms of the kind of products Four Seasons sells (e.g., fresh, natural, healthy, non-GMO, unprocessed). At the very least, the role of bigger players in competing against and helping to foster demand for stores like Four Seasons is quite complex, as Laura J. Miller documents in *Building Nature's Market: The Business and Politics of Natural Foods* (2017).

Rich tries to maintain the quality of his offerings and keep prices as low as possible. Even so, he told me, the larger competitors offer even lower prices. For consumers and for the larger alternative agro-food movement, this is good news. More alternatives, more healthy food, and competitive pressures to keep prices down. For small places like Four Seasons, they can only compete if customers recognize the value of the quality they are selling and/or if more customers seek out such quality. Remember, Casey McKissick pointed this out in reference to his meat-centered business.

Rich's view that small is crucial to quality is echoed by many other engaged sustainers. But not all of them. A few years ago, I met a guy named Kevin who lived on my street and we became friends. Kevin Quandt comes from a family in the food distribution business. For some years after he graduated from Duke (his senior thesis was on Tupac Shakur), Kevin worked for his family's company, Quandt's Foodservice Distributors Incorporated. At some point, he became frustrated with the direction of the company and left. In 2015 Kevin went to work for Sweetgreen, a fast-casual chain of salad and grain bowl restaurants and became its vice president of supply chain and sustainability.

Three Georgetown University graduates founded Sweetgreen in 2007. Their mission statement reads, "Building healthier communities by connecting people to real food."[5] As of January 2020, Sweetgreen had over 100 locations, with plans to double that number within three years. The company reportedly secured the backing of $476 million in venture capital and generated upwards of $300 million in revenue the previous year (Bercovici 2020).

I will say more about Sweetgreen in subsequent chapters. Here, I just want to point out that with respect to distribution, we are seeing genuine innovations. There is broad recognition that supermarkets often fall short in different ways. The trick is to bring together quality, affordability, *and* scale. Achieving two of those goals at once has been accomplished countless times. Four Seasons does a great job with quality and sometimes affordability. Food banks do well with affordability and sometimes quality. Supermarkets and fast food do affordability and scale. Some "natural grocery chains" like Whole Foods and Sprouts Farmers Market offer quality on a large scale. The real challenge is achieving all three goals—quality, affordability, *and* scale—all at once. Sweetgreen is turning heads in this respect. A crucial question for Sweetgreen is how many can afford to eat there. Certainly, a lot of people never get to eat fresh, healthy food at Sweetgreen or anywhere else—a primary concern for Hans Kersten.

HANS KERSTEN: COMMITTED TO
PEOPLE EATING HEALTHY

"God, he is amazing!" The director of the largest food bank in Philadelphia said that about Hans Kersten. He is another person I interviewed who cares about access to healthy food on a large scale. Like Graham, he is not a farmer and doesn't work with supermarkets, restaurants, or farmers' markets. In contrast, though, his main job is pediatric medicine.

Hans has established a successful career as a physician at a children's hospital and professor at an affiliated university and developed an extensive record of publications related to literacy, lead-poisoning, environmental health, evidence-based medicine, tattoos, and piercings. And he is a leader in the effort to address food insecurity.

"Nutritional Powerhouse: Broccoli?" For some reason that struck my funny bone when I read it as a college student in the campus newsletter of the health clinic. It had been written by Hans who had a work-study job in the clinic. (My other friends and I have brought up this important fact basically every time we've been together during the roughly 35 years since those words were written, or to be more precise, one million times.)

I met Hans on my first day of college. He was a sophomore, and I was a first-year student at Earlham College where we met at pre-season tryouts for the soccer team. At 6 foot 7, with a dry sense of humor and open heart, Hans stood out. Over the years, we became buddies. His greatest gift to me was later introducing me to a med school classmate who would become my wife.

The only person more surprised than me that Hans has become such a major player in his field is him. "You will never get into medical school," a professor from a distinguished university told him when he was taking graduate classes after college. But Hans is stubborn—believe me, I know. It took a while, but he did get in and not only completed his training but blossomed. Today, he is extremely accomplished, as demonstrated by various titles, positions, publications, awards, and so on.

I had the pleasure of having a ringside seat as Hans worked hard to get where he is. To this day, if you ask him about his vocation, he will earnestly express surprise as he recalls being admitted to medical school. Something about humility combined with determination, and about grasping the weighty responsibility of his profession, in my informed opinion, has made Hans a special kind of healer.

Hans grew up in Swarthmore, a wealthy suburb of Philadelphia, in a large white family that had less money than most everyone else in the neighborhood. His family was on food stamps, he told me, "back when they were really stamps." "A talented industrial designer," Hans said of his father, "he struggled to find consistent work."

Han's mother was a force of nature who instilled in her four sons and daughter a sense of self-reliance, love of nature, and bottomless compassion, his father a gentle man who spoke volumes through quiet actions. Hans and his three boisterous brothers were "forced" by their parents to bake bread and sell it at their public high school, about which they bitterly complained. Soon after I met Hans, I could see he had to count his pennies but was exceedingly generous toward other people.

He credits his parents, as well as the Quaker college we attended, with the values that energize him. The culture in Hans's family and at our college takes for granted that altruism is an important part of life. Looking out for the left-out is just what you do. By the time I met Hans in college, he knew he wanted to become a physician. Kind-heartedness and engagement with nature were already lessons planted in him by his family that had taken root.

"There's a generation of people who don't know how to cook or store the vegetables," Dr. Kersten told me. "We've had people say, 'What's this?' because they've never even seen broccoli." Turns out he was right—not everyone knows it's a nutritional powerhouse!

North Philadelphia, where he works, is a food desert (Shepelavy 2015). Access to healthy and affordable food is limited. The few markets sell poor quality food at high prices. As I learned at a 2015 conference in Philadelphia, the FreshRX: Fresh Food Symposium: Prescription for a Healthier America, many of the primary and secondary schools there do not even have kitchens (see Poppendiek 2010).

It's hard to serve real food when you have no kitchen in which to cook it. Not being around fresh food, and/or not having the time, energy, or knowledge necessary for food preparation, many people are poorly equipped to feed themselves (see McMillan 2012; Bowen et al. 2019).

Not surprisingly, the food insecurity in that setting is pervasive. Malnutrition has deleterious and cascading physiological and psychological implications. Mothers who endure sustained hunger have a greater chance of developing anxiety and depression and giving birth to babies with a cleft palate or spina bifida. Children who face food insecurity are at higher risk of obesity, diabetes, and hypertension, among other medical problems (Kersten et al. 2018). Practicing in one of the poorest parts of one of the poorest cities in the US, Hans is working at the American ground zero of hunger. Nearly half of all families in North Philadelphia face food insecurity (Shepelavy 2015).

But it would be worse if Hans and his various partners weren't there. This includes a number of the folks who participated in that conference in 2015. Community activists on the ground in Philadelphia and other cities are making a dent in hunger (Gaddis 2020).

Hans reveres his vocation and fellow colleagues in medicine. "There's a lot that we have to do. Being a good physician is a lot." A lot of training, discipline, skill, physical labor, mental labor, emotional labor. It's a lot for one's household, too. I know this from observing Hans's family—more often than not he gets home after most families have already cleaned up the dishes—and from being married to a physician myself. There are long days of work with numerous complex, consequential decisions, strenuous interactions with patients and staff. Keeping up with new research, encountering unfamiliar illnesses, learning different treatments all take time. Navigating changing record-keeping systems, arcane billing procedures, burdensome insurance company practices, and corporate bureaucracy have contributed to a high burn-out rate in medicine. Worrying about patients and medical decisions, managing anxieties about obstreperous or litigious patients after hours comprises a ton of undocumented and unpaid work.

Hans is committed to treating underserved populations. He estimates that at least three-quarters of his patients are on Medicaid. "We need that one-on-one relationship. I need to be able to write letters [to specialists, courts, schools, funding agencies] and advocate from a more personal basis. And so sometimes it's just hard to get out of that because that can be overwhelming. There's just so much stuff they [the patients] need." Meeting that need is his vocation.

But he has a practical streak, too. "I went into medicine," he told me, partly for "a kind of job security because I saw my father who was unemployed a lot." Even so, it was not an easy journey since Hans, like most medical students, accrued hundreds of thousands of dollars of debt. Over the years, some of Hans's colleagues have switched to private practice "because," he said, "they can make more money and spend more time with their family and have an easier life." Not Hans.

"I could keep busy just seeing patients." Doing his best for patients is consuming. His work on food insecurity, as well as lead poisoning and literacy (research areas in which Hans has developed a national reputation) is something else. "This all occurs in other time. I feel like it is part of my calling to help people in this community and the region." After his primary professional obligations are completed, Dr. Kersten goes to work on food insecurity. And he has literally written the book—or at least co-edited a volume—about addressing food insecurity in healthcare: *Identifying and Addressing Childhood Food Insecurity in Healthcare and Community Settings.*

As a physician, scientist, and advocate, Hans shifts his attention back and forth between the details of close interactions with patients and the complexities of the systems at work that provide the context for such treatment. In one chapter in his book, Hans and his coauthors explain the need for a three-tiered response, that includes the provider-based approach of medical personnel directly treating patients, the community-engaged approach of careful, long-term collaboration with other stake-holders and institutions (e.g., schools, libraries, foodbanks), and the advocacy-based approach, which entails involvement with advocacy, education, media, policymakers, and others who have influence over the larger societal patterns of health and nutrition. For example, Hans and his colleagues work with various organizations like The Share Food Program in Philadelphia, The Common Market, Philabundance, the Greater Philadelphia Coalition against Hunger, Lancaster Farm Fresh Cooperation, Solutions for Progress, Pennsylvania WIC (Women, Infants and Children), the National Center for Medical Legal Partnership, Pediatric Health Equity Collaborative, Common Market, Drexel University, and the City of Philadelphia.

Each tier of collaboration includes innovative activities (see Kersten, Beck, and Klein 2018). Hans helped start Farm to Families in North Philadelphia. "There's a lack of access to fresh fruits in this community, so the program is designed to provide fresh produce for families," he told me. "So, it's kind of like a CSA program for inner-city, low-income households. It's geared for anyone who lives, works, or worships in North Philadelphia." A box of fresh vegetables, fruits, and eggs costs between $10 and $15 and can be paid for with SNAP vouchers. Each one comes with recipes in English and Spanish.

He also started prescribing fresh produce. "What we've started at our hospital is called Fresh RX, which is a program for me to write a prescription for a box of food in my office so I can talk about the program to my patients who may have obesity, or may have failure to thrive or may just have food insecurity and say 'here's an opportunity to get fresh fruits and vegetables, here's a prescription for it.' It tells them how to call, and how to contact this program." Echoing many others, Hans said "food is medicine." He sees undernourished patients through his St. Christopher's Grow Clinic, as well as through his regular practice. Records are kept on their health, including the use of Fresh RX (Shepelavy 2015). Hans was one of the first to prescribe fresh produce, I believe. But similar programs are popping up in various other cities as well.[6]

By the way, "RX" is another symbol that has been deployed for marketing purposes. This designation for medical prescriptions derived from the Latin word recipe is used on the breakfast bar brand, *RXBAR*. "No B.S." is part of the marketing for the same product. I like this product. But I always get a whiff of bullshit when legitimate authority is retrofitted into the service of selling some commodity. The most abused such term in connection to food, of course, is "natural." This use of Rx strikes me as a similar abuse. The breakfast bars are not prescribed by physicians.

The opposite is true of the fruits and vegetables offered by St. Christopher's Fresh RX program. More than 100 medical professionals were prescribing food there as of 2015. Other hospitals are now joining this experiment. California is beginning a multiyear study to assess the effects of "food as medicine" in relation to several illnesses across multiple locations (Brown 2018).

One of the most interesting organizations Hans and his team partner with is The Common Market, a nonprofit food distributor. Through Hans, I met Rachel Terry, its National Partnership Director. When I got to interview her in the fall of 2021, she explained how this remarkable organization works. The Common Market is a national organization comprised of regional networks that help family farms get good food to local communities. They have hubs in the Mid-Atlantic, the Southeast, Texas, and soon, hopefully, Chicago, Rachel told me. And they have their eye on seven other regions.

There are several teams totaling more than 40 employees, plus numerous partners on the ground in each location. The Common Market offers sophisticated understanding of logistics, supply chains, value chains, business practices, and communication.

Farmers need to sell as much volume as they can. Many people lack access to good food. There are existing organizations, "anchor institutions," like hospitals, schools, colleges, childcare facilities, and elder care facilities that need good food (thecommonmarket.org) often set in locations with high rates of food insecurity. The Common Market helps make the connections among these interests, communicating carefully with various stakeholders along the way.

According to its website (thecommonmarket.org), in the 2014–2016 school years this organization partnered with 39 public schools in Philadelphia to serve over 14,000 students in free/reduced lunch programs. In 2018, they helped provide more than 4 million meals across all their networks. Over the next three years, that number tripled. By 2022, they were supporting nearly 50,000 acres of farmland involved in sustainable and financially viable production.

In other words, The Common Market is solving problems without getting rich, distributing lousy food, or undermining family farms and their communities. They are building numerous regional systems that foster sustainable agriculture, viable family farms and farm communities, and food security. It strikes me that helping to provide suppliers and buyers with an alternative to Big Food and Big Ag, on a large scale, is a pretty big deal. As such, the multifaceted work The Common Market and its partners are doing exemplifies just the kind of pragmatic and innovative collaboration Hans wrote about in his book.

As noted, the Common Market and The Share Food Program in Philadelphia have been important partners for Hans's hospital, St. Christopher's. "If he has his way," the director of Share told me, St. Chris's "will be the example for hospitals all over the world for how you treat people who are food insecure. He is so committed to this, he is so committed to people eating healthy, and being healthy. I love him. Oh, I love him." Me too.

STEVEANNA WYNNE: EAT GOOD,
DO GOOD, FEEL GOOD

In her 1999 book *Sweet Charity,* the sociologist Janet Poppendieck decried the failures of American food policy, which she argued was unsuccessful in providing reliable sources of nutritious food to our country's population. In addition, Poppendieck criticized the extent to which soup kitchens, food banks, and other stop-gap measures dependent on private voluntarism and charity exacerbate the problems they are intended to address. That is, individual, private emergency programs in many settings have served as a replacement for the degraded and ineffective government programs that should provide a systemic solution.

One of them is the Share Food Program of Philadelphia, where Steveanna is executive director. Philadelphia is rife with food insecurity and Share is the biggest food bank there. Steveanna has a big job working against a huge problem. When I asked her what motivates her, she said "I think partly I'm just a crazy person." As I spoke with her, I could see why some people might agree.

After living in Philadelphia for more than thirty years, it is easy to tell Steveanna is not from there. She speaks with a confident contralto voice in a southern drawl. "My mother was an extremely straight shooter," she told me.

"My father was a little more gentle." As I got to know Steveanna, I figured she had been bragging on both of her parents. Steveanna is large-hearted and takes the commitments of being a neighbor seriously. At the same time, one gets the sense she is comfortable with her own authority and doesn't suffer fools easily. If I said something stupid during our interview, I worried, she would know and say so.

Steveanna talked about growing up in Virginia. Among her peers, she was one of the first to learn to drive. It was mostly in retrospect, she has realized, that she became aware of how segregated by class her community had been. (She is white; race didn't come up in our conversation.) When she and her friends went to games or other events, she would often pick people up wherever they lived. That some were poor, and some were affluent didn't seem important at the time. She just knew they "were all in it together." "Everyone should be able to have a safe place to live," her parents had taught her. "Everyone should have a good environment. Everyone should be able to go to the doctor. Like, that's not too much to ask."

As she pondered those memories out loud, Steveanna told me about a girl who went to school with her for years and sat near her in class from sixth grade through twelfth. Every Friday the school served ice cream. "I never ate ice cream. I still don't eat ice cream." (See? Crazy, right?) "So I would give her my dime, not because she was poor but because she really likes ice cream."

Fast forward many years. As a young adult Steveanna was working in a community action agency in Virginia. The same person, now a young woman, came in for assistance. When she found out Steveanna was the person helping her, "she made a huge deal out of the ice cream." Before that, Steveanna said, "it just never occurred to me that people were poor or rich or whatever. Like, if you have it and don't need it, then you give it away." That was the "aha moment" when her parents' lessons took on real meaning, she recalled, when she started to see the divisions in society that kept some from having what they need.

Steveanna mentioned her son Christopher who has severe dyslexia. For many years, she "made every decision based on what was best for Christopher." Helping him grow up and manage things was the most important work in her life. Over time, things worked out for him. He went to college and got a good job. "Between my work and Christopher, my life was pretty full. And my life needs to be full. I don't do well if I'm not busy." She started thinking about what that might mean after Christopher had grown up and figured out key pieces in his life.

Around that time, in 1984, Steveanna helped start a branch of Share in Virginia. It was then part of a national network of organizations that engaged in food distribution. This was institutionalized neighborliness on a big scale.

She told me that the national organization of Share was founded in 1983 by a Catholic deacon who had worked with Mother Teresa. There were two founding principles, Steveanna said: "everyone in our country should have affordable and consistent food"; and "everyone has a gift, all of us have something to contribute, either to our communities, our street, our families that can make the world a little bit better."

With her son's life stabilized and eager for a new challenge, she moved to Philadelphia in 1989 to work for a Share branch there. As I tried to picture Steveanna's arrival to the City of Brotherly Love, I suggested that maybe folks up north didn't know what to make of this charming and willful gal from Virginia. I could almost hear her grinning over the phone as she confirmed, "they did not." Within a decade or so the national organization would fold, along with most of the other regional branches. Virginia Share closed in 2012. Philadelphia Share endures. Steveanna leads it.

That same year that Virginia Share closed, Greensgrow Farms in Philadelphia posted this on Facebook. "*The Inquirer* chooses Stevanna Wynne from Share as Citizen of The Year, and we heartily agree. This belle of the south has been soothing the waters and rattling the cages of the hunger/food issue in Philadelphia for years and doing it with charm, grace and a few boots inserted in remote places. She runs—and I mean runs—Share with a standard that we should all aim to emulate. Steveanna is the kind of import we need in Philadelphia. Drive that forklift, baby, drive!" Other awards include the MANNA Nourish Award, the Schweitzer Leadership Award from Thomas Jefferson University; and the Hunger Fighter Award from the Greater Philadelphia Coalition Against Hunger.

The main point of Share is to make healthy food available to those without reliable access. In 2018, its website reported that "Share brought 27 million pounds of emergency food relief to low-income Philadelphia residents facing hunger." In 2020, they had over 40 employees and thousands of volunteers, partnered with some 80 organizations, and helped get food to dozens of locations in the city and over 30 in nearby Montgomery County. They were providing food for over a million people a month!

I gleaned a certain sense of ruthless urgency in the way Steveanna thinks about her work. She has little tolerance for nonsense or wasted time. In a certain light, she might simply seem like a hard-charging workaholic who strives to max out the volume of food her organization distributes. She is the kind of boss who knows how to do every job in the organization, works as hard as anyone, and is comfortable telling others to get off their butt.

However, food is not the raison d'etre for Steveanna. Community is. Everyone needs access to healthy food, she told me. "It's a hand up." But they also need smiles and hugs. They need to know they have gifts to offer. "It's about eat good, do good and feel good." And they need to know how their resources are linked to others' resources. "When you do something for others, you do feel better about yourself." Share's work is not just about providing food for hungry people, she explained, but also helping affluent people make the connections. All the different ways neighbors can and should look out for one another came up as we talked. They all revolve around relationships. Even though she is literally surrounded by large piles of food, I got the feeling that the imperatives to "do good" and "feel good" are ultimately much more important to Steveanna. The hope to "eat good" is just one potential avenue for fulfilling those more expansive objectives.

"You have to play with a lot of people to produce any significant change," she reflected. Other chapters of Share folded, Steveanna speculated, because they weren't run like a business—with attention to the bottom line—*and* because they weren't collaborative enough. The Share Food Program in Philadelphia is deeply integrated into the functioning of numerous community organizations and government agencies. As important as collaboration is to Share's ethos and operations, though, if a partnership isn't productive, she ends it.

"There's a real advantage to being 68 years old because you can be very blunt with folks," she declared. "You can move meetings along in a way that you can't when you're twenty or you're thirty. And you can say to people, 'this is crap.' . . . If it's going to produce a result to the people, we're serving then I'm all in!" If not? "I'm not going to be here anymore." I couldn't help but think that Steveanna's terse assertiveness didn't first surface in her sixties. Her mother's straight shooting surely rubbed off on her much earlier. Obviously, her father's kindness did, too.

Share has a knack for getting lots out of volunteers: lots of boxing and bagging food, loading trucks and cars, painting, copying, phone calling, and so much else. The volunteer army includes corporate groups, like the multinational accounting firm, Deloitte, which has a large presence in Philadelphia and a 20-year relationship with Share.

Young people are also involved, from kindergarten on up. "One of the things that happens here," Steveanna explained "particularly with the young folks who think they cannot live or breathe without an iPhone or an iPad or a whatever it is, we just don't allow them to bring it in here. We say, 'that's gotta go, gotta put it in your pocket.' This place is all about participation. Period. If you're here to talk on your phone, you need to go back to school or wherever you came from, because this is not the place.' It's a real problem. Some just laugh and say, 'yeah, I know, Ms. Stevie, I'll get rid of it.'"

More generally, Steveanna promotes service as a way of life. It is sort of a verb enacting the noun community. To commune is to serve, she thinks. Share helps people see that in their own lives. If you babysit grandchildren, volunteer at a school or church, or provide any unpaid labor for someone else, she said to me, that "counts" as service for your community.

When I asked her about why she doesn't burn out like other people in non-profit service work, she told me about a mentor back in Virginia who taught her that "you have to keep your glass filled up," by surrounding yourself with people and activities that give you energy. She mentioned colleagues, family, friends, gardening, and a beloved dog.

As I reflected on our conversation later, though, I realized the whole enterprise energizes her. She practices what she preaches. Or rather she preaches about what she practices. Steveanna has a gift that the world needs, and she knows it. So she shares her gift, but also tries to get others to see the gifts they have to offer. She's giving out fish *and* teaching people to fish.

This brings me back to Janet Poppendieck. In some sense, the amazing achievements of Steveanna and Share represent one side of a heavy coin. On that side, you can see a wondrous image of compassion and wisdom as neighbors commune with one another. On the other side is a dark picture of massive failure. Tens of millions of hungry people in the richest country in human history is a moral disaster. Share is embedded in this failed system and implicated in Janet's book *Sweet Charity* mentioned above, though not by name. Stop-gap measures like food pantries are no substitute for systemic solutions.

When I sat on a conference panel with Janet more than a decade after that book was first published, however, she did something extraordinary few academics ever do. She reconsidered the argument she had made. If the choice is between a systemic public solution to addressing hunger versus private stop-gap measures, *Sweet Charity* strongly favors the former. Again, she originally felt that short-term answers undermine the likelihood of developing long-term answers. After ongoing observation and reflection, though, Janet described it as a false dichotomy and confessed her reassessment of the issue. In fact, she said many of the indefatigable folks working on the frontlines of hunger, make several very important contributions.

First, they help a ton of people with acute needs. Kids who are hungry are often distracted and unsuccessful in school and sometimes get into trouble (Mullainathan and Shafir 2013). Every one of them who gains access to reliable food represents a redirected trajectory of hope. And the same principle applies to grown-ups. I interviewed several folks involved with community meal programs. This includes Jane Lippert, who is the director of Central United Methodist Church's Community Meal Program in Traverse City, Michigan. Through Jane and others I learned how much each meal for each person means: it is a key that unlocks new possibilities for the next day, and thereby all the days that follow. Not that every subsequent door of opportunity will necessarily be unlocked, opened, and walked through. It's just that one is much less likely to get to the second door if the first door is locked. Jane, Steveanna, and their ilk try to make sure the first door revealing tomorrow's possibilities is open.

Second, directors of food banks and soup kitchens learn on the ground what the issues are. They have a distinctive insider's perspective about American food insecurity that is highly informed and therefore credible. Jane talked about challenges for low-income households related to relationships, transportation, housing, work, and cold weather, for example—all issues that tie into access to food. If people can't get to the meal program for whatever reason that may be one less meal they will have. Knowing about those complexities, dilemmas, and tradeoffs is the basis for smart policy and real wisdom. Have you ever heard people complaining about ignorant bureaucrats far away deploying scarce resources on the basis of poorly informed decisions with lousy consequences? Janet Poppendieck realized that such mistakes are much less likely if the powers that be listen to the likes of Jane and Steveanna.

Third, their experience in nonprofit organizations trains frontline workers to be savvy players. Such organizations never have enough money. They know how to do a lot with little. That includes only going to meetings that are productive. They know how to beg, borrow, or steal to make sure their clients, customers, or guests get served. They know how to collaborate, agitate, and advocate. And they change minds, in various organizations like the City of Philadelphia or Deloitte in Steveanna's case, and among countless affluent volunteers in her and Jane's respective activities. Government is not playing the broadly benign role in our food system Poppendieck thinks it should, but it has at times under limited circumstances been a valuable partner.

These three points together, Poppendieck suggested, made such people on the frontlines important allies in the effort to push for more systemic solutions (see also Levkoe 2019; Schor 2011). She offered no false comfort about this dilemma (between short-term and long-term solutions) being conclusively resolved, but rather cautious hope that those working on either end of the spectrum can conceivably collaborate in meaningful, productive ways.

CONCLUSION

As Graham, Rich, Hans, and Steveanna all demonstrate, people get into food distribution for different reasons. Graham and Rich are both running for-profit businesses. Hans and Steveanna both work for nonprofit organizations. For them, food is a means to broader goals, health in Hans's case and community in Steveanna's. All four of these folks share a moral imperative around food. Minimizing harm (e.g., environmental degradation, unhealthy food) and maximizing benefits (e.g., responsible agriculture, sequestering carbon from the atmosphere, distributing healthy calories, building relationships) are strong elements in each case.

As engaged sustainers involved in the distribution of food, these folks exemplify a broad range of activities in this movement, and the diverse settings in which those activities take place. That includes food hubs, stores, restaurants, hospitals, and food banks. Others mentioned in this chapter help distribute food in schools, churches, childcare facilities, elder care facilities, farmers' markets, and various nonprofits. They describe their work in varied ways. Indeed, these are really different kinds of people with different backgrounds working in diverse settings. But these four distributors, Graham, Rich, Hans, and Steveanna, all see their professional endeavors as embedded in a larger movement associated with healthy food.

In different ways, each of them is helping to offer an alternative to the mainstream food system. For Graham and Rich, who run for-profit businesses, the customers gain the opportunity for healthier food that is produced in responsible ways. For Hans and Steveanna, who work for nonprofit organizations, there is an urgency in assisting folks in accessing real food.[7] Both their organizations, St. Christopher's Children's Hospital and The Share Food Program of Philadelphia rely on government (e.g., grants) and corporations (e.g., donations) in different capacities. In some fundamental way, though, the efforts of Hans and Steveanna reflect the fact that the main efforts on the part of government and corporations to oversee our mainstream food system has faltered. If the mainstream food system has a toxic moral footprint, offering alternatives represents moral progress.

What is true for pretty much everyone mentioned in this chapter, including the four featured subjects, is that relationships are central to what they do. Graham is passionate about people—his customers as well as his suppliers and employees. Rich wants to keep his business small so he is connected to everyone there. Hans wants people in his community to eat healthy food— and he has an expansive sense of what that community is. Steveanna has a hard-nosed sense of the bottom line in running her organization, but her real business is people.

NOTES

1. For various patterns related to farmers markets see Schupp (2014; 2019), Hultine, Cooperband, Curry, and Gasteyer (2007), Gasteyer, Hultine, Cooperband, and Curry (2008), Gumirakiza, Curtis, and Bosworth (2014).

2. In general, about 95 percent of farms are run by white people (Horst and Marion 2019).

3. Needless to say, plenty of people do not pay attention to the facts right in front of them, as I acknowledged in the Introduction. But Graham is not alone in betting on the promise of such facts.

4. There is real value in the ideal of organic production, but the regulatory process and actual practice of organic farming is actually a mixed bag. See Guthman (2004), Qazi and Selfa (2005), Tobler et al. (2011), Savage (2016).

5. See sweetgreen.com/mission.

6. A quick internet search of the phrase "foodRX" shows that organizations are doing this in lot of cities across the country, including Anaheim, CA, Baltimore, MD, Boston, MA, Chicago, IL, Dayton, OH, Detroit, MI, Durham, NC, Houston, TX, Portland, OR, Scranton, PA, and Tampa, FL, for example.

7. Hans has at times been affiliated with both for-profit and nonprofit hospitals.

Chapter Seven

Consumption

Remember the last time you were truly, uncomfortably hungry? I have never been hungry for more than a couple days. Yet, it was long enough to know that it is hard to think about much else. Before we evolved into *Homo sapiens*, and before each one of us was even born, we were feeding. It is a fundamental need of all living organisms. The most obvious purpose of grounding, extraction, and processing is to facilitate ongoing consumption.

As innate as the need for food is, its role in our lives is far from simple. Eating is the one basic biological act that we have fully integrated into public life. Mealtime is essential to culture. Whether it is the Eucharist, Seder, Iftar, Thanksgiving, birthdays, wedding receptions, happy hour, teatime, or family dinner, we have incorporated food throughout our lives, the most extraordinary occasions, mundane moments, and everything in between.

Think about your favorite memories of meals, the dishes that make your mouth water, times when you couldn't get the food you wanted, how you feel about your body in relation to food, or how you relate to loved ones around food. Consider how different identities related to gender, race, age, or class are associated with certain foods.[1] Qualities like responsibility, irreverence, piety, stress, and comfort are shaped by and expressed through what we eat. Food is both ubiquitous and complicated.

Plus, it is changing. In an influential essay published in 1999, Juliet Schor described how changing sensibilities around consumption have surfaced in American culture that could be harnessed for a new kind of politics. Several of the aspirations she articulated have become basic elements of the alternative agro-food movement.

"A right to a decent standard of living" (Schor 1999, p. 459) is closely related to the goals of food sovereignty. "Food justice," one engaged sustainer, Owen Taylor, told me, "is the idea of helping everyone have access to healthy food and the ability to grow their own food. Food sovereignty is recognizing that people have a hand in the way they access their food. It's not just an emergency food situation. People have to have agency in accessing

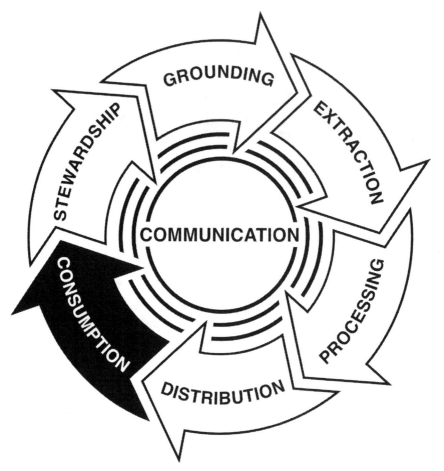

Figure 7.1.   Consumption. Created by Martha MacGregor

food in the creation of food systems and have access to land and culturally appropriate food that looks like comfort food. It's not just about lifestyle and culture."

The emphasis on "quality of life rather than quantity of stuff" (1999, p. 459) that Schor describes is closely related to the concern for lifestyle and health in this movement. Many of Marti Wolfson's affluent clients surely think this way. Overall, the nutrition of what Americans eat, on average, has been improving (see Wang, Leung, Li, Ding, Chiuve, Hu, and Willett. 2014). But healthy calories are distributed unevenly. Working on that problem is partly what animates Hans Kersten's work with low-income families. Everyone deserves quality. People I interviewed who work at food hubs, like

Mother Earth Foods, believe consumers will embrace a "race to the top" in food production and distribution.

At least three-quarters of the people I encountered identified themselves as consumers concerned with health. This is relevant to the "decent standard of living" and "quality of life" Schor mentions. This is surely part of the reason why food companies work so hard to demonstrate the nutritional value of their products, even for things like sugary breakfast cereals, "fruit juice," and meat products, for instance. Think of how much time you spend trying to figure out which products are actually the healthiest.

Schor also mentions the ambition to "democratize consumption practices" (1999, p. 460), which is about having information and options. In terms of food, that means options unavailable among the oligopolistic industries of Big Food. For a lot of the people associated with farmers' markets and CSAs, other food hubs, or farm-to-table restaurants that I encountered, providing an alternative to conventional food is crucial. Some believe sustainable food should be a widely accessible option. Others aspire to entirely supplant conventional, processed foods with the more natural alternatives. The most sophisticated analytical research I know of on farmers' markets is being done by a sociologist named Justin Schupp (see 2016, 2017). He shows that farmers' markets have proliferated across geographical regions, big cities, small cities, towns, and suburbs, and neighborhoods of varying socioeconomic status.

When Schor describes "a politics of retailing and the 'cultural environment'" (1999, p. 461), she is referring to the possibilities of resisting the homogenization of Big Box retail stores. She wants to limit the 24/7 360-degree marketing regime that infests our homes, overwhelms our communities, and commercializes our lives (see also McKibben 1992). Local food systems, including farmers' markets, CSAs, and community gardens, are by definition distinctive and diverse, and a part of local cultural environments.

Schor's invitation to "expose commodity 'fetishism'" (1999, p. 461) is a call for honest appraisal of the moral footprint of production. The fetishism she references holds that "more is always better." This kind of materialism ignores the ethical implications of how things are made and used. Conscientious consumers, in contrast, consider the implications of how food is produced in terms of sustainability, labor, treatment of animals, and so on. Several overlapping social movements (i.e., environmental, labor, animal rights) have converged around this objective. Those invested in sustainable agriculture are very alert to environmental and health issues. Most of the people I interviewed also pay attention to how workers are treated.

Schor calls for "a consumer movement and governmental policy" (1999, p. 461) that is organized and purposeful in advocating for laws and practices that advance "an appealing and humane consumer sphere." Based on what I have seen, I believe the consumer movement is afoot. Local, statewide, and regional efforts are underway to support regenerative farming, to make production practices and labeling more transparent, to facilitate more direct sales from farmers to consumers without corporate skimming in the middle, to bring greater integrity to quality control (e.g., the standards of Certified Organic and other credentialing procedures). I think there is little question that such objectives are being energetically pursued. However, the actual results of those efforts appear to be mixed. Powerful corporate interests and polarized political culture have both undermined this work in real ways. In my conversations with them, a few sustainers referenced the determination of Big Ag and Big Food to suppress competition from smaller operations, as well as the persistent influence of climate change denial.

Schor also mentions the ideal of "ecologically sustainable consumption" (1999, p. 460), which is of course one of the first principles of the movement. All of the sustainers are invested in this ideal. One of the interesting things about those who work on the land is a distinctive sense of time, at least a perspective that is different from a lot of suburban people like me. The labor involves slow work, an awareness of weather, seasons, years, and even decades. The connection to "place" ties farmers to other times and other generations. A piece of land that is meaningful, by definition, involves people who lived here before and, hopefully, people who will live here in the future. I heard pride in the talk of inheritance and legacy. Being ecologically sensitive means paying attention to soil health, clean water, chemical balance, and organic life. Dwelling on sustainability means paying attention over time. Thinking about consumption in this way involves a concern for how extraction affects ecology and sustainability.

Schor offered this agenda about twenty years ago. Needless to say, some of it has not been achieved. But there is in fact a great deal of progress in the alternative agro-food movement relative to most of these elements, as suggested above. There is spreading awareness about the fact that the process of consuming does not occur in a vacuum.

Is it fair to say Americans have never spent more time thinking about what goes into their bodies? I think the answer is clear. If so, then an important question is where do people get their information about food from? What induces consumers to eat one type of food versus another? The most obvious answer is the market itself. Since at least the 1950s, advertisers have been very sophisticated in cultivating the attention, loyalty, and even passion of customers. New technologies, cultural shifts, economic growth, and demographic changes have all contributed to a vast marketing regime shaping the tastes of American consumers. Big Food brands like Doritos, Dole, Jolly Green Giant, Stouffers, and Kraft are put in lunch boxes, on dinner tables and in our mouths every day (see Leon and Ken 2017; 2019). As I suggested in chapter 2, such products are integral to the dominant, ugly story of food in America.

However, that is only part of the picture. The beautiful story of a countermovement is a central theme of this book. The well-known brands that comprise Big Food's core no longer rule consumers' tastes the way they once did. If not Big Food brands, what else holds our attention? What shapes consumers' thinking about what they are going to buy before they ever enter a market? Recent scholarship suggests three kinds of answers (Smith Maguire, Ocejo, and DeSoucey 2022). That is, there are three basic avenues people have, this research indicates, for identifying the main foods they will eat.

The first one is based on very old customs. For thousands of years, people learned from their families and neighbors how to secure and prepare their food. They ate what their grandparents did. This is still true in large parts of the world that retain strong food cultures, well-established methods for procuring ingredients, and culinary traditions. Such habits were always maintained in certain ethnic enclaves in American society, and no doubt still are in some pockets, especially among relatively new immigrants, or segmented ethnoreligious groups (see Counihan et al. 2019). Immigrants from Guatemala, Laos, and Ethiopia, for example, as well as Hasidic Jews and the Amish all have well-defined food cultures.

A more modern source of trust involves institutionally based standards dictated by expert authorities. Such recommendations are often codified in clear, didactic instructions. Since the early 20th century, the U.S. Department of Agriculture has provided official guidelines on healthy food consumption for American households. At times, such guidance was integrated with Big Food brands. "The Basic Four" (Dairy, Meat, Fruits/Vegetables, Breads/Cereals) was a highly regarded typology from 1956 to 1979, for instance. Cereal could be Kellogg's Rice Krispies, which is "fortified with 8 essential vitamins and iron." Need dairy? "Got milk?"

In other words, setting aside the impact of advertising, confidence in certain foods has historically come from esoteric local cultures on the one hand or culturally disembedded institutional authorities on the other—traditional *Gemeinschaft* or modern *Gesellschaft*. That's still true, for sure. However, Smith Maguire, Ocejo and DeSoucey argue that both these scenarios are also less prominent than they once were.

Our era, they suggest, is characterized by vast choices and cultural "omnivorousness." In this context many consumers put a high premium on the concept of "authenticity." This value is reflected in some of Michael Pollan's famous advice: don't eat anything with more than five ingredients or ingredients you can't pronounce, don't eat anything that won't rot, avoid edible food-like substances.

It goes beyond that, too. Consumer perceptions of authenticity are not just derived from what is *in* the food, but also what is *around* it—where the food comes from, who grew it, who processed it, how it is consumed, and so on. Remember, authenticity is a word that farmers use a lot as well. Some of them like Jamie Ager, it seems to me, try hard to do the right thing, want people to know they are doing the right thing, and think creatively about how to attract more attention to such efforts. This may partly account for the shift toward adding more destination qualities to farm operations (e.g., birthday parties, live music, prepared foods, and educational programs). Perhaps it's a little odd that some feel farms need to be enhanced with all these accoutrements to sell consumers on the notion of their authenticity. (It's easy to imagine what Wendell Berry thinks.)

With so many options, so much information, and so much *misinformation*, how do consumers gain confidence in the authenticity of a product? One answer, Smith Maguire et al. suggest, is the "mobile trust regime," which works like this. A group of people bond over their shared preferences. They get to know one another, at least to some extent, through social media and/ or personal relationships. Over time, they form a "taste community," which helps them filter information and establish priorities for making food choices. What defines the boundaries of their community is not (at least not primarily) emotional, political, ethnic, or religious ties, but rather shared tastes. Certain culinary traditions attract like-minded folks around them based on ethnic traditions, regional recipes, or foods that depend on particular ingredients, for example.

Based on my observations of consumers associated with the alternative agro-food movement, Smith Maguire et al.'s emphasis on authenticity sounds right (see also Pratt 2007). It's a word I heard research subjects mention a lot. Among the folks I interviewed, local, fresh, and organic are common qualities that seem to be taken as signs of authenticity.[2] More broadly, there is an awareness of the moral footprint generated by a food product (e.g., nutrition, sustainability, carbon miles, animal welfare, treatment of labor, and/or supporting the local economy). Relationships are also explicitly emphasized— relationships between vendors and buyers, between farms and surrounding communities, or among neighbors. It appears that the point of such relationships is in part to establish trust in the moral footprint of a given enterprise.

I have seen this dynamic in action in relation to dairy products in my hometown in upstate New York, for instance. Like many communities, we have quite a few options for milk. However, two local dairy farms (Battenkill and King Brothers) have generated an exceptional level of credibility. Certain neighbors of mine perceive their products as more "authentic" than other producers.' It's hard to know exactly what makes a particular farm, brand, or commodity become legit, hot, or part of "our community." In the case of King Brothers Dairy, several posts on Facebook each week show images of "regular folks" having fun, cute farm animals, yummy ice cream, and beautiful sunsets, with comments from lots of community residents. Battenkill Valley Creamery talks up the appeal of local farmers' markets (where its products are sold) on its Facebook posts. I've seen proclamations from people at farmers' markets and on social media about both these dairies.

In general, our local farmers' market seems to serve as a key element of this particular taste community, as I suspect is true in other communities. From my conversations with different people, I've learned that some segment of our consumer base tends to think of anything at the farmers' market as more trustworthy than anything at the supermarket. Such trust is facilitated both via in-person and online communications. In some cases, not being affiliated with industrial farming or large corporations functions as a sign of integrity. It's not just who producers are (i.e., local family farms) but who they are not (i.e., distant corporations).

Juliet Schor herself affirmed a broad shift along these lines in her 2011 book, *True Wealth: How and Why Millions of Americans Are Creating a Time-Rich, Ecologically Light, Small-Scale, High Satisfaction Economy.* In it, she extols the achievements of "the leaders of an alternative culture of growing, distributing, preparing, and eating food." That culture, she writes, "respects the earth, nourishes the body, brings people together, fosters creativity, tastes sublime, and satisfies cravings" (p. 128). Not that all the consumers I spoke with are monolithic, but they certainly cluster around the priorities Schor mentioned. Taste matters, of course. Among the consumers I focused on, health, justice, and sustainability come up a lot too.

Again, though, such values don't exist for consumers in a vacuum. They become established through social experience (Brownell and Horgen 2004; Bittman 2021). And then various food products are assessed against those values through social processes as well. Certainly, farmers' markets, community-supported agriculture, and other similar kinds of food hubs are common settings for these interpretive and evaluative processes. In this movement, taste communities form through attachments that consumers share with particular vendors, farms, stores, and restaurants. They also gain confidence in certain food products through particular relationships. A lot of that appears to be mediated online. Many people pay attention to certain national icons like Alice Waters, Mark Bittman, Andrew Weill, Sprouts Farmers Market, or Whole Foods. But trust is also formed through personal face-to-face relationships with friends, neighbors, vendors, or less famous influencers. (I'll say more about this in chapter 9, which focuses on communication.)

It's worth noting that Smith Maguire et al. do not equate the subjective perception of authenticity with actual authenticity in some objective, conclusive sense. Of course, some foods really do have comparatively poor taste, low nutritional value, or toxic qualities. But what our food *means* is largely subjective. The point here is that the ideal of authenticity is in fact a crucial part of the consumption patterns in this movement. For many engaged consumers, an assessment is made of whether a particular food is aligned with that ideal. The ideal is not a fixed standard but revolves around several core themes that are relatively stable but given different weight by different individual consumers. These include sustainability in production practices, carbon miles, nutritious composition of calories, and so on. As documented below, in effect, there are different ways to "keep it real." One of them actually involves hanging out with a bunch of strangers.

ALYSSA MOMNIE: I PERSONALLY LIKE SALTED BROCCOLI

Alyssa Momnie lives on an island in Maine. I crossed paths with her there when my family and I were on vacation in 2018 and we chatted a little bit. Having learned about her I later corresponded with her via email and phone and then visited the island again in 2021 to sit down and interview her. At that time, her eight-year-old son Mateo asked me, "why do you want to talk to my mom?" I took his question to be a matter of mostly curiosity with a hint of protectiveness. He was munching on a cucumber like some folks eat a candy bar. In response to his question, I asked him if he had ever eaten at McDonalds. He scowled and said "No way! McDonalds is bad." I explained that I was curious about what his family eats, which seemed to satisfy him, though he demanded that I mention him in the book. Hi, Mateo! When I asked him what his favorite food is, he thought for a moment and then said, "I personally like salted broccoli." For Alyssa, sustainability and health are core values that shape her consumption patterns. What's on the fork of people like her aligns quite well with each of Juliet Schor's points.

Her outlook on consumption was influenced by experiences "WWOOFing" in several South American countries. The word WWOOF is an acronym associated with several similar phrases, usually Worldwide Opportunities on Organic Farms. Farmers provide simple room and board in exchange for itinerant labor. Alyssa described a subculture of mostly young people traveling on the cheap, folks with a "communal" sensibility, interested in "being off the grid," and "lots of vegetarianism." These are people actively moving away from the "commodity festishism" Schor references.

Along the way, Alyssa was involved in planting, weeding, irrigation, fertilizing, harvesting, cooking, cleaning, and feeding animals, among other tasks. What stayed with her from such travels, she told me, is how possible simple living is and how much fulfillment and joy people in other cultures feel even though they have so much less than affluent Americans are used to. She was especially struck by the harmonious relationship some people have with nature. This same observation was offered by others I interviewed, including Corinne Hansch of Lovin' Mama Farm, mentioned in chapter 3.

Alyssa's conscious and explicit investment in this movement now involves careful consideration of her family's carbon footprint. They buy local, recycle aggressively, and avoid products known to entail ecological harm. From each meal they share, there is a conceptual pathway that goes back in time and one that goes forward in time. Engaged consumers like Alyssa concern themselves with both the antecedent process (e.g., Was the food produced through regenerative agriculture? Was it produced locally? How were the animals treated?) and the ensuing process (e.g., How will this food affect my health? Is the packaging biodegradable? Can the waste be used in any productive way?).

In being aware of such questions, Alyssa is slow in the thoughtful, conscientious, and responsible sense. Like Marti Wolfson, the functional medicine chef who practices elements of Slow Food, Alyssa is a very attentive supply chain angler. For Alyssa, "reading the water" in her part of the stream entails thorough investigation of the ingredients and nutritional value of any given forkful of food. What, exactly, am I eating and feeding my kids, she asks? As a supply chain angler, though, Alyssa gazes way upstream, trying to find out what is in the soil and water that helped generate that food. Such consideration and then the resulting consumer behaviors can have an impact on how farmers farm (Volkova 2022). That is, when consumers pay attention to how their food was generated, farmers are empowered or even incentivized to lean more fully into regenerative agriculture.

It is also true that certain diets, when followed by enough people, contribute to the reduction of greenhouse emissions (see Eshel and Martin 2006). Of course, systemic solutions are ultimately crucial (Poppendieck 1999; Guthman 2011). But there are many ways that little choices individuals like Alyssa make can be a part of larger patterns.

Alyssa explained to me that she is obsessed with what lies downstream as well. What will happen to this food once it's in our bodies? What happens to the waste? That means a lot of energy spent on recycling and composting, as well as avoiding anything that can't be fully recycled or composted. "I'm obsessed with composting food waste," she exclaimed. "It's such a good thing you can do for the environment and it's not that hard."

She also pays attention to the designation of B Corporations. The certification of "B Corporation" (or "B Corp") is attained by private for-profit companies when they meet certain standards of "social and environmental performance." B Lab is the nonprofit organization that oversees the credentialing (see bcorporation.net). As much as Alyssa revels in the research about where her food comes from, which entails learning about the companies she buys from, she sometimes accepts help from this sort of filter too. Ben and Jerry's, Patagonia, and The Body Shop are some well-known examples of Certified B Corps.

Alyssa told me she used to be a hardcore vegetarian but had softened up a bit and now focused more on local sourcing, including some meat. "I guess I'm an omnivore now." She then recalled visiting Ecuador and being so impressed by kids who knew how to kill a chicken, clean it, and use different parts for different purposes. She revealed no squeamishness about that experience. It isn't taking the life of an animal or meat per se that bothers her. She eats meat and would love to raise animals, she said. It's really industrial food processing that is the issue. "I think beef especially is horrific," she declared, her face visibly disgusted. "And I think factory farming is horrific." I thought of my dad's words: "When we eat alongside other creatures and when we take responsibility for the entire network of eating creatures, we may consider our consuming habits very differently" (Brueggemann 2020, p. 29).

I noticed a familiar theme in her patterns. Like Alyssa, many engaged sustainers feel real conviction about certain parameters (e.g., beef and factory farming are horrendous) but quite flexible about lots of other things. Her four-year-old son Andre is a "Pastafarian," she told me. "One love!" Alyssa declared with a knowing gleam in her eye (which I took to mean, *you know, I wish he would eat a more diverse and healthy diet, but parents can only do so much in influencing their children and I'm not too upset about it*). Mateo may dig cucumbers and broccoli but Andre is rather focused on pasta. Their mom is ambitious about what they all eat, but practical. Conviction and flexibility.

After talking inside for a while, we went outside and walked around their small, funky garden, which has no rows, symmetry, or really any discernible order at all. She grinned when I mentioned the apparent disorder. Interesting pieces of wood, which looked like they might have washed up on the beach, were laying around, plus a few children's toys, and a shovel or two. This was not a giant garden, but Alyssa was proud of it. She said her younger son, Andre, liked to help in the garden and Mateo less so. Still, Mateo was flitting about as we talked. It seemed like a happy place where the family spends a decent amount of time. I could tell someone was paying a lot of attention to the plants and removing the weeds, but otherwise embracing a certain amount of chaos. In this case, the conviction was evident in the produce and the flexibility seemed conspicuously exhibited.

As a consumer, it was clear that what really animates Alyssa is the environment. She is energized, informed, and articulate about soil, carbon, waste, and gardening. Being green is fundamental to her conscientious consumption. But she has other concerns.

The health of her family came up several times. She mentioned chemicals in processed foods they studiously avoid. She had apparently convinced her son that fast food is bad business, and fresh vegetables can be delicious—parental achievements that do not just happen without effort in our culture.

More generally, she seems skeptical of normative middle-class, suburban consumption patterns. She hates birthdays and Christmas, she said, because of all the expectations related to material gifts. She recalled trying to teach Mateo about their consumption patterns. "I want to teach him that there's another way of consuming, which doesn't require all this trash."

At one point, she expressed incomprehension about people who don't support Black Lives Matter. Racial justice, at some level, is a no-brainer for her. She alluded to generational wealth and how that has facilitated entrenched inequality, which is at the bottom of a lot of social problems. By the time we were done talking, it became clear that food insecurity is part of Alyssa's thinking, too, even if it's not at the top of the list.

Being a supply chain angler, like Alyssa, is not hard in some intellectual or material sense. We could all study up on sources and waste and make careful decisions. But such efforts are distinctive in the context of our dominant culture.

JIM LIEBERMAN: LIVING OFF THE
LAND, OFF THE GRID

There are of course others who make more radical commitments. My research assistant, Maggie Griesmer, interviewed one such fellow named Jim Lieberman, who represents the other end of WWOOFing. "We get help from the WWOOF program wherein mostly young people come from all over the world to work five or six hours a day in exchange for room and board. It amounts to most of our social life, as well. It is a thoroughly beautiful ongoing experience."

Jim told Maggie by phone that he and his wife of 52 years live on 40 acres of redwood forest in northern California. Their nearest neighbor lives a mile away. Jim is quite different from many folks we encountered. He has strong feelings about the seductive and corrupting influence of capitalism and works hard to avoid its influence. "One of the main functions of market culture," he said, "is to make us dissatisfied with our lives."

He and his family built their own home, they garden, they hunt, they butcher their own deer and chickens, and they collect eggs, he told Maggie. Jim and his wife and son are radical recyclers. He said they fill two garbage cans a couple times a year but use most everything else. He takes pride in speaking multiple languages, playing guitar, being a craftsman, and living off the land.

Jim's first encounter with WWOOFing was in France after his friend Steve had told him about the program. As a traveler himself, he told Maggie, Jim learned how to make cheese and care for berries. "When I got back, Steve said something to the effect of, 'I meant that maybe you could get some help on your place!' I said, "duh!' Then we joined WWOOFUSA and started getting some help on our place." By 2014, when Maggie spoke to him, Jim speculated that he had hosted some 170 people over a five-year period. Jim appears to be something of a maverick, living far away from other neighbors, staying off the grid, and being as self-sufficient as possible. But there is also something deeply social about his experience. Travelling internationally, speaking multiple languages, hanging out with WWOOFers, and making music are all inherently social activities. It's easy to imagine that his critical stance regarding dominant market culture is itself part of a shared ideological identity as well.

In the book *Vocational Vagabond, Volunteer Vacationer,* Astra Lincoln describes WWOOFing at Jim's home. She described him as "a member of the original 'American Back to the Land' movement" (2012). He is radically committed to monitoring his own moral footprint as a consumer. A fellow supply chain angler, like Alyssa, he is also alert to the meaning people make in their consumption habits. "Most of the people" who volunteered on his property, he reported to Lincoln, "want to have meaningful experiences . . . they're trading income for a genuine experience of life" (Lincoln 2012).

Few people I spoke to had any experiences with WWOOFing or other such adventures abroad. But almost all of them share some of Alyssa's sensibilities as consumers. They are eager to know where their food comes from, read labels, study up on ingredients, and buy local. Several live in harmony with the land, growing their own fruits and vegetables and getting their meat from their livestock or hunting and fishing, like Joe Mahay and Naomi Tannen. "I also was quite an avid hunter and fisher," Joe told me, "and most of our meat diet came from game and fish." "We ate bear one whole year," Naomi recalled with a chuckle. In old age they now purchase meat from local farmers. "We buy a whole lamb from a local farm because we want to eat animals," Naomi noted. "We're not vegetarians but we want to eat animals that were treated well and organically. It's lovely to know where your animals come from."

Few of them are as committed as Jim to escaping dominant culture, but sustainers all evince a kind of skepticism related to suburban consumer culture. "There's so many community gardens here" (in Northampton, Massachusetts). "People have plots," one gardener told me. "The city gives people plots for nothing, and it's a plot the size of this room, and they really enjoy taking care of it. And there's a farmers' market every day. So it's very much a part of the culture here."

People like Jim are amazing. I find such choices to be astonishing. They are definitely deeply embedded in this movement. Living largely "off the grid" and "off the land," as it were, makes for a moral footprint that is extraordinary, and thereby demonstrates what is in fact possible. We all make choices, and we could in fact make different choices, as Jim shows. However, we need not emulate such radical behavior to find plausible alternatives.

RICK CHRISMAN: A FLASHLIGHT OF CONSCIOUSNESS

The question of avoiding consumer culture came up again in another conversation I had, this one with a United Church of Christ minister named Rick Chrisman, who was for a time the chaplain at the college where I work. Rick likens consciousness to a small flashlight shining in a dark closet. Its brightness is limited and illuminates only that at which it is directed. Each of us, he suggested to me, chooses where to aim our own consciousness (see McKibben 1992 for a detailed version of this same point.)

White and in their sixties, he and his wife Cindy are very intentional about pointing their consciousness away from mainstream marketing. One result is purposeful consumption, or what my dad calls "mature materiality" (Brueggemann 2020). Rick told me they are "always conscientious" about their eating habits. "We watch sources." Their food tends to be organic, local, fresh, not processed. Their diet is "high on fresh vegetables, low on starches, medium on animal protein (lots of seafood, some pork and beef)." They constantly pay attention to the nutritional value of what they eat. Sustainability is a priority too.

However, Rick acknowledged that "for sustainability we would have to be 100 percent vegetarian, and we are not there." Conviction and flexibility again. They eat a certain amount of salt, sugar, fat, and meat, including red meat. Rick said he happily eats Ben and Jerry's or Newman's Salad Dressing. But he and his wife are *plant-forward* (my term, not his) in their consumption and frequently look for fresh, local, and organic ingredients.

Where did this sensibility come from, I asked him. "My habits were decided long ago listening to my mother read from Adele Davis' *Let's Eat Right to Keep Fit* at the breakfast table, and from reading and hearing Ralph Nader wail away at the corporations." But it seems to me that Rick's consumption patterns still reflect a deliberate kind of practice. He and his wife are generally "oblivious" to mainstream marketing, he said, because they actively, persistently ignore it. They shine the flashlight of their consciousness elsewhere.

Though Rick's eating habits were formed a while ago, lots of folks are increasingly adopting the same commitments. I interviewed a number of people who work in food distribution, including two linked to large corporations, four who work for small-scale for-profit businesses, and a bunch who work in nonprofit settings. They all said the concern for healthy food among American consumers is growing rapidly.

For any individual consumer to direct the flashlight of consciousness away from highly processed foods may sound like a rather modest endeavor. But if we recognize how ubiquitous marketing is on TV, on the internet, on the radio, in the newspaper, on billboards, and how it is integrated with access to other kinds of information, this intentionality starts to sound rather ambitious.[3] As an act of consciousness, Rick's filtering is a valiant move. It's not as bold as the heavy lift of living off the grid like Jim Lieberman or WWOOFing like Alyssa Momnie. But it is a real task more akin to carrying around a 20-pound weight all the time. The steady effort might entail a slow burn, as one studiously avoids intrusive, relentless messages of corporate advertising.

Rick was emphatic in describing this filtering as neither laborious nor heroic on the part of his wife and him. I reckon that understates how powerful dominant culture is, though, and how difficult it would be for most of us to develop other kinds of habits in how we get information. That is, it appears that through some deeply ingrained impulses, Rick and Cindy have developed long-term practices that make their lives feel normal and fulfilling. Like they've been working out for so long that lugging a 20-pound weight around all the time doesn't take much effort. But their deeds would seem arduous or even impossible to most American consumers. Looking away from the constant advertising of Big Food is no small feat. I asked Rick where he and his wife do get information about food. "Word of mouth, local paper," he said.[4] And they frequently visit farmers' markets and roadside stands. That made me think of mobile trust regimes.

That Rick regularly visits farmers' markets is consistent with national data in terms of where they are most available. There are certain factors associated with the presence of farmers' markets (Schupp 2016; 2017; Gasteyer et al. 2008). They are common across geographical regions (though in lower proportions in the Midwest) and as well as big cities, small cities, towns, and suburbs (but less so in rural areas). They are more likely to be in areas where more people are white, affluent, and older. It helps if the local business community and, of course, local consumers buy in. Rick lives in a disproportionately white and upwardly mobile suburban setting in the metropolitan area of a large city.

When we talk about people like Rick Chrisman, Alyssa Momnie, or Jim Lieberman, their individual choices might not sound like a big deal. However, many people in this movement believe the aggregated behavior of American households adds up to something big. Almost every farmer I interviewed referenced the importance of consumer demand (see also Hunt 2007). Roxbury Farms in upstate New York, for example, started with 30 members in its CSA in 1991. Today it has more than 800. Jamie Ager of Hickory Nut Gap thinks that raising a steer in a responsible way—that protects natural resources like soil, water, and air, and produces a healthy animal—absolutely requires informed consumers. Casey McKissick, owner of Foothill Meats, who sells the kind of meat Jamie produces, feels urgent about the same point. Without informed consumers, he has no customers.

The ability of farmers to make a living off a small piece of land by way of regenerative agriculture is hugely affected by consumer demand for food products that have more integrity than what is generally offered by Big Food corporations. We should recall that demand for organic food is currently outpacing the supply. So consumers are not simply responding to more production of fresh, healthy, sustainably generated products, they are also driving it. What I am calling integrity is perceived by many, it seems, to be authenticity. What authenticity means is complicated, as noted above. For now, let's just say it is actually food, as opposed to the notion of food, foodish or food-like.

As I encountered more engaged sustainers, I realized there is a pattern related to religious faith (see McKibben 1998). That Rick Chrisman is a UCC minister is clearly linked to his thoughtfulness about his own moral footprint. The same is true of Dee Lowman, a Methodist pastor. Her commitment to healthy eating is even more prominent in her ministry. For Dee, the context of food production and consumption matters a great deal. "I want my son and I want other people to know that eating healthy and eating vegetables can be fun and growing food can be fun. And I think that's the thing. We had a lot of processed food as kids because I grew up in the 70s. Who didn't eat space food sticks, right? I mean, space food sticks—we're like, 'very cool'! Who knows what was in them? I don't blame my parents. That's the time they were in. You used to put cream of mushroom in everything." Dee talks about the intimacy of growing food and then either consuming it or giving it away and appreciating how it nourishes human bodies.

Although this is a hopeful development, it is not without complexities. For example, on the one hand, informed, affluent consumers have the capacity to impact how our food system operates. They can demand quality, freshness, and sustainability. There is promise in the likelihood of providers responding to such demand. On the other hand, if there were a "race to the top" like this, many low-income households would be left out. This includes farm laborers who are often both crucial to the production of organic and local food and exploited in a big way. Agricultural laborers are frequently excluded from labor laws and therefore do not enjoy many of the protections other workers have, such as minimum pay. As a result, some can't afford to purchase the products they help produce (Gray 2014). More generally, many low-income consumers cannot even afford mass-produced processed foods now (Ehrenreich 2001; McMillan 2012). This problem would be exacerbated if widespread increases in quality are accompanied by increases in cost.

This is one of the most vexing, durable problems in this movement. Structural inequality—vastly uneven distribution of wealth and broadly unequal access to important institutions (e.g., schooling, employment, healthcare, housing, political representation, legal representation)—pose formidable obstacles to true food justice. It is hard to picture genuine, broad, realistic solutions to that problem.

But there are glimmers of light worth focusing on. First of all, the evolving ideal of good food is in any case necessary for low-income households to ever have a chance at food security. Until affluent people recognize and extol the importance of calories that are healthy and sustainable, the notion that low-income households should be afforded the same basic right won't gain much traction. There is some positive momentum in this regard. People across class positions increasingly appreciate the value of good food. In one suburban setting, a food writer told me, "We have started to see the middle-class shopping at farmers' markets alongside folks who are using their food stamps to shop for the same food."

In addition, if "quality" (i.e., taste plus moral footprint) gains a lot of currency, we would expect competitive pressures to drive prices down. Right now, efficiency and quantity are prized goals in the dominant food system. As noted, we already see Big Food companies marketing their food as healthy. But what if there were more transparency and consumers could really tell what products were healthy? And what will such companies do when large numbers of consumers demand sustainably generated products? Perhaps prices would initially go up with demand. But over time if quality endures as a consumer priority, there will be more producers and therefore more supply.

This shift has already started. Growing availability of affordable plant-based foods surely has something to do with this change. There is more plant-based meat in major supermarket chains. The Impossible Whopper now produced by Burger King and McPlant burger in development by McDonalds indicates that even fast food is paying attention. McDonalds, Chick-fil-A, and others have added salads. The new $60 billion fast-casual restaurant sector dominated by the likes of Chipotle is partly based on the appeal of fresh ingredients (Dunn 2020; Technavio 2020). The stunning rise of Sweetgreen, the fast casual salad/grain bowl chain (mentioned in Chapter 5: Distribution) also comes to mind.

KEVIN QUANDT: HEALTHY FOOD THAT
IS CRAVEABLE AND ACCESSIBLE

The main agenda of Sweetgreen is distribution. The company wants to sell food. But we can learn a lot by observing how consumers have made this venture successful. Kevin Quandt, my friend who is an executive at Sweetgreen, told me one of the company's founders has said they want to "make healthy food that is 'craveable' and accessible."

Each Sweetgreen restaurant is unique with a hip, young vibe. The architecture varies but is usually sparse and sort of modern feeling. They make funky salads and bowls with familiar, fresh ingredients as well as combinations that are hard to imagine until you try them. "Sweetgreen is a platform at the intersection of tech and food," Kevin said. "We're going to sell more things than salad through digitalization" (quoted in Martino 2019). This includes digital ordering, home delivery, and loyalty programs, for example.

There is little question their menu is healthy on multiple levels. Sweetgreen advertises local sourcing, nothing frozen, the freshest ingredients possible. As Vice President of Supply Chain and Sustainability, Kevin leads the charge in composting, minimizing waste, and green practices in general, as well.

"Sustainability permeates the company. We operationalize sustainability throughout the entire supply chain. . . . Taste and sustainability go hand-in-hand at Sweetgreen. We're about offering clean, sustainably grown, healthy food with transparent ingredients that tastes delicious. That's the magic of Sweetgreen" (Martino 2019).

The spectacular growth of the company suggests the food is in fact craveable. Over the course of 13 years, the company grew from one location to more than 100 (Dunn 2020). Celebrity chefs make recipes, design firms create appealing spaces, and innovative technologies facilitate distinctive customer experiences, all part of the successful business model. Lines out the door indicate that something special is happening and consumers love it.

Sweetgreen's food is relatively affordable too. It's not as cheap as McDonalds, and it has "carefully cultivated a highbrow brand position" (Dunn 2020), but $15 for a healthy, fresh, locally sourced meal dreamt up by skilled chefs is perceived by many as a good deal. As Kevin noted, "consumers are willing to pay a little more for real food" (Martino 2019). This is not slow food. It is food that is produced fast but with more soundness than fast-food. Efficiency remains a central principle but is blended with ideals of environmental, nutritional and culinary value.

Kevin's job is distinctive. He is in charge of securing resources for a big chain with more than 100 stores geographically spread across the country.

The scale is large. And the goal is to get ingredients from local sources and minimize waste. Sweetgreen partners with many farmers around the country.

For example, Sweetgreen sources organic romaine and broccoli leaf lettuce directly from Full Belly Farm, which is based in Capay Valley, California; fresh berries and three varieties of squash from Ward's Berry Farm in Sharan, Massachusetts; and Columbia river Steelhead from Pacific Seafood in Nespelem, Washington, according to Quandt, who said these and other sourcing partners are chosen because they put the utmost focus on the sustainable production of top-quality food (quoted from Martino 2019).

To my knowledge, this combination in terms of scale and local sourcing has never been tried before.

Another partner is Will Allen, "a farmer of Bunyonesque proportions" (Royte 2009). The six-foot seven-inch retired professional basketball player has become a national leader in the urban agriculture movement. "Creating soil from waste," Allen says, "is what I enjoy most" (Royte 2009). The winner of multiple prestigious awards, including a MacArthur Foundation "Genius Grant," Allen is a farmer based in Milwaukee with a national reputation. For him, the "full circle" is very important, both in terms of sustainable agriculture, but also urban ecology.

Kevin described his meeting with Allen as transformative. Allen spent hours with Kevin showing him how organic urban agriculture works. Kevin came away thinking differently about waste and how it could be systemically deployed in ways that strengthen soil, enhance harvests, and generate healthy food—all in the kinds of urban areas where Sweetgreen operates.

As a retail chain, Sweetgreen is a different kind of business, but their ethos overlaps with that of Allen. The company's website says, "We believe the choices we make about what we eat, where it comes from and how it's prepared have a direct and powerful impact on the health of individuals, communities and the environment."

In this kind of partnership between Sweetgreen and Will Allen, Kevin sees possibilities for altering the market more broadly. The size of Sweetgreen gives the company leverage, Kevin explained to me. For instance, they might get baby greens from a very small grower as well as a very large grower. The company then has the capacity to help the smaller grower, who practices regenerative agriculture, to get bigger fast and/or incentivize the large grower to adopt more sound farming practices. If their partners don't live up to the stated standards, Sweetgreen cuts them loose (see Bercovici 2020). This is the sort of thing big firms have done in many contexts. In the case of Sweetgreen, though, there is an ethic aligned with this movement guiding the leverage.

There are several crucial conditions in place here. First, the company and its customers have a deal: the products will be green (both in terms of being literally comprised of healthy greens and in terms of being environmentally sound). Second, Sweetgreen has devised a distinctive approach that involves local sourcing and large-scale systems. The ethos and vibe of Sweetgreen are surely important too; the food tastes good and Sweetgreen is the place to be.

In 2021, the company committed to reducing its carbon footprint by half within six years, a bold aspiration that involved researching sourcing with every single provider and vendor (Peters 2021) and could only be done in the context of those first two conditions.

This sort of leverage is similar to a point made by the restaurateur and butcher Casey McKissick in chapter 4. Smaller players can influence bigger players by showing that integrity and transparency appeal to increasingly informed customers. In that case, Casey was talking about how meat is produced. But the same point applies to plants, soil, water, and air. When consumers start to care, producers of every size are compelled to care, too.

In sum, Sweetgreen executives believe that they can make money selling sustainably produced food at a reasonable price. Needless to say, this hardly signifies the end of hunger in America. One gets the feeling that if the aim of enhancing communities ever clashes with the goal of revenue, the Sweetgreen founders won't be conflicted about what ultimately motivates them. This is not a social experiment or a philanthropic enterprise; it is through and through a for-profit company. But Sweetgreen's wild success as a business suggests new possibilities in terms of scale, quality, and price. They have effectively tapped into a profound shift in consumer preferences that favor quality. Increasing from one store to one hundred in 13 years is something. Now what? COVID-19 no doubt complicated things for this company as it did for so many. But in spring of 2022, the owners were predicting more than a half billion dollars in revenue.

CONCLUSION

Many of the research subjects I encountered believe that evolving consumption patterns are crucial to this movement. Every engaged sustainer I interviewed is an engaged consumer in one sense or another. Most Americans are very individualistic when they are in consumer-mode. What can I get out of this transaction? Is this a bargain? Do I like how this tastes? We can picture the busy professional or harried household attempting to consume enough calories to keep going. Efficiency is the key. Or a typical customer in a nice restaurant motivated almost entirely by taste. Perhaps they also care about health. Of course, those are reasonable ways to think; for engaged consumers there are broader issues in play as well. A given forkful does not exist simply for the energy or joy humans can extract from it. It shapes one's moral footprint.

Some are extremely diligent supply chain anglers. They matter a great deal by raising the bar, showing what is possible, setting an example, and encouraging more transparency (see Hunt 2007). Others are less ambitious but still important engaged sustainers. A lot of Americans have a growing awareness of how bad our food system is. They do not want to eat or feed their families garbage. They want food that is healthy and tasty. Rick Chrisman is more aligned with that approach to consumption. He is less bold in some ways. Rick isn't really pushing for a paradigm shift. He's just quietly opting out of much of the dominant culture, which is so powerful because it is in some sense quite simple and therefore feasible for a lot of people.

Kevin is certainly part of an ambitious enterprise in Sweeetgreen. They are attempting to blend certain elements—taste, quality, nutrition, localism, and scale—in unprecedented ways. The consumers who frequent Sweetgreeen—and clearly a lot of them do!—show how much those elements appeal. However, Sweetgreen is also somewhat conventional in certain respects—profit and efficiency are central to the endeavor. People like Alyssa and Jim wouldn't love those unalloyed capitalistic values. Again, though, this hybrid model shows what is possible and therefore could be emulated, potentially on a large scale.

The commitments of Alyssa, Jim, Rick, and Kevin all align in different ways with the seven points Juliet Schor made, which I summarized earlier in this chapter. Most certainly we see a commitment to ecologically sustainable consumption and quality over quantity.

The ideal of authenticity is clearly a priority for Alyssa, Jim, and Rick. They each seek independence from what they perceive as the corruption of Big Food. They have each been active members of a global community invested in such freedom.

Sweetgreen looks like a very good example of an organization trafficking in "mobile trust," to borrow Smith Maguire et al.'s terms. This company pulls in lots of information from global sources, curates it by way of celebrity chefs, uses local ingredients, and presents the results in specific, localized dishes to consumers. Sweetgreen leaders think about their employees and customers in terms of "conscious achievers" and "maximized life" (Dunn 2020). The ideals of authenticity and trust are integral to their remarkable success.

NOTES

1. Various identities, roles, and relationships are acted out around food. See DeVault (1994), Julier (2013), Herz (2018), Bowen et al. (2019).

2. See also Pratt (2007), and Tobler, Visschers, and Siegrist (2011).

3. See McKibben (1999), Schor (2004), Chernin (2008), Fielding-Singh (2021).

4. They are not alone. As challenging as it is to maintain a healthy diet, a lot of people do in fact figure out how to do it (see Wang et al. 2014).

Chapter Eight

Stewardship

"The purpose of life is to live it," Eleanor Roosevelt declared, "to taste experience to the utmost, to reach out eagerly and without fear for newer and richer experience." The first part of this claim is basically the theory of evolution: we are evolved to survive. Perhaps the second part is why it's worth the trouble. Stewardship in my reckoning is about preserving the conditions for fulfilling human life over the long run. It is about protecting natural and human resources. If we don't protect natural resources, our species will not endure. If we don't protect human resources in the short run, our food system won't have the labor it needs to function well. If we don't project human resources in the long run, then what is the point of anything?

For a long time, environmentalists have known that when you use something up without replenishing it, sooner or later it will run out. The rest of us, well, some of us, are now starting to grasp this truth. Consumption invites a concern for stewardship. I use this particular word *stewardship* advisedly. It might sound like human arrogance, like our species has supreme dominion over everything. I have something a bit humbler in mind.

Throughout history, the steward is not the person in charge, the ruler or owner. It is the person designated for managing things. Indeed, a steward has often had a relatively high level of responsibility compared to his level of authority. He has to get things done but is not the king. This metaphor notwithstanding, I think of stewarding as a necessarily collective endeavor (which is true of every stage I am describing in this cycle of engagement). Just as no one person can truly possess vast resources, no lone individual can genuinely care for them. It takes a village, or something larger.

Stewardship of natural resources involves conservation, preservation, waste management, securing ecologically sound fuel sources, managing weather impacts, and "green infrastructure." As some Americans have become more genuinely concerned with the consumption of food, and by extension the extraction, processing, and distribution that makes it available, they have given more attention to protecting natural resources, namely,

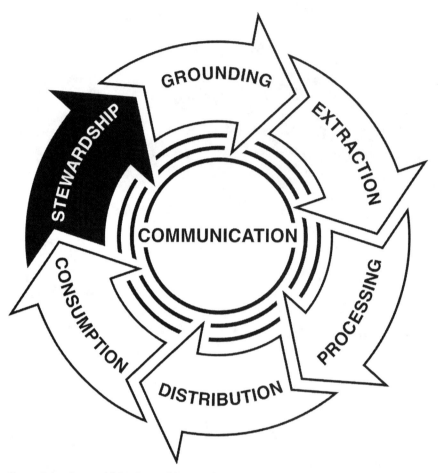

Figure 8.1. Stewardship. Created by Martha MacGregor

arable, and pasturable land, safe water, and clean air. Genuine stewardship is not myopic but thinks in terms of large-scale systems over the long run.

Stewardship of human resources (which is to say, people) protects the fundamental right of physical well-being. Here and now people should have control of and access to reliable sources of healthy food. This kind of agenda requires economic conditions that provide good jobs, a living wage, and a decent standard of living. It has been the raison d'etre of the American labor movement since its inception. More recently, organized labor and college students have been effective in advocating for fair treatment of labor involved with food production among some corporations, including McDonald's, Walmart, and Wendy's (Scheiber 2019). They forced such giants to sign on to the Fair Food Program, which stipulates standards for better pay and conditions for agricultural workers. There is also now a different movement organized around food sovereignty in particular, which seeks to ameliorate the problems extending from food deserts, food apartheid, and food insecurity.

Of course, there have at times been tensions between the stewardship of natural resources and the stewardship of human resources. The environmental movement has not always aligned itself with the interests of workers, and unionists in particular. And the labor movement has not always been concerned with sustainability, especially when such ideals threaten unionized jobs.

For their part, some affluent suburbanites who shop at places like Whole Foods and think of themselves as environmentally progressive may not spend much time worrying about hungry children in the city or country. Conversely, advocates concerned about hunger, those who manage food banks, for example, don't always spend much time thinking about sustainability.

However, there are some signs of hope here. They involve a growing understanding that these different forms of stewardship must be interconnected. One of the first people I interviewed, Tim Storrow, is a farmer and the executive director of the Castanea Foundation. "Castanea Foundation," its mission statement explains, "was established to conserve and protect agriculturally productive and environmentally significant land and water resources in select areas of Vermont and New York. Castanea develops and supports projects designed to conserve the environment and the working landscape by protecting land, and fostering economically viable, environmentally sustainable agricultural practices." What this amounts to in many cases, Tim explained to me when I first met him in 2012, is providing grants to family farms involved in sustainable agriculture to reconfigure their operations to something economically viable under changing market conditions. A common scenario, for instance, is helping dairy farmers get into artisanal cheese.

It became clear to me that the idea of stewardship is evolving and expanding. Naomi, a farmer for decades and a frequent soup kitchen volunteer mentioned in previous chapters, corroborates this. "There's a new cook now," at the soup kitchen, "who's very committed to organic food and vegetables, and not things out of big cans." It seemed to occur to Naomi as she was speaking, "I think that's new . . . the idea that a soup kitchen would be committed to serving healthy organic food. I don't remember hearing that." Others on the front lines of confronting food insecurity reported the same thing: there is growing concern about providing food that is natural, fresh, and healthy.

What is becoming evident is that preserving the land and the community go hand in hand. During a keynote lecture to the Northeast Organic

Farming Association–New York annual meetings in 2018, Richard Ball, the Commissioner of New York State Department of Agriculture and Markets, himself a farmer, addressed this topic. He spoke about seven listening sessions he participated in around New York State in relation to the federal farm bill that was in development at the time. During this tour, he traveled with the Commissioner of New York State Department of Temporary and Disability Assistance and the Commissioner of the Department of Environmental Conservation. Three important state officials respectively concerned with farming, low-income assistance, and the environment gathered in the same room, repeatedly, and listened to different constituencies share their concerns.

Mr. Ball expressed surprise and relief that New Yorkers concerned with farming and New Yorkers concerned with nutrition found common ground. "I didn't hear either folks from the nutrition side or folks from the agricultural side say, 'don't cut us, cut them.' Because I think on the nutrition side people with SNAP benefit concerns and health concerns for an underprivileged population realized they need the healthy agriculture in order to feed the people. And on the farm side, I saw farmers understanding that the people on SNAP benefits and the people who needed the help from the nutrition title were very important customers of theirs. I heard, 'we don't need a smaller farm bill, we need a good farm bill, we need a farm bill that represents all of us and is adequate to what our needs are.'"

This same synergy is evident in the innovative work of The Common Market (mentioned in chapter 6), which has networks in the Mid-Atlantic, the Southeast, and Texas. This organization links up family farmers to communities in need of good food by coordinating with local anchor institutions (e.g., hospitals, schools, community organizations). Thus, the natural resources around agriculture and the human resources of families who are farmers, and their communities, as well as the communities who would otherwise struggle to access good food are both nurtured in this endeavor. By helping with communications, coordination, strategy, and bypassing the rapacious middlemen that extract so much value from our food systems, the Common Market facilitates multifaceted stewardship.

This distinctive work parallels some sensibilities I witnessed several times. I met a number of farmers who spend a lot of energy thinking about their soil and crops, as well as feeding their neighbors, including those facing food insecurity. Some donate food, some volunteer at food pantries or soup kitchens, and others provide free opportunities to learn about gardening or farming. A few people care a lot more about the land and some care a lot more about the people. But most sustainers I talked to think the issues are inextricably linked.

This way of thinking about stewardship aligns with the United Nations' Sustainable Development Goals. The UN articulates 17 such goals related to environmental stewardship, which emphasize several priorities we would expect: clean water and sanitation; industry, innovation and infrastructure; sustainable cities and communities; responsible consumption and production; climate action; life below water; and life on land. But it also sees in sustainability the centrality of human well-being and so also advocates for no poverty; zero hunger; good health and well-being; quality education; gender equality; reduced inequalities; peace, justice, and strong institutions; and partnerships for the goals. A central point in this movement is connectedness. Between nature and people, different species, different peoples, plants and animals, air and soil, urban and rural, here and there, now and later, and so on.

When officials and citizens with different but overlapping interests gather and start thinking systemically about how to find solutions that help "all of us," that is stewardship. Indeed, one of the patterns I noticed among effective stewards is that they find a way to get "in the room where it happens" with the right people who have different but overlapping interests and create the conditions for productive discourse that leads to action (see Garcés 2019; Klein 2022). I found a great example in my hometown.

BARBARA GLASER: CATALYTIC PHILANTHROPY

Barbara Glaser is proud of her roots. She cheerfully invokes the cultural heritage of her family from Sweden, Norway, and Germany. "I am a Viking," she declares, in reference to her own drive and resilience. Like many immigrant accounts, familiar elements are evident in her family's narrative: crossing boundaries, hard work, ethnic loyalty, social mobility, cosmopolitan progression. If the general arc of the story is ordinary, the details of her journey are special. Even as she approached 70, Barbara sounded almost girlish as she spoke exuberantly about her three remarkable parents—her mother, father, and her stepfather.

Her father grew up poor in Minnesota, the son of a streetcar driver. Kenneth Glaser "started his first business," she told me, "then he started a second business, then he started another business, and he kept growing businesses." He would become an owner and CEO of National Car Rental and helped transform the company into a successful enterprise. Barbara's mother, Jeanne Mooty Glaser, was a schoolteacher. After marriage, she became "that classic woman behind the man" but "headed up everything," including Sunday school, Rotarians, the school board, the CPA Wives Club of Minnesota, the Hopkins-Minnetonka Concert Association, Minnesota PEO (Philanthropic

Educational Organization). She and Kenneth were active volunteers and donors for their local church, its choir, the University of Minnesota, and a number of other organizations. "It was the opposite of 'bowling alone.' They were really highly engaged."

The Glasers lived in suburban Minneapolis. Like many of that generation, as children Barbara and her brother were often sent outdoors and told to be home by dinner time. Looking at anthills, collecting birds' feathers, and building forts kept them busy. Barbara's family visited her grandparents' farm several times a year where she helped pick corn and cook meals. They spent a lot of time on Lake Superior and in the woods of that region. All of which helped cultivate a strong resonance for Barbara with the sights, sounds, and smells of wildlife.

While she was in college, her father developed a brain tumor. Adulthood summoned Barbara. She transferred from her preferred college to the University of Minnesota so she could help care for him. "It was hard to leave St. Olaf because I'd just been accepted into that choir. I had gone there to sing in. But I really wanted to be there [with her dad]. So I came home and we took care of him. There was no hospice at the time." Kenneth died when she was 19.

Later, Barbara's mother married her own brother in-law, John Mooty. Jeane's sister, who had been married to John, had died some years earlier. John had worked closely with Kenneth at National and helped with the company's rise. He was a successful lawyer associated with a number of large corporate interests, including Dairy Queen, the Minnesota Vikings, and his own law firm. Like Kenneth and Jean, John was also active in voluntary service and charities.

From her mother, father, and uncle/step-father, Barbara told me, she learned the value of "catalytic philanthropy." Among the varied projects Barbara would be associated with over her life, activities consistently characterized by unsparing generosity and shrewd leadership, one can see a number of threads tied back to her biography.

As Kenneth was dying, he realized good elder care in their community was lacking. The nursing home was "an awful little place," Barbara told me. Figuring out a solution became a mission for him. With Barbara's help, he formed a team of folks who collaborated with local churches and schools, examined elder care facilities in the region, bought some land, and set out to build a state-of-the-art community-based elder care facility.

"So the two years he was dying, recovering, stabilized and then dying," she said, "we were all about figuring out how to make this multi-institutional elder care facility and he died before we broke ground. But the whole thing is built, is still there, still being served by all those different congregations—and the high school kids who come and volunteer and adopt a grandparent. So it was part of his whole being to be purposefully engaged even in that time."

This formative experience of being near her father during his final months helped make death and dying a topic that Barbara has pondered, studied, and worked on ever since. She subsequently studied with Robert Fulton at the University of Minnesota, a pioneering researcher in thanatology, the study of death.

Working with her dad to bring about the new elder care facility also made a lasting impression. This was an institutionalized solution to a systemic problem, which required sustained attention and different kinds of skills to bring to fruition. Barbara watched her father work hard on something he knew would outlast him.

When he died, Barbara told me, she inherited $400,000. "That was a lot of money at the time," she recalled. Over time, the responsibility of such resources weighed heavily on her.

"I like a very low profile. That's been very important to me. Again, because I never, you know, I never felt like I earned this money. I received it. And it was probably in my thirties that I finally confronted it and said, 'okay, I have been made the steward of these resources, what is the highest, best use I can make of them?'"

Deal with what's in front of you. Work hard. Collaborate strategically. Develop lasting solutions. That inherited modus operandi would become a habit for Barbara. When I interviewed her in 2015, Barbara was being treated for lymphoma, including chemotherapy. She credited several projects with keeping her focused and energized, which helped her fight through that difficult period.

For someone like Barbara, what's in front of her is vast. It includes people, near and far. Barbara has become an international leader in the advancement of hospice care, helping to set up numerous organizations in her own communities of Minnesota and New York State as well as other countries. Another early interest was international adoption, which along with hospice care was one of the topics Barbara studied while earning her doctorate in social work at Columbia University. Her first husband, Howard Kirschenbaum, and Barbara adopted a Korean child, who is now a pediatrician and works on international adoption, too.

What's in front of her also includes special places. One of Barbara's first big projects was to preserve two distinctive properties in the Adirondacks. Sagamore and Uncas were compounds built by William West Durant during the late 19th century in the architectural style that later became known as Adirondack great camps. Sagamore was owned by Alfred Vanderbilt and later Syracuse University and Uncas by J. P. Morgan, before both fell into disrepair.

Barbara and Howard rescued Sagamore from a bureaucratic process that was headed toward demolition. When Syracuse University decided to sell the property and New York State agreed to acquire it, the Forever Wild provision of the state constitution dictated that all the buildings be razed. By purchasing the property, Barbara and Howard averted that outcome. They spent years restoring the large, rustic camp and later did the same for Uncas. These achievements helped spur a broader pattern among other stewards of protecting the special historical quality and natural beauty of a number of Adirondack great camps. Over time Barbara helped transform Sagamore into a vibrant not-for-profit educational center, which now employs some 20 staff members and motivates hundreds of volunteers to chip in each year.

Decades later, Barbara restored two buildings in Saratoga Springs, in upstate New York where she and I live, including a hundred-year-old school building with 13,640 square feet. It now houses small nonprofit organizations who pay below market value rent, depending on their resources. This includes The Saratoga Springs Preservation Society, for example. In this capacity, Barbara serves as a talent scout running a nonprofit incubator. The other building is a chapel next door, where she herself works.

Barbara helped start the Open Space Project, which would become Saratoga PLAN (preserving land and nature) an organization that seeks to preserve the natural resources of Saratoga County. After Mt. MacGregor Correctional Facility closed in 2014, she told me, Barbara worked with Saratoga PLAN to help win a battle against developers over 750 acres of woods associated with the prison. Instead of being developed, the land was transferred to nearby Moreau State Park. Over the years Saratoga PLAN has successfully protected more than 5,000 acres of farmland, preserves, conservation easements, and has helped establish miles of green trails. It has secured millions of dollars of grants, conducted studies, held fundraisers, fostered educational programs and generally raised the consciousness in the region about natural resources. Saratoga PLAN is housed in the school Barbara restored, too.

Part of the formula for this success involves what Barbara calls "three-folding," which is pulling together key players from government, the private sector, and civil society. I was told by other folks in our community that Barbara has a knack for drawing well-positioned people together who are adversaries in public discourse and helping them figure out how to collaborate in private, which proved crucial in the conceptualization of the Green Belt Trail—a 24-mile figure-eight shaped pathway being developed in our community.

As I spoke with Barbara, I got tired just listening to her talk about all her work. There is so much. It goes on and on. I asked her what accounts for so many achievements. "Perseverance is a part of it." Underneath that trait, I figured, is a deep well of energy. "About every seven years," she revealed, "I get itchy." In addition to the activities mentioned above, she worked for many years with the Adirondack Council Board of Directors, Adirondack Nature Conservancy, and the Adirondack Land Trust. She recently rescued farmland from development and helped start the CSA it supports. When I interviewed her, her efforts focused on the Women's Global Giving Circle and the Nordlys Foundation. The former consists of some thirty women who gather four times a year to research and plan programs related to international development. The latter funds conservation, education, and community development projects (see *Saratogian* 2012; *Adirondack Daily Enterprise* 2021).

Barbara doesn't go solo. She finds and galvanizes the right people with the right skills. "I know what I don't know," she told me, "and I can procure what I need." This approach was evident when she worked with the farmer Michael Kilpatrick (who I mentioned in previous pages) and a number of other folks, to help start the Pitney Meadows Community Farm.

In this case, city and state government, the private sector, and donors all collaborated to make this 166-acre farm a community hub inside the boundaries of our city. I heard the Board President of Pitney give a presentation to our local school board (of which I am a member) in the winter of 2020. At that time, four years after it was started, he said, there were 100 families gardening in the community garden. Pitney gave away 6,000 pounds of fresh produce to food insecure families the previous year. Large amounts of fresh produce were also sold to our school district (which is subsidized through a special New York State grant).

This joint effort of government, the private sector, and nonprofit organizations is just the sort of creative multilayered collaboration Dr. Hans Kersten (also mentioned in a previous chapter) writes about in connection to food insecurity. In this case, the stewardship relates to the health of human bodies, the viability of soil through regenerative agriculture, and the vitality of community.

Barbara's knack for gathering people together and inspiring them to work hard seems closely related to her collaborative imperative, relentless diplomacy, and persistently low profile (see *Saratogian* 2012). She doesn't vilify adversaries and has resisted various attempts by local political players to link her organizational efforts to partisan politics, she explained to me. "I come from a family of moderate Republicans who did go across the aisle where you would disagree and then go out to dinner and I think that's been really important," she explained. She spoke about all the divisions in society and the need for civic spaces where different people meet, "where you get off your computer" and "you're out of your usual social circles." That is surely one of the most important aspects of farmers' markets in general and, Barbara recalled, why she helped start the one in our town.

However, her tact and neighborliness shouldn't be confused for any sort of aversion to conflict. Barbara has taken a number of stands on controversial issues against powerful actors, including a massively funded effort to add a major expansion to a local casino, and multiple attempts by developers who aspired to encroach on green space. Rather, the low-profile appears to be mostly pragmatic: staying out of the limelight is often strategically effective. I say "mostly" because it seems that something about Scandinavian and Midwestern sensibilities influence this orientation too. ("It was hard for me, sometimes hard for me to be public, hard for me to be the focus of negativity, but it was right at that time to do.") Needless to say, Barbara's conservationist ethic is not derived from any knee-jerk anti-business hubris or naïve tree-hugging delusions. She is proud of her financial acumen and protective of her financial and political independence.

Upon reflection, I realized "a well of energy that feeds the work" is the wrong way to think about it. Just as she sounded youthful as she proudly described her parents' values and accomplishments, her eyes sparkle as she explains her own. Many of us think of our work as sapping our energy. For Barbara, the work—on things that matter—generates the energy. This was true, as she noted, during illness (her father's and hers). Seeing other people—various collaborators, former adversaries, and especially "the next generation of leaders," including her daughter, and other young folks—get jazzed about shared goals does the same.

Barbara has a talent for identifying specific problems and then identifying lasting solutions, a hallmark of stewardship. Protecting large resources can reduce harm and create new opportunities. For instance, saving land from development has enabled more farming. Once the land is available, farmers can then focus on soil, seeds, and crops. In effect, stewardship facilitates grounding.

OWEN TAYLOR: WE HAVE A RIGHT TO CULTURALLY AFFIRMING FOOD

Another steward doing intriguing work is Owen Taylor, a white man who lives in Philadelphia. Like Barbara Glaser, he is interested in protecting a diverse range of valuable assets related to land and people. As I learned about what he does, I started thinking about *Horton Hears a Who!*. Philosophical questions loom large.

When I interviewed Owen on the phone I was in my office, and he was on a farm in Philadelphia. "I am carrying a couple ears of corn that somebody has pulled off the plant and started eating and thinking through how to solve this problem of pests in my corn," he noted as we were talking. Taking time to speak with a researcher is not easy when there are immediate, ongoing problems that need to be resolved on a daily basis—a challenge common to many with whom I spoke. I also noted that he referred to the critters doing the damage to the corn as "somebody," an ennobling characterization of an animal who might be thought of as a vexing enemy.

Having grown up gardening, he recalled to me, Owen had a particularly formative experience working on an organic farm at the age of 19 that stuck with him. During our conversation, he mentioned living in Virginia, Massachusetts, New York, California, and Pennsylvania. Along the way, he picked up an educational background in urban planning and environmental studies. For Owen, being a farmer necessarily ties into community gardening, education, food justice advocacy, and anti-racist activism, all of which have been part of his work for almost two decades.

He spent a large chunk of that time working with East New York Farms! in Brooklyn, NY. They are one of the best urban agriculture programs in the country, he told me. Their website says. "The mission of East New York Farms! is to organize youth and adults to address food justice in our community by promoting local sustainable agriculture and community-led economic development. East New York Farms! is a project of the United Community Centers in partnership with local residents."

Owen explained to me that food justice is about making sure everyone has regular access to healthy food—a seemingly straightforward idea. Food sovereignty encompasses a recognition that "people have to have a hand in the way they access their food," he said. He is especially interested in "culturally appropriate food" that honors the traditions, memories, and stories of a group of people. Certain culinary practices that use specific foods facilitate this connection. If you think about how many people rely on fast food, processed food, have limited access to good, fresh produce, or struggle to pay the bills, it becomes clear that food sovereignty is actually, sadly, a radical idea (see Penniman 2018; Minkoff-Zern 2019).

One of the most thorough statements I've seen about food sovereignty is the Youth Food Bill of Rights developed by an organization I previously mentioned called Rooted in Community. "We have a right," this manifesto claims, to "culturally affirming food . . . sustainable food . . . nutritional education . . . healthy food at school . . . genetic diversity and GMO-free food . . . poison-free food . . . beverages and foods that don't harm us . . . local food . . . fair food . . . good food subsidies . . . organic food and organic farmers . . . cultivate unused land . . . save our seed . . . an ozone layer . . . support our farmers through direct transactions . . . convenient food that is healthy . . . leadership education" (rootedincommunity.org).

Such issues are integral to much of Owen's stewardship. Nature and people are both paramount, as they are for many stewards like Barbara Glaser. He is also interested in preserving distinctive cultures tied to nature and people. In his case, the particular focal point of this three-sided conservation is seeds. Owen is a seed keeper.

He told me that for about seven years he had been actively involved with seed saving. But the story of his connection to a particular bunch of seeds goes back much further. In the 1920s a white man named H. Ralph Weaver began saving heirloom seeds. In an effort to preserve a large, diverse, distinctive set of seeds he carefully documented where they came from and preserved them. When he died unexpectedly in 1956 his grandson William Woys Weaver was nine. At that time, Weaver later remembered, no one paid any attention to the collection.

> As a teenager, I worked summers in West Chester, PA, and stayed with my grandmother. During one of her high-energy housecleaning forays we discovered—at the bottom of the big deep freezer in the cellar—hundreds of baby food jars meticulously labeled and filled with seeds. Those jars contained the core of my grandfather's seed collection. Each jar had a story, and my grandmother was quite amused by my persistence in writing down everything she could remember about each one (Weaver 2008).

Around 1979, William moved his grandfather's seeds to Devon, PA, and named it the Roughwood Seed Collection. It took five years, he has noted, to move the whole collection. By the 1990s, he had become very serious about seed saving. The collection has some 4,000 different kinds of seeds. Weaver had become a well-known gardener, food historian, and author. Fast forward another decade. Owen Taylor joined William Woys Weaver to help care for the collection. Over a four-year period, Owen learned the ropes around seed saving.

The process of preserving seeds can be tedious. One has to know the species, family, life cycle, and pollination method for each kind of seed and take various specific steps depending on all of that. Questions of harvesting, storage, maintenance, and documentation entail more tasks (see Atalan-Helicke, Schneller, Gonzalez, Lois, Alemayehu Mebrate, 2022). Owen told me that most farmers could save seeds if they wanted. But it requires a particular skill set and a ton of time and labor—all of which motivates a very few folks to fool with it. And all of which makes the survival of many kinds of seeds fairly precarious.

The core ethical conviction here is a recognition that very old strains of seeds that evolved through open-pollination, which are by definition not genetically modified, hold distinctive value that is created by long-term natural processes. That kind of lineage is regarded as having special integrity. The great variety of heirloom seeds are linked to particular plants, places, foods, and cultures.

In 2017, Owen founded his own company, Truelove Seeds, which is named after his great, great grandmother, Letitia Truelove (Beurteaux 2018). Owen works with about 20 small farms from which he gathers and processes seeds, and then sells about 80 varieties (Wagtendonk 2018). He knows his company is too small to be noticed by any Big Ag company selling proprietary seeds, but for him what the seeds contain is expansive. In each seed Owen identifies specific cultural heritage—a genetic memory of a particular plant, and a social memory of particular food eaten by a group of people. The seed is a thing, a noun, but it also has internal kinetic motion, a verb, associated with past and future work—the work of the seed growing into a plant, the work of farming, the work of cooking, the work of consuming, and the work of digesting, the work of managing waste.

Each seed is like an adventurous traveler poised to begin a long journey that she will intermittently share with many companions along the way. The converse is true, too. A long journey with lots of teamwork resulted in each seed. Different seeds, different journeys. "For all the farms I work with, the first thing I ask is, 'What is the story?'" Owen said. "Often, that's taken as an ancestral question" (Wagtendonk 2018).

He speaks of "rematriation," which means something like "returning to the mother." It gets used in connection to indigenous people returning to sacred roots and seed savers in particular. Owen learned the word from Roland White, a Mohawk seed saver who coordinates a national network of indigenous seedkeepers (Engel 2018). Seeds connect the present to the past and encompass possibilities for the future.

Following Ralph Weaver's and William Woys Weaver's practices, Owen documents specific stories linking seeds to people. He told me how customers enthusiastically seek out specific seeds so they can make particular foods from their home country or acquire foods their ancestors ate. His website shows vivid photos of a wide range of seeds such as Palestinian Kusa Squash, Paul Robeson Tomato, Lunga de Napoli Winter Squash, and Francois Syrian Molokhia, for example. He references people and plants associated with the African diaspora, Belarus, Bhutan, Burma, Ireland, the Iroquois, Italy, Jamaica, Mexico, the Palestinian West Bank, and Syria, among other contexts.

Owen is embedded in a vibrant community. Truelove Seed's website is full of compelling information and images. Lots of gorgeous seeds and exuberant people. Owen can be seen in many of the pictures surrounded by smiling people. For this vital community, as well as the virtual community of those who sell seeds to and buy seeds from Owen, there is enormous power in each seed. Owen speaks of the promise held in each seed for memory related to identity, nourishment, and love (Engel 2018). Echoing Horton, he imagines a world in each seed.

People with seeds and the wherewithal to make use of them control their own access to food. The intimate connection a person has with a seed, Owen believes, connects that individual to their people's past, the food system in which they live, and future generations. The intimacy facilitates reverence and agency. It motivates more preservation of seeds and enables control over one's food source.

I was made aware of Truelove Seeds by another farmer, Rose Cherneff (mentioned in chapter 4). Rose and Owen share a peculiar orientation. They are each invested in learning about and protecting their own cultural heritage. For Owen, that involves Irish and Italian ancestors. For Rose, it is about Jewish culture. I recently read about another seed saver named Victoria, who shares a similar concern; in her case, though, for Mexican culture (see Minkoff-Zern 2019, p. 149). The twist is that all three of these folks are interested not just in their own heritage but in other people's cultures, too. And they are committed to facilitating the explorations others might make in that regard.

Some cultural preservationists think in terms of zero-sum logic: *if I consider the richness of your culture, mine might be diminished.* In some sense, this has been a great problem of modernization in general: multiculturalism versus fundamentalism. Think of orthodoxies of any stripe. In contrast, Rose, Owen, and Victoria are positive-sum thinkers—like anthropologists who gain more understanding of their own cultures through the study of others. As culturally positive-sum seed savers, Owen and Victoria are each growing a collection of seeds that relates to both their respective traditions as well as cultural traditions that do not intersect with their personal biographies.

In a time when many decry the loss of meaning, the erosion of identity, and the encroachment on sacred traditions, here are people who do not see tension between preserving one's own culture and exploring that of others. Not only does your self-realization not undermine my self-realization, each might say, but both of us can learn from one another and be enriched in our respective journeys. Such cosmopolitanism doesn't water down loyalty to one's own culture, but somehow strengthens it.

It's such a small thing in terms of global issues, but it embodies hope and life itself and when I see communities finding ways to help keep their head up, literally to feed people who are in need of healthy food, and doing it in ways that lift people up and don't see them as deficits or part of the problem but rather part of the solution . . . to focus on the seed, give them another thing to teach self-sufficiency and cultural preservation and pride, and for me it feels like a great way to give back to a movement that I find fulfilling and hopeful. And it feels like a significant and tangible skill-set that people want, so that's why I spend so much time on it (Owen Taylor, interview with author, 2018).

There is something wonderfully pragmatic and idealistic about saving seeds. While Owen learned seed keeping from an expert, William Woys Weaver, he is self-taught as a businessperson. He wants the enterprise to be viable but remains committed to food security, education, and fairness to the growers. He said he pays growers more than most other seed companies. Fifty percent of the money for every seed that True Love Seed sells goes back to the farmer who grew it (Casey 2019). The website includes testimonials of farmers who make more money through working with Owen than they did previously.

Horton hears something from a speck of dust. Owen sees something in a small seed. In both cases, what is perceived is a meaningful world that matters to a group of people and warrants special care. In both cases, the group exuberantly affirms the discerning perception and finds lifegiving sustenance in the special care. In Owen's case, the many seeds hold diverse possibilities in which the expansive potential of nature and vast cultural creativity of humans are bound together.

CHRISTOPHER BOLDEN-NEWSOME: I GET TO WATCH THEM GROW UP AND SOAR

Through Owen, I met his husband Christopher Bolden-Newsome, who helps with Owen's work but is an engaged sustainer and steward in his own right. Chris is the co-farm director of Bartram's Garden in Philadelphia—a farm that purchases seeds from Truelove Seeds. John Bartram (1699–1777) built his estate on an eight-acre property in the Kingsessing neighborhood, three miles from Center City. He was a well-known Quaker, horticulturalist, botanist, and explorer. Today, Bartram's Garden is a 50-acre National Historic Landmark with some 20 employees. Chris's main work is devoted to Sankofa Community Farm, which its website reports is "firmly rooted at Bartram's Garden and in our Southwest Philadelphia neighborhood, with an African focus for our work, strong local leadership guiding our vision, and renewed resources and partnerships to sustain youth development, community health, and food sovereignty" (bartramsgarden.org).

The word Sankofa comes from the Akan culture in present day Ghana and refers to the need for memory, recovery, and restoration. Today in the United States it has become well known in popular culture through dance, film, song, and theater. Chris told me it means, "it is not taboo to go back and fetch what you forgot." As with rematriation, the process of remembering is important.

I got the feeling that this investment in memory is both about acknowledging and undoing harm, but also identifying and preserving beauty.

Chris told me he comes from a multigenerational black farming family in the South that never lost connection to the land. While growing up in Mississippi Delta, Texas, and Oklahoma, his family instilled in him a sense of confidence and ambition related to their being a "sovereign people." "Deep pride and recognition of just the awesomeness and vastness of what my people have created over 300 years of what was supposed to be a death sentence," are a source of exuberant reverence.

Early on in life, Chris was interested in other immigrant groups and ethnic communities. He adopted Spanish as a second language as a kid. He tried different things too—his first job was on "Black Wall Street" in Tulsa, Oklahoma, site of the 1921 massacre of Black Americans, Chris noted. Over time, though, the enduring connection between his African American roots and agrarian culture has remained central to his identity and work.

Such cultural stewardship is common among different groups in the United States. For example, Laura-Anne Minkoff-Zern's ethnographic study (2019) of Mexican immigrant farmers describes other people of color rooted in agrarian traditions in which the land is revered. They have faced extensive racism in the United States and experienced something like "double consciousness" (W. E. B. DuBois' famous term for being caught between two worlds). "As many immigrants explained," Minkoff-Zern says, "they farm in the United States in part to re-create a *recuerdo*, or memory of their former lifestyle in Mexico (2019, p. 104). Like rematriation and sankofa, recuerdo is about preserving the past so as to ground the present and future. "Without our traditions," Tevye (the main character in *Fiddler on The Roof*) said, "our lives would be as shaky as . . . as a fiddler on the roof!"

In each of these cases, vibrant community is regarded as a means to success, and a defining end in and of itself. Mexican immigrants who own farms tend to employ family members. Their operations are generally more labor-friendly and sustainable compared to how large industrial farms are run (Minkoff-Zern 2019).

Sankofa Community Farm lives up to its name. In addition to some two dozen paid employees, the farm "is powered by roughly 20 paid local high school interns." The website indicates that the farm "produces and distributes over 15,000 pounds of food each year, works with more than 50 local families in our community garden, manages weekly neighborhood farmstands and grocery partnerships to sell its produce affordably and locally, distributes over 80,000 vegetable transplants to over 130 farms and gardens around Philadelphia." Here, growing plants and growing community are inseparable processes.

In talking about Sankofa Community Farm, Chris is animated about the young people, who are called Bartram's Incredible Gardeners. A lot of them have been in foster homes, he tells me. Some are refugees. Chris said that the largest U.S. population of Liberians per capita lives in Southwest Philadelphia. Many of them have fled wars or been displaced for other reasons. So, the chance to join this nurturing community and mentoring program is attractive and can be transformative.

Kids have to be committed to be in the program. They are asked to work hard, learn new skills, and collaborate productively. Plus, "no phones are allowed," Chris explained, "and that's the rule. If they want to stay, then they abide by that." As with the volunteers at Share Philadelphia (discussed earlier), something special is happening, needless to say, when young people accept that countercultural restriction.

Chris told me a story of a particular young woman. Like many of the interns, she came from really tough personal conditions, but in her case genuinely "dire circumstances." An older adult associated with the farm, a retired teacher and "community sage," took the young woman under her wing, mentored her, encouraged her, and ended up helping her get a job during her senior year of high school and then gain admission to Cheyney University. Chris said this is not a unique story but a wonderful example of what happens on the farm. "When they fall," he said, "we pick them back up. We are here."

The program gains new interns mostly by the students in the program referring other kids, their friends and siblings. Chris said the adult leadership does not recruit. "We recognized that the young people will be the best judges of who they want to work with, and they never bring us any riff raff." There is a waiting list to join.

Videos of the Bartram's Incredible Gardeners show their exuberance (see Lodewick 2018). "When I first got here, it was unexplored territory for me," Tykia Jerry exclaims. "So it was like making discovery after discovery after discovery." They learn about agriculture, history, relationships, and leadership. "And it was exciting. It was really, really exciting! We are the future. We are the next community leaders." Sade Black points to some tall plants and says, "Those are mine. Me and another student planted those over the summer." She is grinning with pride. "I feel like I am their mom. I feel like a plant-mom. It's awesome. I get to watch them grow up." She makes a big waving motion with her arms. "And soar!"

There is a farmstand for three hours every week during the warm months. "Our goal is not to create wealth from this market," says Dr. Sylvia Briscoe, a community gardener and board member of Bartram's Garden. "Our goal is to create wellbeing in the members of the community. So, we're selling them organic, fresh-picked food" (see Lodewick 2018). Education is central to the mission of Sankofa Community Farm, both in terms of the students but also the community in general. People learn about where food comes from, different varieties of fruits and vegetables, and cultural traditions of agriculture.

While Sankofa Community Farm is focused on preserving African and African American culture, it is also guided by other cultural traditions, including the philosophical approach of the Shumei International Institute based in Japan. "Shumei is dedicated to contributing to the well-being of the world by cultivating spiritual values, the appreciation of art and beauty and the development of a way of life in harmony with nature," its website explains (shumei-international.org). Chris said that approach "is a variation of what our grandparents always did." Again, we see an investment in a particular cultural tradition situated near the exploration of others—just as we did with Owen Taylor and Rose Cherneff—and a recognition of the overlap.

CONCLUSION

Together, the people mentioned in this chapter show how expansive, idealistic, and pragmatic stewardship can be. Barbara protects land, communities, and human bodies. She restores buildings and reduces waste. Owen and Victoria save seeds, the distinctive dishes made from them, and foster human self-sufficiency. Both of them, as well as Chris and Rose conserve cultures and build relationships. All of them are engaged sustainers who get their hands dirty in grounding and extraction of one type or another. As stewards, though, they take care of these valuable materials—natural, human, and cultural resources—for the long run. Like seeds, they are vectors channeling accumulated energy and purpose from the past into new possibilities for the future.

This orientation is similar to what Juliet Schor calls "true wealth" or "plenitude" (2011; see also Anielski 2018). Such concern for broad stewardship, she argues, contradicts "business as usual (BAU)"—the economic practices maintained through U.S. policy and culture. BAU uses up finite resources, regards most things as disposable, and hides the real costs of doing business. Most importantly, BAU puts us at risk of "planetary ecocide." Plenitudinous stewardship, if you will, makes a bold claim that is both very idealistic and very practical: we will not die. By the way, that is ultimately what moral footprints are all about.

One of the most important developments in the alternative agro-food movement is the growing accord among those whose stewardship focuses initially on natural resources and those whose stewardship focuses initially on human resources. In the past, their predecessors were more likely to be antagonistic toward one another. What those folks, previously at odds with one another, shared was a stronger sense that humanity and nature are conceptually separate. To worry about one necessarily meant not paying as much attention to the other. As with many engaged sustainers, stewards now tend to think of that boundary as much more porous: humanity and nature are necessarily entangled. To worry about one requires worrying about the other.

Chapter Nine

Communication

As I introduced the cycle of engagement, I said most of the folks I interviewed are doers, people who handle material stuff and work with human bodies. They do things that make you sweaty. Most, but not all. This movement has another important element that does not directly involve anything physical: communication.

There are rich streams of academic research related to food in agricultural science, anthropology, cultural studies, economics, environmental studies, geoscience, history, management and business, medicine, nutrition, sociology, and other related fields. Scientific investigation, including the senior theses of Environmental Studies majors Elizabeth Forelle and Kailyn Wolfe of Skidmore College or Rose Cherneff of Carleton College, which I mentioned in previous chapters, and the vast body of more advanced research on relevant topics, is part of the communication regime in this movement. Such research provides an analytical evidentiary basis for the claims of the movement. Each drop of scientific findings flows into the river of cumulative knowledge. Of course, it's not a perfect system in which everyone knows the facts and thinks rationally. But it is a movement built on strong empirical foundations. Some of that insight is used by other scientists to build their research on. Some of it is consumed by policymakers. And some of it is distilled for lay people to understand the world in which they live.

That's where evocative words come into play. It is hard to think of a social issue in the 20th century that has been more affected by the use of language. Whether it is scientists, academics, food writers, farmers, cooks, journalists, novelists, or poets, those who write about food have made a difference. People like Mark Bittman, Anthony Bourdain, Rachel Carson, Julia Child, M. F. K. Fischer, Jonathan Gold, Barbara Kingsolver, Wes Jackson, Bill McKibben, Michael Moss, Scott and Helen Nearing, Marion Nestle, Raj Patel, Michael Pollan, Paul Roberts, Jerome Irving Rodale, Upton Sinclair, Andrew Weil, and Pete Wells working in various genres have commanded widespread attention.

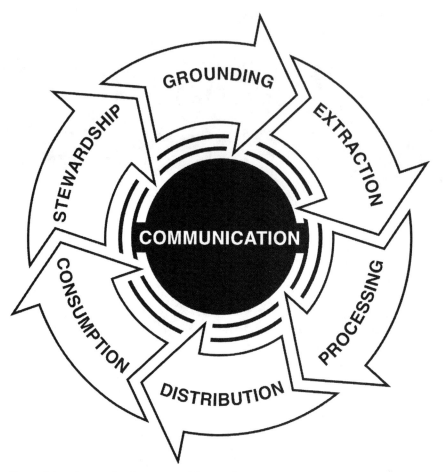

Figure 9.1.   Communication. Created by Martha MacGregor

One of the most iconic writers in this movement is Wendell Berry. My father, Walter Brueggemann, and Berry are friends. Once, when Dad asked Berry if he had seen a certain film, he told me, Berry answered "I don't do screens." That really struck me. Radical in its simplicity. He actually lays out the reasons in a characteristically spare, blunt, and persuasive essay called, "Why I am Not Going To Buy a Computer" (2010). To be honest, as a middle-aged professional with three teenaged children, a certain fidgety anxiety related to the need to get stuff done and have fun, as well as some understanding of how corrosive virtual life is, I find that response haunting.

"I don't do screens," Berry said. Maybe not, but screens do Berry. *Look and See: A Portrait of Wendell* Berry is a professionally crafted documentary about him. Dozens of interviews, talks, and lectures given by Berry are available on the internet. He may not look at screens but he communicates through them. Berry is a seasoned farmer, but the way he got famous, the reason there are so many images of him, is actually the written word. Dozens of poems, novels, essays, and other books contain a fulsome, loving portrayal of rural life and a lacerating critique of modern, industrial market culture.

Berry gets his hands dirty as a grounder and extractor. He is clearly a consumer and steward as well. He is well known for all those activities. Some go to see his farm and break bread with him, like my dad. However, his large cultural influence is really based on communication—his steadfast commitment to the written word, his willingness to use the spoken word, and his reluctant participation in images.

Berry has what Max Weber described as "charisma"—not in the sense of being the boisterous life of the party, but in embodying special, personal qualities that resonate in uniquely powerful ways in a particular historical moment. Such characteristics are by definition exceptionally rare. People like that often say haunting things. So, for an extraordinary person like Berry, he has the capacity to obscure how important the means and content of regular communication are. That is, we might imagine that only exceptional people with singular acuity or celebrity have an impact. However, I think that would be a mistake. Berry represents a conspicuous, vivid example of how words and images can be influential. But there are many other people whose communication contains elements similar to Berry's, whose messages matter, but whose reputations are not as high-profile.

HELEN DENNIS: WITH YOUR FOOD COME STORIES

One such uncelebrated (so far!) writer in this movement is Helen Dennis. "I want to talk about food, and I want to talk about local growing and selling the farmers are doing, and I want to talk about how we can cook locally," she told me. But that is only one side of the story, she said. "I think we need to tell a complete story about what our food systems are. And the fact is that right now we really don't serve a large portion of the population very well." Notice the emphasis on talk. Helen is passionate about food. She develops recipes and works on food insecurity. But she has decided the best way to pursue those interests is through communication. As I write, she is pursuing a master's degree in mass communication at the University of South Carolina, which is supported by a scholarship from the James Beard Foundation.

In explaining her interests, Helen told me about growing up in Georgia, including rural Monticello, urban Atlanta, and suburban Decatur. Her family is white. Both grandmothers were active in the kitchen. Regular family meals have always been part of her life. Helen's parents are each ordained Protestant clergy. Conversation is a family tradition. "We like to talk in my family. We're big talkers."

Having had two grandmothers who were always in the kitchen myself, having lived in Atlanta and Decatur, having two ordained parents, and coming from a family where people never seem to shut up, I have to say there is something familiar about Helen to me, even though I never met her until we spoke on the phone during the interview in 2018. It's not coincidental that our paths crossed because I met her through family connections. Her parents attended the seminary in Decatur where my father taught.

One thing that distinguishes her biography from mine is that she lived in a very small town, Monticello, where agricultural traditions were more vibrant than the suburban settings in which I grew up. Gardening was part of her experience. Farmers were part of her community. "We knew where our food was coming from," she said.[1]

In 2015, Helen graduated from Presbyterian College in South Carolina with a degree in English. One summer during college, she carried out a research project on American food literature. She told me that exposure to M. F. K. Fischer, Anthony Bourdain, and "a ton of other stuff" during that summer was pivotal. After college, she was interested in nutrition and seriously considered pursuing the culinary arts. Yet language called to her. "I loved the words and loved the way people talk about food."

Helen is alert to elemental things. "I mean, on a very basic level everybody eats. But it's more than that. With your food comes stories." She also noticed that in all of the food writing in literature, anthropology, history, and journalism, there wasn't much attention devoted to poverty and hunger. Like many other engaged sustainers (such as Chris Bolden-Newsome, Rose Cherneff, Hans Kersten, Jane Lippert, Anna Woofenden, and Steveanna Wynne), Helen talks about the connections between the beauty and joy of food, the hurt and scarcity related to poverty, and the expansive possibilities of neighborliness. One of the best ways to really grasp how all of that is interrelated, she said, is through stories—connections drawn through telling and showing. Helen explained to me:

> Behind every food we eat, every recipe we make, every meal cooked, there's a person. There's somebody who's provided that product. And when we don't treat our food as though it comes from another human, as though it is provided to us by somebody who is valuable, who deserves to be paid a living wage, who deserves benefits, who deserves to be healthy, who deserves not to be deported or be in fear of losing a job, when we take care of those people, we are able to better appreciate our food and better feed ourselves.

This concern has led to her work with several organizations in South Carolina, including Southern Foodways Alliance as well as End Child Hunger SC, which is located in the University of South Carolina's Center for Research in Nutrition and Health Disparities, where she helps with marketing and communications. Helen is also a regular contributor at *Edible Columbia* ("We tell the story of local food," its website explains) and *Edible Charleston*, digital and print publications in South Carolina associated with *Edible Communities, Inc.*

As with many engaged sustainers, there is something conservative, traditional, and nostalgic evident in Helen's work. In speaking with her and reading her words, I could easily see abiding respect for her family's traditions and her region's culture. Nods to different customs surface in her recipes (e.g., "Eggnog: A History as Rich as the Drink Itself"). She celebrates the agrarian heritage of the setting. "For nearly a century, the same family has tended the land at Keegan-Filion Farm in Walterboro, South Carolina, producing everything over the years from corn to peanuts, and beef to laying hens," begins one essay. In another, she quotes a central lesson of this movement from a local farmer, "know your farmer, know your food."

And as with many sustainers, though, there is also an aspect of Helen's work that is forward-looking, innovative, and fresh. She offers recipes for caprese frittatas, green tomato jam, and summer vegetable tarts. Part of her intent as a writer is to bring savvy messaging, both in terms of content and modes of communication, to this movement. She helps the organizations she works with use social media effectively. In her graduate program, she is learning about how to communicate with different audiences, such as consumers, businesses, or nonprofits. But she is eager to draw connections between different audiences, too. She participated in the Food Access Summit in 2017, which brought together a number of organizations working on food insecurity in South Carolina, including different players who had been working on related issues in proximity to one another without being aware of it.

Communicators like Helen play a potentially pivotal role with consumers. More than ever, we look online for ideas and guidance related to our eating choices. Helen is becoming what some researchers call a "cultural intermediary" participating in a "mobile trust regime" (Smith Maguire, Ocejo, and DeSoucey 2022). As I pointed out in chapter 7 on consumption, figuring out how to "trust" the food we eat is an issue for every consumer. Smith Maguire et al. describe three kinds of mechanisms that help foster trust. Confidence in certain foods has historically come from (1) particular local cultures or (2) bureaucratic institutional authorities.

A relatively new kind of mechanism is (3) the mobile trust regime. Following Smith Maguire et al., I pointed out in chapter 7 that different groups of people form taste communities. They draw information from a vast range of global choices and help one another establish priorities in making food choices. Maguire et al. also suggest that such prioritizing is aided by "cultural intermediaries," which are similar to what some people call influencers. Those intermediaries provide "quasi-personal reassurances" about quality, taste, moral standards, and of course, authenticity. This is like what Mario Batalli did for Italian cuisine, Robert Parker for red wine, and Guy Fieri for pub food. It's not just about global brands, though, and it's not just information flowing down from some guru.

Smith Maguire et al. talk about how locally produced and globally available materials are shared in taste communities and filtered by well-positioned cultural intermediaries. I think it might work in the following way. Say Helen Dennis shares information about locally produced South Carolina culinary traditions to a broader world (including people who do not live in South Carolina), she is informed by some producers (e.g., farmers in South Carolina) and consumers (e.g., people who live there and elsewhere and like her recipes derived from South Carolina traditions). Helen learns about what the taste community likes, but also guides the community in its tastes. Over time, her reputation and the community around her both grow and this mobile trust regime becomes a thing. One can imagine networked consumers who come to know one another, perhaps as social media personas or in more personal ways, all of whom think of Helen as a crucial source of information, and South Carolina cuisine as distinctively appealing.

I recognize this might sound a little convoluted. It is in fact complicated. The point is that key communicators help share information about local sources of food to broader audiences, mediate what the audiences feel about the information, which may well have a significant impact on modern consumption patterns. And, in Helen's case, it is part of what she has been doing in South Carolina through her partnerships.

An element of Helen's effectiveness in facilitating trust is communicating through stories. More generally, stories animate a lot of the effective communication in this movement. My impression is that this explicit concern with sophisticated communication is a growing part of the movement. There are others, like Helen, who realize that drawing the connections in the cycle of engagement—though that's not how they would describe it—is crucially important. They specialize not in agriculture or the culinary arts, but in communication per se.

For instance, I heard a presentation given by Mary Godnick at the 2022 Food Justice Summit sponsored by the Adirondack Health Institute. Mary works for Adirondack Harvest, which is a nonprofit organization associated with the Cornell Cooperative Extension of Essex County, NY. She is an avid gardener, but her educational background is in public relations, and she is the Digital Editor and Communication Coordinator for Adirondack Harvest. In the presentation I heard, she talked about solving communications problems for farmers who are competing against Big Food and Big Ag, especially in terms of relentless corporate advertising. Like Helen, Mary is an active David with a plan to confront the seemingly unbeatable Goliath of modern mass marketing.[2] As in Helen's work, stories anchored in regional collaboration feature prominently in Mary's strategic approach. My hunch is that the kind of work in which Helen and Mary specialize, communications about regional food systems, is becoming a vocation of sorts. If so, their efforts are crucial to this movement.

NANCY FERGUSON: WHAT WILL YOU GIVE? WHAT WILL YOU GET?

There are countless communicators who make a difference as teachers. They provide informed and insightful guidance in the kitchen, in the pulpit, in the examining room, on the internet, on the farm, and of course in the class-room. This includes most of the writers mentioned at the beginning of this chapter. It also includes a number of engaged sustainers I interviewed like Chris Bolden-Newsome, Michael Kilpatrick, Rose Cherneff, Marti Wolfson, Hans Kersten, and Barbara Glaser, all subjects introduced above who think of themselves as teachers.

One of the most remarkable teachers I have ever met, at any level, is known to hardly anyone outside my family's school district. Inside it, though, Nancy Ferguson is a star. She taught my three kids second grade, led each of them on a four-day camping trip when they were fifth graders, and did the same for hundreds of other kids over many years in education. During much of that time, her sister and husband prepared the food for all the kids and chaperones at camp. At least as important, Nancy taught numerous parents about rais-ing children. She has a special gift for discerning who a child is, persuading that child (and the child's parents) that she sees him clearly and that he has value. I interviewed Nancy early on in this project when I was broadly ori-ented toward anyone doing "good work," before the emphasis on food came into focus.

During the camping trips, for which my wife and I each served as chaperones at different times, Nancy revealed herself to be a world-class team-builder. She helps the kids understand and value one another. "I'm a people person," she told me. "That's who I am. I like to talk. I like to listen to people. I like to make people comfortable in an uncomfortable situation." Nancy also knows intuitively what is important about nature and how to help young people grasp it. "Education is all around," she said, "it's not just in your classroom." She does not overtly identify with the sustainable food movement per se, but she has been a leader in our school district related to recycling, serves on the board of directors of a wildlife preserve, has always been involved in the food preparation at the camp, shows the kids how to cook on a campfire, and actively teaches children to value the earth. Rather than being a self-identified participant in the alternative agro-food movement, an engaged sustainer, I would say Nancy is a *latent sustainer.*

What makes her special as a communicator is the ability to help people see connections. The apparent purpose of the fifth grade camping trip is an educational experience with nature. For all the kids, but especially the many who have never spent more than a few hours outside at a time, and had no exposure to camping, hiking, or canoeing, this is a precious gift. An equally important goal is self-esteem and team building. "What will you give? What will you get?" Nancy asked the group each day. One key is that whenever she posed these questions Nancy made sure she had the undivided attention of all 70 kids—a rather impressive feat of communication itself. In a calm moment right before dinner, or late at night while we watched the moon shining on the lake, she would settle the group down, helping everyone appreciate the wonder of quiet, natural sounds. And then she would speak.

"What will you give?" Sometimes she paused in between the two questions. "What will you get?" As if they were each important questions worthy of reflection. Sometimes she didn't pause and asked both questions quickly. As if they were necessarily linked. What I think we all heard was a sense that the world needs something from each of us and that it also has something to give each of us. Over several days of hearing this mantra I found myself pondering generosity, fairness, the Golden Rule, neighborliness, citizenship, patriotism, sacrifice, and other ways that covenant can be woven into our lives. I know the kids saw concrete connections, like between getting dessert and taking a turn cleaning up, but I think they were breathing in the deeper messages, too. The acts of getting and giving feed each other; they are inter-causally related. Nancy frequently extolled the beauty around us and the basis for gratitude. Such reciprocal relations between people, between humans and nature, between resources and labor, are foundational to the alternative agro-food movement.

I saw in Nancy's work what I've seen in other first-rate communicators': explicit, repeated *assertion* of the desired message along with implicit, repeated *demonstration* of the point. She told the kids and showed the kids how the connections work. She didn't just continuously ask about what they would give and receive, she repeatedly gave and received in voluble ways.

I offer all this background about Nancy for several reasons. First, I think she herself embodies a striking combination of excellence and humanity. She is good at what she does and a good person. When Nancy speaks (about anything, as far as I can tell), it is worth listening. That this movement has people like Nancy, latent sustainers, contributing in relevant and productive ways nearby is part of the cumulative effectiveness of the overall effort. Indeed, the latent aspect, the soft touch, may be a distinctly effective means of spreading a certain message. For the purpose of this chapter, though, she exemplifies crucial elements of other communicators: drawing connections by way of telling and showing.

I recently read a terrific memoir from another teacher who works in a very different kind of setting but shares some qualities with Nancy. Stephen Ritz tells his story of teaching in a Bronx high school burdened by high rates of crime and low rates of graduation. It was in his effort to reach his students that he discovered the power of gardening. He developed innovative, impactful teaching methods that center around growing fruits and vegetables. Devotion, creativity, loyalty, *and* close contact with the earth proved decisive. His book (written with Suzie Boss), *The Power of the Plant: A Teacher's Odyssey to Grow Healthy Minds and Schools* (2017) chronicles the rippling effects of his work as a teacher, as he matures from a self-described screw-up, develops neighborhood gardens, heals the soil therein, grows plants with his students, and is transformed by the experience. As an engaged sustainer, Ritz is a communicator par excellence who shows his students, community members, other educators, and policy makers what is possible through "green teaching." "You're showing us how little things are connected to way bigger things and how all of this connects to school," one student exclaims (p. 56).

Dreams for a brighter future are cultivated "one classroom at a time," Ritz says (p. 52). Over time the harvests, literal and metaphorical, have multiplied. The work of Ritz, his students and colleagues, has grown into a larger endeavor, The Green Bronx Machine, which is a multifaceted educational program that involves some 50,000 students across 20 U.S. states every day. Its website declares that "85,000 pounds of vegetables later, our favorite crops include healthy students, high performing schools, graduates, registered voters, living wage jobs and members of the middle class. Our work, vision and mission are as organic and locally grown as it gets—straight from our classroom to our community."

Like Ritz, the engaged sustainers with whom I spoke, who are communicators, all draw connections, and see their work as part of the movement. Those who work in nonprofit and for-profit organizations, even when information is not central to their mission, as it is for Ritz, spend a lot of energy on communication. Many farmers, almost all I interviewed, regard educating the public about what they do as crucial to their long-term commercial success as well as their moral efficacy. The ones who are most ambitious about sustainability believe informed consumers are a key to the movement. More than ever, attention is a prized currency.

Connections in broad organizational networks help with this communication and education, too. Iconic institutions like the Rodale Institute and Polyface Farms loom large both as organizational hubs in the movement and as symbolic guideposts. Several of the people I came across identified those establishments as important influences.

As previously noted, there are tons of other such organizations doing related work that are less well known, including a number with which I had contact. The Glynwood Center for Regional Food and Farming is "a nonprofit organization serving food and farming changemakers from New York's Hudson Valley and beyond." Roxbury Agricultural Institute associated with Philia Farm and Roxbury Farm, both in upstate New York, "is dedicated to sharing information with fellow farmers" and "creating a better food system." CISA (Community Involved in Sustaining Agriculture) of the Pioneer Valley in Massachusetts seeks to strengthen farms and build the local food economy in that region. Singing Frog Farms is an award-winning regenerative farming operation in Sebastopol, California, that many other farmers look to for learning agricultural and commercial methods. Hickory Nut Gap Farm in Fairview, North Carolina, is a cattle farm that draws a great deal of attention too—from other farmers, but also restaurants and distributors. The Maine Organic Farmers and Gardeners Association, the Northeast Organic Farming Association–New York, the Northeast Organic Farming Association—Vermont, and the National Young Farmers Coalition are all networks for farmers helping one another, promoting regenerative farming, and maintaining educational-communication systems.

Each of these organizations does what Nancy and Ritz do: they draw connections by telling and showing. They have personnel working with materials doing things that "make you sweaty" but also folks who traffic almost exclusively in words (written or spoken), images, and sounds. After learning about some famous people and a bunch of unsung engaged sustainers who communicate about food, I started to see a pattern. Writing and teaching about relational narratives connected to food are central to the communications of this movement.

ANNA WOOFENDEN: IT'S ALL CHURCH

Among engaged communicators I noticed another thing, an unexpected theme, which I first heard about when I spoke to Anna Woofenden. Once you start thinking about food, it's hard not to get drawn into conversations about a range of issues like family, economics, politics, community, identity, justice, and religion (see Counihan, Van Esterik, Julier 2019). Anna Woofenden knew years ago that her vocation would involve food. The connections were everywhere. This includes links to her first calling, Christian ministry, which she heard even earlier. What took her some time was figuring out how these two elemental concerns—the nourishing of souls and bodies—would be melded. One gets the sense while talking to Anna that she feels pulled in several different directions and works hard to keep her equilibrium. She is a calm, attentive, empathic listener but I suspect often has many ideas tugging inside her head, eager to get out into the world. (I learned later I was exactly right!) She invokes reverence for certain expressions of faith, texts, rituals, relationships, and memories that make her feel grounded. "I fell in love with the church," she told me. But she is perceptive and a little restless in seeing the limitations of the past. Critique of those problems, innovation, and experimentation do not frighten her. This includes confronting, or at least resisting, the patriarchy, exclusiveness, and material comforts of the Christian church establishment.

With these sensibilities, Anna started a radical ministry using ancient practices in new ways at The Garden Church in San Pedro, CA. For Anna and many of her parishioners, the sharing of food is a deeply meaningful, sacramental experience, and part of "reimagining church."

She told me she was "raised semi-unchurched or anti-church" and then "rebelled in school by going to the local evangelical youth group." (How many kids rebel by moving toward authority?) After that, she became interested in the religious tradition of her grandparents and great grandparents who were members of the Swedenborgian church. She moved from the San Juan Islands in Washington State to attend Bryn Athyn College near Philadelphia, which is affiliated with The New Church (or Swedenborgianism).

As she spoke about her family's heritage, I felt her sense of gratitude, pride and even piety. She takes her own commitment as an adherent in that denomination very seriously. As I suspect of most readers of these words, I had not heard of this sect. This tradition follows the teaching of a 17th century Lutheran Swede named Emanuel Swedenborg. There are about 1,800 members of the Swedenborgian Church in North America. But they claim some rather illustrious "famous Swedenborgians," including Andrew Carnegie, Hellen Keller, Ralph Waldo Emerson, William Blake, and, most fittingly for the purposes of this chapter, John Chapman, AKA Johnny Appleseed! (swedenborg.org).

Anna worked for years in various congregational and denominational positions, all in the more conservative branch of the Swedenborgian church, she told me, which does not allow the ordination of women. During that period, her theological inquiry and her frustration with the church's chauvinistic restrictions both grew deeper. By the time she "heard the call" to attend seminary, Anna had gained significant experience in pastoral work but felt exasperated that she couldn't serve communion because she wasn't ordained and, in that particular branch of the church, was not allowed to become ordained.

This led her to attend first Earlham School of Religion (which is on the same campus as Earlham College, the Quaker school Hans Kersten and I attended, by the way) and then The Center for Swedenborgian Studies at the Berkeley Graduate Theological Union—an institution associated with the more liberal branch of Swedenborgianism (which does support the ordination of women).

Just as she was finding her theological bearings in seminary, Anna was pulled toward another important guidepost that would direct her life. She completed an internship in Washington, DC, at Bread for the World. "Bread for the World is a collective Christian voice urging our nation's decision makers to end hunger at home and abroad," its website declares. "Moved by God's grace in Jesus Christ, we advocate for a world without hunger."

"Part of the puzzle that I want to be a part of was local and on the ground, and connected to sacrament," she explained to me. "Part of my own 'call narrative' was very connected to not being able to serve communion and knowing the power of it."

As interests became passions and then convictions, Anna had an epiphany of sorts. "I call it a vision, carefully, but it was kind of in that waking/sleeping state where I said 'maybe we should have a church in a grocery store' to really bring these two things together. To understand that sacrament is not something that happens in a particular, curated sacred space . . . to bring sacrament into our daily life, in a different way." The extraordinary could be located in the ordinary, the sacred in the profane.

When Anna and I first sat down together, she talked about how Communion has been used at different times in history for exclusion or for inclusion. She reflected on her own exclusion from administering the sacrament even while serving in pastoral leadership roles. She also spoke of the ways churches are segregated by race and class. In her thinking, the issue of such religious division overlaps with concerns about social division in general and unequal access to food in particular. There are many churches, she pointed out, that run food pantries on Friday and hold worship on Sunday, two separate activities—feeding and sacrament—thought of as different aspects of the church serving separate constituencies, but all in the same space.

The apparent rift between these two elemental attachments frustrates her. And, conversely, Anna is interested in how food and sacrament do go together and, relatedly, how religious inclusion relates to cross-class and cross-race connection, sharing, and community. The abstract could be converted to material—and vice versa.

It was in speaking with Anna that I first realized how robust the ties between food and religion are. Of course, this is old and familiar to many. Think of the apple from the Tree of Life, manna from heaven, the bread and the cup, fasting during Ramadan, or observed restrictions on pork, beef, fish, and so on. All great religions emphasize food in their sacred texts and integrate it intimately into important rituals. In these connections, people of faith give thanks to God for creation and sustenance and try to remember who they are by way of cultural markers involving food.

Anna was especially influenced by the teaching of Sara Miles, who is something of a guru in the part of the Christian church that concerns itself with food. *Take This Bread* is a memoir Miles wrote about opening up the doors, pantry, and kitchen of the church, literally, and opening up her own heart to the church, Jesus, and his teachings. This and other books by Miles, according to Anna, influenced her thinking about what is possible.

Wherever you see hunger, you will find religious people trying to ameliorate it. Many religious organizations endeavor to serve the vulnerable. But their efforts so often fall short. Modern poverty is in some sense unnecessary poverty. We put a person on the moon and split an atom. And we have the capacity to generate more calories than our species needs. Yet, there is still poverty—and hunger. Even in the richest country in human history.

Abundant resources in proximity to poverty, the speed and busyness of modern life, the vast menu of religious options, the decline of moral authority, and the mobility of people who change residences for various reasons, are all part of the context for "reimagining church," for rethinking "food as sacrament."

After encountering Sara Miles at the Food Pantry of St. Gregory of Nyssa Episcopal Church in San Francisco, completing seminary, and becoming ordained, the Reverend Anna Woofenden founded the Garden Church in a neighborhood in Los Angeles named San Pedro. On Sunday afternoons, "we work for an hour in the garden," she told me, "then worship starts at 4:00. And it's pretty standard: reading, prayers, community response, Peace and Communion. And we move from our 'sacred meal' to our shared 'community meal.' I don't call *that* church. It's *all* church. We have a meal and then we come back for a closing prayer." Every week, they garden, they worship, they eat together. It's a more spiritual version of the wisdom of Steveanna Wynne from Philadelphia Share who said, "eat good, do good, feel good."

Starting in 2014 Anna led this church for three years. During most of her time there, in addition to her, the church employed a director of community relations and programing, a part-time farm manager, and had some 20 regular volunteers, as well as folks who helped out now and then. The "church" is outside on a piece of leased land between brick buildings in an urban setting, which was bare and shabby when it opened. Now there is an altar, a garden, wooden picnic tables and benches, a portapotty, folding chairs and tables when needed, flowerpots, sculptures and paintings, handmade welcoming signs, and portable heaters. However, images posted online suggest that the space changes a lot, from season to season, of course, but also for art projects, concerts, large gatherings, some in the daytime, some at night. The images suggest fluid but fulsome community. To hear Anna talk about the church or see its fancy website (with lots of images, blog posts, sermons, events, and other information) one can imagine exuberant activities: working, playing, worshiping, eating, talking, singing, learning, and laughing.

When I spoke to Anna in spring of 2017, she reported that the church was producing 45 different crops, and generating some 100 pounds of produce a month—"which is not as good as we could be doing." "We are shifting around our crop management. We are working on it." An average of 36 people were coming each week at that time. Some to work and worship, some just to eat, and some for all of it. There was a core of about 20 and often twice that who came for the meals. The beliefs among those folks, Anna explained, are eclectic, including many committed to religious practice as well as quite a few simply concerned with food, justice, community, or just their own survival.

Beyond the innovative joining of gardening and church, what seems to make this place special is its relational culture. Anna speaks of relationships as "permeable." All are welcome, whether you are more interested in food or worship. Whether you are a Christian or Buddhist or both—or for that matter, an atheist—housed or homeless, drunk or sober, all are welcome. According to Anna, the ethos of the Garden Church revolves around an invitation. Not exactly "if you build it they will come," she said, but close. If we work, grow, offer, serve, share, thank . . . they will come.

The guiding sense of permeability resists clear categorization of parishioners vs. visitors, providers vs. recipients, stable vs. vulnerable, rich vs. poor, and so on. I was reminded of the words of Rose Cherneff from Abundance Farm: "we're really trying to move away from this idea of 'some people are giving, and some are receiving.' . . . I have needs that I need to get from my community and have things that I can give and . . . every person who walks into the farm is giving and receiving." And again, those of Steveanna Wynne: "everyone has a gift."

As much as The Garden Church does, as expansive and flexible as it is, there is some clarity about what it is not: a food bank. "We need to be very clear that we are not a feeding program and not a homeless agency. One of the things we believe is that the best we can give is surrounding our unhoused neighbors with nice, church people and we have found that this has power. About a third of our congregation are unhoused. So, to be a place where the baseline of belonging is that you're a human being, and because of that you have value." They don't just give out food. But all are welcome. And the lives of poor people and affluent people in the neighborhood are a little better because the Garden Church is there.

As in many American communities, this setting has changed a lot over time, and grapples with a number of familiar urban challenges. It is ethnically diverse, including Italian and Croatian families who have been there for decades, and Latino families more recently arrived, African Americans, both established and newly arrived, and others. "It's very mixed," Anna said. Many are employed in the port. Union vs. anti-union tensions simmer. Same with other issues, including homelessness. She explains that quite a few "remember a time when their town was ideal in their mind."

I asked her about all the pressures she navigates while trying to grow momentum in this church. "It's totally messy and I'm a control freak. I had to let go of a lot. Doing a liturgy outdoors. Doing liturgy in a really mixed, really mixed kind of crowd. It's hard. It takes both a letting go and a deep determination."

Can you imagine trying to meditate or pray or speak quietly on a busy city street? "The motorcycle man goes by, and it's so loud, and you acknowledge it. But you keep holding that space." Sometimes, the distractions require a pointed response. "There were two teenage girls, I think actively high, and were maniacally giggling during Communion, and they were actively disruptive." As Anna was in the middle of Communion prayers, she stared directly at them, "the way that a mother says 'I love you, and this is what we are doing. I'm acknowledging you in this place, and I'm not admonishing you, but this is what is happening.'"

On the other hand, sometimes the distraction matters more than what you're doing in the first place. Anna told me about a time Sara Miles came to The Garden Church to participate in worship. "She is preaching about the power of breaking bread together and sharing as this mentally ill, half-dressed, potentially currently drunk man comes in the front gate." A colleague, Connie, leapt up to welcome him, brought him to a table and offered coffee, right near Sara. "In a traditional setting, it would have been like the Easter play. We were literally watching these two sermons, and we are watching Connie do this. These things happen all the time. It was just particularly beautiful how these two things physically connected. It happens all the time. And that changes the community. It's not 'let me tell you a nice story.' People are living it. The work, the church gospel, the transformation, is there."

The Garden Church is a special *space* that matters to Anna. In her work, though, I also witnessed a subtle consideration of *time*. The kind of curiosity about historical roots that drew Anna to her grandparents' religious tradition reflects a broader concern for ancient lessons. Not that she is in any way captive to fossilized relics of past dogmas. She cares about building things for the future too. I think she is thoughtful about developing institutional and cultural arrangements that last.

That is a major theme in her recently published memoir, *This is God's Table: Finding Church beyond The Walls*—a wonderful account of The Garden Church much richer than the brief narrative I am sharing here. As much as she studies the past and plans for the future, though, I was also struck by Anna's talent for being in the present. Right now, in this blessed moment. How else do you worship in a bustling city? How else could you notice that the disturbance on the edge is more important than the intended task in the center?

After Anna left The Garden Church to be closer to her new husband, the pastoral team there added three new clergy, including the Reverend Amanda Riley. In one of her first sermons, Amanda said, "We are doing old things in new ways. We are growing food that no one owns." I keep thinking about that phrase—food that no one owns. It feels like a radical promise as well as a powerful metaphor for other gifts—space that no one owns, time that no one owns, community that no one owns, love that no one owns.

CONCLUSION

In the winter of 2022, I attended a conference in honor of my mom's twin brother, Patrick Dwight Miller, Jr., a distinguished Old Testament Biblical scholar who had recently passed away. "Poems for a Dangerous Time: A Gathering around the Psalms," as it was titled, entailed a stunning set of enriching presentations and conversations. One of the keynote speakers was a Presbyterian minister named Aisha Brooks Johnson. She explained the concept of Sankofa: there is special value in remembering who you are in the face of the forces of cultural amnesia. You'll recall that that is both the name of the community farm in the city of Philadelphia led by Chris Bolden-Newsome and its guiding principle. Johnson then asked the audience: "What are the new songs needed in your life, in your family, community, church, the world?"

It occurred to me upon reflection that what I first learned from Anna Woofenden became visible in many of communicators' stories, including those of Helen Dennis and Nancy Ferguson, and actually in the work of other non-communicator engaged sustainers as well: wonder. Wonderful stories that involve memory and innovation feature prominently here. Recollecting where they have come from while also imaging new possibilities for the future is central to the stories of engaged sustainers.

For Jamie Ager, the story is in the land, in a place that has special meaning to his family. Owen Taylor nurtures numerous precious stories in seeds. Rose Cherneff aspires to be fluent in communicating the stories of plants. Leah

Penniman is invested in the stories of Black, indigenous, and other farmers of color. Hans Kersten, the pediatrician who works on food insecurity, tells stories of little kids who get healthy, partly by eating more fresh produce. Helen Dennis celebrates the stories of southern people who grow and prepare food.

This is grown-up hopefulness. It's known through stories about people who have struggled. It's forged through the vicissitudes that farmers face in fluctuating weather and market patterns, and the vulnerabilities that those who are hungry, sick, or poor know all too well. The experienced sense of triumph is the recognition that, in spite of all those risks and challenges, we must celebrate the meal in front of us and how it is intertwined with profound, mysterious beauty.

I realize this portrayal might sound rather rosy. I don't mean to portray one big happy family. Stepping morally can be pretty complicated. There are plenty of divergent priorities, competitive pressures, and unresolved disputes within this movement. Vegans argue amongst themselves about what is ok, much less with omnivores, and are likewise criticized by other vegetarians. Some farmers are certainly devoted to certain agricultural techniques over others. Many people know their livelihood is wrapped up in beating out neighbors for business. I heard more than one subject suggest that most vendors at my local farmers' markets are Republicans and most customers are Democrats. The tribalist political divide spreading across the nation is relevant in and around this movement, for sure. Plus, it's quite possible that in participating in an interview with a social scientist like me, any given subject might be inclined to put on an extra happy face and describe their relations with others in more harmonious terms than is warranted.

Still, when I think about the anxiety, tension, and strife that permeates our society today, I found the tolerance, flexibility, and unity among all these different folks to be striking. For example, several organic or no-till farmers overtly resisted judgment of others who farm in conventional ways. At different times, vegetarians and meat-eaters acknowledged different consumption patterns among one another without any scorn. Various subjects expressed specific theological convictions and at the same time ecumenical tolerance for others' views. Twice when I pointed out to different gay farmers that they didn't fit the stereotype of an American farmer and then asked them if they had encountered homophobic discrimination in the movement, they reported that they hadn't.

Religiosity, political party, personal tastes, or ideological purity seem to have little bearing on the collaborative spirit. Results matter more than purity. Several farmers I met at the Northeastern Organic Farmers Association–New York are explicitly eager to collaborate with conventional farmers whenever possible.

In short, my interactions with communicators suggest to me that the sustainable food movement includes (1) a diverse group of individuals; (2) a significant degree of unity; and (3) some baseline level of awareness that dominant culture is at odds with what they are doing. In general, gifted communicators like these folks help the rest of us—who don't see as clearly—make the connections among seemingly separate aspects of the world.

Different modes of communication are part of this work. There is a lot of modern scientific analysis at the core of this movement. Farmers and cooks of previous eras were using something like the scientific method before what we know of as "science" even existed—systemic trial, error, and resulting lessons. Oral traditions first allowed the knowledge to be shared and are still important in some contexts. Such insights and traditions are passed on in various narratives.

Engaged sustainers share stories. They show and tell what is important in the stories, often highlighting the value of giving and receiving, relational culture, productive collaboration, and wonder. All of these elements have proven to be fruitful components of the communication regime in this movement.

NOTES

1. Some research suggests that rural consumers are more likely to get produce from farmers they know, which actually makes it harder to run a farmers' market (Hultine et al. 2007). That might be another reason farmers' markets are clustered in population centers.

2. The influence of corporate marketing of food has been well established. See Schor (2004), Brownell and Horgen (2004), and Chernin (2008).

Chapter Ten

Patterns Among
Engaged Sustainers

WHAT THEY HAVE IN COMMON

As I encountered people engaged in generative activities, some explicitly invested in the alternative agro-food movement, others making valuable contributions to it without thinking in those terms, I started to search for patterns. I was especially interested in people who convert ideas into action, beliefs into behavior.

As I've noted, finding such purposeful doers is what drew me into the sustainable food movement in the first place. As a group, engaged sustainers are very diverse, as illustrated in previous chapters. (See also the Appendix A: Methods and Data and Appendix B: Central Cast of Characters.) They are different in terms of activity, identity, biography, race, gender, sexuality, age, education, class, politics, religion, and geography. They vary in terms of how explicit and purposeful their commitment to "the movement" is, too.

However, I also observed a robust pattern of similarities among engaged sustainers. In this chapter I summarize some of the most important ones. The focus here is on behaviors and sensibilities of engaged sustainers per se. This is not about people who do things that help this movement but do not overtly claim the movement, what I have termed *latent sustainers*. Nor is it about social movement activists involved in adjacent social movements (e.g., children's rights, non-food related labor organizing). This is about the central participants in this movement. Not that every engaged sustainer I interacted with reflects every one of these patterns equally. As I spoke to folks, though, a critical mass of them revealed each of the qualities listed here in real ways.

1. Expansively neighborly

I recently reflected on the parallels between Mount Everest and Black Friday. What that place and that time share in common is a kind of activity on the part of otherwise normal people who ignore the well-being of other human beings. Those attempting to summit the highest peak in the world have been known to walk right by others in distress. Those attempting to get the best deal the day after Thanksgiving have been known to be physically aggressive. The consequences for those in trouble on Mount Everest are surely more intense and lasting. The effects of Black Friday, and the growing number of days that resemble it, are more widespread and subtle. The day after we collectively give thanks, something crazy happens that corrodes the idea of neighbors. In both cases, a singular goal erases basic human decency.

Engaged sustainers don't behave this way. They care. They have an expansive sense of neighborliness. This is true in the sense of who one's neighbor is. It could be the family living next door, the person who eats food they produce, or anyone who breathes the same air or drinks the same water. It might even be people who come around long after they are dead.

And it is true in terms of what they might do for neighbors. Sustainers may help them learn about a new technology, sacrifice a bit of profit to sell them something with more quality, pay them more than they have to, or think about their long-term well-being. In general, sustainers are not grasping, detached, selfish, or tribal. They understand community in broad, layered terms. Keri Latiolais of Roxbury Farm said, "We all have these external communities that have shaped how we farm, or participate in a farm, or how we connect through our food."

Naomi Tannen lit up when talking about such connections. "I love gardening, love gathering food that we've grown," she explained. "I mean it's just a joy to me that I can go out and pick some chives if I need it, bring it in, and I really enjoy sharing it. I like giving people pleasure."

She ran a special education school in the Adirondacks from 1967 to 1977. Joe Mahay, who eventually became her husband, was the farm manager. They provided nearly all the food for the staff and students from the farm. "There was an old Catholic retreat center," she recalled, "in Paradox, two miles from our place, and nuns used to work there. I took some of their writing workshops. And I'd come in the morning with a basket this big—they had like 80 people there—and enough food for them all, just piled high, and looking beautiful. And I'd put some flowers in it and I'd walk in with my basket, and everyone lit up just looking at it."

A lot of sustainers feel this sense of interdependence. It takes all kinds. For some of the businesspeople, this is evident in the accounting principle of the "Triple Bottom Line," which factors in the conventional concern for economics, along with social and environmental implications. Success, for these people, is never measured simply in terms of money. Such connectivity is evident in farmers' markets, too. One of the main reasons shoppers go to farmers' markets is to socialize, to interact with other shoppers as well as vendors.[1]

In 2018, the folks who run Roxbury Farm near Kinderhook, NY, were selected by Northeastern Organic Farmers Association–New York as the Farmers of the Year. In his acceptance speech, Jean-Paul Courtens described the requests from friends in Manhattan for fresh produce that motivated the formation of his CSA in the first place. He talked about the importance of nurturing the relationships among the employees and volunteers on the farm. "These stories I'm telling you and sharing with you," he said, "are telling you what it means to be a community." His co-owner Jody Bolluyt explained that Roxbury Farms collaborates with the Rural and Migrant Ministry and the Columbia County Sanctuary Movement "to organize and to offer support to our immigrant neighbors, no matter their immigration status."

"Community" was the most frequent word not explicitly linked to agriculture or food that I heard among engaged sustainers. More than a dozen of them spoke in some depth about how their activities related to agriculture and food implicitly tie into community. All of the respondents involved in food security, including Chris Bolden-Newsome, Hans Kersten, Owen Taylor, Rachel Terry, Helen Dennis, Jane Lippert, Anna Woofenden, and Steveanna Wynne maintain a broadly inclusive sense of community.

Another kind of neighborliness expressed among engaged sustainers involves other species. Many have a strong sense of "mutual creatureliness" (as my dad calls it). Some think of animals' lives as sacred and inappropriate for sacrifice as human food; we humans should not murder them or eat them. Others regard animals as a beautiful part of our world; animals give and take in the cycle of life—they should be treated with humaneness and respect but are a legitimate part of society's food system. Even among those engaged sustainers who think of eating meat as morally reasonable, there is a sense that we different species have overlapping interests; we are in some sense neighbors in a complex community.

2. Collaborative, relational

If neighborliness is about caring, there is also a rational, strategic component here that is about winning. They don't just want to serve; they want to get stuff done. Most of the engaged sustainers think of themselves as being part of a social movement. As I will explain more fully in the next chapter, the sustainable food movement is a young, emerging movement that is situated at the intersection of several other social movements and organizations.

The point here is that many of the people I spoke to believe they are part of a larger story. They have mentors, allies, people who inspire them, teach them, and support them. While many of them are highly motivated self-starters, most do not think of themselves as lone wolves, mavericks, or rugged individualists.

Part of that is about the nature of the work. "No farm is about two people," Jody Bolluyt said. "It takes a community to build and steward a farm." There is the word community again. In this case, though, it is invoked in terms of its utilitarian value. I heard plenty of stories of collaboration, bartering, gift sharing, mentoring, and other collective endeavors focused on farming.

Likewise, any system through which people secure their food has to be just that, a system, which is to say a social system. While some people associated with this movement generate the vast majority of the food they consume themselves, almost everyone is dependent on others in some way for their sustenance, usually with a kind of overt awareness.

I found people willing to work with anybody, whether they identify with the movement or not, sometimes with folks who might be thought of as unnatural allies, or even people who may in some way be adversaries. Steveanna Wynne, the executive director of Share in Philadelphia, said she will work with anyone—in government, the private sector, or civil society—who will help her advance her mission. "If it's going to produce a result to the people we're serving, then I'm all in," she told me. For example, she works closely with Deloitte, a large accounting and auditing firm, which helps Share with warehouse optimization, branding, personnel reorganization, and other management issues.

Part of the collaborative orientation is about reaching beyond *this* acre, meal, time, or place. "It's a national movement," Michael Kilpatrick claimed. He is exuberant about the Young Farmers Conference at the Stone Barn Center for Food and Agriculture. "It's just for young farmers, like thirty and under. It's awesome. The energy is amazing. The place is gorgeous."

The National Young Farmers Coalition is another organization with a related agenda of helping young and/or new farmers. Lots of the younger farmers I encountered expressed a sense of solidarity with others "in the movement." They have an explicit commitment to supporting one another in farming, yes, but also in the larger project of shifting our culture. "We know how to do research and stay connected with the organic farm movement," Corinne Hansch told me. "And that has led us into different veins of research."

While many folks working to advance food security have a rather short-term kind of agenda (e.g., feed as many people today as possible), there are others trying to think more long-term. Collaboration is fundamental to the mission of The Common Market (see chapter 6). Rachel Terry, the National

Partnership Director, explained to me how it works. They have several core teams working in different regions of the country. A core team builds relationships in a given region to develop more sophisticated modes of food distribution. It helps make connections among different stakeholders who need one another, linking them to "anchor institutions" already working on relevant issues (e.g., hospitals, schools, childcare facilities).

In other words, The Common Market develops and manages collaborative relationships. I think this is an especially promising model because through trial and error they have developed an effective strategy that can be applied in a lot of places. The general theory of their approach can be altered depending on specific circumstances on the ground.

Religiosity, political party, personal tastes, or ideology seem to have little bearing on this collaborative spirit. Results matter more than purity. For instance, farmers I met at the Northeastern Organic Farmers Association–New York are overtly eager to collaborate with conventional farmers whenever possible. They may not compromise on a farming technique they think is important but if some other farmer doesn't use that same technique, that doesn't disqualify them from cooperation on some other front.

As someone interested in social movements who works in academia, a setting where many social movements are at least partially anchored, I can say emphatically that this vigorously pragmatic spirit is not typical of all social movements. There are in many cases purity tests that involve ideology or even identity. *If you do not fully embrace every single one of our tenets, then you cannot work with us.*

In a time of ideological polarization, rhetorical excessiveness, and growing competitive pressures to dial up the drama in order to get attention (and after all, what currency has more value right now than attention!), the collaborative spirit of this movement is distinctive. There is something remarkably ecumenical about it.

This is certainly true in the conventional sense of religious ecumenism (i.e., we embrace different approaches to spirituality, including atheism). That might sound obvious since religion is far from being the raison d'etre of the activity—even though, as my subjects made clear, spirituality is actually woven into the lives of most engaged sustainers.

In addition, though, the movement seems quite tolerant in terms of how adherents might be attached to core beliefs of the movement. I take their "deep story"[2] to revolve around the harmonious and porous relationship linking human beings to nature. That conviction is deep in the bones of engaged sustainers. However, even on that score, even as their commitment is passionate, they are tolerant of others' understanding and experience in that regard. That harmonious and porous relationship is elemental, sacred, and beyond question. Yet, different people will relate to it in different ways, they believe. At least, this is my best estimation about how they put it together.

3. Proficient, Skilled

Almost every time I spoke with one of the doers, I learned something, not just about how a specific task gets completed by someone with relevant expertise, but how the world works in general. Many have technical skills, like how to save seeds, fix tractors, or manage finances. Some have significant training in agricultural extension, soil chemistry, hydrology, medicine, finance, supply chains, or the culinary arts. Others have subtle wisdom, about weather or animals, for example. I found the issue of "fluency with plants"—which applies to Rose Cherneff and Joe Mahay, among others—to be especially interesting. Several, like Barbara Glaser, Steveanna Wynne, and Rachel Terry have a nose for sniffing out talent in other people, harnessing it, and deploying it.

I usually got the sense that when one of these people said they know something, they actually do. These are not shallow, ignorant, or unstudied people. I should acknowledge that there is no doubt a kind of selection bias in play here. Why would I seek out or why would someone recommend people who are poorly informed or mediocre in what they do?

Like Michael Kilpatrick, Barbara Glaser, Nancy Ferguson, and Hans Kersten, many of them evince an ideal we extol in liberal arts education: they are lifelong learners. They have problem-solving skills, respect for craft in general, and curiosity about things they don't know. Engaged sustainers of all ages demonstrate a willingness to admit when they don't know something. Most have a specialty (e.g., farming, business, medicine, education), but often seemed like generalists with talents that transcend such categories, like people who are good with machines *and* people, who can do farming *and* fundraising, or are competent at cooking *and* teaching.

A good example is Hans Kunisch. Twenty years ago, he was my student at Skidmore, a sociology major and business minor. Hans always had a quick wit and a twinkle in his eye, but, as he would tell you, he had not yet found his passion in college and struggled to stay focused. During that time he got a job near the college as a chef, which seemed to put a bounce in his step. After he graduated, Hans moved to Tokyo "and cooked at restaurants for two and a half years," he later mentioned to me. He then moved to San Francisco and cooked there for a year. He liked cooking but found the intensive work and low pay frustrating. After that, he did some work in food distribution for three different companies.

Eventually Hans got drawn into the financial aspects of corporate food distribution, he told me. At one point he was managing some $80 million of financial statements in each of two different companies. So beyond all the wonderful things he learned at the college where I teach, he picked up three clusters of hands-on skills—first the culinary arts, then food distribution, and finally financial management. During that same period, he added more tools to his toolbox via an MBA from the University of San Francisco.

As I interviewed Hans in 2017, I loved hearing about his biography. The boy I had known as a college student (who could have passed for a middle-school student) 20 years ago was long gone. "So I got my liberal arts education, went into the real world for a day," he summarized, "and got knocked around and got my MBA. And I think that's a path that certainly worked out very well."

In 2017 Hans was running a consulting company that helps start-up food companies in Silicon Valley and the Bay Area, including Impossible Foods, Kite Hill, Bitty Foods, for example. He worked with management teams on a broad range of issues from finances, supply chain, and marketing, to distribution, he told me—"getting the product from production all the way to the end consumer."

A common focus among companies Hans works with is alternative proteins like plants, nuts, and crickets, the respective emphases of Impossible Foods, Kite Hill, and Bitty Foods. He likes the focus on protein because it "is the center of the plate and the most expensive part of the meal . . . it's also the most damaging part of the meal in terms of what's going on with animals, the environment, the spread of cows, what they're taking up." Notice the perspectives of culinary arts, finance, and environmentalism all in one sentence there.

As we spoke, he mentioned scientific aspects of plant hemoglobin, profits and losses of different companies, nutritional aspects of artisanal cheese, and how cricket production relates to sustainability and food security. He speaks with expertise, confidence, and passion about a range of topics. We will all be eating crickets soon, Hans contends, probably cricket-based flour, partly because it takes only a gallon of water to produce a pound of cricket protein versus 2,000 gallons per pound of beef. (Well, maybe not all of us, according to my department's administrative assistant who always takes an interest in our alums but said she won't ever knowingly eat a cricket.)

Hans is unusual among engaged sustainers because he knows more about finance than most. What is typical about Hans, though, is that he has a range of skills. Perhaps his skillset is unusually broad, but lots of the folks I talked to have multiple clusters of skills. This is true of every farmer I encountered. More generally, most folks I spoke to know a lot about agriculture or food (or both) as well as some other set of skills (e.g., teaching, business, medicine, management, writing). Conversely, I would say it is hard for anyone to be successful in agriculture or food without another set of skills.

There are certainly some young people attracted to the alternative agro-food movement who have not been around very long, don't know a ton, and may not even have the stick-to-it-iveness to stay with it. Can you picture a young, long-haired fellow wearing natural fabrics and earth tones, maybe some tie-dye, waxing philosophical about Ralph Waldo Emerson or Rachel Carson? Perhaps he's a passionate environmentalist, probably enabled by some degree of affluence, and quite naïve. Let's call him NIGEL (i.e., naïve, ignorant, green, enthusiastic, loner), the Hippie Farmer. I heard others suggest that NIGEL the Hippie Farmer is typical of a certain subgroup in this movement. Such folks' commitment is generally uninformed and superficial, and therefore does not last. I think I interviewed one subject like this who seems more interested in a certain identity or the appearance of a lifestyle. His relative ignorance was so conspicuous to me that I realized how much all the other subjects actually know.

But NIGEL is not really who I am talking about here. This summary is about the people who do stick with it—the vast majority of my research subjects. Some are young like Michael Kilpatrick, Marti Wolfson, or Rose Cherneff, but they have already spent many days working hard during a large percentage of their lives, which resulted in the cultivation of multiple skills. The development of such proficiencies relates to a couple other sensibilities that are discussed below.

4. Traditional, Grounded

One of the interesting twists in this research was to find a complex relationship between the past and the future in the minds of engaged sustainers. The past is always whispering to them. Appreciating the earth and how humans are related to it involves an awareness of history, time, and space. In various conversations about farming and cooking, I heard references to God, Gaia, evolution, our ancestors, layers of organically rich soil, strains of seeds evolved over countless centuries, and other ancient species. *This* has all been here for a long time. "It is known," as they say in *Game of Thrones*.

For many, the past is embedded in a particular "place"—a geographical setting that is culturally meaningful to them (see Fitzpatrick and Willis 2015). It's one of the main themes in Wendell Berry's exquisite oeuvre. Can you think of the country, town, property, or even farm where "your people" come from? Why was that setting important? How is it remembered? Does anyone in your family nurture the memory of that place in active ways? The answers to these questions exemplify the significance of place.

For my family, one such place is the Missouri River Valley where my dad lived in various hamlets during his childhood. His father was an Evangelical and Reformed pastor who served different congregations in that region. (The primarily German E&R's would merge with Congregationalists and others to form the United Church of Christ some years later.) As we went from suburban St. Louis to visit my grandparents in the country during my childhood, we drove alongside the Missouri River.

Gazing at the water, the little towns, and the flat fields, which were almost black between crops, my dad would wax nostalgically. More often than not, he would declare, "this is the best soil in the world." He is proud that our German ancestors recognized how special it is. Watching my grandpa on his knees for hours in what to my young eyes seemed like the biggest garden in the world and smelling what my grandma cooked from the garden helped persuade me. I learned later that the widespread grasslands in the temperate area of the Great Plains are bathed in mollisols, in fact some of the most fertile soils on the planet.

Over the years, my dad and other relatives have told and retold stories about our family there. We have visited the different church communities where they lived, including the tiny community of Hudson, KS, where my grandmother and her four brothers were born and raised, my grandparents were married, my grandfather pastored a church, and my dad spent part of his childhood. It is fitting that my grandparents are buried there because like many other rural people they could not imagine living or dying in any other place. Being around the agrarian sensibilities of my grandparents and the esteem my dad felt for them (even as he migrated to suburbia) contributed to my own sense that this place in the Midwest is *our place*. For me, in some lasting vague way, it is known.

This relates to a particular notion of "the land," which is similar to place but is conceptually broader and more abstract. The land may be in one's place or in lots of other, different locations. Wherever it is, the land is a setting that is usually rural, not urban or suburban. It is agrarian and retains some level of natural quality that has not been overly trampled by human designs. A fecund entity, it is a vast resource that gives in generous and mysterious ways. Cultural traditions are embedded in both a particular place and more generally in the land.

Jamie Ager speaks lovingly of the history of the property where his family has maintained Hickory Nut Gap Farm near Asheville, NC. He and his family valorize that place in numerous ways, including in a specific barn where dozens of framed photos of family members on their property over the years hang. That barn is used for education, concerts, celebrations, marketing, and various other events. It is a physical space wherein the sense of that unique place is actively nurtured.

Matt and Corinne of Lovin' Mama Farm express fond memories of the land in multiple places. They respect the earth and the past in some broad sense. Over the course of their lives, however, they have not been rooted in just one place. I got the feeling they love Lovin' Mama Farm, and plan to be there for a long time, but could also be happy in other settings.

I encountered more people like Matt and Corinne than Jamie, more people who want to be close to the land in some lasting way but do not need to be attached to one specific place. This was apparently true of Michael Kilpatrick and Rose Cherneff, who have lived in several different locations, and farmed on various properties. It's also true of Owen Taylor, the seed saver, who has lived in a lot of different settings. Mort Mather, the organic farming guru in Maine has had a long, rich life, residing in varied locales. Naomi Tannen and Joe Mahay farmed the property in upstate New York where their school had been for some fifty years. Yet, as they reached retirement age, they sold it so they could live close to their children in western Massachusetts. I'll also point out that however important the Missouri River Valley has been to my family, none of my grandparents' offspring have lived there for several decades, which is obviously a departure from my grandparents' rootedness.

I don't really know how representative these particular research subjects are of engaged sustainers in general. Based on my sample, though, this is one of the most interesting findings to me. For most of them, no particular place is decisively meaningful. There are exceptions like Jamie Ager and his family, but I mostly encountered people who have lived in different settings over time. This is not to say they don't get attached to a specific farm, property, or community. They do, like any normal family who lives for a long time in a suburban or urban home. But the place does not hold them enough to never consider leaving it.

As much as cultural traditions are embedded in the land, they are also baked into food, both literally and figuratively. Owen Taylor explained how culture is embodied in the life of seeds. Rose told me about community members who come to Abundance Farm to pick certain vegetables for ethnically significant food. Helen Dennis writes about how the recipes she creates and the farmers from whom she gets produce are both grounded in the South Carolina Lowcountry. Leah Penniman (2018) writes about common foods of African heritage, and the history behind them (see also Counihan et al. 2019). All four of them—Owen, Rose, Helen, and Leah—believe that behind every meal there are people with stories. Each plate of food is the culmination of many stories, actually. They are told or written down and document where "our people come from, what our people ate, formal sacred rituals, and informal family traditions.

There are also biological stories of genes, microbes, worms, plants, and other things written into the fabric of such materials by unseen powers. Some folks think a lot about soil and what's deep down there over time such as geomorphological soil experts and farmers, for example. Others think about plants and their lives from seed to harvest, as well as how a field grows over years, such as Rose Cherneff, Joe Mahay, and Mort Mather. These narrative traditions also include cultural stories *about* biological stories like where certain seeds come from, how cattle are strategically bred, family records about how to farm productively, and so on.

In short, a place, the land, plants, animals, and foods all hold cultural meaning. To some significant degree, these material things represent a type of prism through which engaged sustainers view the past. Through that rear-view prism, they nurture memory. (Objects in the prism are closer than they appear!) Their sense of where they come from is refracted through their understanding of those things. As Emile Durkheim taught us, any group that holds together has to maintain some kind of meaningful identity. Knowing where you come from is part of that sustaining process.

As with all cultural meaning, such a prism is what the cultural anthropologist Clifford Geertz called a "model of reality." Symbols in general, Geertz argued, serve as models of reality, a reflection of what is out there, the reality we know, the history we remember. Such symbols provide meaningful context, a sort of map that orients us and grounds us.

In this way, a place, the land, plants, animals, and foods, as well as communities and families, all serve as anchors for certain identities and orientation. They help "us remember who we are." Rose is explicitly exploring her Jewish roots through agriculture. Chris Bolden-Newsome helps lead the educational programs of Sankofa Community Farm explicitly intended to foster cultural Afro-centric memory. Soul Fire Farm also has an Afro-centric educational mission.

Michael Kilpatrick gets animated as he recalls how his family moved to a rural property, he and his siblings began with a small garden, and in the course of a few years turned it into a productive, profitable farm. As he recalls their journey, he shares what they grew, who did the work, how production increased, what he learned, what he hopes others will glean from his experience, and aspirations for the future with respect to his family and farmers in general.

In each of these cases, there are images, words, and gestures that are contained in symbolic forms and organized into stories. The reverence for place, land, plants, animals, foods, and related material things is not some hollow encyclopedic inventorying or merely "just business," but rather a meaning-making, identity-enhancing process (see Counihan et al. 2019). (More on that later in this chapter.) According to Geertz, our most important symbols help organize a coherent, intelligible world for us. This is the value of the past embodied in traditional narratives that is both implicitly known and protected by engaged sustainers.

By the way, there is widespread skepticism among engaged sustainers that such stories, such cultural meaning, can be transmitted through cell phones. Echoing Wendell Berry, that was explicitly evident in comments from Barbara Glaser, Steveanna Wynne, Chris Bolden-Newsome, and Linda Motzkin, all of whom work with young people. They believe getting kids to pay less attention to screens has numerous benefits. It was implicitly expressed by numerous other subjects who pay special attention to aspects of nature they can only discern directly with their own senses.

5. Practical, empirical

"Academia drives me bat shit crazy," Douglas Meyer exclaimed. He is a marketing specialist who works with various nonprofit organizations committed to conservation and sustainability. He was referring to the idealistic but impractical theories of academics in general, as well as a certain impulse on the academic left to find an enemy to target. Rhetorically sticking it to the man, posturing as David confronting Goliath in the name of some theoretical ideal, for some scholars in the Ivory Tower, is more important than solving real problems. That was Douglas's point. I interviewed him in his office, which is located in the large old school building that Barbara Glaser had renovated, which I mentioned in a previous chapter. "Sorry," he added, since I am an academic and he's a nice guy. I told him no apology is necessary because while I love academia, I know he is right.

The kind of problem-solving pragmatism Douglas advocates, in contrast, is standard operating procedure among most engaged sustainers. Although they respect the past, engaged sustainers are generally not captive to it. Nor are they slavishly devoted to particular ideologies, even if environmentalism and neighborliness are important guideposts. A hearty streak of practicality provides a counterbalance to such commitments.

Spoiler alert: if you haven't seen the film *The Martian,* want to see it (you should!), and don't want to know how it ends, you might want to skip this section. Right at the end of the film Mark Watney (the character played by Matt Damon) makes a speech. After being on Mars for 564 days, almost all of it alone, facing countless dire threats, Watney makes it back to earth. Sometime later, in the last scene of the film, he is speaking to a group of aspiring astronauts when he shares this advice.

> At some point, everything's gonna go south on you . . . everything's going to go south and you're going to say, "this is it. This is how I end." Now you can either accept that, or you can get to work. That's all it is. You just begin. You do the math. You solve one problem . . . and you solve the next one . . . and then the next. And if you solve enough problems, you get to come home (Scott, 2015).

He ended up enduring on Mars by improvising a new garden under improbable conditions with the use of his own bio-waste. "I'm going to have to science the shit out of this!" he had exclaimed. Incidentally, a premise in the film is that if he were not a botanist and not doggedly determined, Watney would have had no chance of survival.

The life of a farmer, chef, or small business owner is hardly as dramatic as that of a stranded astronaut but there are in fact parallels. Daily challenges contingent on volatile factors beyond one's control, such as weather, consumer demand, or other market fluctuations can shape one's life in significant and lasting ways. Staying on your feet as such currents swirl around requires a fierce sense of practicality. You solve one problem and you solve the next one and then the next. If you solve enough problems, you get to keep going. "We know how to do research," Corinne Hansch told me, as she described cascading puzzles that confront Lovin' Mama Farm each season. "Soak up information like a sponge," Michael Kilpatrick recommends, "visit other farms, invest in mentoring, read or listen to podcasts. Don't give up!" (Stone Barn Center for Food and Agriculture 2016).

As much as the past is a fundamental and respected backdrop for engaged sustainers, the future is in the front of their minds. They don't adhere to old practices thoughtlessly as a matter of habit or inertia. They add in new stuff that works. Some sustainers embrace tried and true techniques related to farming, for example, combined with digital technology, social media, and modern marketing.

"One of the wonderful things about gardening" Mort Mather said, "is that there are a lot of ways to do it, no one right way" (mortmather.com). This flexibility is a robust pattern among engaged sustainers: the way they do things is based on what solves the problems, what yields the returns, what keeps them going. That includes profits for sure, but other benefits as well, such as ecological soundness and communal solidarity, as noted above. A lot of the folks tend to think like scientists who deductively test hypotheses. That is, they theorize how something might work and apply that theory to an actual case. Depending on the results, they adjust their theory, and apply the revised version. There are certainly guiding principles in play, such as those outlined in the Triple Bottom Line accounting framework. But there is no one theory, ideology, or tribe that has to be served in the work.

The best-selling author Mark Bittman has a section in his book *Food Matters* entitled, "On buying organic, or local, or sustainable, or whatever" about just this point. Within certain broad, healthy guidelines, he advises flexibility as a principle in green, nutritional consumption.

Small farmers can easily play around with different scenarios to see what works. Several I met struck me as particularly data-driven and responsive to what the evidence reveals about successful techniques. They made me wonder if this movement is in some ways more agile in trying new things

compared to the giant corporations in agribusiness whose lumbering bureau-
cracies appear captive to some narrow notion of the bottom line.

The empirical experimentation among engaged sustainers who are farmers and cooks includes a degree of creativity too. In an article for *Edible
Columbia,* Helen Dennis described this sensibility as expressed by a farmer
in South Carolina.

> Computers, weather monitors and regulated environmental controls all point
> to the innovative nature of this farm. But truth be told, innovation is nothing
> without intuition. This farm could not run without Paul Grant observing and
> learning from his success and mistakes. When it comes to farming, and food in
> general he says, "we have to be willing to do things differently. You can't lock
> yourself in." (Dennis 2018).

This point about how intuition and empirical experimentation go together
also brings to mind the TEDx talk Marti Wolfson gave, which I mentioned in
a previous chapter. She conveyed a sense of playfulness in the intuition she
extolled in that talk. There is playfulness and joy in this movement, about
which I'll say more in a bit. But intuition as Paul Grant describes it is more
serious. Numerous engaged sustainers I talked to explained that they are
always testing, learning, and revising in their work. There is often a sense
of urgency. Most of them feel pinched for money, so the experimentation is
more like an engineering problem or medical question than a game.

Naomi Tannen remembered not having enough money to buy stamps for
soliciting letters of referral for her school and farm in the Adirondacks. That's
how tight things were. Hiring someone else to fix a problem was out of the
question (a stance most farmers seem to hold, whether by necessity or not).
So the teachers built the buildings, operated the school, and ran the farm.
"There was this ethos of 'we're going to do it,'" she said. They had 38 head
of Scotch Highland cattle for beef. "All the people had long hair and the cows
had long hair." As well as dairy cows, pigs, chickens, a root cellar, a home
pasteurizing unit, a half-acre garden, and hay. The school had a farm manager, but the students, teachers and their families—about fifty in total—all
chipped in and learned as they went.

Speaking of stamps, Hans Kersten's memory of his family being on food
stamps inspires his work on hunger. In urban Philadelphia, many schools in
low-income neighborhoods do not even have kitchens. How do you prepare
real food without a kitchen? There is an imaginative subculture of medical
professionals, chefs, and educators (I encountered at the FreshRX: Fresh
Food Symposium: Prescription for a Healthier America), including Hans,
working resourcefully to bring healthy food to students. This work emphasizes food that is easily prepared but still nutritious and tasty, fresh produce,

"grab and go meals," and food trucks. Such inventiveness seems to have been effective for skirting bureaucratic hurdles and resisting the temptation to say, "but this is how we've always done it."

In general, the fundamental wastefulness of our society is met by sustainers with frustration, disbelief, or even contempt. Michael Kilpatrick expressed shock at the price tag of Green Mountain College in Vermont. For all that money, "you come out of there and you won't know how to farm." As I'm writing, Green Mountain is going out of business, but his criticism applies to many other well-funded institutions in higher education, too.

"I just really push for people to compost," Alyssa Momnie told me. "Such a good thing you can do for the environment and it's not that hard."

"You have to use all the resources available to you to the very best of your potential," Steveanna Wynne said. That includes time. "You can't be wasteful. Meeting-wise, I really evaluate the results that that meeting will produce, and there's some meetings that I go to and after a while I just don't go back anymore."

Beyond such conventional understanding of waste, though, there is something more ambitious going on here. "Waste nothing!" Casey McKissick decreed. He was referring to parts of a cow or hog in his butcher business. Other sustainers are committed to a similar sense of thrift about material things like different parts of a plant—roots, stalk, leaves, seeds and all.

One of the key points here is that sustainers have a distinctive ontological sense of "waste." "Waste nothing!" doesn't just mean "use all the valuable parts, use the stuff most people think of as waste." It really means "think differently about waste." In the long run, thinking about waste as another valuable resource in a self-sustaining cycle is radically pragmatic.

That was the solution for and advice of Mark Watney in *The Martian.* It is also central the way engaged sustainers think about the relationship between the past and the future. The past is not simply a fixed time that yielded good things we use like food and bad things we discard like waste. Rather, the past is a part of who we were, are, and will be. In some sense, Mark Watney became his own waste. His feces were a decisive component of the food he ate that sustained him. However farfetched a story set on Mars is, this cycle is very real for engaged sustainers, and in some genuine sense for anyone who eats actual food. Cow manure and earthworm castings are different forms of fuel that help generate the food that nourishes us and becomes part of who we are.

In sum, there is a distinctive sense of the relationship between the past and the future for engaged sustainers. Again, Jamie Ager provides a good example. He reveres his family's agricultural traditions. He proudly recounts the history of his people and their commitment to farming. Yet he is also enthusiastic about how his generation is changing things, rethinking the business model, moving toward different emphases in terms of crops and livestock, and adding to the property a multifaceted destination business.

Reflecting upon the importance of both the past (as honored in traditions) and the future (as embraced in innovation) brought to my mind some of two famous sets of stories, one secular and one religious. First, I was thinking it's like watching a performance of a Shakespeare play with the original script but with updated, present-day sets, costumes, blocking, roles, and so on. The author's words are still invoked so the original structure is unchanged. But important adjustments are made in the interest of contemporary relevance.

I also thought of my father's work. Walter Brueggemann is a biblical scholar who has spent his adult, working life deeply engaged with the Christian Bible, specifically the Old Testament. For Dad, the text is like the sun, always shining, pulling his attention, sustaining his strength. He plays in its light, relishes in its heat, and deploys its energy—interpreting and reinterpreting as God moves him, as other readings inspire him, as surrounding circumstances change, for which the needs of the Church and the world call. The interpretation can change, but the text is always there.

Engaged sustainers see the past like a special, unquestioned text. It is not just worth believing in and paying attention to. It is known. It is reality. It just *is*. The past has many gifts to offer, which are worth seeking and understanding. Like the words of the Bible, though, it is not one simple thing that dictates a set of rigid messages in some deterministic way. Hence, interpretation and reinterpretation go along with experimentation, learning new things that shape one's perspective, responding to need, channeling creativity, doing what works. The past provides a foundation on which engaged sustainers innovate for the future.

6. Candid, Outspoken

While such folks are neighborly and collaborative, most of them are not shrinking violets. With few exceptions, which I discuss below, I didn't hear much commentary about others' motives or identities. Nobody I interviewed spent much time talking about enemies, adversaries, or villains. However, I often heard unfiltered criticism of practices that are dumb.

The social movement orientation is important here. Most sustainers have a sense of urgency. Certainly, that involves the need to get tasks done, pay bills, and put food on the table, but it is also about changing the game in general, altering the system. They don't just accept things as they are because this is how we've always done it, someone powerful wants it this way, or we currently don't have the political leverage to change things. If something doesn't work, they say so. This kind of firmness sounded to me like applied hope. *Other things are possible. Let's push for them, hard.*

Perhaps there is something about trafficking in material things versus non-material symbols that makes people more direct in their communication, or at least less inclined toward artifice, pretense, or posturing. There is a reason the thirty-year-old comic strip *Dilbert* is set in a white-collar office setting and remains so relevant. Professionals who traffic in symbols, such as managers, writers, salespeople, advertisers, lawyers, and of course academics spend huge amounts of time thinking about how certain words or images will be perceived. Mark Twain's adage that "there are three kinds of lies: lies, damn lies and statistics" no doubt applies more broadly to such messaging. Most sustainers, especially the doers who handle material things (as opposed to those only involved in communication) don't have time for that. Quite a few actually seem to be rather "plain spoken."

Needless to say, there is great symbolic significance attached to the work of sustainers. Most importantly, the bond between the earth and humanity is sacred. Yet, there is something immediate, concrete, and measurable about the materials most of them deal with: soil, rain, crops, food, sales, overhead, bodies. I don't mean to suggest they are somehow more honest or self-realized, but I definitely witnessed a kind of frankness among many people.

I heard two categories of criticisms directed by some farmers at other farmers. The first one is about NIGEL the Hippie Farmer, previously mentioned. Those we might label as NIGEL are purported to be naïve, ignorant, green (both in terms of environmentalism and inexperience), enthusiastic, and loners (hence the acronym). The stereotype goes something like this. NIGEL doesn't appreciate the hard work necessary over the long run for success in farming. His knowledge base is rather shallow, and he is not terribly interested in knowing what he doesn't know. He is excited about making a difference in the environment. However, he is not very teachable or collaborative. In addition to these purported characteristics, I heard allusions to his affluence (who else can take such risks with capital?), lack of durability and work ethic, and immaturity. I believe I interviewed only one real NIGEL. Several others probably had been NIGELs but through maturation, learning, and work, managed to find their way out of this youthful cul-de-sac.

"We would have these hippies show up and claim that they were farm managers," Naomi Tannen recalled. "They knew nothing about farming. We had one guy decide he wanted to plant brown rice in the Adirondacks. Utterly ridiculous. And all kinds of crazy things. And they would break all of our farm machinery because they didn't know how to use it."

Another common target of disapproval for some farmers are those unwilling to change. We might call this archetype BRUCE (i.e., bull-headed, rigid, unteachable, conventional, experienced) the Old Dog. According to this stereotype, BRUCE the Old Dog's unyielding devotion to traditions is based on many years of hard-earned knowledge about farming. He knows what he knows, and you can't teach him new tricks. I don't think I met any BRUCEs, but I heard about a bunch.

A number of farmers—often the same ones willing to work with anyone— were explicitly critical of BRUCE's unwillingness to consider innovations. They respect BRUCE because he has been at it a long time and shares a lot of experience and perspective with them. They also respect old ways of doing things learned from parents or grandparents. In general, though, that is not simply because those things were done in the past but because they have been demonstrated to be effective. Rotating crops in different fields, moving cattle around different pastures, using natural ingredients for cooking are all examples. The criticism of BRUCE is about his aversion to something new just because it is new. By the way, these invented characters, NIGEL the Hippie Farmer and BRUCE the Old Dog, are both masculine because I only heard such folks described as masculine by the research subjects.

In talking about how a farm might innovate, Michael Kilpatrick noted that it is sometimes easier to "change the farmer than the ideas." BRUCE the Old Dog will sell his farm or hand control of it over to other family members before he will change how he does things. Michael is active in the Young Farmers Coalition. He is passionate about promoting farming among young people. Still, I also heard him speak reverently about several older farmers who have been inspiring mentors for him. His criticism of BRUCE is not about ageism but about ideas.

Tim Storrow, a farmer and director of the Castenea Foundation, described the challenges many farmers face in adapting to all the changes in agriculture since World War II. The Castenea Foundation provides grants to farmers willing to innovate in credible ways that benefit their operation and com- munity. Those willing and able to make the adjustments tend to be younger, he told me.

Matt Leon lamented that a lot of farmers like to feel a sense of control, which they derive from doing things the way they always have, plowing straight, clean rows in a tractor without the mess of no-till techniques and the uncertainty of something new. In Matt's case, he expresses sympathy for those stuck in old ways of doing things but is nevertheless critical of those choices.

I observed other non-farmer sustainers who also communicate in frank ways too. "There's a real advantage to being 68 years old because you can be very blunt with folks," Steveanna suggested. "You can move meetings along in a way that you can't when you're twenty or you're thirty," and you can say to people, 'this is crap.' You need to do what you want to do." Again, my perception was that Steveanna didn't suddenly become blunt in her sixties. I don't know how she got that way, except she told me her "mother was an extremely straight shooter." In any case, I believe the candor with which she speaks to employees, volunteers, and organizational partners in government and the private sector is crucial to the success of the nonprofit she manages, Share Philadelphia.

Phil Korman is the Executive Director of CISA (Community Involved in Sustaining Agriculture) in the Pioneer Valley of Massachusetts. As we spoke, he rattled off a wide range of accomplishments of his agency in measurable terms. They have a nearly million-and-a-half-dollar budget, employ 15 people, and work with some 250 farms. CISA runs a dozen different programs, puts on countless community events, maintains a bunch of funding partners, and provides tons of guidance for farmers, restaurants, and consumers. He was clear about their mission (e.g., supporting local agriculture) and achievements (e.g., strengthening the local food economy), but also what they do not do (e.g., farming). Judging from the hour I spent with him, during which he shared a ton of information and answered my questions quickly, it was obvious he is used to participating in efficient, productive meetings and getting a lot done. Like Steveanna, I thought, he regards time as a valuable resource and is careful about protecting it.

I was struck by the incisiveness with which Hans Kunisch spoke, as well. Remember, two decades before I interviewed him, he was my student—a young college student who seemed extra young in appearance and manner. In addition to multiple distinctive skill sets (e.g., culinary arts, finance), Hans makes a living by giving candid advice to start-up companies. Having known him for a while, I got a definite sense of "don't bullshit a bullshitter."

The other Hans K. I've mentioned, Dr. Hans Kersten, my friend from college, is also comfortable being frank—as I have observed for more than 35 years. I've witnessed his bluntly telling people (including me!) what he thinks, sometimes uncomfortable things, literally hundreds of times.

Numerous others come to mind as well, including Corrinne Hansch, Jane Lippert, Barbara Glaser, each of whom convinced me they have mettle in their character and iron in their voice. I have two working hypotheses about the outspoken character of these folks in general both of which I've mentioned. One is that something about working with material things—soil, plants, animals, and bodies—and navigating through all the circumstances they don't control might contribute to a kind of persistent realism. I think that leads to saying what they mean and cutting to the chase.

In addition, something about being consciously invested in a young social movement may generate a sense of urgency. I have likely encountered the more energetic, committed participants in this movement more than the casually involved performative activists. That is, after all, how I would have found out about them, and may account for why my particular subjects feel a sense of purpose. That drive probably contributes to the outspoken frankness I heard from so many as well.

7. Worldly, realistic

The vast majority of what we do in the academy is, well, academic. We often end a class session, especially in the humanities and social sciences, by acknowledging some thorny question that is unresolved and warrants ongoing, indefinite consideration. *Good work today. Lots to chew on here. Keep thinking about it. Good luck!* For a lot of students and faculty in the Ivory Tower, the topics remain abstract, and the analyses laced with idealism. There is a place in life—there must be such a place—for sustained learning, deep thinking, and ambitious principles without any specific goal. Many of the most important ideas in human history came from this orientation. Nevertheless, we do need our daily bread, as well.

Most of the patterns described above relate to an underlying sense of realism among engaged sustainers. Empiricism, frankness, skills, and collaboration all reflect, at least partly, being grounded in reality. Engaged sustainers often view clearly and humbly the challenges in front of them.

As I've documented, engaged sustainers who are farmers are generally flexible, innovative, empirical, and collaborative. Many feel bound in a synergistic relationship with the earth that has to be managed thoughtfully. So, they are critical of those who they see as overly unrealistic or rigid. NIGEL is unrealistic. BRUCE is rigid.

Just as some people want to be close to the land but are in fact not cut out for farming, some who go into the culinary arts, love eating, and want to be around food but don't have the kind of stamina it takes for making a living out of it. Those are not the people who stick with it.

I perceived very little naiveté or fragility among engaged sustainers. They seem to comprehend the technical challenges of what they are trying to do in grounding, extracting, and processing, for example. Perhaps most importantly, in comparison to many would-be social activists, they are practical about the financial challenges of what they hope to achieve. They are attentive to business returns, fundraising, budgets, and finance. This is often related to patterns mentioned above such as being proficient, empirical, and candid. "I'm also super passionate about the business," Corrinne Hansch exclaimed.

At the center of this orientation is an honest sense of the organic realities of food. A viable ecosystem and a viable food system both encompass death. Death is hard. It involves suffering and loss. The production of food and handling of waste inevitably have repulsive aspects. Mud, excrement, urine, detritus, blood, guts, waste. It's not that engaged sustainers like all that, they just don't hide from it, which puts them at odds with mainstream American culture. Our "indoorsy" society obscures such necessities and sanitizes some basic ugly truths of life. Not true of engaged sustainers.

After I spoke with many folks and discerned this pattern of realism, I puzzled over how it was melded with the sort of idealism that can make someone think they will make a real difference one acre or meal at a time. Then I came across a quote from the Dalai Lama that described what I think I had observed: "Optimism does not mean being blind to the actual reality of a situation. It means maintaining a positive spirit to continue to seek a solution to any given problem. And it means recognizing that any given situation has many different aspects—positive as well as problematic." Almost every word in this statement relates to engaged sustainers.

The general spirit among them is optimism, but I kept witnessing recognition of "the actual reality" in various circumstances. Engaged sustainers working in the private sector understand they have to balance ideals of sustainability, fair treatment of employees, and communalism with low overhead and competitiveness. Richard Frank, owner of Four Seasons Natural Foods, and Graham DuVall, co-owner of Mother Earth Foods, both said this. Matt Leon and Corrinne Hansch are using both no-till and organic techniques on their farm, which is a tricky combo, partly because they think it will make them more competitive in the local farmers' markets. Michael Kilpatrick talked about how farmers have to find a niche. "You've got to be focusing on growing a business, researching new stuff, doing stuff only you can do." Tim Storrow helps farmers do just that. A farmer himself, he leads the Castenea Foundation whose mission is partly to help farmers reinvent their enterprises in response to market changes. He helps dairy farms that have produced milk, for example, shift over to a focus on artisanal cheese where demand has been growing.

Those working on food insecurity get huge doses of reality every day. One challenge described to me several times is the goal of being pragmatic in trying to help poor people without being paternalistic. Anna Woofenden, previously pastor of The Garden Church, and Steveanna Wynne, executive director of Share in Philadelphia, Rose Cherneff, farm manager of Abundance Farm, and Jane Lippert, head of a Methodist soup kitchen, all explicitly mentioned this challenge. They are intimately familiar with the struggles of food insecure people.

Each of them has a subtle sense of the relational nature of their work. We all have gifts and needs, they believe. And none of them thinks that any specific step forward in confronting hunger, whether it is offering this meal or helping that person, is any sort of panacea. Food insecurity is all about instability related to poverty. To work on food insecurity, they each expressed in different ways, is to offer a bit of stability through food *and* relationships. It's not just about calories. What I learned from them is that once people become relational and connected, they start to grasp the give and take that is possible and necessary for all of us. The challenging circumstances in which Anna,

Steveanna, Rose, and Jane all work do not allow for purity—not purity of purpose, character, or strategy. Real neighborliness requires realism.

Steveanna has maintained a long-term relationship with a global corporation, Deloitte, which has been mired in numerous controversies over the years, *because* they deliver as a partner for Share Philadelphia in terms of volunteers and donations.

Rose speaks of "blendy" work that involves openness to different experiences and relationships. Abundance Farm where she works is a Jewish organization and Rose is deeply invested in her Jewish roots. She contends, however, that everyone connected to this community farm, including gentiles and food insecure people, have both gifts to share and needs that require attention. Relationships across social boundaries are as important to her, I sensed, as her explorations into her own ethnoreligious heritage.

Anna pastored a Christian church that includes regular visitors who are Buddhists or agnostics. Her church actively works on food insecurity through the shared experience of gardening and eating but is explicitly not a soup kitchen or food pantry.

Jane explained how important conflict resolution is in her work. Some of the folks who come to her soup kitchen get drawn into violent confrontations with one another. She prides herself on being effective in dealing with fights and has to use those skills on a regular basis.

Barbara Glaser is very good at a different sort of conflict resolution. You'll recall that she is the conservationist and community organizer in my hometown who has restored aging buildings, protected green space, and helped start a farmers' market and CSA, among many other achievements. She has a knack for bringing active citizens who are adversarial toward one another in public life together so as they can privately collaborate on issues where they have common ground.

Casey McKissick runs the restaurants and butcher businesses focused on responsibly produced meat in Asheville, NC. He is ambitious about his own businesses and making a difference in terms of sustainability but is unequivocal in his belief that the alternative agro-food movement is ultimately not scalable to the point of feeding the world.

Mort Mather, the organic farming guru in Maine, has a similar sensibility. He cares a great deal and wants to convince others to join him in sustainable agriculture. Even so, he is adamant that he can only ultimately control his own choices.

Finding the right balance for many sustainers is hard. And not all of them always land on the side of the angels. Corrinne Hansch pointed out that a "dirty secret about organic farms" is that "they're relying on interns, which they pay hardly anything." Rose Cherneff mentioned how she had been exploited during one job on a farm, having been asked to "work, work,

work" to produce as much volume as possible, without much pay. I should point out that a major gap in my research is not having a much deeper pool of information from farm workers. The vast majority of farmers I interviewed were owners of farms. I did not hear a lot about this sort of exploitation, but it is documented in other research. See, for example, Margaret Gray's book, *Labor and the Locavore* (2014), which reveals the widespread exploitation of agricultural workers in the Hudson Valley.

People I interviewed shared painful stories of financial struggles, dishonest business associates, organizational dysfunction, marital disruption, loss of pets, illness, the death of loved ones, and violent behavior from people they were trying to help. As I met more sustainers, I was struck by how many genuine real-life challenges they had faced, including the kind of experiences that tend to foster skepticism, bitterness, or despair. The effect I found, though, in most cases, was realism. There is a fine line between idealism and naiveté on the one hand and between cynicism and realism on the other. The hopefulness I encountered seemed clearheaded. Again, I think this is just what the Dalai Lama had in mind: optimism not blind to the actual reality of the situation. It's like engaged sustainers live right near those lines but tend to stay on the good side. Why? Keep reading.

8. Mesoscopic or Multiscopic

Some people only see what's in front of them. Missing the forest for the trees is a common hazard in our over-scheduled, achievement-oriented, multitasking culture. How many people do you know who breathlessly race from one thing to another, whether it is soccer practice, piano lessons, book clubs, religious services, and all the other activities that keep so many Americans frenzied? Often, the busyness is comprised of sound, worthwhile endeavors. There is just too much of it. The result, for some, is a frantic, unbalanced life in which none of the activities are fully experienced or appreciated.

Others only contemplate the forest and never pay attention to the trees. In academia, for example, there are tons of absent-minded professors who dwell on the big picture, but can't seem to show up on time, prepare for a meeting, or make a concrete contribution outside the Ivory Tower. Lots of engagement with abstract ideals, as stated above, and little to show for it in terms of concrete achievements. I know what I am talking about here since I have worked in the academy for about 30 years and have at times fit this profile myself.

Engaged sustainers are different. I spoke to many who keep a close eye on their particular agenda, see the whole thing they are working on from different angles, but scrupulously avoid looking beyond the boundaries of their purview. For instance, a number of farmers are working on an acre or two and they do all they can to be successful in that endeavor, dealing with soil, irrigation, pests, harvesting, marketing, and finance. They are neither microscopic in examining the trees, nor macroscopic in looking out over the forest. Rather, they are *mesoscopic*, with a mid-range view of things, gazing on their section of the forest. They intentionally don't look too far or take on too much. "Each farmer can only know and love so much land," declared the agricultural economist John Ikerd (quoted in Roberts 2008, p. 280).

Mort Mather, the organic farmer from Maine, is like this. He writes books and blogs about farming. Yet, when I asked about other social issues, he was candid about not knowing much. Rich Frank, owner of Four Seasons Healthfood stores, said he made a deliberate decision to not expand his business past what he could personally manage. Most of the self-employed sustainers like Marti Wolfson, Casey McKissick, and Graham DuVall are like this as well. They certainly have awareness of a big picture but focus on staying in their lane.

A particular version of this orientation was described to me by a photojournalist and activist named Lawrence White. He has been involved in various social movements over the years, including work with Cesar Chavez and the United Farm Workers, he told me. Lawrence relayed a well-known story about a boy walking on the beach.

> There's been this extremely high tide and all these fish, thousands and thousands of fish, have washed up on the shore and they're flopping around and he's walking by and he's picking one up after the other and throwing them back in the water. And these two men come by and they go, "young boy can't you see it's hopeless? You can't possibly help them all." And he picks up the one fish and he goes, "well, I helped that one. Well I helped that one." And that's how I also am.

That tale brought to mind Albert Hirschman's notion of "petites idées" (see Adelman 2014, p. 441).[3] A German Jew and polymath intellectual, Hirschman was very familiar with large-scale human projects that didn't work well, including fascism, state socialism, and neo-liberal development efforts, the failures of which he witnessed firsthand. This led him to make a case for confronting problems one at a time with creative, experimental solutions and thereby avoid overly ambitious grand designs that seem appealing in theory but often flounder in application. This orientation, which Hirschman called "possibilism," is based on a commitment to the "right to a non-projected future" (see Adelman 2014, p. 451).

Helen Dennis advocates this approach, as she explained when I interviewed her.

> That's the thing. If we split this up and if we work in small enough groups that it is a manageable issue then we have so much more potential than if we're like

"everybody in American is hungry, everybody in America's obese, what are we going to do?' . . . You know you look at it on a smaller scale and say, 'Alright, ten kids out of the 40 in this class are not getting enough food. How can we help those 40 kids? How can our local government get together to better serve these kids and their families?' Because that is a huge issue and once it's resolved, then a lot of other things follow.

As self-conscious activists who see themselves as part of a movement, though, some take to heart other wisdom articulated by the Dalai Lama: "If you think you are too small to make a difference, try sleeping with a mosquito." Matt Leon, Corinne Hansch and Michael Kilpatrick, Owen Taylor, and Marti Wolfson definitely think about their modest plans disrupting larger systems in such ways. Again, it's not that engaged sustainers don't see the forest, most do. But they focus on their small part of it.

As McDonalds was developing the McPlant burger, Frank Bruni of the *New York Times* memorably called it a "McOxymoron." But that is how real change happens. Something doesn't seem possible, until it does. And it's surely what the Dalai Lama had in mind. Even McDonalds, the ultimate bastion of processed factory food, is being forced by the proverbial mosquito to wake up and rethink things.

I once invited a writer named Rebecca Stott to guest lecture in a class I was teaching. She had written a couple interesting books about Charles Darwin, who was central to the course. In that lecture, she aptly described Darwin as "lurching" between diligent investigation of small things and expansive consideration of large things. He would examine the tiny details of plankton, barnacles, or earthworms, endlessly, and then ponder how they might fit into a larger explanation of evolution, which ended up changing his life and how we all understand life in general.

I interviewed people whose thinking shifts from earthworms to scalable food systems, or from specific medical problems of one person to the collective health of the U.S. population. These lurchers, who consider the minutia, the gargantua, and everything in between can be thought of as *multiscopic*. They see connections between the proverbial "trees" of here and now (e.g., microbes, food ingredients, paying the bills) and the "forest" of there and later (e.g., government policies, social change, the earth, posterity, divinity), as they shift their focus back and forth. Remember the comment of the student of Stephen Ritz? "You're showing us how little things are connected to way bigger things and how all of this connects to school" (Ritz 2017, p. 56).

The environmental movement has this special kind of vision deeply embedded in its ethos. Serious environmentalists persistently trace the symbiotic relations between particular flora and fauna and larger ecosystems. Those who mock efforts to save endangered species, like the spotted owl, are blind to this way of seeing things. Conservationists like Barbara Glaser and Douglas Meyer who worry about threats to flora and fauna are not. Likewise, those who preserve distinctive genetic strains of plants like the seedsaver Owen Taylor see small things and large things, too. Like Horton hearing the folks of Whoville in the speck of dust, Barbara, Douglas, and Owen have a special kind of alertness and patience. They see the promise of vital neighborhoods, ecosystems, and cultures through the prism of restored buildings, preserved species, and seeds, respectively.

Hans Kersten, the pediatrician working on food insecurity in Philadelphia, also notices the trees and the forest. Because I know Hans so well, I know that for him each patient is not simply part of a caseload, a targeted quota, or workday, but an individual person. He surely hears in some of them an echo of his own childhood during which his family was on food stamps. Each hungry child he treats has what C. Wright Mills called "personal troubles," in this case food insecurity and its medical implications. But Hans also pays attention to the systemic context, what Mills called "social issues," that surround those troubles.

Mills described the value of thinking about how the troubles and issues are interrelated, which is what Hans does. A kid may be malnourished, or have diabetes, because her family doesn't have access to fresh produce, due to food apartheid. Hans has carefully studied the individual problems on the ground, the systemic problems around them, built partnerships to address the linkages between the two, and produced articles, presentations, and a book about proven solutions for others to emulate.

The same lurching process characterizes the work of Kevin Quandt, supply chain manager for Sweetgreen, Steveanna Wynn, executive director of Share Philadelphia, and Rachel Terry, National Partnership Director of The Common Market. Those who work in large systems, whether it is a vast medical organization, a national corporation, a large urban food bank, or a national network of family farms partnering with local communities, have to think in both small and big ways, if they are good at what they do.

In sum, lots of engaged sustainers carve out a consequential niche in which they can make a difference, and often a living—the mesoscopic sustainers. Those folks tend to be self-employed or working in small operations. Others lurch between the small and the large, working to understand the linkages between the two and how solutions extend from those connections—the multiscopic sustainers. This seems to be especially true of engaged sustainers associated with large organizational systems. As I interviewed dozens and observed hundreds of subjects, here is what I did not see: people who exclusively pay attention to trivial minutia or intractable, abstract problems.

I think both the mesoscopic and multiscopic orientations entail keen perception—picture a highly trained scientist, who knows very well how her vision-enhancing instruments work, carefully adjusting the lens to view her subject just the way she wishes—which is conducive to the kind of realistic optimism described by the Dalai Lama. I will also add that in my own attempt to be multiscopic, I observed specific stories unfolding in the lives of engaged sustainers grappling with various challenges, as well as a larger movement they comprise heading toward something good.

9. Committed, Ambitious

Over the years, I've heard numerous students complain about how grim sociology is. We just seem to talk about awful problems all the time. Perhaps counterintuitively, there is actually an optimistic premise embedded in our discipline. Most of us sociologists think that we, as a society, can do better. Most sociological research is implicitly looking for solutions. The first thing you have to do in order to develop a solution is clearly identify the specific problem. That is partly how critical thought works. Among those who accept this premise, the next question then is often, "ok, what can I do about it?" The sustainers answer like this: make a commitment.

I remember getting seeds for flowers and vegetables when I was about 12. I was going to grow a bunch of stuff. How cool would that be? Well, not cool enough for me to stay with it, apparently. My interest faded within days. A bunch of sustainers explained to me that it was around that age when their initial interest surfaced. Unlike me, though, they didn't quit.

Maybe being meso- or multiscopic doesn't seem that special. In the context of American culture in general, though, I think these are distinctive perspectives. Our society has normalized shrinking units of attention, escalated entertainment value, and celebrated narcissism. Hence the rise of social media like Twitter, Tik Tok, and Instagram, cable news with brightly colored sets, dramatic music, and stylish anchors, the proliferation of "reality TV," the common use of Photoshop to enhance physical features of real people. Plus, jobs in which speed or the latest fads are valued above all else.[4]

A lot of plants are genetically modified by agribusiness so that they are easier to produce and transport and will look better to consumers. That might sound reasonable and has at times generated certain benefits (e.g., larger amounts of affordable food), but not without significant costs. This includes unsustainable production methods that use too much water or harm soil as well as food that is ultimately less tasty and healthy (Patel 2007; Bittman 2021; Jackson and Jensen 2022).

Such shortcuts have proven hugely profitable to a few. It's no wonder that Jeff Bezos has become one of the richest people in the world through his Amazon empire. All of the Amazonification that privileges speed, disposability, and short-term gratification works against the alternative agro-food movement. Or more to the point, engaged sustainers swim against the force-ful currents of dominant culture. Certainly, many of them try to be efficient in their endeavors. Some engaged sustainers who run food hubs are banking on efficiency as an enduring value in our culture as they deliver fresh food to people's doorsteps. Others converse and move with a sense of haste—they've got stuff to do!

That said, the more common disposition I witnessed was "slowness" as in a conscientious, responsible, and deliberate pace. As I've indicated in talk-ing about their sense of the past and the future, engaged sustainers are often philosophically contemplative. They tend to be reflective about what they are doing, thinking carefully about time, space, what their mission is, and what it isn't. Farmers worry about seasons, weather, consumer demand, acre-age, yields, place, and the land. Chefs worry about sourcing, supply chains, overhead, price structures, recipes, what sells. Nonprofits like Community Involved in Sustainable Agriculture, The Garden Church, the community kitchen at Central United Methodist Church in Traverse City, Michigan, and The Common Market all have clear parameters dictating activities adjacent to their core missions, in which they do not engage. A well-defined mission is part of the commitment evinced by many engaged sustainers.

A lot of them feel their primary work overlaps almost entirely with the goals of this movement—the two agendas are rarely at odds. This is true for farmers like Michael Kilpatrick, Matt Leon, Corrinne Hansch, and Mort Mather, distributors like Graham DuVall and Rich Frank, and communicators like Helen Dennis and Anna Woofenden.

People who farm or cook for a living work hard. I routinely heard talk of 50-, 60-, or 70-hour work weeks. Some farmers don't take a day off for years. For a lot of engaged sustainers, paying the bills requires working more than one job. "I used to handpick potato beetles every morning before I'd go off to work," one gardener told me. "I'd go out in the garden and just go down the rows and pick up all the potato beetles and eggs and larvae and kill them in my hands."

Hans Kersten said his work on food insecurity is mostly "extra." It's linked to his pediatric practice, but not central to it. The same is true for the clergy with whom I spoke. Growing and serving food is entangled with their minis-try but not required of them.

Lots of people attached to this movement work in other jobs, as teachers, artists, nonprofit managers, but take their work related to food seriously as an avocation. I interviewed two men employed fulltime by Skidmore College where I work, Steve Otrembiak and Peter Kobor, who run small farms as well. I also spoke to Chip Alleman who works fulltime in high-end hospital-ity management but has also been associated with the Glynnwood Center for

Regional Food and Farming, serving for some time as the chair of its board of directors.

But even those who participate in this movement only part-time are very committed. Oscar Wilde once said, "the trouble with socialism is that it takes up too many evening meetings." That's actually true of most social movements. They certainly don't all think of themselves as socialists, but many engaged sustainers attend a lot of "evening meetings." That is, they work hard on things above and beyond normal working hours, especially those overtly invested in the movement per se, like Jamie Alger, Michael Kilpatrick, Barbara Glaser, Mort Mather, Matt Leon, Corinne Hansch, and Phil Korman. Whether it is fulltime focus on farming and the movement, attaching movement-related elements to their normal jobs, or being committed to an avocation like gardening or nonprofit work on top of their primary job, this is a busy bunch of people.

Some regard their connection to this movement not as a vocation or avocation, but as a lifestyle. That is especially true of thoughtful consumers like Alyssa Momnie, Rick Christman, and Richard D'Abate. Just because their engagement in the movement is not part of a primary job or serious past-time does not mean they are not invested, because it is woven throughout their lives in daily choices. Remember the metaphor for consuming wisely in the face of the 360-degree 24/7 marketing regime Big Food maintains? Carrying around a 20-pound weight all the time. In this day and age, that's what it means to consistently think about the moral implications of the food you eat.

The main point here is that I kept encountering people who have strong convictions, a robust work ethic, and lots of energy. Like I said, most of them are not naïve about what they are doing. They comprehend the financial challenges relative to how hard they have to work. Most seem to have an honest appraisal of how far away systemic transformation really is. Rome wasn't built in a day, but it required persistence, they know. They continue to work hard, develop new skills, solve the problems of today, while endeavoring to plan for the long term. Like most social movements, participants in the alternative agro-food movement want to win—in this case, they want to achieve their goal of transforming how we produce food. They want Rome built. Still, they are realistic enough to know that it ain't going to happen in some global way any time soon.

Moreover, the deep story for many engaged sustainers doesn't focus on a linear race toward a finish line but rather something more ambiguous, imaginative, or even spiritual, like harmony or resonance. Maybe Rome is the wrong metaphor because some part of this work is never finished. The goal is not to achieve victory over nature but to move toward alignment with it. Jean-Paul Courtens, the award-winning organic farmer from upstate New York, strives to "really think about the bigger picture." In this sense, commitment is both a means and an end. For people like him, the work certainly drains their energy, but it also generates it.

I interviewed a small handful of folks who say they care about a lot of these things, but only volunteer, garden, or cook a little. We might think of them as *reticent sustainers*. They dabble in this work here and there, on the weekend, during a certain phase in their lives, or perhaps once in a while with a more dedicated friend. I know even more who are happy to "like," "share," or affirm some other positive gesture on social media, or even write a check.

Engaged sustainers are different because they are engaged. For all the engaged sustainers I observed, commitment is a defining quality: work hard, learn more, study stuff outside your comfort zone, network with others, draw connections, tell the world, find reasons to keep at it, don't give up.

10. Joyfully Reverent

There is one other thing that is essentially universal among the sustainers. They feel a sense of reverence for nature, humanity, and what binds one to the other. This sensibility is likely related to most of the other patterns outlined above. Believing in the harmony of nature and humanity drives the commitment, neighborliness, creativity, and candor. Imagine knowing something deep in your bones—like the love of your parents or your children—not just believing it but knowing it. This is how the deep story works. It is a reality taken for granted, like breathing in air, that shapes every other part of a person's life.

I interviewed half a dozen Protestant clergy and another dozen religiously observant Christian laypeople for whom this movement is very important. They think of the earth as God's creation. They consider people to be God's children, worthy of love and nourishment. For most of them, food is central to their religious practice—to commune with the divine, fellow adherents, and neighbors in general. For all of them, consuming responsibly is important.

Dee Lowman, the Methodist minister I mentioned previously, is part of the same church-based food movement as Sara Miles and Anna Woofenden. "I think I always had my hands in the dirt," she told me. "Anywhere we lived we tried to plant a little garden or a big garden. Every parsonage we ever lived in, we always said we're going to have a garden." That includes the front yard of a recent home in an affluent, suburban neighborhood.

Food has been central in the worship Dee led. "I wanted people to recognize how much of an impact our food has on the environment, but that it impacts our spiritual life too. And it connects us with the people who help prepare the food. And that's a bigger circle for us rather than just sitting down eating our food and then going into a Bible study, that there's a connection in our spiritual life with the animals who give their lives for our food. I'm a vegetarian but others aren't. So, honoring the source of our food. Honoring the abundance that we have and knowing that there are those who don't have that kind of abundance."

What Dee helped me see is that this connection Christians have to food is not just a matter of the Eucharist, soup kitchens, food banks, or a few foodie pastors. It's a legitimate, substantial movement within the church.[5] "The Dinner Church Collective is a nationwide community of mealtime missionaries spreading the word about a simple, effective, and historic approach to starting new forms of church." The website of this particular organization (dinnerchurch.com) shows a map with hundreds of congregations that are part of this network. "We're reaching out to communities for whom traditional church isn't really their thing. And so we're making something out of nothing," Dee said.

Another sign of this movement's momentum among American Christians is the integration of such matters into theological education. Sustainable agriculture, responsible consumption, and food justice are now woven into programming at a number of schools, including Anabaptist Mennonite Biblical Seminary, Asbury Theological Seminary, Duke Divinity School, Methodist Theological Seminary, Princeton Theological Seminary, Wake Forrest University School of Divinity, and Yale Divinity School.

I also interviewed a half dozen Jews, who draw a link between sustainable food and their religious practice too, including Naomi Mahay and Rose Cherneff, as mentioned in previous pages. By the way, Jewish Theological Seminary also has growing programs related to food. Various ideals in Judaism mandate humane treatment of animals. "Tza'ar ba'alei chayim" is a conceptual imperative to prevent the suffering of living creatures. Some believe that necessitates a commitment to vegetarianism or veganism. For instance, SHAMAYIM: Jewish Animal Advocacy is a nonprofit organization that promotes animal welfare and veganism.

At one point, I was speaking with a friend of mine, Rabbi Linda Motskin. She talked about the work of her temple's bakery, which is led by her husband, Rabbi Jonathan Motskin. He was a baker before seminary. "They bake Challahs for the Sabbath on Friday night. They also make granola, they make cookies, they make bagels, they make different sweetbreads," Linda told me. The bakery is staffed by volunteers, "of all different ages and abilities," some members of the congregation, some not. It's "so satisfying to get your hands into it. And also the sense of doing good, you know, baking something delicious that people will enjoy, that is healthy." They use locally sourced ingredients "whenever possible," including maple syrup. The proceeds all go to charitable causes, "including hunger relief." Linda talked about the beauty of the food, the value of the revenue, the experience of the volunteers, and the network of people attached to this activity through supply chains, sharing, and consumption. Again, it overlaps with the wisdom Steveanna Wynne shared: "eat good, do good, feel good."

Linda also told me about being a Sofer, a Jewish scribe who makes Torahs. It is a rare talent that requires a great deal of training to prepare for and enormous skill to carry out. The craft is practiced mostly by men and by "no more than a dozen women in the world today," she estimated. Most of them are not rabbis, which makes Linda even more distinctive. To do this work, Linda prepares her own parchment from deerskin and uses a feather quill for the calligraphy. She tries to set aside an hour each day. "For me, it's a spiritual discipline. Like when I sit down for an hour and try to do it first thing every morning to write. It's in a quiet room. No radio, no internet, no computer, no telephone. It's fully focused concentration on the shaping of each letter to make it as beautiful as it can be without mistakes. The closest thing I can think of is meditation." Working at this rate for several decades, Linda told me, she will complete one Torah in her lifetime. It will be worth upwards of $50,000 and then she will give it away to a Temple who needs it.

Like others, Linda is alert to basic things: in her case, making bread, writing sacred words, sharing with neighbors, as well as her work as a rabbi, of course. "We're disconnected from the earth," she said of modern culture. "We're disconnected from one another. We're disconnected from the things that communities used to work cooperatively to make together for the benefit of all of them." Getting deerskin from nearby hunters, eggs from local farmers, labor and donations from neighbors all connects these two rabbis (a scribe and a baker) to their community. It all seemed especially poignant to me, as she and I were speaking, when Rabbi Jonathan called Rabbi Linda to inform her that one of their congregants had just committed suicide. As she rushed out, it felt heavy.

In general, this awareness of deep meaning is one of the most interesting things I learned through talking to engaged sustainers. They see the little stuff as environmentally, historically, metaphysically, or theologically significant. Of course, this connection to deep meaning is important for religious believers like Anna Woofenden, Helen Dennis, Rik Christman, Shane Ash, Jane Lippert, Michael Kilpatrick, Rose Cherneff, and Linda Motskin. They see God's hand at work (see Graham 2005).

But the wonder in this movement is not just felt among those who are observant in formal religion. Being in harmony with the earth arouses awe and devotion. It is absolutely related to putting food on the table (both literally and figuratively), but it is obviously not just utilitarian. The work is entangled in deep, mysterious meaning that defies any simple explanation. We need to work urgently toward transforming our food system so it is viable for the long-term, sustainers believe. In any event, though, each harvest, each plant, is its own miracle, and end in and of itself.

One farmer suggested that a farmer is to a plant, for a time, as a parent is to a child.

"There's this period when they're just needy, when you're being very tender . . . making sure they get the exact right amount of sunlight and handpicking bugs off them . . . and then there's this moment. I can't explain exactly what it looks like but you're like, 'oh, ok you're going to be fine.' (I'm not a parent, but I think there's a moment when your child is a teenager when you're like 'oh, you don't need me in the same way anymore'). 'And you have deep enough roots, and you're photosynthesizing on your own, you don't need to add nutrients'"

This pleasant imagery shouldn't be confused for some naïve notion that the sense of nature here is akin to one big happy family. A few months down the road, Rose will rip those same plants out of the ground and eat them. Remember the urban community farm where they confront pests who threaten crops by creating a friendly habitat for the pests' predators. The perspective on the beauty is more expansive than some sanitized understanding of endless harmony. It is about life, yes, but also death and ultimately wondrous mystery.

Some are proactive in their spiritual engagement, like Jean-Paul Courtens of Roxbury Farms. He helps run a 450-acre farm, so it is a big operation with lots of employees. During his keynote lecture at the 2018 Northeast Organic Farming Association of New York Annual Conference, he described their morning routine that began about 20 years ago—getting up early, gathering the crew, and starting the day's work. He and others recognized at some point that they were not connecting as human beings. Since then, Jean-Paul explained, they made changes.

Each morning they gather together and share a verse from the book *Calendar of the Soul* by Rudolph Steiner, a 19th-century philosopher and architect who wrote about organic farming, medicine, art, architecture, and spirituality (see Bittman 2021). Each day as they read, Jean-Paul's team shifts the language between English, Spanish, and Dutch. They do several rounds of breathing exercises and touch base to see if anyone has anything going on that might distract them from the work. This, he said, brings them together, grounds them, prepares them for work, including use of heavy machinery, reminds them of what's important, and how their labors are embedded in a larger, meaningful world.

Corinne Hansch and Matt Leon explained to me that the name of their farm, Lovin' Mama Farm, has layered meanings, including a reference to Mother Earth. Catholic roots in Corinne's family, who venerated the Virgin Mary, Corinne's and Matt's appreciation of their mothers and grandmothers, Corinne's role as a mother who gave birth and raises children, and the generosity of the earth are all integrated sources of sacred meaning, which have placed the divine feminine at the center of their lives. "We are very spiritual," she said of her family.

Leah Penniman, cofounder of Soul Fire Farm, spends many pages in her book *Farming While Black* on this theme, including the chapter "Honoring Spirits of the Land." Several other engaged sustainers expressed similar feelings about their relationship to the earth.

Not everyone is as intentional or disciplined as the folks at Roxbury Farm, Lovin' Mama Farm, or Soul Fire Farm, but this explicit awareness of how each human body and soul, the community, and the land are connected is common. I asked most of the interview subjects about the role of religion and spirituality in their lives. Many of them refer to traditions they grew up in or were exposed to but moved away from. For quite a few, there is no longer a substantive connection to any explicit religious or spiritual traditions.

Nevertheless, there is a tone and vocabulary in their speech that connotes reverence. A sense of mystery, awe, and gratitude permeates the ways they describe their work. I often found myself listening to someone speaking with increasing animation, even joy, as they described what they do. When I asked Michael Kilpatrick what it's like to grow food people will eat, he grinned and exclaimed, "it makes you happy!" As much as many engaged sustainers work very hard to make a living, there is a sense of abundance in such neighborly acts (see Brueggemann 2020).

Humor came up a lot too. I shared a laugh with multiple subjects. Jane Lippert manages a church soup kitchen that feeds a lot of people facing very serious struggles with homelessness, joblessness, mental health, addiction, and other challenges. Steveanna Wynne runs the largest food bank in a major city with huge rates of food insecurity. Both mentioned the value of humor—and cracked me up several times.

Giving to and getting from a dynamic flow of beautiful and valuable things energizes people. "What will you give? What will you get?" Nancy Ferguson asked. This was a robust pattern among most everybody I spoke to: they find expansive wonder in the little things tied into the cycle of life that inspires their work. For a lot of them, that wonder also ties them to "the movement."

More broadly, the movement includes intentional cultural carriers who preserve particular historical traditions. Rose Cherneff promotes ancient, Jewish ethical practices in farming and education. At the same time, though, Rose actively seeks out lessons and insights from other cultural traditions. It was Rose who drew my attention to Owen Taylor, the food justice advocate, farmer, and seed-saver who collects, processes, organizes, and distributes seeds from various geographical, cultural settings. Leah Penniman quotes Owen in her book about Soul Fire Farm, which is, among other things, a farming manual for African heritage people. For Rose, Owen, and Leah, some seeds hold more of "our" past in them than others, but all culturally laden seeds are worthy of safeguarding and respect.

Likewise, Alyssa Momnie, the WWOOFer, was captivated by the joy that people in other parts of the world feel even though they have so much less stuff than most Americans—a feeling she has endeavored to bring to her own family in connection with their consumption patterns.

Unlike the presumptive zero-sum games that permeate dominant western culture—as in "if you win, I must be losing" or, as we sometimes see today, "I have to demean your culture to really advance mine"—I got the sense of a different calculation from these folks. It's not one seed versus another, one agricultural technique versus another, one place versus another, one way to consume versus another. Those identified with this movement and cultural sensibility constitute a "we" that includes individuals adherent to varying religious traditions and agnostics, of different racial and ethnic backgrounds, straight and gay, folks who live in the city and country, north, south, east, and west, and so on. I interviewed, observed, or read about a number of people across these boundaries.

"While I study and cherish the Torah, I felt a great and expansive joy to learn that my Indigenous African ancestors had an oral sacred literature as long and deep as several Torahs combined," Leah Penniman wrote (2018, p. 56) right before she described the worship of nature in the teachings of Vodou and Odu Ifa, religious traditions practiced in different parts of Africa and the Caribbean.

Some demographics are overrepresented among the subjects I met, like white people living in the country near population centers, but there is definitely a diverse cast of characters in this movement. This is consistent with analytical research on farmers markets (Schupp 2016; 2017). What these varied cultural carriers seem to resist most is not the other mores of one another, but amnesia, apathy, and cynicism.

What binds a lot of them together is deep meaning embedded in the land, in the recognition that the production and consumption of food inherently entails a partnership among neighbors, and between people and nature. There is no food without both nature and culture. Food is by definition a social thing. Often the result of generations of people working, learning, sharing. Abundance is a triumph of life. In speaking to engaged sustainers, I heard this deep story expressed in dozens of different ways.

"I love it because I love to watch things grow," Joe Mahay told me about farming and gardening. "I love to make an environment in which something will grow and grow well and grow healthily. It gives me a lot of pleasure to do that." By the way, it's also true that love literally makes food taste better. Recent research suggests that just thinking about love can make food taste sweeter (see Herz 2018, p. 290).

Amidst feelings of fatigue, anxiety, uncertainty, and humility, I frequently witnessed joy among engaged sustainers, people who garner genuine satisfaction from what they are doing. My sense is that working with basic things, as farmers, cooks, and medical practitioners do, makes work meaningful. No doubt being a part of a larger purpose, as those who think about the movement, the environment, human well-being, or God's creation, does too. Lots of research is now showing that happiness is dependent on physical work, strong relationships, a sense of purpose, and close encounters with nature— all themes that typify who engaged sustainers are.[6]

David Chandler, the Syracuse hydrologist, observed that "experimenting and toying with how you manage your crops and breeding, that's where the joy in agriculture lies. In addition to eating it!" He suggested that those who have a lot of control over what they are doing, like gardeners and "gardener-farmers," do the work in order to get food but also because it's fun and interesting. Conversely, it's easy to imagine that those who are embedded in large systems in which they have less control or less direct connection with what they produce feel less meaning. Among most of the people I interviewed, those who regard their work as an avocation or a vocation, there is a robust contextual narrative. The story they tell about what they do has a kind of weight, gravitas, that grounds them and guides them.

CONCLUSION

Ten themes emerged among the engaged sustainers I encountered. Despite lots of differences, as a group, they are together:

1. Expansively neighborly
2. Collaborative, relational
3. Proficient, skilled
4. Traditional, grounded
5. Practical, empirical
6. Candid, outspoken
7. Worldly, realistic
8. Mesoscopic or multiscopic
9. Committed, ambitious
10. Joyfully reverent

In isolation, each of these themes is not especially striking as a descriptor. One need not be an engaged sustainer to manifest any one or even several of these qualities. I was recently giving a talk about these findings, for example, when a retired engineer pointed out that most of these characteristics apply to engineers, too.

Still, there are several notable things about this list. One distinctive finding pertains to a particular factor, the last one. The mixture of joy and reverence engaged sustainers evince has not been documented in just this way elsewhere. Lots of people like their jobs. Some folks explicitly traffic in meaning like clergy, artists, and teachers. Others garner great satisfaction through helping others, like medical personnel and social workers. But most engaged sustainers spend most of their time working with stuff—soil, plants, animals, food. My guess is that the key to the special meaning is the combination of working with elemental things, and seeing how they are tied to human well-being.

As a whole, this set of qualities evident across a diverse group of research subjects implies something about how this movement works. While each of these characteristics is visible among many people who are not engaged sustainers, the whole combination is not very common. For instance, not everyone who is bluntly outspoken is a good neighbor, needless to say. Many who revere traditions are reluctant to try new things through empirical experimentation. Lots of altruistic people who value neighborliness in a big way are not very realistic. Plenty of those same people never develop any real skills. Having grown up in a family of clergy, I know some religiously observant people, especially those with an otherworldly bent, who are not very practical and do not develop many concrete skills either. My informed guess is that religious and spiritual people often do not converse in candid ways about worldly matters in realistic terms. In addition, a lot of extremely practical and realistic people do not express a lot of joy.

Based on this research, I am not really able to state conclusively that this list of factors represents patterns across the entire alternative agro-food movement. What I really know is that they are embodied in the people I myself encountered. However, these observations provide a distinctive vantage point for some credible conjecture. It is only speculation, but on that basis, I would guess that this list of factors has contributed to the success of the movement writ large. I'll highlight three relevant patterns.

First, the combination of collectivism (expansively neighborly and collaborative, relational) and concentration (practical, empirical, and mesoscopic or multiscopic) makes for a kind of social efficacy. It's hard to get stuff done by yourself or in a disorganized group without much focus. Second, the mixture of idealism (expansively neighborly and joyful reverence) and pragmatism (practical, empirical and worldly, realistic) enables people to navigate the pitfalls of naiveté and cynicism. Third, the strong sense of meaning (committed, ambitious, and joyfully reverent) appears to supply a kind of motivational fuel, which all social movements need.

Individuals comprise groups and groups shape individuals. As I just noted, these particular qualities of individual engaged sustainers appear to contribute to the success of various groups in the alternative agro-food movement. It is also the case that the success of those groups has likely fostered such qualities in many engaged sustainers. That is the subject of the next chapter.

NOTES

1. There seems little question that more substantive social interaction occurs at farmers' markets compared with supermarkets. See Gumirakiza, Curtis, and Bosworth (2014), Schupp (2014).

2. This idea of a deep story comes from Arlie Hochschild (2016), who thinks of it as a narrative people tell themselves about their identity, values, hopes, fears, and disappointments. A deep story feels true.

3. See also Schumacher (1973), Brueggemann (2016).

4. See Bryman (2004), Brueggemann (2012a), Honor (2004), and Stone (2021).

5. A lot of this work is enacted on the ground in churches, among neighbors. But there is also a trove of relevant writings that inspires and bears witness to the movement, which is part of the communication regime. See, for example, Graham (2005), Wirzba (2011; 2022), Bahnson and Wirzba (2011).

6. Mark Anielski summarizes ancient wisdom and new research supporting these connections in *An Economy of Well-Being* (2018).

Chapter Eleven

Social Sources of Engagement

THE SOCIAL SELF

"You want to wear a jersey to the game?" Paul asked me. In the back of his car, my old friend Paul Schroeder had several authentic St. Louis Cardinals jerseys. Many years after we grew up together in suburban St. Louis, both of us in our fifties, we were on our way back to Busch Stadium to see the Cards play. His basement is brimming full of Cardinals memorabilia he has collected for decades, including baseball cards, cups, bobble heads, programs, posters, pennants, hats, and a bunch of jerseys. A true fanatic. Another friend of mine has been a leader in the national effort to deal with homelessness. As head of the Atlanta Task Force for the Homeless (where I was employed for several years) and the National Coalition for the Homeless for decades, Anita Beaty has been an indefatigable and unyielding "warrior of goodness" (as my father described her), facing one battle after another for those without a roof over their heads. My wife's closest friend in her pediatric medical residency was named Jamie McElrath. A physician now employed at Johns Hopkins, Jamie is certified by the American Board of Medical Specialties in pediatrics, pediatric critical care, anesthesiology, and pediatric anesthesiology. Among numerous other remarkable skills, Jamie handles anesthesiology during cardiac surgery on infants. Each of these people is peculiarly interesting.

As their friend, I love them all. As a sociologist, I find each of them fascinating. How did they get this way? They arrived into the world as infants with certain biological and psychological proclivities, but from a sociological perspective a blank slate. Then, their biographies began and led them toward pathways that crossed mine, but also along other trajectories far afield from mine. I know them all well and have always been interested in the things that animate them. What makes someone become devoted in such ways?

The sociological lens can help in revealing the details of who someone is. But only so much—partly because biological and psychological factors (forces mostly outside the sociological imagination) are so important in any person's make-up. Sociology is better suited for understanding patterns among groups of people, including zealous sports souvenir collectors, prophetic advocates for social justice, or extraordinarily trained medical specialists. This chapter is about the social contexts that shape the people active in this movement. Most of the people I interviewed are truly interesting individuals and many are downright quirky. All of them are in some fundamental way ordinary, though. They are not super rich, powerful, or famous. Still, they make at least some choices in life that are countercultural, which is what makes them exceptional. It is what they share as a group, the way their weirdness is normalized, that I find especially distinctive. The common ground that they share across diverse backgrounds, varied skills, and geographical miles is foundational for this movement. (Such patterns are detailed in the previous chapter.)

People do not become engaged or sustainers in a vacuum. While every person has a particular biography that shapes who they are, there are patterns among the people I observed that influenced such behaviors, how they feel, think, and live in relation to these issues.

As I talked to people, I asked a series of related questions. *How did you get interested in such issues? What is your background that has prepared you for this work? Have you had important mentors, allies, or collaborators? Do you think of yourself as part of a social movement, or cultural shift?* The answers to these questions that folks offered give a hint to the larger question of "why?"

A few people spoke about their beliefs without much context. Most engaged sustainers, however, articulated how they see the world in connection to specific experiences, relationships, and groups.

Why Do People Get Invested?

In one of the most cited academic sociology journal articles of all time, "Culture in Action: Symbols and Strategies," Anne Swidler offers a useful way to understand culture—as a sort of "'toolkit' of symbols, stories, rituals, and worldviews, which people may use in varying configurations to solve different kinds of problems" (1986, p. 273). Depending on various factors, such tools can be wielded with a heavy hand through concerted ideological claims, employed more subtly by observing tradition, or maintained with a light touch just by following "common sense." What accounts for which way such tools are deployed?

At certain times, during social churn when many people have "unsettled lives," the marketplace of cultural tools is vibrant, even frenetic. There is uncertainty, competition, passion, and fluidity. Extrapolating from Swidler's logic, we can observe this "unsettled" quality in American life in such moments as 1909, 1935, or 1962. "Bursts of ideological activism," she suggests, "occur in periods when competing ways of organizing action are developing or contending for dominance. People formulate, flesh out, and put into practice new habits of action" (p. 279). The explicit formulation reflects a kind of intentionality and ambition.

The formation of the National Association for the Advancement of Colored People in 1909, the establishment of the Congress of Industrial Organizations in 1935, and the Port Huron Statement written in 1962 all fit the bill.

Such periods of dynamic change generate new strategies for transforming social order. "Such cultural models are thus causally powerful, but in a restricted sense. Rather than providing the underlying assumptions of an entire way of life, they make explicit demands in a contested cultural arena" (p. 279). Assertions are made, for example, about the urgency of equality for Black Americans (in the early 20th century), how workers of varying skill levels should have broader rights in the workplace (as industrial unionists argued in the 1930s) or the value of participatory democracy and nonviolent civil disobedience (in the 1960s).

In other contexts, Swidler explains, "settled lives" are more normative. The status quo is more likely to be taken for granted. Change is both harder to picture and less likely to be on people's minds. The cultural tools in play in those moments are more subtle. "In settled lives," she wrote, "it is particularly difficult to disentangle cultural and structural influences on action" (p. 281). The official message coming out of formal organizations is internalized into the minds of people on the street. "Settled cultures are thus more encompassing than are ideologies, in that they are not in open competition with alternative models for organizing experience. Instead, they have the undisputed authority of habit, normality, and common sense" (p. 281). In such a context, say the 1920s, 1950s, or 1980s, one is less likely to encounter ideas at odds with the establishment being posed in the headlines, from the pulpit, in classrooms, at parties, and so on.

In distinguishing between settled and unsettled settings, Swidler is talking about society or large swaths of society in general. Hypothetically, the level of settledness can vary across time in society, or between parts of that society, or between separate societies. So we could look at mainstream American society in the 1950s versus 1960s. Or compare what things are like in a tradition-laden setting steeped in history and old money like Charleston, South Carolina, to Bohemian, artsy places like Greenwich Village. Or look at closed societies like Saudi Arabia and open societies like Italy, where out-smarting government regulations seems to be a national sport.

We can also borrow Swidler's logic for more specific focus. One broadly defined kind of social setting that tends to be more "settled" in general is institutions. Institutions are by definition stable establishments with fixed norms and purpose. They usually develop mechanisms to motivate people connected to them to follow the rules, both the formal, written ones like a code of conduct or mission statement, as well as the informal norms. Durable institutions have strong mechanisms that motivate compliance with the rules, often by way of utilitarian incentives, or emotional persuasion (see Etzioni 1975). In stable contexts where institutions and the lives connected to them are settled, the cultural tools are used frequently without much conscious-ness. In that kind of circumstance, people take for granted the legitimacy of the rules, the authority of the organization's leaders, and the wisdom of the dominant way of seeing things.

When enough people feel that existing organizations are not responsive to their concerns, we often see collective action, sometimes in a sustained way that gives rise to a social movement. Social movements usually occur outside existing structures of authority like government, organized religion, or private companies. They involve some critical mass of people who share a grievance, usually because they want something in society to change, or they want to defend something from changing. The people involved get organized to an extent—enough so that their action is collective and ongoing, but not so much that the movement becomes a fixed institution (see Snow and Soule 2010).

A social movement, by definition, has a degree of continuity but also an element of fluidity. The fluid aspect gives it (1) potential to "move," as in social *movement*, to do something radical, and (2) a certain kind of vulner-ability to repression, cooptation, implosion, or exhaustion. Social movements therefore take place on a kind of continuum between atomized individuals unconcerned about or unaware of any strong feelings other individuals have on one end, and highly stable, bureaucratized organizations on the other (see Snow and Soule 2010). Once a social movement becomes so solidified it is a formal organization, it is not really a social movement per se. It is in the middle of the continuum where the consequential social movement activity takes place.

These phenomena are complex and contingent enough that it is difficult to make clear predictions. In some general sense, though, we can expect more social movement activity in "unsettled" times and places. That is when the impulse to mobilize is likely to be the strongest, and the capacity to resist social movement activity on the part of established organizations is likely to be the weakest. Thus, people articulate shared grievances, embed them into ideological claims, develop a narrative or "frame" for what they are doing, cultivate networks of likeminded participants, and advocate for or resist some kind of change. They may, for example, try to restrict abortion, advance reproductive rights, legalize marijuana, reform the criminal justice system, or protect gun rights. In the context of such unsettled social order, they are more likely to gain traction. The unsettledness is like a disorganized soccer team defending its goal, providing the other team with a window of opportunity to score.

Swidler has in mind that a social setting in a given period tends to be either settled or unsettled. As I've suggested above, though, I think we can also talk about aspects, spaces, or regions of a society that are more or less settled at the same moment. If we honor Swidler's intentions, we'd have to recognize that our society today is in some broad sense deeply unsettled. Trust in dominant institutions is low. Political divisions are intense. Confidence in the nation's future has been rattled. Various industries (e.g., energy, education, security, digital technology, and food!) are in flux. If that is all on target, it means that what is taken for granted as common sense in social life is mostly not universal. And it means that we should expect to encounter different kinds of ideological claims about how the world works and varied proposals for how we should act on the basis of those claims.

SPHERES OF SOCIAL ACTION

The sources of engagement described above—culture, organizations, and social movements—influence all kinds of people's behavior. The subjects I interviewed led me to believe that they are no exception. Of course, the lived experiences of these folks are actually messier than the kind of tidy theoretical categories Swidler provides. For most people, the engagement is not simply the straightforward consequence of joining some organization. It involves a conjuncture of experiences in relevant settings over time.

Below I summarize the types of collective containers that shape people's behaviors relative to the alternative agro-food movement. One way to think about such activities is in terms of three spheres: government, market, and civil society.[1]

Government

The role of government in managing our food system is complicated, to say the least. This includes the different levels of government and the various institutions at each level. In some broad sense, government's connection to food is mired in the problems of American political institutions in general: lots of good work but too much lumbering bureaucracy and too much money influencing policies in favor of specific, powerful stakeholders.[2] As a result, we don't normally associate agility, innovation, and responsiveness with government. As I sought out research subjects, people I spoke to would constantly recommend someone else with whom I should speak, which often included farmers, nonprofit managers, business owners, and teachers. I think it is not coincidental that not one person recommended a government employee.

Trying to take the measure of the overall impact of farm bills over the years is extremely difficult, but there is a lot of evidence to suggest that farmers both resent the endless hurdles imposed by government regulations and depend on government for various kinds of aid and protections. State and federal government institutions have often acquiesced to the influence of Big Food and Big Ag in a way that is detrimental to our food system. The subsidizing of a small number of crops (e.g., corn, soy, wheat) favored by Big Food apparently occurs at the expense of a broad range of other crops with a better moral footprint. The embrace of massive Concentrated Animal Feeding Operations that make for unhealthy animals and questionable food, and disastrous handling of waste also makes the list.

Overall, the system overseen by government has to be regarded in some sense as a failure in relation to two of the most significant problems of our era: climate change and social inequality. The use of fossil fuels in producing and transporting food is a documented problem. The science is clear that in this way human beings are contributing to devastating climate change. Because the science is clear, this is a well-understood self-inflicted wound that implicates generations of government officials. In the richest country in the history of the world, tens of millions of Americans do not have reliable access to healthy food, reflecting rates of food insecurity higher than most any other industrialized country, another self-inflicted wound that has to be attributed, at least in part, to government's ineptness. (See chapter 2 for discussion of that ongoing debate as well as other problems related to government and food.)

Still, this case is more complicated than a simple guilty verdict. Government has at times been enormously effective in managing natural resources, supporting responsible agriculture, and helping to feed people. Both the U.S. Department of Agriculture and the Environmental Protection Agency have in some moments achieved great things that strengthened our food system in lasting ways. Helping to protect clean water and healthy soil are good examples. Whatever its flaws, the Supplemental Nutrition Assistance Program (SNAP) or "food stamps" has been immensely consequential in alleviating food insecurity. Research on nutrition led by the USDA is crucial to that success.

In terms of my direct observations, I encountered several pertinent patterns. The most common was how often farmers collaborate with university agricultural extension programs. The National Institute of Food and Agriculture (NIFA) is part of the U.S. Department of Agriculture. Across the country, state universities linked to the NIFA help farmers monitor the health of their soil, manage various pests, and learn about new techniques informed by current research. I heard directly about such connections in nine different states. Government's positive impact on agriculture in this regard is in fact vast and profound.

One of the problems with government in the eyes of many farmers is how difficult regulations make it to do the right thing and be successful. Numerous farmers explained that they follow a standard different from Certified Organic that is at least as responsible. On the other hand, there was recognition that natural resources need active protection on the part of government.

Remember what Michael Kilpatrick said? He resents government intrusion and regulation, but also recognizes that government should play an active role in safeguarding the best farmland from development. Such ambivalence appears to be common. I heard as much from Suzanne Carreker-Voigt, who was for some time the coordinator of the farmers' market in my town. She portrayed mixed feelings along these lines among various farmers she knows.

Different subjects described numerous partnerships with local government related to community farms, farmers' markets, food banks, and other nonprofits. The most interesting scenarios I heard involved local collaborations with government in generating creative solutions. I've mentioned Pitney Meadows Community Farms in my hometown of Saratoga Springs, NY. This multifaceted 166-acre nonprofit community farm was created through a partnership of a private business previously run by the Pitney family, the City of Saratoga Springs, and various local nonprofit organizations. The Cornell Cooperative Extension of Saratoga County subsequently helped secure a Farm-to-School Project grant from New York State, which has enabled expansive collaborations between Pitney Meadows Community Farms and surrounding school districts. That has led to a relaxation of elaborate restrictions on the sources of school food in those districts. As a result, huge quantities of fresh produce flow from the farm to the schools. In some cases, students learn about farming and cooking, as they eat good food. The rippling implications are wondrous.

The City's Open Space Fund and easement in support of the formation of the community farm was crucial. Cornell University is a distinctive institution that is a private Ivy League University but also a land-grant research university with three state-supported colleges inside of it. New York State is out front in recognizing the win-win-win promise of investments like Pitney Meadows. Michael Kilpatrick, Barbara Glaser, the community leader mentioned previously, and Margaret Sullivan, the Saratoga Springs City School District Lunch Program Director, and various other local community members with whom I spoke were all involved in bringing these ambitions to fruition.

Some of the effects of the Pitney Meadows collaboration include an investment in sustainable agriculture and all its cascading consequences for healthy soil and clean air, inroads on food insecurity in local school districts, ongoing educational programs that help young and old in the community see the connections, protection of green space, including farmland as well as space for trails and recreation, and sourcing of ingredients for local restaurants. Without federal, state, and local governments offering assistance, none of this would be possible.

What the federal and state governments do on a large scale has huge implications. As Janet Poppendieck, Marion Nestle, Raj Patel, and numerous other researchers argue, the large systems related to supply chain, distribution, access, and so on, matter immensely. What my research shows, though, is that some of the most effective and imaginative work is done on the ground through local collaborations. As distinctive as Pitney Meadows Community Farms appears to my proud neighbors, I do not think it is terribly unique. These sorts of creative projects are popping up all over the place (see Fitzpatrick and Willis 2015). They often revolve around esoteric local concerns and opportunities, but also have some common characteristics. One is that they usually involve the support of government institutions in some capacity.

Another example I came across is Sankofa Community Farm. This four-acre farm is situated on the 50-acre National Historic Landmark operated by the nonprofit John Bartram Association in conjunction with the City of Philadelphia Department of Parks and Recreations. Sankofa works on sustainability, food sovereignty, education, horticulture, history, and education, all within the city limits of Philadelphia. Chris Bolden-Newsome, who I interviewed, is the farm director there.

Hans Kersten, the pediatrician at St. Christopher's Children's Hospital, and Steveanna Wynne, director of Share, have also worked closely with the City of Philadelphia to address food insecurity in that city as well.

What strikes me about a lot of such productive partnerships I encountered is that some large amount of the imaginative energy comes from the ground. There is now a substantial research literature on the efficacy of local problem-solving projects. Benjamin Barber's books, *If Mayors Ruled the World: Dysfunctional Nations, Rising Cities*, and *Cool Cities: Urban Sovereignty and the Fix for Global Warming*, James and Deborah Fallows' *Our Towns: A 100,000-Mile Journey into the Heart of America,* and Rik Scarce's *Creating Sustainable Communities: Lessons from the Hudson River Region*, are some notable examples.

The big solutions to our most significant challenges necessarily involve government, partly due to the scale of such problems. In the context of global patterns in weather, conflict, markets, underground economies, and pandemics, there is no way around that. We need only look to the racial history of the United States, from the Civil War to the various efforts currently under way in multiple states to suppress voting rights among people of color to recognize that localism has its limitations. For now, however, the most interesting items in the mixed bag of government achievements related to food appear to involve local government in collaborative partnerships.

Market

If our political institutions involve cross-cutting trends in terms of addressing problems in our food system, the market encompasses even more extreme contradictions. Of course, we expect private firms to focus on the bottom line. For-profit companies seek profit. There is nothing wrong with that (see Smith 2022). However, when the goal of profit obliterates all other principles, we have a problem. The most damaging patterns do appear to be driven by Big Food and Big Agriculture: production, transportation, and distribution systems that aggravate environmental degradation and social inequality. Greed, corruption, and inertia are embedded into the Industrial Food Complex. That is central to the ugly story. Multinational corporations account for the overwhelming majority of our arable land, factories, distribution centers, and calories. And they have made quite a mess of the whole situation. (Look back to chapter 2 for more details.)

Again, the central claim of this book is that a beautiful story is unfolding. Against this vast, execrable current, there is a dramatic countertrend, a trickle of clean, lifegiving freshness that is rapidly gaining strength. Elements of the private sector are implicated in the ugly story, but other elements of the private sector are crucial to the beautiful story. This includes, most importantly, farms. From the people I spoke to directly, others they mentioned, and secondary research, it seems clear to me that many farmers care deeply about the land, what they produce, how they produce it, and its consequences for consumers.

There are no doubt greedy, cynical farmers out there knowingly doing harm to the land and consumers. How else can we explain such long-term trends? The number of farms across the United States is shrinking and the average size is growing, and many of them use unsustainable practices to generate dicey outcomes. Nevertheless, I do not think greed or cynicism is generally common among the people with whom I spoke, even if they succumb to the human impulses to secure surplus resources and portray themselves in a positive light.

The grounders (see chapter 3) and extractors (see chapter 4) I interviewed emphasize the bottom line, but not *only* that. There were several revealing "tells" among them, providing a kind of corroborating evidence of their broader claims. For starters, there is a demonstrated sense that "less is more." Many, like Steve Otrembiak, Corinne Hansch, Peter Kober, and Mort Mather, work no more than a few acres. Lots of them want to grow their business, but they know that keeping the enterprise relatively small is necessary for a certain level of integrity. I kept hearing about earthworms, particulates, and microbes as decisive issues. Any farmer who cares about earthworms ain't all bad. It's like a shibboleth of agrarian integrity.

They also spoke about relationships, as I highlighted in the last chapter. They referred to the need to work with other people (e.g., suppliers, slaughterhouses, market executives, consumers) who are trustworthy and the desire to be regarded themselves by others as trustworthy. The importance of limited size and personal relationships are of course correlated. One can only know, support, and be personally accountable to so many individuals. McDonaldization, Disneyization, and what I've called Amazonification all make such familiarity, care, and responsibility implausible.

Perhaps the most important relationships linked to farmers involve their customers. On the production end of the private sector, farmers are clearly the most crucial players. I repeatedly heard from them about the importance of informed consumers, and I witnessed efforts to educate those who buy their products. They want people to see how their operations work and why it matters. Such intentional transparency is another tell. If you work with people you know, you are much more likely to be honest (see Hunt 2007).

Not that all large companies lie or that all small operations are fully truthful. For example, Kellogg's has been lauded for its ethical business practices, on one hand (see Schroeder 2021). On the other, Hoangson "Sonny" Nyugen is a farmer in Manning, South Carolina, who had 20,000 of the chickens on his farm murdered; he was allegedly one among several farmers in the area victimized by a ruthless competitor, quite likely in charge of a smallish operation (Leonard 2015).

Nevertheless, personal relationships depend on a degree of trust, which is sustained by dependability and accountability and smaller operations tend to have more of all of that. The flow of information about their processes and products through education and personal relationships sharply contrasts with the opaque character of many Big Food companies that do not let people see production processes, ask employees to sign nondisclosure agreements, and deliberately spread misinformation.[3]

In addition to some for-profit agricultural operations in the private sector that are integral to this movement, it is worth highlighting the role of food hubs, farm-to-table restaurants, and health food stores. There are a lot of engaged sustainers in the movement, who are not farmers, trying to make a buck. Rich Frank of Four Seasons Natural Foods in Saratoga Springs, New York, Graham DuVall of Mother Earth Foods in Asheville, North Carolina, Joshua Mather who runs Joshua's Restaurant and Bar in Wells, Maine, Casey McKissick, owner of Foothill Meats in Black Mountain, North Carolina, and Marti Wolfson, the functional medicine chef, all want to make a living and make the world a better place.

As they all know, a crucial segment of the private sector that is working to advance this movement is consumers. We are all part of the market whenever we buy something. So, every time someone purchases food, they are having an impact on this movement one way or the other. One hundred percent of the after-tax profits from the brand Newman's Own go to charitable causes, which include projects that work on safe water and food security. Every time you dip a chip into Newman's Own salsa, you're doing something nice in addition to enjoying a snack. Better yet, every time you buy a fresh vegetable from a local farmer instead of a supermarket chain, you are in all likelihood reducing the use of fossil fuels, supporting the local economy, potentially strengthening your local community, and maybe even helping to sequester CO_2 from the atmosphere (see Schupp 2014; 2016). In contrast, each Big Mac or package of Kraft Mac and Cheese helps advance the movement and its goals a lot less.

Now, of course it's actually more complicated than all that. Newman's Own is not a perfectly green company. Its packaging is not always ideal, and it transports ingredients over large distances, for instance. Local farmers don't always practice regenerative agriculture. And both McDonalds and Kraft have made forays into more responsible production. But the basic distinction still holds. What's harder is figuring out all the shades of gray between such extremes. Tons of products make various claims about their moral footprint and it's not always easy to discern what is true.

Still, there are growing numbers of consumers who work hard to sort through the chaos to purchase food that does in fact have a benign moral footprint. And the market responds to them, as the numerous extractors and communicators I interviewed explained. The organizational impact of the private sector is therefore channeled through each consumer.

In chapter 7 on consumption, I highlighted several individuals who have become conscious participants in this movement as consumers and who represent a cultural shift in consumer behaviors more broadly. Supply chain anglers, like Alyssa Momnie and Jim Lieberman, are on the leading edge of this movement. Rick Chrisman shows how impactful some straightforward behavioral choices, like ignoring mainstream marketing, can be. Kevin Quandt's company, Sweetgreen, has created a scaled-up model that facilitates engaged consumption.

Beyond these folks, I know numerous families who are having active conversations about their consumption patterns relative to their moral footprint. Four households in particular come to mind. They include individuals who have become vegetarians as well as family members who continue to eat a lot of meat.

As responsible and healthy consumption becomes more normative, it is easier to make wise choices. That is, there is more information, more access to healthy food options, and more role models. *Look what the Joneses are eating!* But households divided this way—with some vegetarians and some meat-eaters, or perhaps some who avoid processed foods and some who don't—suggest that it isn't all that easy. By the way, in each of these four households the vegetarians have told me how challenging it is. Finding appealing vegetarian recipes is not always easy, they sometimes crave meat, and a household preparing multiple kinds of dishes for different diets adds work to lives that are already hectic. In any case, the motivations are sufficiently strong for a lot of people to make this effort to move toward consumption patterns that favor sustainability and health. And every one of them is in some sense an agent of the market.

There is another less direct way that the market has to get credit for contributing good things to our food system. The alternative agro-food movement includes numerous settings where neighbors interact with one another. Some of those contexts have been described as "third places."[4] If home is the "first place" and work is the "second place," other public spaces, mostly ungoverned and unregulated, provide a different environment for social interaction.[5] In *The Great Good Place*, Ray Oldenburg identifies the pockets of such activity still alive and kicking. In coffee shops, bookstores, and bars, for example, there is conversation, belonging, and playfulness—all elements of valuable social capital that help people build relationships, cultivate self-esteem, and work through problems.

In *Building Communities through Food* (2019), David Purnell shows how food is central to such interaction. This includes various settings associated with the alternative agro-food movement in particular. There, people gather without a specific goal and bond over food. Neighbors are much more likely to speak with one another at a farmers' market than a supermarket. CSAs allow for substantial interaction between vendors and customers. Coops are, well, cooperative (see Knupfer 2013). Religious settings that serve food, whether in the form of a community soup kitchen, or a broader sort of interaction are third places too. This was evident in the Garden Church started by Anna Woofenden and Abundance Farm where Rose Cherneff is the farm manager. Various farms have become destinations, but also just places where people hang out. That is true of Hickory Nut Gap Farm in Asheville, NC, as well as Saratoga Apple near Saratoga Springs, NY. A lot of what goes on in these settings feels like civil society (which is discussed below). But there is a decidedly commercial element in many of them too, so the market has been credited with this contribution as well.

However problematic certain private companies are in terms of sustainability, health, and social justice, we have to acknowledge that the market is in fact an important organizational hub for the alternative agro-food movement.

Civil Society

Just to reiterate, as much as government and the private sector are contributing in terms of sustainability, health, and social justice, they are falling well short of what they could or should be doing. In terms of comparative sustainability, according to Yale's composite Environmental Performance Index (Wendling, Emerson, Sherbinin, and Esty 2020), the United States does not look good. We are one of the least green countries in the industrialized world both in terms of government policy and corporations based here. Our record on hunger is not impressive either; more than 40 million Americans are food insecure.

If these great institutions, government, and the market, are such a large part of the problem, how is it that this movement has any momentum at all? The answer is civil society, where the most focused and ambitious efforts to change how we eat are influenced. Civil society is comprised of voluntary associations, nonprofit organizations, and other civic groups.[6] Organized religion, labor unions, and social movements are important examples relative to food.

The modes of motivation in government and the market tend to be rather severe. Ultimately, government relies on coercion. If you don't do what the government wants, that is, if you don't follow the law, you may pay a fine, surrender your freedom, or even lose your life. The logic in the private sector is not quite as harsh, but it's still very concrete. Everyone has a price, the market says. So, the ultimate mode of incentivizing people to participate in the private sector is bribery. Elements of civil society can be tough too, but the more common mode of motivation is persuasion. Different agents in civil society use pride, shame, guilt, honor, flattery, and other normative appeals to draw people into their designs (see Wright 2010).

From my observations, it appears that the most important institution in civil society that binds this movement is the family. It's not that progressive ideas about a person's or society's moral footprint related to food originate in the family. Most mothers and fathers don't sit around thinking about how their farming techniques can be more regenerative, or how they can force others to use fewer preservatives in food production. What happens in the family is that the values people have, which are usually derived at least in part from other settings, are transmitted to other individuals. That is, parents, children, siblings, and grandparents think about how they can spread the values they hold to others in their family.

Somewhere in their relationships with other people, the anchors of the alternative agro-food movement developed an investment in sustainability. They learned to feel a particular way toward nature. In addition, for most of them, an interest in the linkage between nature and humanity evolved into an active sense of commitment. What they *felt* was transformed into the need to *act*. They are almost all doers who regularly interact with material objects, including soil, water, plants, animals, food, and human bodies.

When I asked them where these sensibilities came from, a lot of them, especially farmers and gardeners, described being drawn into planting early in their lives by older family members. Quite a few recollect a specific moment or a window of time when the seeds were planted, both literally and figuratively. The director at Sankofa Community Farm, Chris Bolden-Newsome, talked about his extended family's southern agrarian roots, for example. Jamie Ager is part of the fifth generation running Hickory Nut Gap Farm. William Woys Weaver got drawn into seed-saving by way of his grandparents.

Likewise, in speaking with people about what food they purchase, how it is prepared, who prepares it, and what mealtimes are like, I heard numerous stories about family (see also Ochs and Shohet 2006; Purnell 2019). Not every adult reproduces the same familial practices around food they encountered in their childhood. However, a preponderance of respondents who are thoughtful about such matters referred to formative experiences with parents and grandparents.

Hope Casto is an avid gardener and cook.[7] Using fresh ingredients for scratch cooking and sitting down for long meals with lots of conversation is a habit she learned in childhood. "This is deeply embedded in my family traditions," she told me. When her family gathers, the food is a big deal. She explained that "planning the meal, the procurement of the food, and preparation of the meal," all with great care, are part of the intergenerational traditions.

Marti Wolfson was her mother's little sous-chef. Helen Dennis' family got fresh eggs and produce from local farmers, and she learned to cook at home. The annual conferences of the Northeast Organic Farming Association of New York are family-friendly events with multiple generations in attendance.

The same is true of neighborliness. Numerous subjects, like Hans Kersten, Steveanna Wynne, Barbara Glaser, and Helen Dennis, all mentioned their families as being decisive in this regard. *When you have more than enough, you share*, each of them learned from family members, in one form or another.

The transmissive role of family in this movement is thus very strong. Again, though, that is not really where the values originate. In so far as they think about it, a parent doing weekly shopping for groceries enters the market with the objective of purchasing food stuff that is aligned with their family's values.

The most ambitious research related to farmers' markets has been conducted by the sociologist, Justin Schupp (see 2014; 2016; 2019). He explores what motivates shoppers to visit a farmers' market and identifies several factors. The desire to eat fresh, healthy, tasty food, support the local economy including farmers, and build community are all demonstrated factors. No doubt some of these and other values shape preferences of shoppers in conventional supermarkets as well.

But where do the goals come from? What makes a shopper look down to see what the ingredients are on a label? What makes them ponder the supply chain, look upstream to where resources come from, and downstream to how waste is handled? Such perspective doesn't just emerge from the dinner table.

The answer is in some sense necessarily speculative. Each of us forms values from numerous sources and channels them into our behavior in complex, fluid, contingent ways. Nonetheless, conjecture about the answers can rest on a firm evidentiary basis, as mine does. Where do the values come from? My observations suggest primarily from a particular group of social movements and organizations in civil society.

The social force behind this movement that was mentioned most frequently is the environmental movement.[8] More broadly, the concern with nature, the land, sustainability, and reducing harm of human activity relative to the earth is widespread among engaged sustainers. Many of them are consciously linked to the environmental movement. Some farmers care a great deal about the land, both their property and the earth more generally, but don't think of themselves as environmentalists per se. Among my research subjects, most do but not all. Some engaged sustainers are latent environmentalists. That is, they care about sustainability and ecology but don't overtly identify with the movement. In effect, the environmental movement has helped foster a cultural atmosphere that encourages behaviors aligned with its goals even when the person in question does not explicitly identify with the movement.

I also heard references to different social movements focused in one way or another on food security. That is at the forefront for the food sovereignty movement, as emphasized by Capital Roots, Soul Fire Farm, and The Glynwood Center for Regional Food and Farming all in upstate New York, for example.

In various conversations, I heard explicit mention of the labor movement, the consumer rights movement, and the children's rights movement. Each of these efforts ties into what I have called the stewardship of human resources, mostly in connection with food security, but also dignity and equity in general. In addition, a lot of subjects referenced issues implicitly tied to those movements with attaching themselves in overt ways.

For example, some farmers spoke about fair pay and working conditions for employees, obviously key concerns of the labor movement, but did not speak in terms of union organizing. Several healthcare professionals and educators emphasized the need for children to have reliable access to nutritious food, which is a core issue for the children's rights movement, though they never mentioned that movement. Lots of consumers and farmers want more transparency in connection with the production and sale of foodstuff (see Hunt 2007), obviously a primary goal of the consumer rights movement, but that movement is not prominent in their rhetoric.

In each of these examples—the labor movement, the children's rights movement, and the consumer rights movement—there are diffuse efforts that have unfolded across decades. In those endeavors, a discourse around the core concerns mentioned above has been maintained.

The stewardship of human resources is also an overriding consideration in the Judeo-Christian food movement. I interviewed individuals associated with several groundbreaking organizations: Abundance Farm, the Jewish farm and community center in western, Massachusetts, the Garden Church in Long Beach, California, New Beginnings Church in Kansas City, Missouri, and the Simple Church (part of the Dinner Church Collective) in Grafton, Massachusetts, have each done impactful work in this respect. Such religious organizations are often intertwined with those working on the front lines of anti-hunger efforts. Sharing food is considered sacred in many of them. Soup kitchens and food banks are commonly housed in religious organizations.

But the most ambitious efforts to address food insecurity are more likely to be energized by a social movement orientation than an organizational mission statement. Thinking back to Anne Swidler's notion of a cultural toolkit and the context for bold ideological claims, it makes sense that a social *movement*, which is by definition more "unsettled," will often advocate for more expansive goals than a formal organization, which is by definition more "settled."

The food sovereignty movement is engaged in a strategic process of "frame bridging" (see Benford and Snow 2000, p. 624). The phrase *food sovereignty* is implicitly both critical of hunger, insecurity, and scarcity, and affirming of freedom, autonomy, and abundance. The idea of food sovereignty thus bridges these two frames (i.e., critique of hunger and affirmation of freedom).

It's not a matter of nibbling on the edge of the issue by having the affluent hand out some crumbs to the poor. Rather, the goal of food sovereignty is to radically reconfigure social systems so that the relationships between food systems and communities encompass collective security and health (see McMichael 2014). The Food Project and Rooted in Community (two organizations based in Boston), Think&EatGreen@School (in Vancouver, British

Columbia), Sankofa Community Farm (in Philadelphia), all maintain vibrant educational programs that actively make this connection.

Lots of organizations make a difference in terms of hunger every day, groups like the Share Food Program in Philadelphia, Central Methodist Church in Traverse City, Michigan, the Presbyterian New England Congregational Church in Saratoga Springs, New York, and the Atlanta Center for Self Sufficiency, by distributing food to many people who need it—by giving a man a fish, as it were. For that man, on that day, the fish is a big deal. In contrast, the food sovereignty movement wants to reimagine the whole situation—rethink the role of the fishing industry in society, if you will.

Interestingly, Abundance Farm and the Garden Church are in some sense both formal organizations *and* social movement organizations. Rose Cherneff in the former setting and Anna Woofenden in the latter, each spoke explicitly about the different ways members of a community can be empowered to both give and receive, even across boundaries like class and race. A fixed institutional structure, in part, makes those groups organizations, but this porous sense of such boundaries exemplifies social movement ambitions.

The social movements mentioned in this chapter so far—the environmental, labor, children's, consumer rights, and food sovereignty movements—are in some sense traditional social movements that revolve around "contentious politics" (see Haenfler, Johnson and Jones 2012). They tend to focus on public battles, confronting established authorities, collective efforts, and measurable goals. The objective in each case is often a new law, more inclusion, or realizing some expansion of social justice. *Regulate how environmental waste is generated and handled. Make sure workers are paid a living wage and treated fairly. Provide children with nutritious calories. Let people see how products are made and what ingredients are in them.* What all those endeavors have in common is the hope to change power relations in lasting ways. How government and corporations operate are often central to that focus.

There is, however, another, different element in the alternative agro-food movement. In addition to contentious politics, the cycle of engagement is closely tied to a "lifestyle movement," especially in all the activities that relate to consumption (see Haenfler et al. 2012). Such endeavors tend to emphasize individual, private, ongoing action. The focus is more likely to be cultural practices rather than specific institutions, laws, or policies.[9] Consumers who think about their own personal moral footprint in terms of sustainability, health, waste, treatment of animals, and labor relations are central to the lifestyle element of the alternative agro-food movement. Locavores, vegans, advocates of Slow Food, the Dinner Church Collective, and those who practice voluntary simplicity are all examples of this orientation that are integral to the larger alternative agro-food movement.

Richard D'Abate and Mort Mather moved to Welles, Maine, consciously to cultivate a lifestyle closer to the land. Alyssa Momnie, who coincidentally lives on an island near Welles, is deeply invested in a green lifestyle. Numerous farmers I spoke to, including Corrinne Hansch, Matt Leon, Joe Mahay, and Naomi Tannen, relish how intimate their connection is to the earth in daily life. In so far as they think of their individual behaviors as being relevant to broader cultural currents, these folks are all part of this lifestyle movement.

It's easy to surmise that the average organic produce section, health food store, farm-to-table restaurant, farmers' market, or community-supported agriculture is frequented by lifestyle movement participants, people with expansive conscience about their moral footprint as consumers. If such a sensibility is indeed crucial in all those settings, as I believe it is, individuals concerned with their identity in this respect are absolutely crucial to this movement as a whole.

It is tempting to conjure up an image of the stereotypical tofu-munching, yoga-practicing, chai-latte-sipping suburban soccer mom who dabbles in green lifestyle choices—and mock her. Certainly, those who fuss over where their milk comes from, and buy Certified Organic, while relying on massive amounts of fossil fuels, exploiting workers, and adding to landfills with disposable goods may deserve a bit of ridicule. Nevertheless, reasonably thoughtful consumers who spend some time pondering their choices are vital to this movement. In fact, the movement only has life because there are so many of them following this lifestyle to one degree or another. And their impact is growing.

If we think back to the analogy of harm reduction, it is obvious that a gas-guzzling SUV-driving suburban consumer who worries about where their food comes from is better than a gas-guzzling SUV-driving suburban consumer who doesn't. Moreover, very few Americans have a moral footprint relative to consumption that is completely noble, very few indeed. Hardly any of us are truly innocent.

Picture this. We find out about different ingredients, new products, alternative places to shop. Maybe we meet new people, friends of friends, parents of our kids' friends, work associates or colleagues, and find out what they are doing. The Joneses with whom we try to keep up change over time. Keeping up might mean being greener. Or perhaps we hear messages from a pastor or rabbi, read books, or watch documentaries. The internet is at once a vast encyclopedia with a kind of traffic cop guiding us to different information, depending on what sorts of information we have sought out before. Maybe we get guided toward new ways to think about food.

As I discussed in previous chapters, a lot of us develop symbiotic relationships with social influencers, who both gather information from those "around them" (their followers, "friends," and others), and guide us toward information they think we will want. Many of us breathe in such culture—the knowledge, perspective, sensibility, and convictions—sometimes without making a conscious choice to do so. And for some of us, the culture becomes part of our identity and adds value to this movement.

These two categories of social movements, those that revolve around contentious politics versus those that emphasize lifestyle, are conceptually distinct. Each can partly be understood in contrast to the other. However, that doesn't mean a person cannot be active in both categories. I encountered plenty of folks who dabble in both kinds of movement activity. Helen Dennis, the chef, food writer, and activist in South Carolina, is intentionally trying to shape the culture of her region by preserving agricultural and culinary traditions. Such work is mostly about lifestyle. On the other hand, she is deeply invested in the battle against hunger in that region too, which ties into contentious politics. Owen Taylor, Chris Bolden-Newsome, Barbara Glaser, and Leah Penniman similarly advocate for both political and lifestyle changes relative to the larger movement.

Remember what the New York Commissioner of Agriculture, Richard Ball, observed. In a listening tour of his state, he found significant alignment and resonance among the farmers, environmentalists, and social justice advocates. No doubt there are activists among each group committed to contentious politic: farmers concerned about farm bills, environmentalists worried about government regulations, and social justice advocates pushing for food sovereignty, for example. It is also clear that each group relies on the commitment of consumers worried about lifestyle. Some customers want to buy from local farmers, both for ecological reasons and in support of farming communities. Some think about their carbon footprint. And others may only buy products that involve union labor or Fair Trade.

We can imagine tensions that are political, logical, or emotional between advocates of contentious politics work versus cultural lifestyle commitments. The former might regard the latter as fake, soft, disingenuous, or even undermining their efforts. *You're a Locavore who lives in a giant energy-inefficient McMansion and posts green messages on Instagram. Adorable hypocrite.* And the latter might regard the former as too radical, angry, divisive, or even quixotic. *Right, Americans are going to stop eating meat, wearing leather, or buying products generated by low-wage workers! What planet are you living on?* I don't want to be naïve about the risks of those potential tensions. They are real.

However, most people I observed seem to be erring on the side of a big, inclusive tent. I did not hear about purity tests or alienation from others who are too radical or too timid. Indeed, the folks I spoke to often went out of their way to express a sense of tolerance or inclusion toward allies with different priorities.

THE BIG PICTURE

In sum, this is how I think this story is unfolding. Figure 11.1 shows a visual image of my speculations about the social forces that contain this movement. Elements of the market (i.e., farmers, consumers, health food stores) and government (e.g., the U.S. Department of Agriculture, land-grant universities, local government) have at times helped spur progress in support of this movement. The main forces that enable regenerative farming and responsible consumption, though, come from civil society. The family is a crucial channel for transmitting the values of the movement.

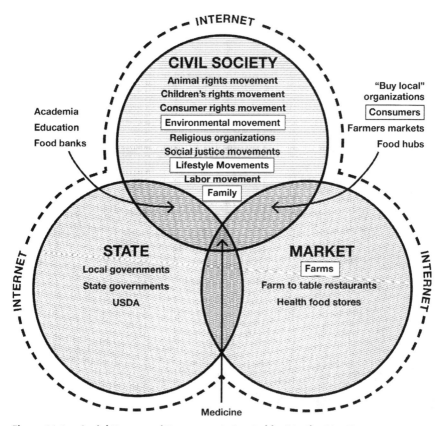

Figure 11.1.   Social Sources of Engagement. Created by Martha MacGregor

However, those values originally come out of other institutions and social movements in civil society, including most importantly the environmental movement and different lifestyle movements. Academic, educational, and religious organizations help nurture such values, too. These movements and institutions have in recent decades made powerful ideological claims that have gained traction. Many citizens who are both consumers and voters have been persuaded by such claims and carry the values embodied in them as they enter the private sector and participate in the political system. That is, engaged sustainers shop and vote with those values in mind. They didn't learn about healthy soil, responsible waste, and the nutrition of fresh food inside the supermarket or voting booth.

Such behaviors then gain momentum by being further institutionalized in market logic and government policies. Hence, farmers move toward regenerative agriculture partly because that is what their customers want. Supermarkets expand their produce section, then their organic section, then their local section. Farmers' markets and CSAs thrive. Officials elected by engaged sustainers work on policies that support responsible agriculture, sound production regulations, and food security. With elements of the market and the polity on board, showing what smart practices and laws can do, more institutions, social movements, and individuals in civil society grasp broader possibilities. Local government and specific communities have been more agile in embracing such opportunities.

This combination of organizational contexts, as depicted in Figure 11.1, is crucial to the overall movement. Some of the most consequential activity occurs where the two or three spheres of the market, government, and civil society overlap, where organizations in one sphere partner with organizations in another, where individuals wear multiple hats at once, or realize they need others with different skills and perspectives to get things done. The engaged steward Barbara Glaser calls collaboration across these three spheres "three-folding." Hans Kersten, Steveanna Wynne, Rachel Terry, Helen Dennis, and other engaged sustainers routinely work on such creative coordination with other players in their communities.

Needless to say, the internet has been hugely important in this movement, as it is in most every social setting now. It is harder to hide certain information from the world now that we are all wired into the internet. Of course, that doesn't mean that all information is helpful. As I've demonstrated, there is a great deal of misinformation efficiently spread across the internet. But images of factories and grocery stores, government reports and other kinds of data, and networks of likeminded people are all easier to find on the internet than they were in a previous era.

Social media platforms enable social influencers and mobile trust regimes to channel information to and from taste communities. Various taste communities, lifestyle subcultures, and movements based in contentious politics all find ways to develop solidarity, clarify agendas, and frame their claims by way of digital communication. Groups as diverse as the Young Farmers Coalition, Northeast Organic Farmers Association of New York, Adirondack Harvest, Sweetgreen, and Common Roots all use digital technology in effective ways to advance their mission.

You will see that consumers, the environmental movement, families, farms, and lifestyle movements are all highlighted in Figure 11.1. This emphasis reflects the significance engaged sustainers I encountered attached to those factors.

CONCLUSION

Taken all together, this is the organizational and cultural basis of the alternative agro-food movement. It is wellspring of the beautiful story. Needless to say, though, as much momentum as that story has, it is not unfolding in a vacuum.

All this time, the ugly story still festers. Big Food, Big Ag, and others with vested interests in the status quo scramble around trying to protect business as usual. They are well-resourced, clever, and have for a long time been comfortably nestled into the halls of power. But now they are anxious. Some adapt and retool. Thus, Tysons is phasing out human antibiotics and Pepsi cut out aspartame for a time. In fast food, we have the Impossible Whopper, the McPlant burger, and Beyond-Meat "chicken" at KFC. There is no question that this movement is affecting Big Food in ways that are positive for human and natural resources.

So far, however, it seems like just nibbling on the edges. The largest corporations have too much at stake in their conventional practices. Pepsi brought aspartame back for Diet Pepsi. The Whopper and the Big Mac remain iconic. KFC's experiment with Beyond Meat is a temporary project for now. And the efforts to keep the influence of the alternative agro-food movement as small as possible remain energetic and strategic (see chapter 1). Yes, that is all true.

Still, I would not want to be an executive in one of the Big Food companies—for a lot of reasons! First, I would be afraid of the power of this movement. I would watch the large automobile companies as they clamber to make greener cars, wondering if they will have any future in the world ahead of us. I would think carefully about whether my company should do what we have always done. As I pondered that, I suspect several questions would vex me, including strategic ones and personal ones. *Is there any sign that the organizations and cultural trends upending the status quo are likely to peter out? If not, will my company be intact in a decade? Can we afford to really rethink*

what we do? Can we afford not to? Should we try to be seen as more respon-
sible? Should we actually be more responsible? Can I serve my own children
the products my employer produces? How will I answer when my loved ones
who have come into contact with this movement ask me about what I do? Will
they see me as part of the problem? Am I in fact a part of the problem?
The structural and cultural foundations of this movement are solid. Groups
who care about the environment, health, and taste are strong and not going
anywhere. Those who focus on equality and justice have less traction, in my
opinion, but they aren't going anywhere either. The values and ideologies
nurtured and disseminated by such groups appear to have staying power too.
If I were such an executive, yes, I would be afraid.

NOTES

1. This is a common way social scientists think of the institutional world. See Wolfe (1991), Persell (1994), Wright (2010), Flora, Flora and Gasteyer (2018).

2. For a small taste of the extensive research on this, see Roser (2020), Sattler (2022), Flora, Flora and Gasteyer (2018), Bittman (2021), Smith (2022).

3. See Foer (2009), Patel (2007), Nestle (2013; 2017; 2018), Moss (2014).

4. The value of "third places" has been articulated by Oldenburg (1989; 2001). See Purnell (2019) for how food ties into third places.

5. At different times, various societies have had a broad range of cafes, coffee-houses, beerhalls, taverns, and pubs for social interaction, places where people can catch up, relax, and rejuvenate, or just belong. As fun as all that is, such experiences also have enormous utilitarian value for groups of people trying to get along, solve problems, and maintain psychological health (Oldenburg 1989). But with the spread of suburbia, especially after World War II, such spaces have not always been widely available in American social life.

6. See Wolfe (1991), Wright (2010), Brueggemann (2012; 2014b), Flora et al. (2018).

7. Hope is a friend and colleague at the college where I work. She teaches in the Education Studies Department.

8. See also Gasteyer (2008), Schor (2011), Schupp and Sharp (2012), Ritz and Boss (2017), Bittman (2021).

9. See Haenfler et al. 2012), Starr (2010), Zukin and Smith Maguire (2004).

Chapter Twelve

So What?

FINDINGS

The alternative agro-food movement encompasses a distinctive combination of institutions and organizations that emphasize modes of production, distribution, and consumption that are different from our mainstream food system. The individuals involved are ordinary people doing extraordinary things together, which adds up to genuine progress on a range of measurable outcomes.

In chapter 11, I described ten characteristics embodied among the research subjects I interviewed and observed. As a group, engaged sustainers are:

1. Expansively neighborly
2. Collaborative, relational
3. Proficient, skilled
4. Traditional, grounded
5. Practical, empirical
6. Candid, outspoken
7. Worldly, realistic
8. Mesoscopic or multiscopic
9. Committed, ambitious
10. Joyfully reverent

As noted, the blended sensibilities of being traditional (#4) and practical (#5) are interesting—the past is respected but the future is in the front of their minds. I believe the last quality (#10) of being joyfully reverent is also notable. It appears that the work of engaging with elemental things (e.g., soil, water, sun, air, plants, animals, food, and human bodies) and the recognition of humanity and nature being inextricably linked make for a profoundly meaningful perspective. More generally, it is the peculiar combination of all these factors that differentiates the attitudes and behaviors of this group of people.

In chapter 11, I offered some informed speculation about the key social settings in which activity related to the alternative agro-food movement occurs. It appears that the majority of it unfolds in civil society. In particular, the various social movements that flow into the alternative agro-food movement take place there, most importantly the environmental movement. Social movement organizations associated with environmentalism have effectively engaged in contentious politics, and thereby impacted various policies and practices in favorable ways.

In addition, the family is a crucial institution in civil society where the values associated with environmentalism and other movements are transmitted. Those values help shape a certain lifestyle in which daily choices related to agriculture and food are enacted.

The market is also an important context for relevant activity. A lot of individuals shaped by the values of different social movements enter the market as consumers with that lifestyle in mind. Thus, the relevant lifestyle movement, which originated in civil society, affects the choices of consumers in the market.

Inside the market, other players advance the goals of the movement as well. This includes restaurants, health food stores, and most significantly farms. Farmers themselves have shaped the choices of those consumers. In effect, the demand of consumers and supply of farmers are intercausally associated.

In addition, different elements of government have been collaborative partners in this movement. This includes at times the U.S. Department of Agriculture, state level actors, and local governments. Cooperative extension programs based in land-grant universities are fundamentally important for farming across the country. Numerous creative initiatives have involved different combinations of actors from government in conjunction with the private for-profit and nonprofit sectors. There are other organizational elements of this movement, as detailed in chapter 11, but these are the most important ones.

The one other factor that has been so crucial is the internet, which makes all kinds of relevant communication possible. The alternative agro-food movement would not look like it does without the internet. A key element shaping consumers' tastes appears to be the formation of mobile trust regimes (as described in chapter 7), which is partly facilitated by online interactions.

One other substantive finding in this research is that three important groups of people who previously disagreed on more things than they agreed upon now appear to have converging priorities. As I mentioned in chapters 8 and 11, farmers, environmentalists, and food justice advocates are finding more and more common ground. They appear to be increasingly aware of their directly overlapping interests, and their mutual strategic value. That is, a lot of farmers are worrying more about biodiversity and new markets for their products, environmentalists see famers as potentially important collaborators, and pay attention to the well-being of human beings as well as other species, and advocates for food justice realize that the key is good calories (not just any calories) derived from nutrient-rich foods, which are dependent on biodiversity. Again, this is not to say that there are no tensions, but rather the dominant trend is one of converging priorities.

These are the main findings of this research as derived from primary empirical investigation and consultation of secondary materials. So how does all this fit into broader theoretical considerations and why should anyone care?

Moral Damage and Expansive Market Culture

Near the beginning of this book, I laid out two theoretical frameworks, one pertaining to moral foundations in general and one related to the market culture of our society in particular (see chapters 1–2). The significance of those ideas has been implicitly demonstrated in the intervening chapters. Here, I revisit those themes more explicitly, and explain how they relate to the beautiful story of the cycle of engagement.

Every viable society must figure out certain moral questions and find the right balance in its foundational moral arrangements. That is the central premise of moral foundation theory (see chapter 1 for details). Not that every single person has to fully agree with how society is set up, but a critical mass has to embrace the moral situation for the collective to have enough trust, confidence, stability, and buy-in to keep going. For every foundational issue, there is a risk that things will be arranged badly and, as a result, there will be strife and potential collapse. The basic tradeoffs look like this:

Care versus harm
Fairness versus cheating
Liberty versus oppression
Loyalty versus betrayal
Authority versus subversion
Sanctity versus degradation

I believe there is plenty of evidence to indicate that these foundations are precariously arranged in our society today. As I asserted in the first chapter, *The soil has been depleted of fertility and vast tracts of land are no longer suitable for life.* This statement is true both literally and figuratively. Social patterns in dominant western culture have contributed to the degradation of soil. Weakened soil fertility has affected the moral well-being of society.

Lasting damage to finite resources, such as soil, water, and air, is evidence of extensive *harm*. Forty million people without reliable access to healthy food is also incriminating.

Companies that contribute to such damage, get rich doing it, and hide the fact that they are doing so are considered by many to be *cheating*. It's bad and a lot of people know it.

Likewise, profitable companies that pay fulltime employees so little they need government aid, or that maintain productive processes with unsafe working conditions, are engaged in *oppression*. Those consumers who buy products from them, despite lots of opportunities to know what is going on, are implicated here, especially affluent consumers with alternative choices. In a country as wealthy as ours, with more calories per capita than we need, hunger is another form of oppression, which can be laid partly at the feet of government.

Various corporations, including acclaimed companies with storied histories, have demonstrated little allegiance to the consumers to whom they sell, the workers they employ, or the communities in which they operate. When executives won't let their own families eat the products they make, and when companies leave the settings they occupy worse off than they found them, it's *betrayal*. When politicians let them get away with it, that is too. Anyone who turns a blind eye to such behavior and helps to reelect such officeholders, for whatever reason, is complicit.

Lobbying efforts of Big Food and Big Ag, and their hired flunkies in politics and research who spread misinformation, sometimes undermine the credibility of known experts related to nutrition and climate change. Anyone trying to promote such confusion is engaging in *subversion* of facts, truth, and trust.

What is uglier than the willful poisoning of human bodies and knowing destruction of precious resources? The defiling of our land, water, and air is *degradation*. I think that is true at face value. (I use the term "our" intentionally here as these finite resources ultimately belong to everyone.) It's also the case that the natural world is regarded as very important, or even holy, by most organized religions. Those who sully it are often at odds with their own religion's teachings.

These patterns aren't in play everywhere at all times, of course. But the analytical empirical evidence indicating that they are unfolding on a large scale is formidable. They collectively comprise a moral failure. Our moral footprint is dirty and deep.

Why? What has motivated people to participate in such destructive behavior? As I've said, there are numerous factors. In my view, though, the most important explanation involves expansive market culture. As detailed in Chapter 2, several issues have become prominent in our society and have overwhelmed other important principles. These include efficiency, profit, consumption, individualism, competition, and short-term thinking. I believe it is the prevalence of these themes in our attitudes and behaviors that are behind the weakening of moral foundations.

The corrosive arrangement of moral foundations described above, and the expansive market culture behind it comprise the main elements of the ugly story of American food. Our failing dominant food system is at the heart of crumbling moral foundations largely because of expansive market culture. Powerful leaders of large institutions associated with government and corporations, especially, as well as ordinary consumers are implicated in this mess. That is the bad news.

Moral Vitality and Sustainable Culture

And yet! There is also good news to be found in the beautiful story. The alternative agro-food movement provides evidence that expansive market culture is under pressure from a small, but rapidly growing current flowing in a different direction. We see in the work of engaged sustainers alternative patterns that support viable moral foundations.

Engaged sustainers who are neighborly model deep *care.* Loving an acre of land, growing nutrient-rich crops, treating animals humanely, and cooking tasty, nutritious foods are acts of care.

The culture of sharing, reciprocity, and collaboration among engaged sustainers is all about *fairness.* Trying to remove the rapacious intermediaries in our food system, and bringing more transparency to food production all serve the ideal of fairness.

Understanding that every person has a right to good food, culturally resonant food, and influence over how they get it represents a commitment to *liberty.* Freedom from hunger has rippling implications. Any alternatives to the dominant food system this movement can help generate (e.g., farming techniques, food distribution choices, nourishing foods) advances the goal of freedom, too. Every such alternative weakens the mainstream system— including the taxpayer-funded subsidies to Big Ag.

Those who take care of the land, and their neighbors evince *loyalty*— not to some backstabbing adversary or to narrow self-interest, but to a broader concern.

To respect the knowledge scientists generate is to acknowledge genuine *authority.* Trusting farmers to grow their own crops with integrity, and helping them to be independent of coercive oligopolistic forces, is too. More to the point, to work with nature, rather than trying to conquer it, is to embrace a profound source of authority.

Comprehending the elemental meaning of nature, being humble before it, and finding joy in it, is to feel *sanctity.*

Most engaged sustainers are committed to these foundations. Some of them, though not all, think explicitly in these terms. But there is another, perhaps more concrete, way that they understand the world—or rather a way that they *know* the world. Just as expansive market culture partly explains why our mainstream food system is failing, an alternative sort of culture can account for the countertrend. That is, an alternative culture nurtured by engaged sustainers facilitates a different sense of the moral foundations.

Chapter 2 summarized the problems with expansive market culture, the failings in our food system extending from overemphasis on efficiency, profit, consumption, individualism, competition, and short-term thinking. Again, it's not that all those goals are inherently problematic. It's just that they are out of balance relative to other ideals.

For each of those issues, we can see in the behavior of engaged sustainers an alternative cultural alloy, additional ideals that offer more balance.[1]

> Efficiency . . . meaning
> Profit . . . need
> Consumption . . . creation
> Individualism . . . community
> Short-term thinking . . . long-term thinking

Several times I described engaged sustainers who think and behave in "slow" ways—with thoughtfulness and care. Such activity makes for alertness to *meaning.* By thinking about how to grow plants, how to cook food, and how to relate to neighbors, engaged sustainers attach themselves to a larger context. Here and now grows in significance. This place and time become linked to our past and future, and to other settings.

Every time a farmer, cook, or consumer sacrifices some money for another ideal, in all likelihood they serve a certain *need.* The need of other species, the neighborhood, culinary arts, or even just the principle of integrity. People who give food away, volunteer, pay more to keep a known business associate thriving, or pay more to keep employees prosperous, are complicating the most fundamental goal of market culture, profit.

We have to consume to survive. Nothing is more basic than that. Ultimately, however, consumption is dependent on *creation.* The practice of leaving the place better than you found it, which is to say with healthier soil, bodies, and communities, as many engaged sustainers know, is to participate in sacred creation.

The strange condition of *Homo sapiens* being at once a social and an individual sort of species is endlessly fascinating and tricky. Engaged sustainers understand that "it takes a village" to do most good things. No agriculture or food system will ultimately work with a group of atomized individuals scurrying around trying to get as much as they can. As previously noted, *community* is the most common word (not directly related to agriculture or food) I heard mentioned by engaged sustainers.

Slow thinking is closely akin to *long-term thinking*. In both cases, the broad sense of time ties into a capacious sense of space, as in the land, the ecosystem, the earth, the elements. I heard numerous references to the past and the future, as described in chapter 10. Whereas the market thinks in terms of quarterly reports, one-day sales, what the stock market did this morning, and getting the order delivered on time, this movement realizes that what really matters has a much larger context that transcends this moment.

THE UGLY STORY VERSUS THE BEAUTIFUL STORY

Our mainstream food system is a mess, a great, big, seemingly intractable mess. It's like a huge, flat, polluted river that slowly, inexorably drifts through population centers, picking up more filth along the way and tainting everything it touches. Some people might swim, bathe, or fish in it. But it's spoiled by toxic waste. The dirtiest tributaries are contaminated with sewage.

Wherever you look at the Toxic River, from one location or another, it looks pretty much the same. Some people are invested in keeping it the way it is. They don't want to stop doing the things that make it so foul. Many others are so used to it—it seems to be everywhere—they barely notice the stench. Familiarity can be comforting, even if it is kind of gross. At any rate, it's hard for many to imagine anything different.

A little ways in the distance there is another, smaller stream. It is fed by numerous tiny brooks. They start from natural springs in high places that spill down steep hills over rocks. As they flow through gullies and gorges, they are joined by other creeks. The central channel quickly grows in volume. Its sparkling, clear freshness is a wonder. Most people who see the Fresh Stream up close fall in love.

One waterway is huge and never changes. The other is much smaller, even in its largest stretch, but grows every day. Only some people, who are adventurous and observant, have seen the Fresh Stream. Lots of them wonder why the Toxic River isn't as pleasant. They hope the little one will flow into the big one downstream and help make it cleaner. However charming it is, though, some of them are skeptical that the little one will amount to much. There are, after all, reasons to think it will ultimately be absorbed by the big foul river. Or maybe the little one is just a temporary rivulet that will dry up soon.

In effect, our dominant food system is rife with potent moral garbage. The alternative agro-food movement is relatively small, but it is appealing and gaining strength. Whether it will end up being broadly transformative is impossible to know. As dynamic and energetic as it is, there are in fact significant impediments. I'll mention several that I think are at the top of the list.

The first issue is logistical, the question of scale. Can regenerative agriculture be scaled up to produce enough healthy calories to feed the world? How much healing of all the damaged soil and air can regenerative agriculture pull off?

Some of my research subjects are skeptical, like Casey McKissick, the butcher and restaurateur, and David Chandler, the hydrologist.[2] There are certainly impressive examples of good work being done on a large scale, like St. Christopher's Children's Hospital in Philadelphia, the land-grant university cooperative agricultural extensions, Sweetgreen, and The Common Market. But the vast majority of engaged sustainers I observed are working on a rather small patch. Whether they can collectively take it big, or many more will join them, remains to be seen.

A related issue is the limitations inside the movement itself. Engaged sustainers are more active in some places than others. Organic cropland is concentrated on the coasts and in the upper Midwest. Farmers' markets tend to be located in population centers and involve folks who are disproportionately white, affluent, and old. Those operated in low-income settings tend to have fewer choices, and products of inferior quality. The best health food stores are not very affordable or accessible for large portions of the population.

There is a racist streak among some in this movement, perhaps most conspicuously exemplified by Joel Salatin (see Philpot 2020a). He is a renowned doyen of regenerative agriculture, celebrated by Michael Pollan, among others, for the amazing work he has done as a farmer and teacher. Several of my subjects spent time at his farm in Virginia to learn about effective farming techniques.

In various settings, Salatin has dismissed the historic racism behind the unequal distribution of wealth (including the hundreds of acres he inherited) and denied that systematic racism in the United States exists today. He has paid tribute to William "Buffalo Bill" Cody, who is famous for perpetrating systematic violence and theft against Native Americans. He has suggested that the collapse of the family in Black communities is more consequential than racism, and that people of color who think they don't have enough opportunity in America should "return to their tribal locations and domiciles" (quoted in Philpot, 2020a).

How widespread racist sensibilities are in this movement I don't know. I encountered none of that from the people with whom I spoke. Nevertheless, it's easy to imagine the problem is not trivial in a movement that is disproportionately white and has such a strong localist bent. The Fresh Stream is not entirely pristine.[3]

Another closely related topic involves conditions external to the movement. That is the social inequality outside the movement that many engaged sustainers are trying to ameliorate. The food sovereignty movement is a force to be reckoned with. However, the powers that maintain our dominant stratification system are formidable, to say the least. Many small-scale farmers are realizing substantial success. Competing in markets dominated by Big Ag and Big Food, though, is always an uphill battle.

I know plenty of people who think it is easier to picture civilized society entirely falling apart than it is to imagine multinational corporations giving up any real ground in terms of the influence they wield, including the exploitation of workers around the world. Greed endures. So does racism. It's not just powerful executives who maintain the status quo. Lots of Americans are not convinced that all citizens, let alone all people, deserve to eat healthy food.

The final wrinkle I have to acknowledge is a rather large elephant in the room, which I have barely mentioned in these pages. The American political system is massively dysfunctional, which makes solving other problems especially difficult. Widespread corruption through lobbying, campaign finance, and graft is stunningly visible and often legal. Dissemination of misinformation and willful ignorance poisons democratic processes. From corporate taxation, to gun safety, healthcare, and a range of other issues, we see numerous surveys indicating what majorities of Americans want. Yet, little gets done. All of those layered problems in the polity, especially at the federal level, will surely get in the way of any comprehensive change in our food system.

With such daunting obstacles, it's tempting to surrender to cynicism, to forget about our common life, and just look out for Number One. However, the most committed, persuasive, engaged sustainers in the movement won't yield. They are like George Bailey in *It's a Wonderful Life* during the bank crisis. Everyone in the town is upset and wants to withdraw their money from the savings and loan. George implores his neighbors to trust him and to trust one another. By working together, and not succumbing to the fears of all the horrible things right in front of them, he exclaims, they can manage.

To pull that off, George basically describes their "inescapable network of mutuality" (to borrow Martin Luther King's memorable phrase). "You're thinking about this place all wrong, as if I had the money back in a safe. The money's not here. Why, your money's in Joe's house. That's right next to yours, and in the Kennedy house, and in Mrs. Maplin's house, and a hundred others." He identifies his neighbors by name, the challenges they all share, the particularity of their specific hardships, and what would happen if Mr. Potter had more control over them. "Can't you understand what's happening here? Don't you see what's happening? Potter isn't selling. Potter is buying. And why? Because we're panicking and he's not. That's why. We can get through this thing alright. We've got to stick together, though. We've got to have faith in each other."

Potter controls the bank, bus-lines, and department stores. He's like the Toxic River—our dominant food system. The Bailey Savings and Loan is like the Fresh Stream—the alternative agro-food movement.

On its best days, the alternative agro-food movement is a radical act of imagination being instantiated one neighbor, acre, and meal at a time. Like George Bailey, it invites a fresh take on things. A different way to think about our lives, one another, and our relationship to the big picture. Through the lens of this movement, we can grasp that what I eat is dependent on what you grow and vice versa, what we eat and grow is dependent on the health of the soil, and vice versa, the vitality of my community is dependent on what I put into it, and vice versa. A network of mutuality, indeed.

Scale is a key issue, as noted above. It is tempting to think about minutia in my neck of the woods—*what exactly is on my fork right now?!*—to the neglect of other issues. Of course, we can't lose track of the whole forest, the systems on which all people rely. The systems ultimately matter a great deal. For various reasons, however, I have come to think of the preoccupation with scale and the ambition to completely transform our system as potentially immobilizing.

That is, some would wait until there is a comprehensive plan. They delay taking one single concrete step until the theory of how such change can be implemented is fully articulated. They argue against little steps because such incremental shifts might undermine broad transformation. History has proven that that is often a legitimate concern. In this case, though, I believe it is misguided.

The mesoscopic and multiscopic engaged sustainers I met have led me instead to appreciate the orientation of "possibilism." This is the approach Albert Hirschman based on a commitment to "the right to a non-projected future." Hirschman came to believe in "petites idées" or little ideas. Take on one problem at a time. Then another.

That's how Mort Mather, the old organic farmer in Maine, thinks. He focuses on what he can control, but he shares the fruits of his labor (literally) with his son and his community. Michael Kilpatrick wants to build a movement but advises each farmer to emphasize what they are good at. Barbara

Glaser has had many projects but has a knack for really bearing down on what's in front of her. Rick Chrisman, the Protestant minister and thoughtful consumer, knows that our consciousness can pay attention to only so much. Marti Wolfson encourages us to experiment while cooking—if it works, keep doing it. Anna Woofenden has a gift for being in the present as a loud world swirls around her. Helen Dennis says we should look at hunger "on a smaller scale" and take on slivers of the problem "in smaller groups." These are all little brooks flowing into the Fresh Stream.

During the bank crisis, George Bailey doesn't try to get rid of Potter. He has no grand scheme. He's certainly not trying to get rich. He just wants the Bailey Savings and Loan, and all the members of his community, to survive the day intact. His determination proves contagious.

Mary, his wife, is initially reluctant to do anything. "Don't look now but there's something funny going on over at the bank, George," Burt, the cab driver, says. "I've never really seen one, but that's got all the earmarks of being a run." Mary says, "George, let's not stop. Let's go." She's only thinking about George and her. "Please, let's not stop, George!" A few minutes later, as George pleads for his clients not to panic, his neighborliness proves contagious. Mary steps up and offers up their honeymoon money. Like George, she becomes willing to make a personal sacrifice on that day for the greater good. It's just a little idea—that matters a lot on that day and makes other subsequent little ideas viable. That's why George and the gang celebrate after they get to closing time and put the only two single dollar bills they have left in the safe with fanfare. They made it through the crisis. They solved one problem.

One of the things I have loved about that film since my friend Paul Schroeder (remember the Cardinals paraphernalia hoarder?) dragged me to see it in college ("yes, it's old and black and white but I guarantee that you'll love it!") is that a bunch of little victories, interspersed with many defeats, adds up to . . . a wonderful life!

Several times I have mentioned a common orientation in the practice of social work called harm reduction. It is based on the premise that people are flawed, some are addicts, and that the goal is not to fix everything, but to do as much as you can. That's what possibilism is about.

And that's my hope for the alternative agro-food movement. Bad stories are seductive and in some sense infectious. But good stories are also seductive and infectious. Engaged sustainers enact and embody good stories. And each one flows into a broader narrative.

With all of that in mind, here are some suggestions as to how each of us might add to the Fresh Stream. I offer these thoughts as someone who is not a farmer, professional cook, nutritionist, or supply chain expert, but as a layperson who wants a wonderful life for us all. That said, though, I think that the probability of every one of these suggestions leading to something wonderful is supported by solid empirical research.

1. Reimagine how your family eats. Established habits are not easily changed. And food means different things to different people. But the first step is recognizing that change is possible. Baby steps and flexibility are important for most people who try to redefine their patterns.

2. Prepare home-cooked meals and sit down together to eat them slowly. It's not easy and certainly harder for some than others. Nevertheless. I sincerely believe this may be the single most important habit that my wife and I have maintained as parents and aspiring engaged sustainers.

3. Talk to people—farmers, cooks, neighbors, and especially your loved ones. Discuss what is healthy, affordable, tasty, and ecologically sound. Cultivate buy-in from household members. Pick the right "Jones" to "try to keep up with."

4. Find out where your food comes from and goes to. Become supply chain anglers who learn about how ingredients were produced (relative to soil, labor, animals, etc.), and what happens to them after they are consumed (relative to nutrition and waste). You've heard it before: think globally, act locally. If you can't do the work yourself, find smart shortcuts, like B Corporations or social influencers you trust.

5. Try something funky. Start a garden. Join a community garden. Buy directly from farmers. Find new recipes with foods you haven't used before. Volunteer at farmers' markets, food banks, soup kitchens, coops, and other nonprofit organizations. Breaking out of routines and taking risks is part of the reimagining process. "Everyone can do something," Ellen Kelsey (2020) said. "And then something else."

6. Join community, regional, and national organizations. It takes more than a village to transform our food system. Social capital is a prerequisite for most solutions in social life. There is nurturing community, fulfilling purpose, and satisfying accomplishment waiting to be enjoyed in such settings.

7. Learn about the most formidable obstacles. Is it a matter of powerful political bullies? Or entrenched habits of regular people? Lack of information or access? Which barriers are actionable? Based on what you learn, you can then be strategic. Perhaps you have to kill them with kindness, elect different people, connect various players so they can coordinate, or study at the feet of others who have overcome the challenges.

8. Play the long game. Rome wasn't built in a day. Keep track of where you've been, where you are, and where you hope to go in terms of the

cycle of engagement but maybe don't take responsibility for doing everything possible.

You'll notice that none of these items is rocket science. Anybody can take action on any of these fronts. That doesn't make it easy. The Toxic River is all around us and its cultural current is strong. But the Fresh Stream is available to each of us if we are willing to let it flow into our consciousness. Every one of these actions is doable either in small, incremental steps or as broad, ambitious leaps. Moreover, if you look at most successful social movements or favorable cultural shifts, and consider the moments of their greatest triumph, and then work backwards to see how it all unfolded, you will often see at least some incremental steps similar to these.

I love food and through this research have come to revere those who make it available. I find this movement to be stirring, both in terms of what it is doing for our food system, but more importantly for all the lessons it offers for how neighbors can live together. I think this story is both credible and wondrous. Perhaps most importantly, it affects how I think about other stories. Don't you see what's happening? We've got to have faith in each other.

NOTES

1. The moral foundations (i.e., care, fairness, liberty, loyalty, authority, sanctity) are presented as juxtaposed against morally disruptive circumstances (e.g., harm, cheating, oppression, betrayal, subversion, degradation) because they are inherently opposites. Hence the use of the word "versus." The elements of expansive market culture (i.e., efficiency, profit, consumption, individualism, short-term thinking) are not portrayed here exactly in juxtaposition with the themes of sustainable culture (i.e., meaning, need, creation, community, long-term thinking) because their relationship is more complex. I believe the two sets of values have been in tension but are not mutually exclusive.

2. Plenty of other observers are too. See, for example, Poppendieck (1999), Guthman (2004; 2011), Brown and Getz (2008), Newman (2019), Bowen et al. (2019).

3. For various objectionable elements that are in play in this movement, see also Guthman (2004), Gray (2014), Newman (2019), Weiss (2021), Bowen et al. (2019), Schupp (2017).

Appendix A
Methods and Data

When I studied sociology in college, we learned no formal social scientific methodology. My advisor was a superb teacher, revered by students and respected by colleagues. But he had no time for the technical stuff. Our attention was drawn to important books and big ideas. However, one of the requirements was a senior thesis for which we were expected to study a social phenomenon in some depth. There was one on Rastafarians (as I expect there was at a lot of colleges during those years). Another classmate was trying to study car crashes in Kenya. I'm still not sure what that was about. My topic involved some vague notion about "dichotomous thinking."

As I began that project, I consulted my father, who had been a sociology major himself. Even then, I knew my teacher was not providing enough guidance. Dad suggested I find six people and interview them about the questions I had. That seemed way too hard for me. Who would I find? How would I get them to speak with me? What would I ask?

Well, things turned out OK (though my senior thesis stunk). I finished college and went on to pursue sociology in graduate school. There I was introduced to real methods and epistemology. After a couple courses about Thomas Kuhn, inductive and deductive methods, multivariate analyses, and the like, my dad's suggestion was not only demystified; it seemed quaint. Six people! What can you learn from six people? You would be stuck with the "Small N Problem," I realized. I wrote, or rather I should say I completed (the argument leaned more on numbers than words), a master's thesis using social survey data. Dozens of variables for thousands of cases spared me from the Small N Problem. The first time I saw my work in print, I felt enormously proud—even a tad immortal. But I also felt funny about what I had learned. That is, I wasn't at all clear what it was. It didn't matter, though, because I had statistical significance and a "pub" in hand.

Most of my scholarly endeavors for the next 20 years used comparative historical methods. I would study old documents, archives, and primary sources to identify patterns in social history that generated theoretical arguments. More recently, I realized I wanted to learn about something unfolding right now, which could not be revealed through archival research and was too subtle for large data sets. Having consumed quite a bit of social science based on a wide range of methodological approaches, I now have a deeper sense of some of the tradeoffs. What I needed to do, I realized, was talk to people. Find six people! But when I recognized that direction could be useful, it felt so hard.

I came to understand that the best qualitative researchers were doing something very tricky. Find the right people. Make sure they have something in common that makes them comparable. Make sure they have some differences that make them interesting. How do you get them to agree to be interviewed? How do you make them comfortable, lead them to the right topic, evoke their candor, and protect what they want protected, all at once? It was daunting. But it paid off.

This research is informed by three kinds of sources. The most important primary evidence comes from a series of semi-structured interviews. I also conducted participant observation at conferences, farmers' markets, community-supported agriculture operations, and soup kitchens. In addition, I consulted numerous secondary sources, including scientific research, government documents, journalistic accounts, and various treatises and essays.

For the interviews, I used an approach called convenience or snowball sampling. I started by approaching farmers at the farmers' market in my hometown in upstate New York, alums from my institution I knew were in relevant industries, contacts in eastern Pennsylvania (where my in-laws live) and western North Carolina (where my mother lives). Over time, through this inductive process, I gained more clarity into what I was looking for.

Any time I interviewed a research subject with pertinent information, I asked them if they could think of others who might be helpful. This led to formal interviews with some 60 people that my undergraduate research assistants and/or I conducted between 2013 and 2022 (the vast majority between 2017 and 2020). Three of them were interviewed by my assistants without my presence. The interviews generally lasted an hour, though sometimes more.

The snowball sampling led to interviews of subjects who live in California, Maine, Massachusetts, Michigan, New York, North Carolina, Pennsylvania, South Carolina, and Vermont. Half of the respondents are fulltime farmers, part-time farmers, or avid gardeners. Nine are chefs or serious cooks. Four work in medical professions. Six work in for-profit (non-farm-based) businesses. Twelve work for nonprofit organizations linked to food or sustainability. Fourteen of them think of themselves as educators in one form or another.

Fifteen of them are published writers. Twelve are committed volunteers or activists. Four are serious artists.

I spoke with many other people, about 40 of them, in less formal circumstances. And I observed dozens more in different settings. None of those subjects are listed in the primary Cast of Characters (see appendix C), but the information they shared is integrated into this account.

Three research subjects I interviewed explicitly identify as people of color (two Black people and one Asian Indian American). Most of the others identify as white. The racial and ethnic identity of a small handful is not known to me. While this movement is disproportionately white, this skewed racial distribution is a significant shortcoming in my sample. However, I did seek out extra sources at conferences for participant observation to help provide a fuller perspective. I spoke more informally and/or observed a dozen people of color who are associated with this movement. I also consulted particular texts to help provide more context for questions of diversity in relation to this movement.

Twenty-four respondents identify as female and thirty-seven as male. I did not seek out a lot of information about religion, but I did learn that six of my research subjects are mainline Protestant clergy. Three people in the sample are associated with Evangelical traditions. Five identify as Jewish, including one rabbi.

Beyond the interviews and informal conversations, I observed dozens of people involved in this movement during participant observation. Multiple visits to a half dozen farmers' markets and half a dozen farms were part of this work. Several other settings provided valuable perspective as well. The annual meetings of the Northeast Organic Farmers Association of New York, the Community Outreach Program of Central United Methodist Church in Traverse City, MI, the RX: Fresh Food Symposium: Prescription for a Healthier America, the Uprooting Racism in the Food System workshop, and the Food Justice Summit sponsored by the Adirondack Health Institute stand out in this regard. Between these two primary sources of evidence (interviews and participation observation), plus the secondary sources, I acquired a good sense of a lot of things going on in the alternative agro-food movement as a whole.

It is the case, however, that in light of the fact that my primary evidence comes from 60 interviews, and observations of several dozen other people, what I really know is only what I heard and saw myself. Even that involves a subjective, interpretive process. What food means to people, what they think and say about it, is complicated. So many experiences, feelings, and identities are wrapped up in our food. So, the portrait I am presenting, as informed by people I interviewed and observed, is just a snapshot refracted through their own sense of the world, a subjective way of describing it to me, and my own interpretation.

For that reason, I have endeavored to give the research subjects a strong voice in this text. They are quoted and paraphrased extensively. I also intentionally placed myself in the text, overtly sharing my own perceptions and observations along the way, as well as analogies, metaphors, and anecdotes intended to clarify various points.

As a group, the research subjects reveal a great deal of information. But they do not constitute any sort of representative sample. The secondary research literature I consulted, including more ambitiously analytical studies, aligned with what I personally encountered in a number of ways. Any generalizations I have made beyond those I interacted with, however, are necessarily speculative.

I emphasize the word *snapshot* here because what I have tried to capture is also temporally delimited. I started this research a decade ago. People's lives change, relationships evolve, prices fluctuate, and weather patterns shift. Not to mention the global pandemic. No doubt some of what I have described is no longer exactly the way it was when I observed it. For instance, I know my subjects' lives have been touched by changes in jobs, financial gain and loss, relocation, aging, the birth of children, divorce, illness, and death. Based on how robust the patterns were and how they were corroborated by secondary sources, though, I do not think the main account here is at all obsolete.

On top of these inherent limitations, I believe the evidentiary basis of this book has two major weaknesses. The first pertains to race, as noted above. The other is that I was not able to garner much information from workers. Most of the observational evidence comes from owners, managers, or volunteers. The biggest gap in this regard is agricultural workers. How do they think about this movement? What is their role in it? In this research, I offer little commentary in response to those important questions. I did seek out secondary evidence on this topic and shared some of that information in the text. Still, the shortcoming remains.

Appendix B

The Central Cast of Characters

These are the thirty-five people with whom I had direct contact who factor most prominently into my thinking. I have listed the activities in the cycle of engagement I heard each person discuss. I believe most all of these folks are thoughtful consumers, but I have listed consumption as one of their activities only in the cases where I explicitly heard them mention it. Twenty-three of them have their own section. The other eleven are described in less detail but are still important. Dozens of other subjects not listed here inform my overall sense of things. See Appendix A: Methods and Data for more information on the sample as a whole.

A number of these subjects are referenced in multiple chapters, but I have listed the main ones where their work is described in some detail.

Jamie Alger—Farmer, co-owner of Hickory Nut Gap Farm in Fairview, NC, near Asheville. Engaged in grounding, extraction, communication. See Chapter 4: Extraction.

Richard Ball*—New York State Commissioner of New York State Department of Agriculture and Markets, farmer, owner of Schoharie Valley Farms in Schoharie, NY. Engaged in grounding, extraction, communication. See Chapter 8: Stewardship.

Christopher Bolden-Newsome—Farmer, educator, Sankofa Community Farm in Philadelphia, PA. Engaged in grounding, extraction, distribution, stewardship, and communication. See Chapter 8: Stewardship.

Hope Casto—Gardener, cook, college Professor of Education Studies at Skidmore College. Engaged in grounding, extraction, consumption, and communication. See Chapter 11: Social Sources of Engagement.

Rose Cherneff—Farmer, educator, Abundance Farm in Northampton, MA. Engaged in grounding, extraction, communication. See Chapter 4: Extraction.

Rick Chrisman—Pastor, St. Eliot Church of Newton (United Church of Christ). Engaged in consumption. See Chapter 7: Consumption.

Jean-Paul Courtens*—Farmer, educator, co-owner Roxbury Farm in Kinderhook, NY. Engaged in grounding, extraction, communication. See Chapter 10: Patterns among Engaged Sustainers.

Helen Dennis—Writer, cook, activist, pursuing a graduate degree in communications at The University of South Carolina. Engaged in processing, consumption, stewardship, and communication. See Chapter 9: Communication.

Graham DuVaul—Co-owner and manager of Mother Earth Foods based in Asheville, NC. Engaged in consumption and distribution. See Chapter 6: Distribution.

Nancy Ferguson—Schoolteacher, conservationist based in Saratoga Springs, NY. Engaged in stewardship and communication. See Chapter 9: Communication.

Richard Frank—Owner and Manager of Four Seasons Natural Foods health store in Saratoga Springs, NC. Engaged in distribution and consumption. See Chapter 6: Distribution.

Barbara Glaser—Philanthropist, volunteer, activist in multiple states in the United States and multiple countries, based in Saratoga Springs, NY. Engaged in stewardship, communication. See Chapter 8: Stewardship and Chapter 11: Social Sources of Engagement.

Corinne Hansch—Farmer, co-owner of Lovin' Mama Farm in Amsterdam, NY. Engaged in grounding, extraction, consumption. See Chapter 3: Grounding.

Hans Kersten—Pediatrician at St. Christopher's Children's Hospital in Philadelphia, PA. Engaged in distribution and communication. See Chapter 6: Distribution.

Michael Kilpatrick—Farmer, educator, activist, co-owner Kilpatrick Family Farm in Middle Granville, NY. Engaged in grounding, extraction, stewardship, communication. See Chapter 5: Extraction and Chapter 11: Social Sources of Engagement.

Hans Kunisch—Business consultant, chef based in Los Angeles. Engaged in processing, communication. See Chapter 10: Patterns among Engaged Sustainers.

Kevin Quandt—Vice President of Supply Chain and Sustainability with Sweetgreen. Engaged in distribution. See Chapter 6: Distribution and Chapter 8: Consumption.

Matthew Leon—Farmer, co-owner of Lovin' Mama Farm in Amsterdam, NY. Engaged in grounding, extraction, consumption. See Chapter 3: Grounding.

Jim Lieberman—Farmer living off the grid in California. Engaged in grounding, extraction, stewardship, and consumption. See Chapter 7: Consumption.

Jane Lippert—Minister and Community Outreach Coordinator, Central Methodist Church in Traverse City, MI. Engaged in distribution, stewardship. See Chapter 6: Distribution.

Dee Lowman—Methodist pastor, gardener, cook. Engaged in grounding, extraction, processing, consumption, communication. See Chapter 11: Patterns among Engaged Sustainers.

Casey McKissick—Restaurateur, butcher, ex-farmer, ex-teacher based in Asheville, NC. See Chapter 6: Processing.

Mort Mather—Farmer, consultant, and author based in Maine. Engaged in grounding, extraction, and communication. See Chapter 4: Grounding.

Alyssa Momnie—Gardener, cook, mother of Mateo and Andre, WWOOFer, based in Maine. Engaged in grounding, extraction, consumption. See Chapter 8: Consumption and Chapter 10: Patterns among Engaged Sustainers.

David R. Montgomery*—Gardener, geomorphologist based at the University of Washington, author of numerous books, including *Dirt: The Erosion of Civilizations* and *Growing a Revolution: Bringing Our Soil Back to Life*. Engaged in grounding, extraction, communication. See Chapter 2: The Ugly Story of the American Food System.

Marion Nestle*—Professor of Food Studies based at New York University, author of numerous books, including *Food Politics: How the Food Industry Influences Nutrition and Health, Soda Politics: Taking on Big Soda,* and *Unsavory Truth: How Food Companies Skew the Science of What We Eat.* Engaged in consumption and communication. See Chapter 2: The Ugly Story of the American Food System.

Leah Penniman*—Farmer, co-owner of Soul Fire Farm near Albany, NY, educator, author of *Farming While Black, Soul Fire Farm's Practical Guide to Liberation on the Land.* Engaged in grounding, extraction, processing, consumption, stewardship, communication. See Chapter 10: Patterns among Engaged Sustainers.

Janet Poppendick*—Sociologist based at Hunter College, author of numerous books, including *Sweet Charity? Emergency Food and the End of Entitlement* and *Free for All: Fixing School Food in America.* Engaged in stewardship, communication. See Chapter 6: Distribution.

Tim Storrow—Farmer, Director of the Castenea Foundation, which supports family farms. Engaged in grounding, extraction, stewardship, communication. See Chapter 8: Stewardship.

Naomi Tannen—Gardener, soup kitchen volunteer, retired teacher, ex-farmer based in western, MA. Engaged in grounding, extraction, stewardship, communication. See Chapter 4: Extraction.

Owen Taylor—Seedsaver, farmer, owner of Truelove Seeds, based in Philadelphia, PA. Engaged in grounding, extraction, stewardship, communication. See Chapter 9: Stewardship.

Rachel Terry—National Partnership Director of The Common Market. Engaged in distribution, stewardship. See Chapter 6: Distribution.

Marti Wolfson—Chef, consultant, teacher. Engaged in processing, consumption, communication. See Chapter 5: Processing.

Anna Woofenden—Ordained minister in The New Church, founder of The Garden Church in Los Angeles, author of *This is God's Table: Finding Church Beyond the Walls*. Engaged in grounding, extraction, communication. See Chapter 9: Communication.

Steveanna Wynne—Director of The Share Food Program in Philadelphia, PA. Engaged in distribution and stewardship. See Chapter 6: Distribution.

* These are important sources I've heard speak in public but have not interviewed.

Appendix C

Glossary

Business as usual (BAU): A term developed by Juliet Schor (2011, p. 4) that refers to "current economic rules, practices, growth trajectory, and ecological consequences of production and consumption." See Chapter 2: The Ugly Story of the American Food System and Chapter 8: Stewardship.

BRUCE the Old Dog: A label for a hypothetical mature farmer who is committed to old agricultural techniques and traditions and unwilling to try new things. The acronym BRUCE stands for bull-headed, rigid, unteachable, conventional, experienced. Some research subjects described such older farmers they know as resistant to change. See Chapter 10: Patterns among Engaged Sustainers.

Communication: The one element of the cycle of engagement that is not fundamentally material in character. The activity of *communication* is to help more people grasp the connections among the different stages in the *cycle of engagement*, and the root idea at the center of it all, that humanity and nature are necessarily bound up in overlapping interests. *Engaged sustainers* who participate in relevant *communication* include researchers, teachers, journalists, filmmakers, writers, clergy, storytellers, and others who use the spoken and written word or images to share ideas. This part of the *cycle of engagement* extends from and connects to all elements of the cycle. See Chapter 9: Communication.

Consumption: I have used this familiar term in several different ways. Of course, it has an everyday connotation related to food, basically the act of eating it. It is also relevant to the conventional understanding of the economy (i.e., the linear sense of production, distribution, and consumption). The premise in that context is that there is a certain carelessness or even irresponsibility associated with depleting resources. The most important usage of the term here, though, is as one of the stages of the *cycle of engagement*. Consumers who are *engaged sustainers* tend to be more thoughtful with respect to their habits compared to normative, mainstream American consumers. Some of them are *supply chain anglers*. As an activity in *the cycle of engagement, consumption* is about getting good food into oneself or other people. *Consumption* is the direct result of *distribution* and/or *processing*. See Chapter 7: Consumption.

Cycle of engagement: A set of activities at the center of the alternative agro-food movement based on a particular sense of the economy. Instead of business as usual, this perspective encompasses different stages (i.e., *grounding, extraction, processing, distribution, consumption, stewardship, and communication*) that feed into one another. These activities are carried out by engaged sustainers who tend to think of the economy in broader terms that are harmonious, synergistic, and generative. See especially chapters 3–9.

Distribution: One of the stages of the *cycle of engagement*. Natural resources have to be transported from the location where they are generated to the place where people will acquire them for use. And there must be some system for figuring who will get what. That is the task of *distribution*, which is carried out by restaurants, supermarkets, health food stores, farmers' markets, community-supported agriculture, food banks, soup kitchens. Most distributors are concerned with whether people actually eat the food they get, but their main goal is to get the food distributed. Thus, restaurants care more about how much food is purchased versus actually eaten. *Distribution* and *processing* both extend from extraction and lead to consumption. Sometimes *processing* precedes *distribution*, like when wheat is milled into flour before it is taken to a store. And sometimes *distribution* precedes *processing*, like when fish are taken to a restaurant before they are cooked. See Chapter 6: Distribution.

Engaged sustainer: A person actively involved in the *cycle of engagement*. They care about sustainability in connection with agriculture and food. They do more than just think and talk about it but take concerted action. They tend to think of themselves as participants in the alternative agro-food movement or some related collective endeavor. I sometimes refer to an engaged sustainer involved in a particular stage of the cycle of engagement in terms of their specific activity, like an engaged grounder, and engaged consumer, and so on. See especially chapters 3–9.

Expansive Market Culture: A particular set of themes enacted in individuals' daily lives and built into social institutions. The dominant values in expansive market culture are efficiency, profit, consumption, individualism, short-term thinking. Market culture is not inherently rotten to the core. It can be part of a viable social system when situated among other countervailing institutions and cultural norms. It is the expansive part that makes it problematic. These values are out of control in our society and thereby flow through most aspects of our lives, overwhelming other ideals. This situation is documented in my 2012 book, *Rich, Free and Miserable: The Failure of Success in America.* See Chapter 1: Moral Foundations and Market Culture, Chapter 2: The Ugly Story of the American Food System and Chapter 12: So What?

Extraction: One of the stages of the *cycle of engagement* focused on generating natural resources that people can use directly or indirectly for food. This includes farming, gardening, foaling, milking, fishing, slaughtering, and reaping, for example. *Extraction* leads primarily into *processing,* though sometimes to *distribution.* It is dependent on *grounding.* See Chapter 4: Extraction.

Food apartheid: Social systems that separate people from reliable access to healthy food. This concept is closely related to the concept of food deserts. But the key distinction is that whereas a desert is a naturally occurring viable ecosystem, various arrangements of the American food system are the result of human designs (see Sevilla 2021). The word *apartheid* means "separateness" or "aparthood." This term, *food apartheid*, implies a degree of intentionality behind the stratified food system of our society, which disproportionately impacts communities where people of color and/or low-income families live. Other social arrangements, such as employment, education, criminal justice, healthcare, legal representation, and political representation, are all entangled with the prevalence of *food apartheid.* See Chapter 2: The Ugly Story of the American Food System.

Grounding: One of the stages of the *cycle of engagement. Grounding* is about trying to affect the human impact on natural resources, including plants, animals, earth, sun, water, and air, in a benign way. Developing alternative energy or sophisticated inputs for agriculture are examples. *Grounding* leads directly into *extraction.* It is dependent on *stewardship.* See Chapter 3: Grounding.

Latent sustainer: A person who is aligned with the goals of the alternative agro-food movement and participates in behavior that helps the movement but does not explicitly identify with the movement as such. *Latent sustainers* add value to the movement by advancing its goals and serving as role models for others. Unlike *engaged sustainers,* though, they do not seek out collaborators in the larger movement. In addition, by not labeling what they do in terms of an agenda or movement, they do little to help with the communication and framing related to the movement. See Chapter 9: Communication.

Moral footprint: A hypothetical, composite measure of a person's or group's impact in the world in terms of the long-term well-being of human beings and nature. The smaller and cleaner, the better. The notion of morality being used here comes from Jonathan Haidt's categories in moral foundation theory (see Haidt 2006; 2007; 2012; Haidt and Graham 2009; Haidt and Joseph 2004). They are care, fairness, liberty, loyalty, authority, and sanctity. In effect, the more of those foundations built into social behaviors, the better the moral footprint. See The Introduction, Chapter 1: Moral Foundations and Market Culture and Chapter 12: So What?

Mesoscopic engaged sustainers: People who actively participate in the alternative agro-food movement by keeping their focus on a medium-sized project. For example, one could farm an acre, which is a more ambitious endeavor than a tiny garden but less ambitious than a giant ranch. Or one could own one small health food store, which is sort of in between selling vegetables from your small garden versus running a multinational corporation. See Chapter 10: Patterns among Engaged Sustainers.

Multiscopic engaged sustainers: People who actively participate in the alternative agro-food movement by using multiple lenses for thinking about what they do. In effect, their gaze toggles between little things and big things. They collect information about lots of little things, which informs their thinking about much broader concerns. As they ponder the bigger issues, that affects how they think about the narrower issues. For example, a medical professional could pay close attention to the physiological details of a patient's well-being and think about how they are linked to public health patterns and environmental conditions on a large scale. Or a farmer could measure the health of soil on her property and consider how it relates to long-term $CO2$ emissions. See Chapter 10: Patterns among Engaged Sustainers.

NIGEL the Hippie Farmer: A label for a hypothetical person who is attracted to the imagery and lifestyle of farming but not really committed to the learning and work that is necessary. The acronym NIGEL stands for naïve, ignorant, green, enthusiastic, loner. Some research subjects described such people as young people who look like hippies. See Chapter 10: Patterns among Engaged Sustainers.

Processing: One of the stages of the *cycle of engagement*. This is the work of converting the natural resources gathered through *extraction* into food ready for consumption. This includes, for example, de-hulling, milling, dressing, butchering, cleaning, washing, fermenting, pickling, pasteurizing, refining, jarring, canning, preserving, packaging, or, most importantly, cooking. It is usually followed by *distribution*, though sometimes it precedes *distribution*. See Chapter 5: Processing.

Stewardship: One of the stages of the *cycle of engagement.* This is about protecting natural resources (e.g., plants and animals) and human resources (i.e.,
people) on a large scale, over the long run. Thus, it includes conservation,
preservation, waste management, securing ecologically sound fuel sources,
managing weather impacts, and "green infrastructure," on one hand, and fair
treatment of workers, food security, and sovereignty, on the other. The depletion of resources by way of *consumption* leads directly into the concern for
restoring resources by way of *stewardship.* The protection of large units of
resources (e.g., safeguarding many acres of arable land, strains of seed species, communities) allows for particular efforts to invest in natural resources
(e.g., helping the soil in a particular field to become more nutrient rich). Thus,
stewardship leads directly into *grounding.* See Chapter 8: Stewardship.

Supply chain angler: An especially conscientious consumer who pays attention to the past, present, and future significance of *consumption* patterns.
Unlike the common experiences of mainstream consumers who often think of
their own consumption in very narrow, individualistic terms, or perhaps don't
really think very much about their consumption at all, supply chain anglers
recognize that consumption is inherently a social activity. The word *angler*
refers to someone fishing with a rod, line, and hook. *Angle* is an old word for
hook. Like a person fishing in a stream, a supply chain angler looks carefully
around where they are, up the stream and down the stream to see how the
water is flowing, and how they can get what they are looking for. A supply
chain angler looking upstream is mindful of how food is produced. Looking
downstream involves concern with nutritional benefits and then waste.
Paying attention to what is nearby reflects awareness of the immediate circumstances of consumption. Another layer here is that supply chain anglers
consider various perspective and implications—or angles—in relation to consumption patterns. See Chapter 5: Processing and Chapter 7: Consumption.

Sustainable Culture: a particular set of moral ideals enacted into individuals'
daily lives and built into social institutions. In contrast to *expansive market
culture,* sustainable culture emphasizes meaning, need, creation, community,
and long-term thinking. It is not necessarily better in every respect than other
cultural systems. Even this label is imperfect. Other cultural systems with
different combinations of values, sensibilities, and habits can be sustainable
too. But this particular set of organized norms emphasizes ecological sustainability per se, and the well-being of the neighborhood. And it contrasts with
the currently dominant values in expansive market culture of efficiency, efficiency, profit, consumption, individualism, short-term thinking. See Chapter
12: So What?

References

Abundance Farm. 2021. "Abundance Farm–Partners." abundancefarm.org/partners.

Addison, Corbin. 2022. *Wastelands: The True Story of Farm Country on Trial.* New York: Knopf.

Adelman, Jeremy. 2014. *Worldly Philosopher: The Odyssey of Albert O. Hirschman.* Princeton, NJ: Princeton University Press.

Adirondack Daily Enterprise. 2021. "Glaser is Council's Conservationist of the Year." adirondackdailyenterprise.com. June 9.

Ager, John Curtis. 1991. *We Plow God's Fields. The Life of James G. K. McClure.* Boone, NC: Appalachian State University.

Anderson, Lessley. 2014. "Why does Everyone Hate Monsanto." *Modern Farmer.* modernfarmer.com. March 4.

Andreyeva, Tatiana, Inas Rashad Kelly, and Jennifer L. Harris. 2011. "Exposure to Food Advertising on Television: Associations with Children's Fast Food and Soft Drink Consumption and Obesity." *Economics and Human Biology.* February.

Anielski, Mark. 2018. *An Economy of Well-Being: Genuine Wealth and Happiness.* Gabriola Island, British Columbia: New Society Publishers.

Atalan-Helicke, Nurcan, Andrew J. Schneller, Clarivel Gonzalez, Carolyn Lois, and Helen Alemayeh Mebrate. 2021. "Seed Libraries in the U.S.: Regulations, Seed Saving, Seed Sharing, and Seed Sovereignty." Pp. 163–182 in Administering and Managing the U.S. Food System: Revisiting Food Policy and Politics, edited by A. Bryce Hoflund, John C. Jones, and Michelle C. Pautz. Lanham, MD: Lexington Books.

Barbas, Samantha. 2002. "Just Like Home: 'Home Cooking' and the Domestication of the American Restaurant." *Gastronomica.* 3(4): 43–52.

Barber, Benjamin R. 2013. *If Mayors Ruled the World: Dysfunctional Nations, Rising Cities.* New Haven, CT: Yale University Press.

Battistoni, Alyssa. 2012. "America Spends Less on Food than Any Other Country." *Mother Jones.* February 1.

Bahnson, Fred and Norman Wirzba. 2011. *Making Peace with the Land: God's Call to Reconcile with Creation.* Downers Grove, IL: InterVarsity Press Books.

Bell, Michael Mayerfield, Loka L. Ashwood, Isaac Sohn Leslie, and Laura Hanson Schlacter. 2020. *An Invitation to Environmental Sociology.* New York: Sage. (6th Edition).

Benford, Robert D. and David Snow. 2000. "Framing Processes and Social Movements: An Overview and Assessment." *Annual Review of Sociology.* 26: 611–639.

Beurteaux, Danielle. 2018. "Truelove Seeds Offers a Connection to Culinary Heritage and Food Justice." *Civil Eats.* civileats.com. August 27.

Bercovici, Jeff. 2020. "Your $14 Salad's not as Eco-friendly as Advertised—But Sweetgreen's Trying." *Los Angeles Times.* latimes.com. January 15.

Berry, Wendell. 2009. *Bringing it to the Table: On Farming and Food.* Berkeley: Counterpoint.

———. 2010. *What are People For? Essays.* Berkeley: Counterpoint

Bilger, Burkhard. 2006. "The Lunchroom Rebellion." *The New Yorker,* newyorker.com/magazine/2006/09/04/the-lunchroom-rebellion.

Bimbo, Francesco, Alessandro Bonanno, Gianluca Viscecchia, and Rosaria Nardone. 2015. "The Hidden Benefits of Short Food Supply Chains: Farmers' Markets Density and Body Mass Index in Italy." *International Food and Agribusiness Management Review.* 18(1): 1–16.

Bittman, Mark. 2009. *Food Matters: A Guide to Conscious Eating with More Than 75 Recipes.* New York: Simon and Schuster.

———. 2021. *Animal, Vegetable, Junk: A History of Food, from Sustainable to Suicidal.* New York: Houghton Mifflin Harcourt.

Bowen, Sarah, Joslyn Brenton, and Sinikka Elliott. 2019. *Pressure Cooker: Why Home Cooking Won't Solve Our Problems and What We Can Do About It.* New York: Oxford University Press.

Brooks, David. 2001. "The Organization Kid." *Atlantic Monthly.* 287 (4): 40–55.

Brown, Patricia Leigh. 2018. "Cod and 'Immune Broth': California Tests Food as Medicine." *New York Times.* nytimes.com. May 11.

Brownell, Kelly D., and Katherine B. Horgen. 2004. *Food Fight: The Inside Story of the Food Industry, America's Obesity Crisis, and What We Can Do about It.* New York: McGraw-Hill.

Brown, Sandy and Christy Getz. 2008. "Towards Domestic Fair Trade? Farm Labor, Localism, and the 'Family Scale' Farm." *GeoJournal.* 73: 11–22.

Brueggemann, John. 2002. "Racial Considerations and Social Policy in the 1930s: Economic Change and Political Opportunities." *Social Science History.* 26: 139–177.

———. 2012a. *Rich, Free and Miserable: The Failure of Success in America.* Lanham, MD: Rowman and Littlefield.

———. 2012b. "Reflections on the Morality of Food." *Tikkun.* tikkun.org. June 4.

———. 2104a. "Morality, Sociological Discourse, and Public Engagement. *Social Currents.* 1: 211–219.

———. 2014b. "The Role of Organized Labor in Civil Society." *Sociology Compass.* 8): 1033–1044.

———. 2016. "Two Stories about American Food. *Tikkun.* 31(2): 10–13.

Brueggemann, John, and Cliff Brown. 2003. "The Decline of Industrial Unionism in the Meatpacking Industry: Event-Structure Analysis of Labor Unrest, 1946–1987." *Work and Occupations* 30(3): 327–360.

Brueggemann, John and Walter Brueggemann. 2017. *Rebuilding the Foundations: Social Relationships in Ancient Scripture and Contemporary Culture.*

Brueggemann, Walter. 2020. *Materiality as Resistance: Five Elements for Moral Action in the Real World.* Louisville: Westminster John Knox.

Bryman, Alan. 2004. *The Disneyization of Society.* New York: Sage.

Carleton College. 2017. "Food Truth." *Carleton College.* carleton.edu/ccce/issue/environment-energy/food-truth/.

Carman, Tim. 2017. "Fast Casual Nation: The Movement That Has Changed How America Eats." *Washington Post.* washingtonpost.org. August 29.

Casey, Haly. 2019. "Saving Seeds, Saving Cultures." *Mother Earth Gardener.* motherearthgardener.com. Spring.

Catton, William R. Jr. 1980. *Overshoot: The Ecological Basis of Revolutionary Change.* Urbana: University of Illinois Press.

Chernin, Ariel. 2008. "The Effects of Food Marketing on Children's Preferences: Testing the Moderating Roles of Age and Gender." *Annals of the American Academy of Political and Social Science.* 615: 102–118.

Christen, Caroline. 2021. "Meat Consumption in the U.S. Is Growing at an Alarming Rate." *Sentient Media.* sentientmedia.org.

Clark, Lara P., Dylan B. Millet, and Julian D. Marshall. 2014. National Patterns in Environmental Injustice and Inequality: Outdoor NO2 Air Pollution in the United States. *PLoS One.* plos.org. April 15.

Common Market. 2021. thecommonmarket.org.

Confino, Jo. 2012. "Beyond environment: falling back in love with Mother Earth." *The Guardian.* theguardian.com. February 12.

Counihan, Carole, Penny Van Esterik, and Alice Julier (editors). 2019. *Food and Culture: A Reader.* York: Routledge.

Curran, Erica Jackson. 2021. "Seven Unexpected Benefits of Eating Together as a Family, According to Science" *Parents.* parents.com

Cusser, Sarah, Christie Bahlai, Scott M. Swinton, G. Phillip Robertson, and Nick M. Haddad. 2020. "Long-term Research Avoids Spurious and Misleading Trends in Sustainability Attributes of No-Till." *Global Change Biology.* 26(6): 3715–3725.

Dennis, Helen. 2018. "A Balance Made on Freshly Grown Farms." *Edible Columbia.* ediblecommunities.com. October 19.

DeVault, Majorie. 1994. *Feeding the Family: The Social Organization of Caring as Gendered Work.* Chicago: University of Chicago Press.

Diamond, Jared. 2011. *Collapse: How Societies Choose to Fail Or Succeed: Revised Edition.* New York: Penguin.

Dimitri, Carolyn, Anne Effland, and Neilson Conklin. 2005. "The 20th Century Transformation of U.S. Agriculture and Farm Policy." United States Department of Agriculture. usda.gov.

Dunn, Elizabeth G. 2020. "In a Burger World, Can Sweetgreen Scale Up?" *New York Times.* nytimes.com. January 4.

Edwards, Bob and Adam Driscoll. 2009. "From Farms to Factories: The Economic Consequences of Swine Industrialization in North Carolina. Pp. 153–175 in *Twenty Lessons in Environmental Sociology,* edited by Kenneth A. Gould and Tammy L. Lewis. New York: Oxford University Press.

Ehrenreich, Barbara. 2001. *Nickel and Dimed: On (Not) Getting by in America.* New York: Holt.

Engel, Tagan. 2018. "Truelove Seeds and Owen Taylor." *The Table Underground.* thetableunderground.com. February 9 podcast/article

Eshel, Gidon and Pamela Martin. 2006. "Diet, Energy and Global Warming." *Earth Interactions.* 10(9): 1–17.

Estabrook, Barry. 2018. *Tomatoland: From Harvest of Shame to Harvest of Hope.* Kansas City, MO: Andrew McMeel Publishing.

Etzioni, Amitai. 1975. *Comparative Analysis of Complex Organizations.* New York: Free Press.

———. 1996. *The New Golden Rule: Community and Morality in a Democratic Society.* New York: Basic Books.

European Commission. 2014. "Towards a Circular Economy: A Zero Waste Programme for Europe. ec.europa.eu/environment/circular-economy/pdf/circular-economy-communication.pdf

Evans, David. 2011. "Beyond the Throwaway Society: Ordinary Domestic Practice and a Sociological Approach to Household Food Waste." *Sociology.* 46 (1): 41–56.

———. 2014. *Food Waste: Home Consumption, Material Culture and Everyday Life.* London: Bloomsbury.

Evans, David, Daniel Welch, and Joanne Swaffield. 2017. "Constructing and Mobilizing 'The Consumer': Responsibility, Consumption and the Politics of Sustainability." *Environment and Planning A: Economy and Space.* 49(6): 1396–1412.

Fallows, James and Deborah Fallows. 2018. *Our Towns: A 100,000-Mile Journey into the Heart of America.* New York: Pantheon.

Fielding-Singh, Priya. 2021. *How the Other Half Eats: The Untold Story of Food and Inequality in America.* New York: Little, Brown, Spark.

Fitzpatrick, Kevin M. and Don Willis. 2015. *A Place-based Perspective of Food in Society.* New York: Palgrave Macmillan.

Flora, Cornelia Butler, Jan L. Flora, and Stephen P. Gasteyer. 2018. *Rural Communities: Legacy and Change.* Routledge. (Fifth edition.)

Foer, Jonathan Safran. 2009. *Eating Animals.* New York: Penguin.

Foley, Jonathan. 2013. "It's Time to Rethink America's Corn System." *Scientific American.* scientificamerican.com/article/time-to-rethink-corn/. March 5.

Food and Water Watch. 2013. "Grocery Goliaths: How Food Monopolies Impact Consumers." foodandwaterwatch.org.

———. 2015. "Factory Farm Nation." foodandwaterwatch.org.

Forelle, Elizabeth and Kailyn Wolfe. 2018. "The Various Effects of Various Tilling Practices on Long-Term Soil Health in the Capital Region of New York." Senior Thesis. Environmental Studies Program. Skidmore College.

Fountain, Henry. 2020. "Belching Cows and Endless Feedlots: Fixing Cattle's Climate Issues." *The New York Times,* October 21.

Freedhoff, Yoni. 2012. "Is Obesity Simply about a Lack of 'Balance'? Why Big Food Wants You to Be Fit." *PloS Medicine.* plos.org. July 5.

Fukuyama, Francis. 1996. *Trust: The Social Virtues and the Creation of Prosperity.* New York: The Free Press.

Gaddis, Jennifer. 2020. "Why Are You Still Packing Lunch for Your Kids?" *The New York Times.* nytimes.com. February 10.

Galt, Ryan E. 2011. "Counting and Mapping Community Supported Agriculture (CSA) in the United States and California: Contributions from Critical Cartography/GIS." *ACME: An International E-Journal for Critical Cartographies.* 10(2): 131–162.

Garcés, Leah. 2019. *Grilled. Turning Adversaries into Allies to Change the Chicken Industry.* New York: Bloomsbury Sigma.

Gasteyer, Stephen P. 2008. "Agricultural Transitions in the Context of Growing Environmental Pressure over Water." *Journal of Agricultural and Human Values.* 25: 469–486.

Gasteyer, Stephen P., Sarah A. Hultine, Leslie R. Cooperband, and M. Patrick. Curry. 2008. "Produce Sections, Town Squares, and Farm Stands: Comparing Local Food in Community Context." *Southern Rural Sociology.* 23(1): 47–71.

Genoways, Ted. 2016. "Close to the Bone: The Fight over Transparency in the Meat Industry." *The New York Times.* newyorktimes.org. October 4.

Golembiewski, Kate. 2022. "How Chewing Shaped Human Evolution." *New York Times.* newyorktimes.org. August 17.

Graham, Mark E. 2005. *Sustainable Agriculture: A Christian Ethic of Gratitude.* Eugene, OR: Wipf and STOCK.

Gray, Margaret. 2014. *Labor and the Locavore: The Making of a Comprehensive Food Ethic*. Berkeley: University of California Press.

Greenaway, Twighlight. 2018. "No-Till Farmers' Push for Healthy Soils Ignites a Movement in the Plains." *Civil Eats.* civileats.com. February 13.

Guthman, Julie. 2004. *Agrarian Dreams: The Paradox of Organic Farming in California.* Los Angeles: University of California Press.

———. 2011. *Weighing In: Obesity, Food Justice, and the Limits of Capitalism.* Los Angeles: University of California Press.

Gumirakiza, Jean Dominique, Kynda R. Curtis, and Ryan Bosworth. 2014. "Who Attends Farmers' Markets and Why? Understanding Consumers and their Motivations." *International Food and Agribusiness Management Review.* 17(2): 66–82.

Haenfler, Ross, Brett Johnson, and Ellis Jones. 2012. "Lifestyle Movements: Exploring the Intersection of Lifestyle and Social Movements." *Social Movement Studies.* 11(1): 1–10.

Haidt, Jonathan. 2006. *The Happiness Hypothesis: Finding Modern Truth in Ancient Wisdom.* New York: Basic Books.

———. 2007. "The New Synthesis in Moral Psychology." *Science.* 316 (May 18): 998–1001.

———. 2012. *The Righteous Mind: Why Good People are Divided by Politics and Religion.* New York: Pantheon Books.

Haidt, Jonathan and Craig Joseph. 2004. "Intuitive Ethics: How Innately Prepared Intuitions Generate Culturally Variable Virtues." *Daedalus.* (Fall) 55–66.

Haidt, Jonathan and Jesse Graham. 2009. "Planet of the Durkheimians: Where Community, Authority, and Sacredness Are Foundations of Morality." Pp. 371–401 in *Social and Psychological Bases of Ideology and System Justification*, edited by John T. Jost, Aaron C. Kay, and Hulda Thorisdottir. New York: Oxford University Press.

Hall, Peter A., and David Soskice. 2001. *Varieties of Capitalism: The Institutional Foundations of Comparative Advantage.* New York: Oxford University Press.

Harari, Yuval N. 2015. *Sapiens: A Brief History of Humankind.* London: Vintage.

Haskell, Meg. 2016. "How Homesteader, Activist, Writer Mort Mather Found Happiness in Maine." *Bangor Daily News.* bangordailynews.com. July 22.

Herz, Rachel. 2018. *Why You Eat What You Eat: The Science Behind Our Relationship with Food.* New York: W. W. Norton and Company.

Hetherington, Marc J. 2005. *Why Trust Matters: Declining Political Trust and the Demise of American Liberalism.* Princeton, NJ: Princeton University Press.

History Extra Podcast. 2021. "Food History: Everything You Wanted to Know. *BBC History Magazine.* historyextra.om. August 29.

Hochschild, Arlie. 2016. *Strangers in Their Own Land: Anger and Mourning on the American Right.* New York: The New Press.

Honore, Carl. 2004. *In Praise of Slowness: Challenging the Cult of Speed.* New York: Harper Collins.

Horst, Megan and Amy Marion. 2019. "Racial, Ethnic and Gender Inequities in Farmland Ownership and Farming in the U.S." *Agriculture and Human Values.* 36: 1–16.

Hossfield, Leslie H., E. Brooke Kelly, Amanda Smith, and Julia F. Waity. 2015. "Towards Economics That Won't Leave: Utilizing a Community Food Systems Model to Develop Multisector Sustainable Economies in Rural Southeastern North Carolina." Pp. 83–102 in *A Place-based Perspective of Food in Society*, edited by Kevin M. Fitzpatrick and Don Willis. New York: Palgrave Macmillan.

Hosseini, Khaled. 2003. *The Kite Runner.* New York: Riverhead Books.

Hunt, Alan. 2007. "Consumer Interactions and Influences on Farmers' Market Vendors." *Renewable Agriculture and Food Systems.* 22(1): 54–66.

Hunter, James Davison. 2010. *To Change the World: The Irony, Tragedy, and Possibility of Christianity in the Late Modern World.* New York: Oxford University Press.

Hribar, Carrie. 2010. "Understanding Concentrated Animal Feeding Operations and Their Impact on Communities." *National Association of Local Boards of Health.* cdc.gov.

Hultine, Sarah A., Leslie R. Cooperband, M. Patrick Curry, and Stephen P. Gasteyer. 2007. "Local Food: A Case Study of the Local Food Project in Fairbury, Illinois." *Journal of the Community Development Society.* 38(3) p. 61–76.

Intergovernmental Panel on Climate Change. 2014. "Assessment Report." ipcc.ch/reports/.

Jackson, Robert B., Kate Lajtha, Susan E. Crow, Gustaf Hugelius, Marc G. Kramer, and Gervasio Pineiro. 2017. "The Ecology of Soil Carbon: Pools, Vulnerabilities, and Biotic and Abiotic Controls." *Annual Review of Ecology, Evolution, and Systematics.* 48: 419–445.

Jackson, Wes and Robert Jensen. 2022. *An Inconvenient Apocalypse: Environmental Collapse, Climate Crisis, and the Fate of Humanity.* Notre Dame, IN: Notre Dame Press.

Jones, Jeffrey M. 2022. "Confidence in U.S. Institutions Down; Average at New Low. *Gallup.* gallup.com. July 5.

Julier, Alice. 2013. *Eating Together: Food, Friendship, and Inequality.* Champaign, IL: University of Illinois Press.

Kalaichandran, Amitha. 2018. "The Doctor is Cooking." *New York Times.* nytimes.com. May 22.

Kearns, Cristin E., Laura A. Schmidt, and Stanton A. Glantz. 2016. "Sugar Industry and Coronary Heart Disease Research: A Historical Analysis of Internal Industry Documents." *Journal of American Medical Association.* 176(11): 1680–1688.

Kelsey, Ellen. 2020. *Hope Matters: Why Changing the Way We Think Is Critical To Solving the Environmental Crisis.* Vancouver: Greystone Books.

Ken, Ivy. 2014. "Profit in the Food Desert: Walmart Stakes its Claim." *Theory in Action.* 7(4): 13–32.

Kersten, Hans, Andrew F. Beck, and Melissa Klein (editors). 2018. *Identifying and Addressing Childhood Food Insecurity in Healthcare and Community Settings.* New York: New York.

Kilpatrick, Michael. 2016. "Kilpatrick Family Farm." *Stone Barns Center.* Stonebarnscenter.org

Kilpatrick Family Farm website. */michael-kilpatrick.com/kilpatrick-family-farm/.*

Kimmerer, Robin Wall. 2015. *Braiding Sweetgrass: Indigenous Wisdom, Scientific Knowledge and the Teachings of Plants.* Minneapolis: Milkweed Editions.

———. 2021. "Serviceberry: An Economy of Abundance." *Emergence Magazine.* emergencemagazine.org.

Klein, Ezra. 2022. "The Hidden Costs of Cheap Meat." *The New York Times.* (The Ezra Klein Show). nytimes.com.

Klinenberg, Eric. 2013. *Going Solo: The Extraordinary Rise and Surprising Appeal of Living Alone.* New York: Penguin Books.

Knupfer, Anne Meis. 2013. *Food Co-ops in America: Communities, Consumption, and Economic Democracy.* Ithaca: Cornell University Press.

Kristof, Nichalos. 2021. "The Ugly Secrets behind Costco Chicken." *New York Times.* nytimes.com.

Kucinich, Elizabeth. 2014. "Monsanto: Enemy of the Family Farm." *Huffington Post.* huffpost.com. December 6.

Lehtokunnas, Taru, Malla Mattila, Elina Narayanan, and Nina Mesiranta. 2020. "Towards a Circular Economy in Food Consumption: Food Waste Reduction Practices as Ethical Work." *Journal of Consumer Culture.* June: 1–19.

Leon, Kenneth Sebastian and Ivy Ken. 2017. "Food Fraud and the Partnership for a 'Healthier' America: A Case Study in State-Corporate Crime." *Critical Criminology*. 25: 393–410

———. 2019. "Legitimized Fraud and the State-corporate Criminology of Food—A Spectrum-based Theory." *Crime, Law, and Social Change*. 71: 25–46.

———. 2022. "Regulatory Theater in the Pork Industry: How the Capitalist State Harms Workers, Farmers, and Unions." *Crime, Law, and Social Change*. February.

Leonard, Christopher. 2014. *The Meat Racket: The Secret Takeover of America's Food Business*. New York: Simon and Schuster.

———. 2015. "Who's Murdering Thousands of Chickens in South Carolina?" *Bloomberg*. bloomberg.com.

Levin, Sam. 2018. "Monsanto 'Bullied Scientists' and Hid Weedkiller Cancer Risk, Lawyer Tells Court." *The Guardian*. theguardian.com. July 19.

Lincoln, Astra. 2012. *Vocational Vagabond, Volunteer Vacationer*. Bloomington, IN: Booktango.

Lesser, Lenard I., Cara B. Ebbeling, Merrill Goozner, David Wypij, and David Ludwig. 2007. "Relationship between Funding Source and Conclusion among Nutrition-Related Scientific Articles." *PloS Medicine*. plosmed.org. January.

Levkoe, Charles Z. 2019. "Learning Democracy through Food Justice Movements." Pp. 510–524 in *Food and Culture: A Reader*, edited by Carole Counihan, Penny Van Esterik, and Alice Julier. New York: Routledge.

Lodewick, Colin. 2018. "A Safe Place to Grow." *Philadelphia Citizen.* thephiladelphiacitizen.org. September 27.

Lynas, Mark. 2020. *Our Final Warning: Six Degrees of Climate Emergency.* London: Fourth Estate.

Lucas, Amelia. 2022. "Sweetgreen Losses Widen Despite 67 Percent Jump in Quarterly Sales." *CNBC.* cnbc.com. May 5.

MacDonald, James, and William McBride. 2009. "The Transformation of U.S. Livestock Agriculture: Scale, Efficiency, and Risks." *Economic Information Bulletin* No. EIB-43, United States Department of Agriculture.

Martino, Victor. 2019. Sweetgreen Builds Customer Experience and Growth Around Sustainability and 'Deliciousness.'" *CO.* uschamber.com. July 15.

Mcgillis, Alec. 2021. *Fulfillment: Winning and Losing in One-Click America.* New York: Farrar, Straus and Giroux.

McKibben, Bill. 1998. Hundred Dollar Holiday: The Case for a More Joyful Christmas. New York: Simon and Schuster.

Mather, Mort. 2019. Personal website. mortmather.com.

Markowitz, Lisa. 2019. "Expanding Access and Alternatives: Building Farmers' Markets in Low-income Communities" Pp. 480–491 in *Food and Culture: A Reader*, edited by Carole Counihan, Penny Van Esterik, and Alice Julier. New York: Routledge.

Maya-Ambia, Carlos J. 2015. "Agricultural Industrialization and the Presence of the 'Local' in the Global Food World." Pp. 37–58 in *A Place-based Perspective of Food in Society*, edited by Kevin M. Fitzpatrick and Don Willis. New York: Palgrave Macmillan.

McKibben, Bill. 1989. *The End of Nature*. New York: Random House.

———. 1992. *The Age of Missing Information.* New York: Random House.

———. 1998. *Hundred Dollar Holiday: The Case for a More Joyful Christmas.* New York: Simon and Schuster.

———. 2004. *Deep Economy*. New York: St. Martin's Griffin.

McGrath, Maggie. 2017. "World's Largest Food and Beverage Companies 2017: Nestle, Pepsi and Coca-Cola Dominate the Field." *Forbes.* forbes.com. May 24.

McKnight, John and Peter Block. 2010. *The Abundant Community: Awakening the Power of Families and Neighborhoods*. San Francisco: Berrett-Koeler Publishers.

McMichael, Phillip. 2014. "Conclusion: The Food Sovereignty Lens." Pp. 345–364 in *Globalization and Food Sovereignty: Global and Local Change in the New Politics of Food*, edited by Petger Andree, Jeffrey Ayres, Michael J. Bosia, and Marie-Josee Massicotte. Toronto: University of Toronto Press.

McMillan, Tracie. 2012. *The American Way of Eating: Undercover at Walmart, Applebee's, Farm Fields and the Dinner Table.* Simon and Schuster.

Metzl, Jonathan. 2019. *Dying of Whiteness: How the Politics of Racial Resentment Is Killing America's Heartland*. New York: Basic Books.

Miller, Laura J. 2017. *Building Nature's Market: The Business and Politics of Natural Foods.* Chicago: University of Chicago Press.

Minkoff-Zern, Laura-Anne. 2019. *The New American Farmer: Immigration, Race, and the Struggle for Sustainabilty*. Cambridge, Mass.: MIT Press.

Montgomery, David R. 2017. *Growing a Revolution: Bringing our Soil Back to Life.* New York: W. W. Norton & Company.

———. 2022. Personal correspondence.

Montgomery, David R. and Anne Biklé. 2016. *The Hidden Half of Nature: The Microbial Roots of Life and Health.* New York: W. W. Norton & Company.

Moss, Michael. 2014. *Salt Sugar Fat: How the Food Giants Hooked Us.* Penguin Random House LLC.

Nation, Allan. 2005. *Grassfed to Finish: A Production Guide to Gourmet Grass-finished Beef.* London: Green Park Press.

———. 2015. *Grassfed to Finish: A Production Guide to Gourmet Grass-Finished Beef.* London: Green Park Press.

National Public Radio. 2017. "The Ground beneath Our Feet" *1-A* (podcast). the1a. org/segments/2017-12-04-the-ground-beneath-our-feet/.

National Resources Conservation Service. 2016. "Reduction in Annual Fuel Use from Conservation Tillage." United States Department of Agriculture. usda.gov. August.

Natural Resource Conservation Service. 2016. "Reduction in Annual Fuel Use from Conservation Tillage." *United States Department of Agriculture.* usda.gov.

———. 2020. "Animal Feeding Operations." *United States Department of Agriculture.* usda.gov.

Nestle, Marion. 2013. *Food Politics: How the Food Industry Influences Nutrition and Health.* Los Angeles: University of California Press.

———. 2017. *Soda Politics*. New York: Oxford University Press.

———. 2018. *Unsavory Truth: How Food Companies Skew the Science of What We Eat.* New York: Basic Books.

New York Times. 2018. "An Extremely Detailed Map of the 2016 Election." nytimes. com.

Newman, Chris. 2019. "Small Family Farms Aren't the Answer." *Medium.* medium.com. July 15.

———. 2020. "Everything I Want to Do Is Racist." *Medium.* medium.com. September 4.

Ochs, Elinor, and Merav Shohet. 2006. "The Cultural Structuring of Mealtime Socialization." *New Directions for Child and Adolescent Development* 2006(111): 35–49.

O'Connor, Anahad. 2012. "Sweetgreen Makes Healthful Food Fast—But Can You Afford It?" *New York Times.* nytimes.com. July 26.

Oldenburg, Ray. 1989. *The Great Good Place: Cafes, Coffee Shops, Bookstores, Bars, Hair Salons, and the Other Hangouts at the Heart of a Community.* Philadelphia: Perseus.

———. 2001. *Celebrating the Third Place: Inspiring Stories about the "Great Good Places" at the Heart of Our Communities.* New York: Marlowe and Company.

Olmstead, Larry. 2016. *Real Food/Fake Food: Why You Don't Know What You're Eating and What You Can Do About It.* Chapel Hill, NC: Algonquin Books.

Oreskes, Naomi and Erik M. Conway. 2011. *Merchants of Doubt: How a Handful of Scientists Obscured the Truth on Issues from Tobacco Smoke to Climate Change.* London: Bloomsbury Publishing.

———. 2014. *Merchants of Doubt. How a Handful of Scientists Obscured the Truth on Issues from Tobacco Smoke to Climate Change.* London: Bloomsbury.

Patel, Raj. 2007. *Stuffed and Starved: The Hidden Battle for the World Food System.* Brooklyn, NY: Melville House Publishing.

———. 2008. *Stuffed and Starved: The Hidden Battle for the World Food System.* Hoboken, NJ: Melville House Publishing.

Patel, Rajeev C. 2012. "Food Sovereignty: Power, Gender, and the Right to Food." *PloS Medicine.* plos.org. January.

Penniman, Leah. 2018. *Farming While Black: Soul Fire Farm's Practical Guide to Liberation on the Land.* White River Junction, VT: Chelsea Green Publishing.

Persell, Carol Hodges. 1994. "Taking Society Seriously." *Sociological Forum.* 9(4): 641–657.

Peters. Adele. 2021. "How Sweetgreen Plans to Cut its Carbon Footprint in Half in the Next Six Years." fastcompany.com.

Pew Research Center. 2022. "As Partisan Hostility Grows, Signs of Frustration with Two-Party System." pewresearch.org. August 9.

Philpott, Tom. 2020a. "Joel Salatin's Unsustainable Myth." *Mother Jones.* motherjones.com. November 19.

———. 2020b. "White People Own 98 Percent of Rural Land. Young Black Farmers Want to Reclaim Their Share." *Mother Jones.* motherjones.com. June 27.

Plumer, Brad. 2013. "No-Till Farming is on the Rise. That's Actually a Big Deal." *The Washington Post.* washingtonpost.org. November 9.

Polyface Farms. 2020. "Polyface Farms Guiding Principles." polyfacefarms.com/ principles.

Poppendieck, Janet. 1999. *Sweet Charity?: Emergency Food and the End of Entitlement.* New York: Penguin Books.

———. 2010. *Free for All: Fixing School Food in America.* Los Angeles: University of California Press.

Pratt, Jeff. 2007. "Food Values: The Local and the Authentic." *Critique of Anthropology.* 27(3): 285–300

Press, Eyal. 2012. *Beautiful Souls: Saying No, Breaking Ranks, and Heeding the Voice of Conscience in Dark Times.* New York: Farrar, Strauss and Giroux.

Purnell, David F. 2019. *Building Communities through Food: Strengthening Communication, Families, and Social Capital.* Lanham, MD: Lexington Books.

Qazi, Joan A. and Theresa L. Selfa. 2005. "The Politics of Building Alternative Agro-Food Networks in the Belly of Agro-industry." *Food, Culture, and Society.* 1(1): 45–72.

Ritz, Stephen. 2019. stephenritz.com.

Ritz, Stephen with Suzie Boss. 2017. *The Power of the Plant: A Teacher's Odyssey to Grow Healthy Minds and Schools.* New York: Rodale.

Ritzer, George. 2020. *The McDonaldization of Society.* New York: Sage.

Roberts, David. 2018. "What Made Solar Panels So Cheap? Thank Government Policy." *Vox.* vox.com.

Roberts, Paul. 2008. *The End of Food.* Boston: Houghton Mifflin.

———. 2009. *The End of Food.* New York: Houghton Mifflin Harcourt.

Royte, Elizabeth. 2009. "Street Farmer." *New York Times.* nytimes.com. July 9.

Roser, Max. 2020. "Why Did Renewables Become So Cheap So Fast?" *Our World in Data.* ourworldindata.org.

Rooted in Community. rootedincommunity.org.

Saratogian. 2012. "Saratoga Springs Preservation Foundation to honor Barbara Glaser, Nick Palmetto and Randy Martin." saratogian.com. May 5.

Sattler, Sandra. 2022. "U.S. EIA Annual Energy Outlook 2022 Reveals No Reduction in Emissions to 2050." *energypost.eu: the Best Thinkers on Energy.* energypost.eu.

Savage, Steve. 2016. "Why I Don't Buy Organic, And Why You Might Not Want To Either." *Forbes.* forbes.com. March 19.

Sayer, Andrew. 2015. "Time for moral economy?" *Geoforum.* 65: 291–293.

Sayre, Laura. 2011. "The Politics of Organic Farming: Populists, Evangelicals, and the Agriculture of the Middle. *Gastronomica.* 11(2): 38–47.

Scarce, Rik. 2015. *Creating Sustainable Communities: Lessons from the Hudson River Region.* Albany: State University of New York Press.

Scheiber, Noam. 2019. "Why Wendy's is Facing Campus Protests (It's About the Tomatoes)." *New York Times.* nytimes.com. March 7.

Schor, Juliet. 1992. *The Overworked American: The Unexpected Decline of Leisure.* New York: Basic Books.

———. 1999. "The New Politics of Consumption." *Boston Review.* Summer.

———. 2004. *Born to Buy: The Commercialized Child and the New Consumer Culture.* New York: Simon and Schuster.

———. 2011. *True Wealth: How and Why Millions of Americans are Creating a Time-Rich, Ecologically Light, Small-Scale, High Satisfaction Economy*. New York: Penguin.

Scott, James. 1998. *Seeing Like a State: How Certain Schemes to Improve the Human Condition have Failed*. Yale University Press.

Scott, Ridley. 2015. *The Martian*. 20th Century Fox.

Schroeder, Eric. 2021. "Kellogg, PepsiCo Garner Accolades for Commitment to Business Integrity." *Food Business News*. foodbusiness.net. February 25.

Schnell, Steven M. 2007. "Food with a Farmer's Face: Community-Supported Agriculture in the United States. *The Geographical Review*. 97(4): 550–564.

Schumacher, E. F. 1973. *Small is Beautiful: Economics as if People Mattered*. New York: Harper and Row.

Schupp, Justin, and Jeff Sharp. 2012. "Exploring the Social Bases of Home Gardening. *Agriculture and Human Values*. 29(1): 93–105.

Schupp, Justin. 2014. *Just Where Does Food Live? Assessing Farmers Markets in the United States*. Ohio State University. Dissertation. Department of Sociology.

———. 2016. "Just Where Does Local Food Live? Assessing Farmers' Markets in the United States." *Agriculture and Human Values*. 33(4): 827–841.

———. 2017. "Cultivating Better Food Access Outcomes? The Role of Farmers Markets in the Local Food Movement in the United States." *Rural Sociology*. 82(2): 318–348.

———. 2019. "Wish You Were Here? The Prevalance of Farmers Markets in Food Deserts: An Examination of the United States." *Food, Culture and Society*. 22(1)111–130.

Sendhil Mullainathan, Sendhil and Eldar Shafir. 2013. *Scarcity: Why Having Too Little Means So Much*. New York: Times Books.

Sevilla, Nina. 2021. "Food Apartheid: Racialized Access to Healthy Affordable Food." *NRDC*. nrdc.com. April.

Shanker, Deena. 2017. "There Aren't Enough Slaughterhouses to Support the Farm-to-Table Economy." *Bloomberg*. bloomberg.com. May 23.

Shepelavy, Roxanne P. 2015. "Combatting the Food Desert." *The Philadelphia Citizen*, April 28, thephiladelphiacitizen.org/freshrx-combatting-the-food-desert/.

Shulman, Robin. 2015. "Sowing the Seeds of Syria: Farming Group Rescues Plant Species Threatened by War." *The Guardian*. guardian.com. November 4.

Sierra Club. "Why Are CAFOs Bad?" sierraclub.org/michigan. (Michigan Chapter).

Smith, Lindsey P. Shu Wen Ng, and Barry M. Popkin. 2013. "Trends in US home food preparation and consumption: Analysis of national nutrition surveys and time use studies from 1965–1966 to 2007–2008." *Nutrition Journal* 45: 2–10.

Smith, Noah. 2022. "How We Will Fight Climate Change." *Noahpinion*. noahpinion. substack.com/p/how-we-will-fight-climate-change. July.

Smith Maguire, Jennifer, Richard E. Ocejo, and Michaela DeSoucey. 2022. "Mobile Trust Regimes: Modes of Attachment in an Age of Banal Omnivorousness." *Journal of Consumer Culture*. 0(0): 1–20.

Snow, David and Soule, Sarah. 2010. *A Primer on Social Movements*. New York: W. W. Norton.

Snyder, Benjamin H. 2016. *The Disrupted Workplace: Time and the Moral Order of Flexible Capitalism.* New York: Oxford University Press.

Starapoli, Nicholas. 2016. "No-till Agriculture Offers Vast Sustainability Benefits. So Why Do Many Organic Farmers Reject It?" *Genetic Literacy Project.* Geneticliteracyproject.org.

Starr, Amory. 2010. "Local Food: A Social Movement?" *Cultural Studies ⌈ Critical Methodologies.* 10(6): 479–490.

Stone Barn Center for Food and Agriculture. 2016. "Farm Case Study: Kilpatrick Family Farm." stonebarnscenter.org/resource/farm-case-study-kilpatrick-family-farm/.

Stone, Brad. 2021. *Amazon Unbound: Jeff Bezos and the Invention of a Global Empire.* New York: Simon and Schuster.

Stout, Jeffrey. 2010. *Blessed are the Organized: Grassroots Democracy in America.* Princeton, NJ: Princeton University Press.

Stull, Donald D., and Michael J. Broadway. 2012. *Slaughterhouse Blues: The Meat and Poultry Industry in North America.* Cengage Learning.

———. 2013. *Slaughterhouse Blues: The Meat and Poultry Industry in North America.* Boston: Cengage Learning.

Sumner, Jennifer. 2015. "Ways of Knowing the World: The Role of Knowledge and Food Movements in the Food-Place Nexus." Pp. 83–102 in *A Place-based Perspective of Food in Society,* edited by Kevin M. Fitzpatrick and Don Willis. New York: Palgrave Macmillan.

Swidler, Ann. 1986. "Culture in Action: Symbols and Strategies." *American Sociological Review.* 51(2): 273–286.

Taylor, Mark. C. 2014. *Speed Limits: Where Time Went and Why We Have So Little Left.* New Haven, CT, Yale University Press.

Technavio. 2016. "Fast Casual Restaurants Markets in the US 2016–2020. technavio. com. October.

———. 2020. "Fast Causal Restaurants in the US Grow by $150.10 Billion in 2020." businesswire.com.

Tobler, Christina, Vivianne H. M. Visschers, and Michael Siegrist. 2011. "Organic Tomatoes Versus Canned Beans: How Do Consumers Assess The Environmental Friendliness of Vegetables?" *Environment and Behavior.* 435(5): 591–611

U.S. Department of Agriculture. 2020. "Farms and Land in Farms 2019 Summary." usda.gov. February.

Ulijaszek, Stanley J. and Hayley Lofin. 2006. "Obesity in Biocultural Perspective." *Annual Review of Anthropology.* 35: 337–360.

Valasquez-Manoff, Moises. 2018. "Can Dirt Save the Earth?" *New York Times.* April 18. nytimes.com.

Ver Ploeg, Michelle, Lisa Mancino, Jessica E. Todd, Dawn Marie Clay, and Benjamin Scharadin. 2015. "Where Do Americans Usually Shop for Food and How Do They Travel To Get There? Initial Findings from the National Household Food Acquisition and Purchase Survey." *United States Department of Agriculture.* usda.gov.

Volkova, Anastasia. 2022. "Making Food Production More Sustainable—What Does It Mean?" *Forbes.* forbes.com. March 16.

Wagtendonk, Anya van. 2018. "Truelove Prizes Seeds and Stories from around the World." *Philadelphia Inquirer.* inquirer.com. July 2.

Walker, Polly, et al. 2005. "Public health implications of meat production and consumption" *Public Health Nutrition.* 8 (4): 348–356.

Wallis, Claudia. 2006. "The Multitasking Generation" *Time.* March 27 pp. 48–55.

Wang, Dong D., Cindy W. Leung, Yanping Li, Eric L. Ding, Stephanie E. Chiuve, Frank B. Hu, and Walter C. Willett. 2014. "Trends in Dietary Quality among Adults in the United States 1999–2010." *JAMA Internal Medicine.* 174(10): 1587–1595.

Warde, Alan, Shu-Li Cheng, Wendy Olsen, and Dale Southerton. 2007. "Changes in the Practice of Eating A Comparative Analysis of Time-Use." *Acta Sociologica.* 54: 363–385.

Washington, Harriet A. 2019. *A Terrible Thing to Waste: Environmental Racism and Its Assault on the American Mind.* New York: Little, Brown, Spark.

Weaver, William Woy. 2008. "Gardening with Heirloom Varieties." *Mother Earth News.* motherearthnews.com.

Weber, Max. 2010. *The Protestant Ethic and the Spirit of Capitalism.* New York: Oxford University Press. (Stephen Kalberg, translator).

Weiss, Rebecca Bratten. 2021. "Homegrown Nationalism," *Christian Century.* August 25: 22–25.

Wendling, Zachary, John Emerson, Alex de Sherbinin, and Daniel C. Esty. 2020. "Environmental Performance Index 2020." *Yale Center for Environmental Law and Policy.* epi.yale.edu.

Wirzba, Norman. 2011. *Food and Faith: A Theology of Eating.* New York: Cambridge University Press.

———. 2022. *Agrarian Spirit: Cultivating Faith, Community, and the Land.* Notre Dame, IN: University of Notre Dame Press.

Wolfe, Alan. 1991. *Whose Keeper? Social Science and Moral Obligation.* Los Angeles: University of California Press.

Woods, Timothy and Matthew Ernst. 2017. "Community Supported Agriculture: New Models for Changing Markets." *United States Department of Agriculture.* usda.gov.

White, Monica A. 2019. *Freedom Farmers: Agricultural Resistance and The Black Freedom Movement.* Chapel Hill: University of North Carolina Press.

Wright, Erik Olin. 2010. *Envisioning Real Utopias.* New York: Verso.

Wu, Tim. 2018. *The Curse of Bigness: Antitrust in the New Gilded Age.* New York: Columbia Global Reports.

Yaffe-Bellany, David. 2019. "For Dairy Farmers, A Crisis Within." *The New York Times.*

Zimring, Carl A. 2016. *Clean and White: A History of Environmental Racism in the United States.* New York: New York University Press.

Zukin, Sharon and Jennifer Smith Maguire. 2004. "Consumers and Consumption." *Annual Review of Sociology.* 30: 173–19.

Index

African American. *See* Black people; race
agriculture, 2, 8, 22, 27, 34, 43, 45–46, 50, 51, 60, 69, 71, 75, 80, 81, 82, 84, 87, 103, 108, 120, 154, 162, 175–76, 185, 199, 203, 207, 214–15, 232, 241, 244, 260, 265; sustainable agriculture, 57, 66, 86, 107, 108, 128, 140, 154, 161, 169, 218, 224, 227, 242; urban, 154, 169. *See also* extraction; farming; no-till farming; organic
Almond, Steve, 5–6
Amazon, 29, 108, 223, 244
animal, 4, 14, 21, 27, 28, 33, 35, 36, 44, 46n2, 50–51, 55, 56, 60, 66–72, 97, 98, 104–7, 140–51, 163, 169, 199, 202–3, 207, 215, 226, 233, 240, 248, 259, 270; rights, 51, 140; slaughtering, 31, 51, 56, 66, 70, 75, 93, 105, 238; welfare of, 28, 65, 66, 71, 105–8, 121, 140–45, 227, 251, 263
authenticity, 6, 68, 117, 142–44, 151, 156, 184, 235

Barber, Benjamin, 242
B Corporations, 71, 146, 270

beautiful story, 10, 49, 141, 242, 243, 256, 261, 263, 265
Berry, Wendell, 57, 79, 95, 142, 154, 180–81, 204, 207–8
Bezos, Jeff, 29, 223. *See also* Amazon
Big Agriculture, 28, 31, 40, 42, 55, 64, 66, 102, 128, 140, 171, 185, 240, 243, 256, 262–63, 267. *See also* business
Big Mac, 109, 118, 245, 256. *See also* McDonalds
Big Food, 28, 31, 32, 33, 35, 39–42, 55, 64, 83, 102, 107, 115, 117, 119, 120, 128, 139–41, 150–52, 156, 161, 185, 225, 240, 243, 244–45, 256, 262, 267. *See also* business
Bittman, Mark, 143, 179, 209
Black Lives Matter, 147
Black people, 174, 176, 193, 195, 230, 237, 266. *See also* race
BRUCE the Old Dog, 213–14
Brueggemann, Walter, 17, 180, 212
Bryman, Alan, 29
Buddhist, 65, 90, 192, 218
business, 68, 71, 78, 105, 108, 134, 150, 163, 183, 218; corporation, 8, 42, 55, 64, 99, 102, 117, 119, 125, 131, 140, 150, 164, 185, 196, 202, 243, 267. *See also* Big Agriculture, Big Food

carbon, 3, 8, 62, 71, 134, 147; carbon
    dioxide (CO2), 119, 245; emissions,
    3, 72; footprint, 13, 16, 145, 155,
    153; miles, 13, 95, 106, 109,
    115, 142, 144
Carson, Rachel, 179, 204
cell phone, 6, 42, 75, 117–18, 131,
    180–81, 207, 208
Certified Organic: change, 9, 36, 44,
    64, 119, 140, 240, 242, 262. *See
    also* organic
Child, Julia, 179
Christianity, 7, 18, 78–79, 120, 189–92,
    198, 204, 205, 212, 218, 224,
    226–27, 250, 251. *See also* religion;
    spirituality; United Church of Christ
church, 1, 14, 20, 25, 60, 132–34, 149,
    164, 189–94, 204, 205, 212, 217,
    218, 224–27, 230, 234n5, 246, 250–
    51. *See also* religion; spirituality;
    United Church of Christ
civil society, 18, 166, 200, 239, 247,
    249, 255, 260
class (social), 88, 100, 108, 110, 129,
    137, 139, 147, 152, 187, 190–97,
    251, 266. *See also* inequality;
    labor; poverty
climate, 163
communication, 21, 22, 51, 127, 179–
    96, 213, 234n5, 256, 260
community-supported agriculture
    (CSA), 36, 65, 69, 73n1, 79, 82,
    84, 86–87, 103, 105, 113, 115, 117,
    126, 139, 143, 151–52, 167, 199,
    218, 246, 255
compost, 54, 57, 62, 65, 146,
    153–54, 211
computer, 42, 167, 180–81, 208,
    210, 228. *See also* internet; social
    media; website
Concentrated Animal Feeding Operation
    (CAFO), 27–28, 35, 44, 65–66, 70,
    108, 120, 240
consumption, 9, 13, 17, 23, 26–46, 51,
    66, 72, 80–81, 86, 90–93, 98, 100,

107–10, 117–22, 137–59, 163, 183–
    87, 195, 209, 223–28, 231, 243–64,
    263, 264, 271n1. *See also* mobile
    trust regime
contentious politics, 251, 253, 256, 260
cooking, 34, 36, 42, 50, 51, 58, 86,
    93–103, 116, 124, 145, 171, 179,
    196, 202, 204, 214, 241, 248, 263,
    269; cooks, 34, 58, 102, 100, 124,
    179, 196, 210, 232, 270; home, 38,
    99, 103, 104, 270
Cooperative Extension, 57, 61,
    185, 241, 260
COVID-19, 155
cycle of engagement. *See*
    communication; consumption;
    distribution; extraction; processing;
    stewardship

Dalai Lama, 217, 219, 221, 223
Darwin, Charles, 221
De Tocqueville, Alexis, 21
Diamond, Jared, 4
diet, 34, 44, 66, 87, 96–99, 100, 121,
    145–49, 246. *See also* nutrition
dirt, 2, 8–10, 55, 83, 120, 226.
    See also soil
Disneyization, 29, 244
distribution, 15, 26, 29, 37, 45, 51, 67,
    113–39, 150–53, 159, 201, 212–23,
    242, 243, 259, 263, 266
Durkheim, Emile, 21, 207

Earlham College, 60, 123, 190
engaged sustainers, 56, 59, 64, 72, 81,
    90–91, 95, 98, 106–7, 110, 116, 119,
    122, 134, 140, 146, 149, 151, 156,
    163, 173, 176–77, 182–85, 188,
    195–236, 236, 245, 249, 255–56,
    259, 263–71
environmentalism, 13, 17, 19, 28, 31,
    43, 49, 53, 68, 70, 72, 79, 86, 90,
    123, 134, 140, 146, 154, 155, 161,
    163, 169, 179, 199, 203–4, 210, 213,

221, 228, 231, 240, 243, 247, 251, 253, 255–57, 260–61
Eucharist, 137, 227
extraction, 51, 75–91, 93, 137, 140, 159, 176–84

Fallows, Deborah, 242
Fallows, James, 242
family, 8, 15, 19, 23–30, 34–35, 38, 39, 40, 42, 68, 75, 78–79, 82, 91, 99, 105–6, 120, 122–28, 132, 137, 139, 143–48, 161–67, 170, 174, 182–85, 189, 194, 195, 198, 204–7, 210, 211, 214, 222, 229–33, 241, 246–48, 255, 256, 260, 266, 270. *See* also gender
farmers' market, 1, 36, 51, 60, 65, 77–79, 86, 93, 97, 98, 102–3, 105, 109, 113–17, 123, 139, 143–44, 149–50, 152, 168, 195, 199, 196n1, 217–18, 231, 234n1, 241, 246, 249, 252, 255, 266, 270
farming, 3, 26, 27, 40–44, 50, 51, 53, 55–68, 77–93, 102–5, 116–17, 128, 135n4, 140, 143, 146, 155, 162–63, 168, 171–75, 188, 192, 195, 199–200, 201, 202, 204–25, 228–32, 241–42, 247, 248–50, 252–55, 260, 263–67; as a destination, 68, 69, 79, 142, 212, 246. *See also* agriculture; extraction; no-till farming; organic
fast-casual restaurants, 65, 103–4, 123, 153
fast food, 28, 29, 30, 36, 40, 42, 69, 98, 103–4, 109, 118, 123, 144, 147, 152, 154, 169, 221, 256. *See also* Big Mac; McDonalds
Faulkner, William, 31
food apartheid, 38, 39, 161, 222. *See also* food desert
food as medicine, 96, 97, 98, 127
food desert, 34, 36–37, 125, 161. *See also* food apartheid
food hub, 51, 104, 113, 115, 116, 117, 119, 120, 134, 139, 143, 224, 244

food insecurity, 34, 37, 38–39, 116, 123, 125–33, 147, 161, 162, 167, 173, 182–83, 190, 195, 200, 210, 217–18, 222, 224, 230, 242, 245, 249, 250, 255. *See also* hunger
food justice, 13, 87, 137, 152, 169, 185, 227, 230, 260, 261
food sovereignty, 38, 51, 137, 161, 169, 173, 242, 249, 250, 251, 253, 267
food stamps, 29, 115, 124, 152, 210, 222, 240
fossil fuel, 4, 13, 17, 23, 36, 43, 44, 240, 245, 252

Gaffigan, Jim, 30, 54, 102
Genetically Modified Organism (GMO), 41, 49, 83, 117, 121, 122, 169
gender, 6, 7, 8, 19, 137, 163, 197. *See also* family
glyphosate, 41, 44, 64
government, 3, 18, 19, 23, 27, 33, 34, 36, 64, 66, 80, 81, 84, 116, 128, 131, 133–34, 140, 166–67, 200, 215, 221, 238, 239, 240–43, 247, 251, 253, 255, 256, 260–63, 267; policies, 221, 247, 255
greenhouse emissions, 3, 145
Green Revolution, 27, 46, 75
grounding, 49, 50, 51, 53, 54, 69, 72, 75, 137, 168, 176, 216

Haidt, Jonathan, 14, 16, 24n3
Harari, Yuval Noah, 2
Hirschman, Albert, 220, 268
homelessness, 26, 192, 193, 230, 235. *See also* poverty
hunger, 17, 37, 115, 125–26, 130, 132, 155, 161, 163, 182–83, 190, 191, 210, 217, 227, 247, 250–53, 262–63, 269. *See also* food insecurity; poverty

immigrant, 18, 141, 163, 174, 199
industrial, 3, 4, 17, 27, 28, 37, 43, 45, 46, 71, 75, 95, 98, 115, 119, 124,

146, 181, 237, 240, 247; farming, 3, 28, 44, 117, 143, 174, 243; Industrial Food Complex, 26, 115, 243; industrialization, 43; industrialized meat, 27, 43, 66, 69; industrial production, 45, 55; Industrial Revolution, 2, 26. *See also* Big Agriculture; Big Food, business
inequality, 8, 24n3, 30, 38, 147, 152, 163, 240, 243, 267
internet, 22, 135n6, 150, 181, 185, 228, 252, 260. *See also* cell phone; computer; social media; website
iPhone. *See* cell phone
It's a Wonderful Life, 17, 267

Judaism, 7, 18, 85–91, 141, 172, 207, 218, 220, 227–31, 250. *See also* religion, spirituality

Kimmerer, Robin, 45, 90
King Jr., Martin Luther, 7, 267
Kraft, 32, 39, 40, 102, 140–41, 245

labor, 3, 14, 18–21, 30, 31, 36, 49, 51, 55, 80, 82, 83, 115, 120–21, 125, 132, 140, 142, 145, 150, 152, 159, 161, 170, 174, 186, 197, 219, 228–29, 247, 249, 250, 251, 253, 268, 270. *See also* class; inequality; organized labor; union
land, 2, 3, 4, 13, 25, 31, 41, 43, 45, 49, 50, 56, 61–65, 68–72, 77, 78, 82, 83, 84, 85, 86, 88, 89, 91, 138, 140, 147–51, 160–71, 174, 176, 183, 192, 195, 205–7, 216, 218, 220, 224, 230–31, 241, 243, 249, 252, 261, 262–65
latent sustainers, 187, 197
Latino/a, 174, 193
LGBTQ+, 7, 18, 196, 231
lifestyle movement, 251–52, 255, 256, 260
low-income, 30, 31, 36, 38, 39, 84, 87, 100, 115, 126, 130, 133, 139, 152, 162, 210, 266. *See also* food stamps; inequality; poverty

market, 1, 13–24, 18–28, 32, 37–40, 58, 60, 61, 62, 71, 72, 77, 78, 83, 101–9, 114, 117, 122, 125, 141, 154, 161, 166, 168, 195, 209, 217, 233, 239, 243–49, 255, 260, 261, 265, 271n1; culture, 9, 10, 13, 18, 20, 24, 25, 26, 44, 120, 148, 181, 261, 263, 264; logic, 18, 21, 24, 26, 40, 255
marketing, 26, 33, 34, 35, 41, 51, 60–61, 68–72, 80–81, 105, 107, 113, 115, 120, 127, 139, 141, 149, 150, 152, 183, 185, 196n2, 203, 205, 208, 210, 218–20, 225, 245
Marx, Karl, 22
McDonalds, 28, 30, 39, 102, 109, 144, 152–53, 160, 221, 245; McDonaldization, 29, 244. *See also* Big Mac
McKibben, Bill, 75, 179
mesoscopic engaged sustainers, 219, 220, 222, 233, 259, 268
methods, 10, 28, 62, 63, 64, 141, 187, 188, 197, 223
Mills, C. Wright, 222
mobile trust regime, 142, 143, 150, 156, 183–84, 256, 260
Monsanto, 40–41, 64, 83, 102
Montgomery, David, 2–3, 43, 53–54, 73n2
moral footprint, 14, 16, 17, 24, 28, 36, 45, 72, 106, 110, 134, 139–43, 148, 149, 151–52, 156, 176, 240, 245–47, 251, 252, 262
moral foundations, 4, 5, 9–11, 14, 17–18, 21, 24n3, 261, 262–64, 271n1
moral hardware, 19, 20
morality, 8, 13, 16, 24
moral software, 20
Moss, Michael, 32, 179
multinational corporations. *See* business
multiscopic, 219, 221, 222, 223, 232, 233, 259, 268

multiscopic engaged sustainers, 221, 268
Muslims, 7

nature, 2, 13, 21, 22, 30, 39, 41, 43, 45, 46, 53, 60, 61, 64, 66, 70–72, 80, 82, 103, 104, 106, 120, 122, 124, 145, 163, 166, 167, 170, 173, 176–77, 186, 200, 201, 208, 210, 217, 225–56, 229, 231, 232, 248–49, 259, 264
Nestle, Marion, 34, 41, 179, 242
NIGEL the Hippie Farmer, 204, 213, 214, 216
no-till farming, 58, 61, 62, 63, 65, 77, 81, 195, 214, 217
nutrition, 3, 14, 25, 28–29, 32, 36, 38, 42, 44, 53, 66, 70, 76, 80, 82, 97, 100–102, 107, 113, 115, 123–26, 128, 136, 139, 142, 144–45, 149, 154, 162, 169, 179, 182, 183, 203, 209–10, 240, 250–51, 255, 262–63, 270. *See also* diet

obesity, 23, 32, 35, 40, 41, 92n1, 125, 127
Oldenburg, Ray, 246, 257nn4–5
organic, 2, 8, 35, 36, 41, 51, 55, 57, 59, 62, 63, 71, 80, 81, 92n3, 108, 113, 117, 119, 135n4, 140, 142, 145, 149, 151, 152, 154, 187, 204, 209, 216, 217, 220, 255; Certified Organic, 57, 61, 62, 72, 77, 80, 81, 106, 121, 140, 241, 252; cropland, 77, 79, 266; farming, 57, 59, 63, 80, 83, 86, 92n3, 102, 115, 135n4, 145, 169, 188, 195, 199, 200, 201, 206, 218, 220, 225, 229, 248, 256, 268; food, 119, 151, 161–62, 169, 175, 252; movement, 49. *See also* regenerative agriculture
organized labor, 3, 18, 19, 160. *See also* labor, union

Patel, Raj, 179, 242
Penniman, Leah, 54, 55, 86, 195, 206, 230, 231, 253

people of color, 7, 18, 31, 37, 86, 174, 243. *See also* Black people; race
petites idées, 220, 268
place, 3, 4, 10, 14, 21, 25–26, 30, 37, 43–45, 50, 51, 58, 59, 62, 69, 70–72, 77, 78, 84, 85, 86, 91, 99–103, 106–7, 115, 117, 121–22, 129, 130, 131–34, 140, 147, 148, 155, 161, 164–65, 171, 175, 192–93, 195, 198–201, 204–7, 216, 224, 237, 238, 242, 245, 246, 252, 257nn4–5, 260, 264–65, 266, 267
Poe, Edgar Allen, 50
Pollan, Michael, 53, 95, 141–42, 179, 266
Poppendieck, Janet, 128, 132–33, 242
possibilism, 220, 268, 269
poverty, 20, 30, 34, 116, 163, 182, 191, 195, 217. *See also* class; food insecurity; inequality; hunger; low-income
processing, 31, 51, 66, 80, 93–95, 105, 108, 109, 116, 120, 137, 148, 159, 216
Purnell, David, 246

race, 3, 6, 8, 86, 88, 129, 137, 147, 190, 191, 197, 230, 251; discrimination (racial), 38; racism, 174, 266, 267. *See also* Black people; white people
ranches, 28, 73n6
recuerdo, 174
regenerative agriculture, 13, 49, 55, 65, 68, 71, 79, 82, 85, 91, 119, 121, 145, 151, 154, 167, 245, 255, 266
religion, 3, 6, 8, 15, 18–19, 23, 51, 61, 99, 88, 137, 141, 149, 151, 189, 190–91, 197, 201, 204, 212, 226, 228, 230, 232, 238, 247, 262. *See also* Christianity; church; Judaism; spirituality; United Church of Christ
rematriation, 171–74
reticent sustainers, 226
Ritzer, George, 29
Roberts, Paul, 27, 28, 43, 179

Rodale Institute, 79, 188

Salatin, Joel, 67, 79, 266
sankofa, 84, 173–76, 194, 207,
    242, 248, 251
Scarce, Rik, 242
Schor, Juliet, 45, 137–40, 143–
    44, 156, 176
Schupp, Justin, 78, 139, 249
seder, 137
slaughterhouse, 105, 108–9, 244
Slow Food, 49, 90, 98, 109,
    145, 153, 251
slowness, 90, 98, 145, 154, 224, 264
Smith, Adam, 21
social media, 3, 6, 8, 38, 72, 142, 143,
    183–84, 209, 223, 226, 256. *See also*
    cell phone; computer; internet
social movement, 49, 56, 59, 62, 85,
    140, 197, 199–201, 212, 215, 220,
    225, 233, 236–39, 247, 249, 250–55,
    260, 271. *See also* Black Lives
    Matter; civil society; contentious
    politics; lifestyle movement;
    organized labor; union; Vegan;
    vegetarian
soil, 2, 3, 4, 5, 8–9, 17, 36, 43, 44, 50,
    51, 53, 57–58, 62–65, 70, 71, 72,
    73n2, 75, 82, 98, 119, 140, 145, 147,
    151, 154–55, 162, 163, 167–68, 187,
    202, 204–6, 213, 215, 220, 223, 233,
    240–42, 248, 255, 259, 261–62, 264,
    266, 268, 270. *See also* dirt
spirituality, 19, 56, 65, 88, 91, 201,
    225–30, 233. *See also* Christianity;
    Judaism; religion
state. *See* government
stewardship, 51, 68, 84, 159–63, 167,
    168, 170, 174, 176, 249, 250
stories, 1, 2, 5, 8, 18, 25, 30, 31, 32, 35,
    45, 49–50, 58, 75, 80, 100, 104, 163,
    170–71, 175, 181, 183, 187, 194–95,
    200, 201, 206, 211–12, 220, 225,
    226, 231–34, 254, 256, 271. *See also*
    beautiful story; ugly story

supply chain, 97, 105, 106–10, 123,
    127, 153, 202, 203, 222, 224, 227,
    242, 249, 269
supply chain angler, 107, 145, 147, 148,
    156, 245, 270
sustainability, 65, 70–71, 97, 103, 110,
    116, 119–23, 140, 142, 143, 144,
    149–53, 161, 163, 188, 203, 208,
    217, 218, 242, 246–51
sustainable culture, 65, 263, 271n1
Sweetgreen, 64, 122–23, 152–56, 222,
    245, 256, 266
Swidler, Anne, 236–39, 250

Triple Bottom Line, 67, 198, 209
Trump, Donald, 3, 5, 6, 16, 41, 77
trust, 10, 14, 21, 81, 83, 109, 110, 116,
    141–44, 156, 184, 139, 244, 261,
    262–63, 267, 270

ugly story, 5, 10, 25, 45, 46, 141, 243,
    256, 263, 265. *See also* beautiful
    story; stories
United Church of Christ, 149, 204. *See
    also* Christianity; church; religion;
    spirituality
United States Department of Agriculture
    (USDA), 41, 76, 105, 115–16, 118,
    240. *See also* cooperative extension;
    government
union, 18–20, 161, 193, 237, 247,
    250, 253. *See also* class; labor;
    organized labor

vegan, 49, 71, 121, 195, 227, 251
vegetarian, 49, 55, 104, 121, 144, 146,
    149, 195, 227, 246. *See also* Vegan

waste, 14, 17, 19, 28, 31, 45, 50, 53, 98,
    104–8, 145–47, 153, 154, 159, 171,
    176, 208, 211, 216, 240, 249, 251,
    255, 265, 270. *See also* compost
Waters, Alice, 143
Weber, Max, 30, 51, 181

website, 58, 68–69, 79–81, 82, 86, 106, 117, 118, 128, 130, 154, 169, 171, 173–74, 176, 183, 187, 190, 192, 227. *See also* computer; internet; social media

Weill, Andrew, 143
white people, 31, 37, 59, 67, 78, 84, 114, 124, 266. *See also* race
Wilde, Oscar, 83, 225

About the Author

John Brueggemann is a professor in the Department of Sociology at Skidmore College. He researches, teaches, and writes about inequality, social movements, social theory, labor history, and food. His previous book, coauthored with his father, Walter Brueggemann, is *Rebuilding the Foundations: Social Relationships in Ancient Scripture and Contemporary Culture*. He earned his BA in sociology and anthropology from Earlham College, and masters and doctoral degrees in sociology from Emory University. The best thing he ever did was marry Christina. John is father to three amazing human beings, Emilia, Anabelle, and Peter. He loves food.